LIVES OF THE MASTERS

Saraha

POET OF BLISSFUL AWARENESS

Roger R. Jackson

SHAMBHALA

Shambhala Publications, Inc.
2129 13th Street
Boulder, Colorado 80302
www.shambhala.com

Frontispiece: Mahasiddha, Saraha; 19th century; Tibet or Mongolia;
Pigments on cloth; 27 × 18 inches; Donor: Dhondup Khangsar
Asian Art; Rubin Museum of Art; c2002.35.5

Excerpts from *First Thought Best Thought: 108 Poems*
by Chögyam Trungpa used with permission from
Carolyn Gimian and Diana Mukpo.
See the notes for complete source credits.

Cover art: Robert Fenwick May, Jr.
Cover design: Gopa and Ted2, Inc.

9 8 7 6 5 4 3 2 1

FIRST EDITION
Printed in Canada

Shambhala Publications makes every effort
to print on acid-free, recycled paper.
Shambhala Publications is distributed worldwide by
Penguin Random House, Inc., and its subsidiaries.

LIBRARY OF CONGRESS CATALOGING-IN-PUBLICATION DATA
Names: Jackson, Roger R. (Roger Reid), 1950– author. |
Sarahapāda, active 8th century. Dohākośa. Selections. English.
Title: Saraha: poet of blissful gnosis / Roger R. Jackson.
Description: Boulder: Shambhala Publications, 2024. |
Includes bibliographical references and index.
Identifiers: LCCN 2023040662 | ISBN 9781611806069 (trade paperback)
Subjects: LCSH: Sarahapāda, active 8th century–Criticism and interpretation. |
Apabhraṃśa poetry—History and criticism. | Religious life—Buddhism—Poetry. |
Didactic poetry, Apabhraṃśa—History and criticism.
Classification: LCC PK1428.9.S2 Z75 2024 | DDC 891/.29—dc23/eng/20240403
LC record available at https://lccn.loc.gov/2023040662

To the memory of two mentors: James Helfer Stone (1933–2021), who introduced me to Saraha, and Geshe Lhundub Sopa (1923–2014), who gave me tools for understanding him.

Mind is luminous, O mendicants, and the defilements that defile it are accidental.

Pabhassara Sutta, Aṅguttara Nikāya

Truth is an arrow and the gate is narrow that it passes through.

Bob Dylan, "When He Returns"

The songs that erupt
Are gist of the poesy,
Come by themselves, hark,
Stark as prisoners in a cave
Let out to sunlight.

Jack Kerouac, *Mexico City Blues*

Contents

Series Introduction

BUDDHIST TRADITIONS are heir to some of the most creative thinkers in world history. The Lives of the Masters series offers lively and reliable introductions to the lives, works, and legacies of key Buddhist teachers, philosophers, contemplatives, and writers. Each volume in the Lives series tells the story of an innovator who embodied the ideals of Buddhism, crafted a dynamic living tradition during his or her lifetime, and bequeathed a vibrant legacy of knowledge and practice to future generations.

Lives books rely on primary sources in the original languages to describe the extraordinary achievements of Buddhist thinkers and illuminate these achievements by vividly setting them within their historical contexts. Each volume offers a concise yet comprehensive summary of the master's life and an account of how they came to hold a central place in Buddhist traditions. Each contribution also contains a broad selection of the master's writings.

This series makes it possible for all readers to imagine Buddhist masters as deeply creative and inspired people whose work was animated by the rich complexity of their time and place and how these inspiring figures continue to engage our quest for knowledge and understanding today.

KURTIS SCHAEFFER, *series editor*

Preface

I FIRST READ THE SONGS of the Buddhist poet-yogin Saraha, also known to Tibetan tradition under several other names, including the Great Brahmin and the Archer, in 1971, as a mysticism-besotted undergraduate religion major at Wesleyan University. He quickly joined my disparate pantheon of ancient and modern culture heroes, which also included Zhuangzi, Nāgārjuna, Śaṅkara, Meister Eckhart, D. T. Suzuki, Carlos Castaneda, Hermann Hesse, Alan Watts, Norman O. Brown, Martin Heidegger, William James, Gary Snyder, John Cage, and the Grateful Dead. Read through the rose-tinted glasses of the Perennial Philosophy to which I was partial at the time, all these figures, including Saraha, could be seen to be making the same point: the mind/self/soul is pure, and spiritual freedom can be achieved only through an ecstatic transcendence of what Heidegger called "calculative thinking" through a process of "meditative thinking." Saraha was a particularly attractive figure because of his apparently countercultural lifestyle and his critical stance on society, religion, and rationality, making him seem like something of a Beat Buddhist *avant la lettre*.

In the years after college, I traveled to Asia and began to study Tibetan Buddhism seriously, at Kopan Monastery near Kathmandu, Nepal, and the Library of Tibetan Works and Archives in Dharamsala, India. Back in the United States, I entered the graduate program in Buddhist studies at the University of Wisconsin. Although my studies there, under Geshe Lhundub Sopa, a renowned Gelukpa scholar, were largely doctrinal and philosophical in orientation, Saraha continued to fascinate me, and several of my graduate seminar papers focused on the charismatic Indian tantric Buddhist great adepts, or great perfected ones, the *mahāsiddhas*,[1] of whom Saraha was perhaps the most celebrated, or on Tibetan Buddhist traditions, such as the Kagyu, that preserved and developed the mahāmudrā, or great seal, teachings traced to Saraha and the "mad yogin" lifestyle of Saraha and other mahāsiddhas.

Ever since, my academic writings—not to mention my personal interests—have tended to oscillate between the "scholastic" pole of Buddhism so consummately incarnated in Geluk philosophy and the "yogic" pole symbolized in India by the mahāsiddhas and in Tibet by mahāmudrā traditions wherever they might be found. Along the way, I wrote essays on Saraha that analyzed translations of his key works by Herbert Guenther and explored his ethics, his place within the Geluk tradition, and his status as a philosopher. I also published my own translations of two of his collections of *dohās*.[2] My own writings on Saraha form an exceedingly minor star cluster within the larger galaxy of pioneering works on his life, writings, and ideas that have been produced by scholars for the past century or so—not to mention the much vaster cosmos of great Tibetan scholarship on Saraha that, over the past millennium, made him into the exemplary tantric adept that we know today—even as his reputation in India, like Buddhism itself, faded into the background.

Tibetan work on Saraha is far too vast to survey here,[3] but a brief overview of significant modern scholarship devoted to him may prove useful, in part as a way of contextualizing the present book. It may be that Saraha is mentioned in one or another nineteenth-century work of Orientalist scholarship, but he does not appear in Brian Hodgson's reports on his research in Nepal between 1820 and 1858, Alexander Csoma de Körös's pioneering dictionary of

1834, Eugène Burnouf's 1844 history of Indian Buddhism, Heinrich Jäschke's 1881 Tibetan-English dictionary, or L. Austine Waddell's compendious 1895 account of Tibetan Buddhism. Indeed, the first mention of Saraha in modern scholarship may not have come until the twentieth century, when, in his 1902 Tibetan-English dictionary, the Indian scholar, explorer, and spy Sarat Chandra Das defines *sa ra ha pa* adjectivally as "of an Indian saint."[4] Just a few years later, the first writings attributed to Saraha—a handful of Apabhraṃśa-language verses cited in the Sanskrit *Compendium of Good Sayings* (*Subhāṣitasaṃgraha*)—were published in Calcutta by Cecil Bendall.[5] In 1916, Albert Grünwedel published a German translation of the biographies of eighty-four mahāsiddhas, attributed to Abhayadatta, which includes a brief account of Saraha's life and deeds.[6] That same year, the Bengali scholar Haraprasād Śāstrī published unedited transcriptions of Apabhraṃśa texts he had discovered in Kathmandu, including a version of Saraha's *Dohā Treasury* (*Dohākoṣa*) extracted from a Sanskrit commentary on the text composed by Advayavajra, and an anthology of songs by the mahāsiddhas, the *Treasury of Performance Songs* (*Caryāgītikoṣa*), which includes four songs attributed to Saraha.[7] It was not until 1928, with the appearance of Muhammad Shahidullah's *Les Chants Mystiques de Kāṅha et de Saraha*, that the material found by Śāstrī was edited, compared to Tibetan versions, and translated into a Western language, in this case French.[8] In 1929, Prabodh Chandra Bagchi found in Nepal two fragmentary short dohā collections attributed to Saraha, as well as a more correct and complete version of the *Dohā Treasury* first published by Śāstrī; he published his results, along with the Advayavajra commentary, in part in 1935 and in full in 1938.[9] In the meantime, Giuseppe Tucci had published in 1930 an account and edition of a Sanskrit guru-lineage he had located in Nepal, which is focused on Nāgārjuna but mentions Saraha.[10] Also, in 1934, Rāhula Sāṃkṛtyāyana located at Sakya Monastery in Tibet an Apabhraṃśa manuscript of a long

Saraha *Dohā Treasury* that only partially overlapped the one discussed by Śāstrī, Shahidullah, and Bagchi—although he did not publish it until over two decades later.[11]

After World War II, scholarship on Saraha accelerated. In 1946, Shashi Bhushan Dasgupta published his monumental study of Indian esoteric movements, *Obscure Religious Cults*, which drew liberally on the Apabhraṃśa works of Saraha and other mahāsiddhas,[12] and in 1954, David Snellgrove provided the first English translation of the *Dohā Treasury*, in an anthology of Buddhist texts in translation.[13] Around the same time, the great German Tibetologist Herbert Guenther published *Yuganaddha: The Tantric View of Life*, in which he became the first scholar to draw from the large corpus of Tibetan translations of works attributed to Saraha that lie beyond texts preserved in Apabhraṃśa.[14] Sāṃkṛtyāyana's 1957 *Dohā-Koś* made available the long Apabhraṃśa version of the *Dohā Treasury* he had discovered at Sakya, along with transcriptions and Hindi translations of much of the Saraha corpus preserved only in Tibetan, and a very helpful set of appendixes. In 1969, Guenther published his translation (from Tibetan) of Saraha's *Dohā Treasury: A Performance Song* (*Dohākoṣacaryāgīti*), referred to by Tibetans as the *King Dohā* (the title I will henceforth use), along with the commentaries of both South Asian and Tibetan authors.[15] In 1977, Per Kvaerne produced a new analysis, edition, and translation of the Apabhraṃśa *Treasury of Performance Songs*, incorporating perspectives from the Tibetan translation and Munidatta's Sanskrit commentary.[16] Abhayadatta's biography of the eight-four mahāsiddhas, including that of Saraha, was translated into English for the first time in 1979, by James Robinson,[17] and four years later David Templeman provided another, later biographical account of Saraha in his translation of the Tibetan scholar Tāranātha's *Seven Instruction Lineages*.[18] In 1993, Guenther published the first English translation of all three Tibetan versions of Saraha's Dohā Trilogy (*Doha Kor-*

sum), or Essential Trilogy (*Nyingpo Korsum*), consisting of the *People Dohā*—which is roughly equivalent to the *Dohā Treasury* studied by Śāstrī, Shahidullah, Bagchi, and Snellgrove—along with the *Queen* and *King Dohākoṣas*, for which we have no Indic-language originals.[19] In 1997, H. C. Bhayani expanded on Sāṃkṛtyāyana's 1957 work by editing the Apabhraṃśa of the Sakya version of the *Dohā Treasury* and providing it with a Sanskrit gloss and a rough English translation; he also produced a fresh edition and translation of the *Treasury of Performance Songs*, in which, as noted, Saraha is represented four times.[20]

With the turn of the twenty-first century, Saraha scholarship intensified still further. In 2004, I published a fresh translation of the Bagchi edition of the Apabhraṃśa of the *Dohā Treasury*, supplemented by translations of verses found in Tibetan but not in Bagchi's edition;[21] the book also included translations of *Dohā Treasuries* by Kāṅha/Kṛṣṇācārya and Tilopa. The next year, Kurtis Schaeffer published a landmark work in Saraha studies, *Dreaming the Great Brahmin*, which argues convincingly that even if Saraha was an Indian, his importance is due largely to the way in which Tibetans imagined his life, work, and lineage; the book also includes a translation of the *People Dohā* as embedded in the early Tibetan commentary of Chomden Raldri.[22] In 2005, Thrangu Rinpoche published a new translation of, and commentary upon, the *King Dohā*.[23] Marco Passavanti published and discussed in 2008 a newly discovered thirteenth-century account of the lives of numerous mahāsiddhas, which includes an important early version of the life of Saraha.[24] Also in 2008, Julia Stenzel completed an MA thesis (still unpublished) on Saraha's role in the Kagyu lineage of Tibet, which includes a brief survey of works attributed to him in the Tibetan Tengyur, a translation of his *Mahāmudrā Pith-Instructions*, and an intriguing study of his place in Kagyu rituals as practiced by Western retreatants in France.[25] In 2012, I presented the first

English translation of the *Queen Dohā* since Guenther's almost two decades earlier, while in 2014 Lara Braitstein broke entirely new ground in Western-language scholarship with her critical edition and translation of Saraha's mahāmudrā-oriented vajra-song collections, the *Body Treasury* (*Kāyakoṣa*), *Speech Treasury* (*Vākkoṣa*), and *Mind Treasury* (*Cittakoṣa*).[26]

Most recently, in 2019 Klaus-Dieter Mathes provided a useful perspective on Saraha's *People Dohā* through the lens of the great Kagyu commentary by Karma Trinlepa.[27] In 2020, Keith Dowman brought out a small volume of translations of mahāsiddha poetry that includes Saraha's *King* and *Queen Dohā Treasuries* and one of his performance songs; and starting the same year, Karl Brunnhölzl began publishing an ongoing and quite extraordinary multivolume study and translation of the massive anthology of mahāmudrā-related texts compiled by Tibet's seventh Karmapa, Chödrak Gyatso, which includes most, if not all, of Saraha's poetic works, and is a gold mine of information on texts and traditions surrounding the Great Brahmin, especially but not solely as he is understood in Tibetan traditions.[28] In early 2024, Klaus-Dieter Mathes and Péter-Dániel Szántó published the most important work in many decades on Saraha's seminal work, the *Dohā Treasury*, including fresh editions of several little-studied versions of the text, and a new edition, and English translation, of Advayavajra's Sanskrit commentary and the Tibetan version (the only one available) of Mokṣākaragupta's commentary, which are seminal sources for Indic and Tibetan versions of the text, respectively.[29] As of this writing, at least one other important Saraha-related work is nearing completion—Lara Braitstein et al.'s translation of the *Alphabetical Dohās* for the 84000 Project,[30] and at least one key project is in preparation: the late Thrangu Rinpoche's translation and discussion of the *People*, *Queen*, and *King Dohās*, based on Karma Trinlepa's commentary, edited by Michele Martin.

With a century's worth of distinguished scholarship behind it, this book is anything but groundbreaking. It does, however, have several distinctive features that set it apart from previous work. Foremost, it is the first attempt to produce a monograph that focuses on Saraha as a whole: his life, his works, his teachings, and his influence. To a greater degree than previous scholarship, it tries to view Saraha through the lens of virtually all the texts attributed to him in Indic and Tibetan tradition, uncertain as the authorship of some of those texts may be. Accordingly, in the translation portion of the book, I range widely. I include not just the texts for which Saraha is best known, such as the *People*, *Queen*, and *King Dohā Treasuries*, his performance songs, his *Mahāmudrā Pith-Instruction* (*Mahāmudropadeśa*), or his *Body*, *Speech*, and *Mind Treasuries*, and not just lesser-known mahāmudrā works that received scholarly attention only sporadically but also several of Saraha's more straightforwardly "tantric" works, including a portion of his immense commentary on the *Buddhakapāla Tantra* and two tantric practice-texts (*sādhanas*)—the latter being a staple of the corpus of almost any latter-day-Indian (or Tibetan) master.

More specifically, in line with most other works in the Lives of the Masters series, the book is broadly divided into two parts: a series of analytical chapters and a set of translations.

In the first part, the introduction supplies some basic information about Saraha and establishes his historical importance; raises the "problem" of ascertaining actual details of his life, works, and teachings; and, with caveats firmly in place, attempts to roughly situate him as a Indian Buddhist tantric master in the late first millennium CE.

Under the rubric of "Life," chapter 1 provides a general overview of biographical material that we possess about Saraha, a translation and analysis of two prominent "early" (from the twelfth–thirteenth centuries) life stories devoted to him, an indication of other ways in which he has figured in the Indian and Tibetan imagination, and a discussion of the problem of figuring out who, exactly, he may have been.

Under the rubric of "Teachings," chapter 2 surveys the corpus of texts attributed to Saraha on either side of the Himalayas, discussing first the handful of writings that survive in Indic languages, especially Apabhraṃśa, and then the larger collection of works found only in Tibetan translation, whether within or outside the Tengyur, the translated treatises of Indian Buddhism; the chapter also addresses the problem of the authorship of, and cohesion (or lack of it) within, the corpus. Chapters 3 and 4 attempt to build on the material discussed in the previous chapters so as to present Saraha's overall social, philosophical, and religious message, through an explanation of various "guises" he has assumed for his audience. Chapter 3 analyzes Saraha as a poet-singer, exploring his relation to oral tradition, his prosody, and his use of images and symbols. Chapter 4 focuses on Saraha as a religious teacher, treating in turn his role as a critic; his notion of the ultimate; and aspects of his teaching that show him as, variously, a radical gnostic, a tantric yogin, and a mainstream Buddhist. Chapter 5 looks briefly at Saraha's aesthetic and religious legacy in South Asia, the Tibetan cultural sphere, and the modern world.

The second part of the book presents full or partial translations, primarily from Tibetan, of twenty-one works attributed to Saraha.

Chapters 6–8 contain translations of the texts comprising the "Essential Trilogy." Chapter 6 is a rendition of the canonical Tibetan *Dohā Treasury Song*, or *People Dohā*, with variants found in the standard Apabhraṃśa version translated in the notes. Chapters 7 and 8 contain the *Queen Dohā* and the *King Dohā*, which are available only in Tibetan.

Chapters 9–15 focus on works with a strongly esoteric flavor. Chapter 9 is a translation of the tantric devotional text *Stages of Self-*

Blessing. Chapter 10 contains excerpts from Saraha's *Buddhakapāla Tantra* commentary, while chapter 11 is a Buddhakapāla sādhana, and chapter 12 is a sādhana of the form of Avalokiteśvara called Trailokyavaśaṃkara Lokeśvara (The Cosmic Lord Who Subdues the Three Worlds). Chapter 13 contains the *Alphabetical Dohās*, chapter 14 a dohā-treasury song entitled *Ornament of Springtime*, and chapter 15 the four Saraha songs found in the *Treasury of Performance Songs*, with variants found in the Apabhraṃśa or "Old Bengali" version translated in the notes.

The remaining chapters, while certainly replete with tantric imagery and terminology, may best be characterized as centering on Saraha's notions of the great seal, mahāmudrā. Chapter 16 contains the popular *Mahāmudrā Pith-Instruction*. Chapters 17, 18, and 19 present his often quite technical "treasuries" of mahāmudrā instructions related, respectively, to the "three doors" of Buddhist anthropology: the *Body Treasury*, *Speech Treasury*, and *Mind Treasury*. Chapter 20 contains a related text known as *Cognitive Disengagement from Body, Speech, and Mind*. Chapters 21–26 constitute a series of brief songs: chapter 21 includes two short, untitled songs; chapter 22 a special mahāmudrā instruction for those on the verge of death; chapter 23 a dohā song called *The Summit of Instruction on Suchness*; chapter 24 the *Dohā Song of View, Meditation, Conduct, and Result*; chapter 25 the *Twelve Verses of Instruction*; and chapter 26 a collection of symbol-songs known as *Key Instructions*.

There are many people to thank for helping bring this book to light. First and foremost are the Tibetan masters who have taught me so much about how to read and think about Buddhist texts through a traditional lens, especially H.H. the Fourteenth Dalai Lama, Lama Thubten Yeshe, Thubten Zopa Rinpoche, Geshe Lhundub Sopa, Ganden Tri Rinpoche Losang Tenzin, and Yangsi Rinpoche. Hardly less important are my other teachers of Indic and Tibetan languages and literature: Leonard Zwilling, Frances Wilson, Sheela Verma, Usha Nilsson, Stephan Beyer, and V. Narayana Rao. In matters directly connected to Saraha, I might never have known of his songs had I not been alerted to them by two inspiring teachers at Wesleyan University, James Helfer Stone and George Curth (whose name is still inscribed in my well-used and much-loved copy of Guenther's *The Royal Song of Saraha*). Needless to say, I am greatly beholden to the trailblazing Saraha scholars of earlier generations, such as Haraprasād Śāstrī, Muhammad Shahidullah, P. C. Bagchi, Rāhul Sāṃkṛtyāyana, Shashi Bhushan Dasgupta, David Snellgrove, H. C. Bhayani, and the inimitable Herbert Guenther. And in my own time, I have had the fortune to learn from the work of—and often befriend—scholars who continue to expand and deepen our understanding of the Great Brahmin, including Lara Braitstein, Karl Brunnhölzl, Matthew Kapstein, Per Kvaerne, Michele Martin, Klaus-Dieter Mathes, Kurtis Schaeffer, and Péter Szántó. More broadly, I have benefited immensely from the work on Indian and Tibetan Buddhist Tantra produced by scholars such as Alex Wayman, Robert Thurman, David Snellgrove, Stephan Beyer, Alexis Sanderson, Harunaga Isaacson, Francesco Sferra, Giacomella Orofino, Ronald Davidson, Christian Wedemeyer, David Gray, Charles Manson, and my go-to guy on all matters Indically obscure and esoteric, John Newman. I also have learned much from the work on non-Buddhist Indian tantric traditions, song traditions, or both by the likes of Douglas Brooks, John Stratton Hawley, Glen Hayes, Linda Hess, David Lorenzen, June McDaniel, and David White. I'm grateful to Kurtis Schaeffer for inviting me to write this book (even though he is far better equipped for the task than I); to Casey Kemp for being a persistent, supportive, and good-natured editor throughout its early stages; to Michael Wakoff for shepherding it though the later stages with extraordinary acuity and grace; to Michael Russem for designing the book's interior; and to LS Summer for preparing the index. Nikko Odiseos has been wonderfully supportive from the book's inception right through to its publication. Finally, unending thanks to my wife, Pam Percy, for her amazing ability to encourage my scholarly obsessions while at the same time showing me that there's far more to life than is contained even in the most sprawling of libraries or the worthiest of academic projects—a view she might almost be channeling from Saraha himself.

Technical Note

On Words and Spellings in Indic Languages and Tibetan

Sanskrit and Apabhraṃśa words are spelled according to the standard conventions for transliteration. Unless the context requires it, I will refer to Indic-language terms and names in their better-known Sanskrit forms rather than the Apabhraṃśa forms they often take in South Asian versions of Saraha's works, for example, *svabhāva* rather than *sahāva* and *mahāsukha* rather than *mahāsuha*. When referring to Indian mahāsiddhas, I will typically utilize the Tibetan transcription of an adept's Indic name, for example, Śavaripa rather than Śabari, Tilopa rather than Tillipāda, Nāropa rather than Nāḍapāda, or Maitrīpa rather than Maitrīpāda. In conformity with the style of the Lives of the Masters series, in the body of the text Tibetan names and terms are not transliterated using the Wylie system but are rendered phonetically, so as to approximate their pronunciation in the Lhasa dialect of the language. In the endnotes, I generally use Wylie spellings.

On Verse Numbering

In this book, Saraha's poetic texts are typically cited with the abbreviated title followed by the verse number. Thus, for example, *Queen Dohā* verse 24 would be cited as QD 24. It must be emphasized that the original-language versions of Saraha's texts, whether in

Apabhraṃśa or Tibetan, are almost never numbered, so nearly all systems of enumeration are the creations of modern scholars. It is slightly easier to enumerate Apabhraṃśa verses because the meter and end rhymes help to delineate the boundaries of a verse. Still, because of differences among various Apabhraṃśa editions, numbering schemes are by no means uniform, especially with regard to Saraha's most important work extant in Apabhraṃśa, the *Dohā Treasury* (S. *Dohākoṣa*). In Tibetan, where end rhymes are not employed and metrical differences that may have been present in the Indic original are sometimes effaced, determining where a verse begins and where it ends can be difficult, especially when we lack an Indic equivalent—which is most of the time. A Tibetan verse typically consists of four lines, but this is not always the case, and so the numbering of Tibetan verses is even more arbitrary than in the case of Indic-language texts. All this is to say that the verse-numbering system I use is my own and will not, in many cases, exactly correspond to those of other translators.

Abbreviations

Full bibliographic details for the texts listed here may be found in the first part of the bibliography, "Indic and Tibetan Sources," which is arranged alphabetically by abbreviation, rather than by author or title.

A.	Apabhraṃśa
AD	*Alphabetical Dohās*
AP	*Scriptural Commentary on the "Dohā Treasury"*
AV	*Commentary on the Essential Meaning of the "Dohā Treasury"*
BK	*Buddhakapāla Tantra*
BT	*Body Treasury: An Immortal Vajra Song*
C	Coné edition of the Tibetan canon
CB	*The Gnostic: A Commentary on the "Buddhakapāla Tantra"*
CC	*Commentary on Consecration*
CD	*Cognitive Disengagement from Body, Speech, and Mind*
CS	*Essential Realizations of the Eighty-Four Mahāsiddhas*
D	Dergé edition of the Tibetan canon
DN	*Gdams ngag mdzod: A Treasury of Instructions and Techniques for Spiritual Realization*
DT	*Special Mahāmudrā Instruction for Death Time*
DZ	*Eight Dohā Treasuries*
EA	*Explanatory Notes on the "Alphabetical Dohā"*
ES	*Offering Rite for All Elemental Spirits*

GG *Garland of Golden Drops: Vajra-Song Experiential Pith-Instructions*
H Lhasa edition of the Tibetan canon
HT *Hevajra Tantra*
IT *Indian Texts on the Mahāmudrā of Definitive Meaning*
KD *Dohā Treasury: A Performance Song* (*King Dohā*)
KI *Key Instructions*
KT *Do ha skor gsum gyi tshig don gyi rnam bshad sems kyi rnam thar gsal bar bston pa'i me long*
MB *Illumining the Stages of the Offering Rite of Glorious Buddhakapāla*
MD *Melody of the Precious Reality Body beyond Thought*
MM *The Mahāmudrā Pith-Instruction Called "Dohā Treasury"*
MP *Scriptural Commentary on the "Dohā Treasury"*
MT *Mind Treasury: A Vajra Song on Nonarising*
N Narthang edition of the Tibetan canon
OS *Ornament of Springtime: A Dohā-Treasury Song*
P Peking edition of the Tibetan canon
PD *Dohā Treasury Song* (*People Dohā*)
PDM Dpe bsdur ma version of the Dergé edition of the Tibetan Tengyur
PM *Praise of Mahākāla*
PS *Treasury of Performance Songs*
QD *The Inexhaustible Treasury: A Song of Instruction* (*Queen Dohā*)
S. Sanskrit
SB *Sādhana of the Glorious Buddhakapāla*
SI *The Summit of Instruction on Suchness: A Dohā Song*
SL *Sādhana of Lokeśvara Who Subdues the Three Worlds*
SM *Secret Songs of the Mind*
SO *Song of the Overflowing Inexhaustible Dohā Treasury*
SS *Stages of Self-Blessing*
ST *Speech Treasury: A Gentle Vajra Song*
T. Tibetan
TR *Teachings Received*

TV *Twelve Verses of Instruction*
US *Two Untitled Songs*
VJ *Vajra Songs of the Siddhas*
VM *Dohā Song of View, Meditation, Conduct, and Result*
VS *Vajra Secret Song: A Pith Instruction on Mahāmudrā*
VY *Sādhana of the Glorious Vajrayoginī*

Saraha

Introduction

Saraha's Indian Context

In Search of Saraha

Ashish Nandy begins his brilliant book on South Asia's favorite sport by observing that "cricket is an Indian game accidentally discovered by the English."[31] We might, with equal justification, say that Saraha is a Tibetan saint who was accidentally born in India. Yes, there are a number of Indic-language texts—usually in the late first-millennium CE Prakrit known as Apabhraṃśa—in which an author refers to himself, or is identified, as Saraha;[32] and yes, a twelfth-century collection of biographies of Indian Buddhist mahāsiddhas, including Saraha, is credited to an Indian master named Abhayadatta;[33] and yes, the name Saraha appears in at least one uncontestably South Asian lineage list from early second-millennium Nepal;[34] and yes, the Tibetan corpus of Buddhist texts translated from Indic languages contains well over thirty works attributed to Saraha, as well as commentaries on his works by Indian authors. But, as Kurtis Schaeffer has convincingly argued, it was really in Tibet that Saraha "was dreamed into existence":[35] it was in Tibet that most if not all the biographies of him that we have were written, in Tibet that his texts were not only translated but in some cases transcreated, in Tibet that his identification as the human fountainhead of the mahāmudrā transmissions so influential on the plateau occurred, in Tibet that his works were quoted and commented upon by masters of every tradition, and in Tibet that he became a figure that appeared not only in ancient songs and stories but in the visions and dreams of devout practitioners too.

Still, just as cricket really was a game invented in England, so the name Saraha probably designates a person who did reside at some point in India—though where, when, and how he lived, what he verifiably sang, said, or wrote, and whether he was a single individual all remain something of a mystery. Depending on the sources we consult, he was from the east, south, north, northwest, or possibly even the west of the subcontinent. The range of dates claimed for him extends from several centuries BCE to the eleventh century CE, although most modern scholars date him to somewhere between the eighth and tenth centuries, probably on the later side of that span.[36] He was the author of anything from a handful of poetic works to nearly three dozen writings in a wide range of literary genres. And he may have been a single individual or a series of individuals who adopted the same name—just as several different authors seem to have appropriated (or been assigned) the names Nāgārjuna, Āryadeva, and Candrakīrti over the course of Indian Buddhist history.

For now, let us simply remark that Saraha was a name to conjure with, and that the most famous work associated with that name, the *Dohā Treasury* (*Dohākoṣa*), had likely been edited in some form by early in the tenth century, for it was quoted and commented upon by both Indian and Tibetan scholars active or born in that century, including (working backward in time) Atiśa Dīpaṃkāra (982–1054), Nāḍapāda (or Nāropa, 956–1040), and Bhavabhaṭṭa (mid-tenth century).[37] If our dates for these figures are correct, and the works in which they cite Saraha are rightly attributed to them, then it is likely that the Great Brahmin lived no later than the mid-tenth century CE. An earliest possible date is harder to determine, but references within the *Dohā Treasury* to terms, practices, and deities related to the yoginī tantras, which seem first to have appeared in the eighth century,[38] and the inclusion in the *Dohā Treasury* of at least one verse that matches a passage in the *Hevajra Tantra* (ninth century),[39] would suggest that he may not have lived before the eighth century—or perhaps even the ninth. More will be said in this and subsequent chapters about who Saraha was: where and when he might have lived, what he might have written, what he may have taught and practiced, and whether he was a single individual—although the reader expecting definitive answers to any of these questions will come away disappointed. For the moment, let us simply affirm that there is a single name that is attached to a variety of works likely produced in India (or, in certain cases, Tibet) sometime between the eighth and eleventh century CE, and that with that scant—and potentially suspect—information in hand, we may tentatively suggest something about the historical, social, cultural, linguistic, literary, and religious context in which a person or persons designated by that name may have lived. For the sake of convenience, I will treat him for now as a single individual.

Before delving into Saraha's lifeworld, it is worth pausing to consider his name. The form in which it is typically found in Indic texts is simply "Saraha," which is a *bahuvrīhi* compound that means "arrow shooter," or archer, where the Apabhraṃśa *sara* (S. *śara*) means "arrow" and *ha*, derived from the Sanskritic verbal root *hā* (or *hi*), means, among other things, to "impel" or "shoot. This was the reading accepted by most Tibetan scholars. An alternative—though decidedly minority—reading was offered by the fifteenth-century Tibetan Sakya master Drakpa Dorjé, who argued that "Saraha" should be read as a contraction of Sara[gra]ha, that is, "arrow holder" or "arrow handler" (T. *dadzin*). This, he says, comports better with the common Tibetan belief—derived from the hagiographical tradition—that Saraha was an arrow *maker* rather than an arrow *shooter*, or archer.[40] Occasionally, Saraha is referred to in South Asian texts as "Sarahapāda," which adds to his name a common Indic honorific (sometimes shortened to *pā*) indicating the "feet" (*pāda*) of a master worthy of being touched by one's head—in other words, worthy of veneration.

In Tibetan texts, the Indic *sa ra ha*, a simple transliteration, is frequently encountered, but at times, too, the name is translated into Tibetan as *danun*: "one who pierces with an arrow," or "arrow shooter," or simply "archer."[41] As suggested already, Tibetans often refer to Saraha by a moniker suggested by his presumed caste origin, the "Great Brahmin" (*bramzé chenpo*)—an epithet, so far as I know, not found in Indic sources associated with Saraha. Also unattested in Indic sources known to me is another name encountered in Tibetan texts, Rāhula (or Rāhulabhadra)—a reference either to the Buddha's son or a disciple of the Buddha's son (which would push Saraha well back into the BCE period) or, more often, to a poet of the second century CE named Rāhulabhadra, who is best known as the author of a famous song of praise to the goddess of perfect wisdom, Prajñāpāramitā.[42] In any of these cases, Rāhula(bhadra) is reputed to be the teacher of the great philosopher Nāgārjuna, who is himself variously asserted to be either the teacher or disciple of Saraha, though the latter is more common in Tibetan traditions.[43] Further confusion is added when we consider that reference is sometimes made to "Saraha the Elder" and "Saraha the Younger," with the latter typically referring to the mahāsiddha Śavaripa (or Śabari), typically regarded as an important disciple or granddisciple of "our" Saraha—that is, Saraha the Elder. Compounding the problem, the appellations Śabareśvara (T. Ritrö Wangchuk) and Mahāśabara (T. Ritröpa Chenpo) may refer either to Saraha or Śavaripa, and we also encounter the name Mahāśabara Saraha, which *probably* refers to Saraha the Elder but could also be identified with Śavaripa as a conveyor of Saraha's teachings.[44] Here, I will typically refer to "our Saraha" as "Saraha," but for the sake of variety, I will occasionally utilize "the Great Brahmin."

As may already be clear from the number of qualifications littering this introduction, contextualizing Saraha is no easy matter. We know he was Indian, but the range of possible dates for him, even if narrowed to the last centuries of the first and the very beginning of the second millennium CE—what we might call "the medieval period"[45]—still leaves us with many, quite distinct eras in which he might have lived. Furthermore, the fact that (a) his hagiographers variously assign him to nearly every part of India[46] and associate him with a variety of kings, not all of whom are historically traceable, and (b) the language in which his extant Indic-language works are written is either a western or an eastern form of Apabhraṃśa, or perhaps a mixture,[47] leaves us quite uncertain where he was born, where he lived, what language or languages he spoke or wrote, what kings he may have served or confounded, where he might have studied and traveled, or where he died. Nevertheless, we can affirm that the general milieu in which Saraha seems to have flourished was that of the Buddhist culture of India sometime between the eighth and eleventh centuries, and even with parameters as broad as these, we may say something about his historical, social, cultural, linguistic, literary, and religious context.

Historical, Social, and Cultural Contexts

Although linguistic and historical uncertainties loom large, we may begin to home in on Saraha's possible milieu by making two observations. First, the various forms of the language of most surviving Indic texts attributed to him, Apabhraṃśa, were most common in north India, where they served as something of a historical "bridge" between Prakrits such as Pāli and Gāndhārī on the one hand and modern vernaculars like Bengali, Hindi, Gujarati, and so forth on the other. The term *Apabhraṃśa* is a complex one that, depending on time and context, may refer either to a spoken or a written language and, as noted, admits of regional variations, often being divided into eastern, western, and southern branches—which, especially in later times, are not always clearly distinguishable on grammatical grounds.[48] We do know, however, that the Buddhist texts extant in Apabhraṃśa are, by dint of cultural, historical, and other references, most commonly associated with eastern India. Second, for a variety of political, economic, and cultural reasons, in the period between 700 and 1100 CE, the regions of India in which Buddhism remained most vibrant were the mountainous areas of the far northwest (for example, Kashmir, Gandhāra, and Swat, or Oḍiyāna) and the northeastern plains, hills, and shores drained by the Ganges and Brahmaputra rivers as they descend to the Bay of Bengal (for example, the eastern part of present-day Uttar Pradesh, Bihar, Bengal, Orissa, and Assam).[49] This means that if we are to "locate" Saraha in time and space, we may do best to focus on northeastern India between approximately 700 and 1100 CE—which would situate him more or less within the bounds of the Pāla empire. The Pālas, to varying degrees, controlled northeast India (and sometimes considerably more) between 750 and 1161 CE—and were notable, among other things, for being the last great pre-Muslim Indian dynasty to patronize Buddhism. Even if Saraha did *not* live within the Pāla domain but rather in Oḍiyāna, or somewhere in the west or south, an examination of late-first millennium north Indian Buddhism, with a special focus on the Pāla, will help provide some sense of the general cultural milieu in which he probably lived.

It is evident from reading any history of India that the northern part of the subcontinent was, between 700 and 1200 CE, marked by political instability, nearly constant warfare, social and cultural upheaval, and religious ferment and contestation.[50] Of course, this could be said of most periods of India's history, in which eras of tranquillity were few and far between, being confined mostly to certain stretches when most or all of the north was under the long-term control of a single dynasty, as by the Mauryas between 322 and 185 BCE, the Guptas between 319 and 467 CE, and the Vardhanas, under Harsha, between 606 and 647 CE—and even these eras were far from being turbulence free. The period in the north during which Saraha probably lived—the eighth through the eleventh centuries—saw a constant reshuffling of power relations among several different regional dynasties, most notably the Rāṣṭrakūṭas of the western Deccan (present-day Maharashtra), the Gujara-Prātīharas from the far west (present-day Gujarat and Madhya Pradesh), and the Pālas in the eastern territories of Magadha, Bengal, and Kaliṅga (portions of present-day Bihar, West Bengal, Odisha, and Bangladesh). Other forces contending in the north during this period included the Bhaumakaras of Odisha, the Coḷas from the southeast (present-day Tamil Nadu), the Gāhaḍvālas of the upper Ganges area (present-day Uttar Pradesh), the rulers of Kāmarūpa (present-day Assam), the Newārs of the Kathmandu Valley of Nepal, and, across the Himalayas, the Tibetans. But most of the struggle in north India was among the "Big Three"—the Rāṣṭrakūṭas, Prātīharas, and Pālas—whose fortunes waxed and waned as they took and retook territory from one another, with their efforts often centered on Kanauj (in present-day Uttar Pradesh), which controlled the upper Gangetic plain and had served as Harsha's capital up until his death in the mid-seventh century.[51]

Narrowing our focus to the Pālas,[52] we find that, in terms of territory, they reached their zenith under the second and third rulers of the dynasty, Dharmapāla (reigned circa 775–812) and Devapāla (reigned circa 812–50), who expanded dynastic control far beyond Bengal, to Kanauj toward the northwest, Kāmarūpa in the far northeast, and Odisha to the southeast. One of the subsequent rulers associated with Saraha in later hagiographies, Ratnapāla, ruled in the early-to-mid-tenth century. Later, after a period of decline, Pāla fortunes were revived by a king also associated with Saraha,

Mahipāla, or Mahāpāla, who ruled from the late tenth through the early eleventh centuries. He succeeded in regaining some of the territory controlled by the Pālas in earlier centuries, especially in Bengal and Magadha, though he was engaged in constant warfare with the Coḷas and other groups, and most of what he regained was lost by his weaker successors. The dynasty persisted in name until 1214, but well before that, it had been supplanted by the Hindu-friendly Sena dynasty, and, in the late twelfth century, Bengal was invaded by Turkic Muslims led by the Ghurid general Bhaktyār Khaljī (d. 1206), whose forces reputedly destroyed Vikramaśīla (1193), Oḍantapuri (ca. 1200), Nālandā (1202), and other Buddhist monasteries, thereby undermining the major institutional base of Buddhism in the east and paving the way for the religion's near disappearance from the subcontinent over the succeeding centuries, first in the Gangetic plain and eventually in the south.

Like most empires of medieval north India, the Pāla was organized along the lines of what has been called "*samānta* feudalism,"[53] whereby a king, emperor, or supreme monarch (*raja* or *rājādirāja*) employed local rulers (*samānta*s, literally, "neighbors," that is, minor *rāja*s) to extend their power—often exercised from afar—right down to the grass roots. The samāntas, who have been likened to vassal lords, viceroys, or governors (and who themselves typically had their own set of subordinates), were usually recipients of land grants. They were given a fair degree of autonomy in ruling their domains, for instance, in organizing agriculture, collecting taxes, dispensing justice, sponsoring public works, or supporting religious institutions, but in turn they were expected to offer to the king not just fealty and obeisance but a yearly tribute, as well as troops in times of war. The administrative structure of the Pāla and other medieval Indian empires was far more complex than this, but the king-samānta relationship was in some ways the crux of the system: when it functioned smoothly—typically under the aegis of a strong monarch—it assured a certain degree of stability and predictability in the lives of everyone from farmers to nobles, but when the monarch was weak or (as so often happened) royal succession was disputed, samāntas often exploited the situation, breaking their feudal bonds and pursuing higher ambitions, typically at the expense of peace and order and even the integrity of the kingdom itself. Not incidentally, Ronald Davidson has argued persuasively that the system in its ideal form—with consecrated monarchs ruling over circles of samāntas—provided an "imperial metaphor" for the development of Buddhist (and other) tantric systems, with the consecration or initiation (*abhiśeka*) ceremony through which a tantric disciple was recreated as a buddha standing in for a royal coronation and the circle of feudatory samāntas serving as a basis for imagining the circle or circles (*maṇḍala*) of deities who populate the palace, or domain, of the consecrated practitioner.[54]

Despite the absence of a single overarching imperium during the medieval period, the economic and social patterns of north India in general and the Pāla domains in particular remained more or less as they had been for centuries.[55] Thus, the economy was—as still is the case in the subcontinent—above all agricultural, with wheat the predominant crop in the west and rice in the east, and with various vegetables, fruits, and fish (or, more rarely, meat) rounding out people's diets. Pastoralism persisted in lands unsuited for tillage, and other forms of production ranged from cultivation of nonstaple agricultural products such as spices and medicines, to metallurgy and textiles. Cities and towns, although far less populated than rural areas, continued to serve as political, commercial, and cultural hubs. Trade, both overland and by river, remained important, and for the Pālas, situated as they were by the Bay of Bengal, sea trade with Southeast Asia was an important source of wealth, not to mention cultural contact with the Indian-influenced lands of that region, many of which were oriented toward Buddhism.

The absence of a strong central authority, not to mention constant warfare, did perhaps interfere with agricultural life, slow the growth of cities, or impede commerce both at home and abroad, but north India in the medieval period was not especially economically distressed.

As it had been for nearly two millennia, the fourfold *varṇa* (or "caste") system was the normative (and, for Hindus, religiously sanctioned) social ideal, with brahmins, at the top, devoted in principle to religion, ritual, and education; the *kṣatriya*s, the warriors and administrators, responsible for establishing and maintaining order; the *vaiśya*s, representing a range of professions, including, notably, agriculture, manufacturing, and trade; and the *śūdra*s making up the servile class. This ideal, however, had been articulated in vastly different political and economic conditions than obtained in the late first millennium CE—or, for that matter, the late first millennium BCE, since as conditions changed and Indo-Aryan civilization came to dominate more and more of the subcontinent, a variety of new peoples were assimilated into the hegemonic culture and a multitude of new occupations emerged. Each of these ethnic or occupational groups received their own designation as a "birth-group" (*jāti*), and often was assigned a slot in the varṇa system, although in fact the jātis formed part of a vastly more complex network that reflected how Indians "on the ground" conceived social groupings. Furthermore, although śūdras occupied the bottom rung of the varṇa-based hierarchy, other groups regarded as especially impure because of their employment in "polluting" occupations such as fishing, butchering animals, working with leather, washing clothes, presiding over cremation grounds, drumming, or even cutting hair, eventually were relegated to even lower positions, such that they were generally regarded as "untouchable" (*asparśya*) by those of the three highest varṇas. Many (though not all) untouchables were members of tribal groups that, over the centuries, were assimilated into the Indo-Aryan mainstream, finding themselves at the bottom of the social heap in somewhat the same manner as immigrants to the United States often have had to enter American society at the bottom of the social hierarchy. It is important to note that although social groups were, in principle, defined by occupation and ranked according to their ritual purity, there was more room for change, or advancement, within the system than is often believed. Thus, brahmins might sometimes receive land grants and engage in agriculture, vaiśyas or even śūdras might present themselves as kṣatriyas on the basis of a concocted royal lineage and rule great kingdoms, and members of lower castes might "reinvent" themselves in an urban or commercial context far from where people knew their original status.

The norms and deviations we have just described were set out with men in mind, but there was an entire genre of sociological analysis devoted to *strīdharma*: the duties incumbent upon women. In such normative texts as the *Laws of Manu* (*Manovnadhamaśāstra*), women were primarily restricted to the domestic sphere and were clearly subordinated to men: in the most extreme instance, it is said that a woman must be subject to her father in childhood, to her husband during marriage, and to her sons when she is widowed.[56] This was a prescription applied most consistently to higher-caste women, especially brahmins and kṣatriyas. Lower-caste or untouchable women, on the other hand, were presumed to be less pure, hence often less restricted than their higher-caste sisters. It is from their ranks, it seems, that many (though not all) of the human (as opposed to divine) yoginīs celebrated in tantric lore were drawn. One other point about social groupings: although the "caste system" was decidedly Hindu in origin, and aspects of it, such as the observance of untouchability, were rejected by Jains and Buddhists, it was rarely the case that the system as a whole was rejected by any religious community—it was, for the most part, assumed by almost everyone in the subcontinent that caste in general (if not in all its details) was the natural order of society.

The towns and royal courts of medieval north India, including those of the Pālas, were hubs of artistic and literary activity, some of it for everyday use, much of it religious. Although originally produced for Indian temple settings, Pāla religious art—much but certainly not all of it Buddhist—spread along land and sea routes to other parts of Asia, including present-day Nepal, Tibet, China, Myanmar, Thailand, and Indonesia, creating what has been called the "Pāla international style." The brilliance of Pāla architecture is evident in India in the ways in which imperial artisans refurbished such Buddhist institutions as the "monastic university" at Nālandā and the Mahābodhi temple at Bodh Gaya and built such new monastic centers as Oḍantapuri and Somapur. Also influenced by the Pāla style were such spectacular sites as Samyé and other old temples in Tibet, the temple complexes of Bagan in Myanmar and Angkor Wat in Cambodia, and the great stūpa of Borobudur on the island of Java. Pāla artisans also produced countless sculptures in stone and metal intended primarily for ritual and decorative purposes in Buddhist (or Hindu or Jain) temples, and here again, the Pāla style spread beyond India to other parts of Asia. Another religious art form was painting, whether on cloth, palm-leaf manuscripts, or walls; although extant examples are scant in India, their style may be inferred from datable examples found in Nepal, Tibet, and other Pāla-influenced regions of Asia.[57]

In linguistic and literary terms, north India, including the Pāla regions, presented a complex picture.[58] Remarkably, for all the literary remains we have, we usually do not know precisely what the spoken language of any given region was. We can only surmise that it probably lay somewhere between Apabhraṃśa—which although once spoken in various regional forms, had by this time become a quasi-standardized, primarily literary language—and the modern vernaculars that emerged in the first half of the second millennium. A reasonable guess might be that, within the Pāla domain, for everyday purposes people spoke "proto" versions of Bengali, Maithili, Bhojpuri, Hindi, Assamese, or Oriya. As already noted, we do have literary remains from this era in Apabhraṃśa, consisting mostly of Jain texts from western India—especially hagiographies and moral-tale collections—and Buddhist texts (especially "songs") likely from the east, although the language also was incorporated (and had been for centuries) into Sanskrit plays as a way of marking a speaker as lower class. Some literature continued to be composed in older Prakrits such as Pāli and Jain Mahārāṣṭrī, but this was less common late in the first millennium than in the late BCE and early CE periods. Indeed, as it had been for centuries, classical Sanskrit was the common literary language of the north (and, to some degree, of the south, as well), the *lingua franca* in which most official records, chronicles, and religious, philosophical, and literary works were composed. Thus, regardless of what language was spoken in the kitchens and on the streets in a particular locale, and regardless of one's religious or cultural identity, Sanskrit provided a culturally unifying factor—at least for the literate minority—much as Latin did from the end of the Roman Empire until the late Middle Ages in Europe.

Religious Contexts

As had been the case since the mid-first millennium BCE, religious groups in India in the medieval period were broadly divided into the native categories of *brāḥmaṇa* and *śramaṇa*.[59] The former comprised those following the vast array of ideas and practices contained nowadays under the umbrella term "Hinduism," including

- devotees of Viṣṇu (both in himself and in his incarnations as Rāma and Kṛṣṇa), Śiva (also known by such names as

Maheśvara, Mahādeva, and Śaṃkara), or one or another goddess (*devī*);

- philosophers of many stripes;
- ritual officiants at anything from royally sanctioned great sacrifices (*mahāyajña*) to small-scale local offering-ceremonies (*pūjā*);
- a variety of ascetics, monastics, and other contemplatives, whether living in communities of like-minded practitioners (*āśramas*) or in solitary retreat in forests, mountain caves, cremation grounds, or other out-of-the-way places; and
- authors of texts that ranged from sectarian narratives (*purāṇas*), to treatises on society (*dharmaśāstras*), to devotional songs (*gīti*), to esoteric manuals (*tantras*).

Although those later classified as "Hindu" were a disparate lot, they tended for the most part to agree that (a) the Vedic religious corpus, consisting of the Saṃhitās (most notably the *Ṛg Veda*), Brāḥmaṇas, Āraṇyakas, and Upaniṣads, was divinely revealed authoritative tradition par excellence; (b) the caste system, governed in part by notions of hereditary occupation and in part by a concern with ritual purity and impurity, was divinely sanctioned and represented the natural social order; and (c) the ultimate goal of human striving was to escape a beginningless series of more or less unsatisfactory rebirths (*saṃsāra*) through proper ritual and ethical action (*karma*), devotion to a deity (*bhakti*), or correct knowledge (*vidyā*, *jñāna*) of the nature of reality (as, for instance, the unchanging *ātman* or *brahman*), or all three, and in the end attain a state of spiritual liberation (*mokṣa*) in which rebirth is brought to an end and the greatest possible "happiness" enjoyed for eternity, sometimes expressed as a state of perfect existence, knowledge, and bliss (*sat-cit-ānanda*).

The term *śramaṇa* (literally, "striver," sometimes glossed as "ascetic") is, like *brāḥmaṇa*, or *Hindu*, also an umbrella term, which referred to anyone who

- rejected the authority of the Vedas, substituting for them their own set of scriptures;
- denied the divine origins of the caste system and criticized many of its assumptions and practices, especially the observance of untouchability;
- organized themselves into distinctive communities (*saṅghas*), in which monasticism or some other form of organized asceticism played a central role; and
- prescribed a variety of ideas and practices that would lead one from the morass of saṃsāra to the eternal respite of liberation from uncontrolled rebirth.

In this sense, śramaṇa traditions agreed with Hindu groups that the basic problem facing sentient (especially human) beings is subjection to unwanted and repeated rebirth, the solution is attainment of a state of eternal spiritual freedom, and the method for attaining that freedom is to be found in some combination of affective, ethical, intellectual, and contemplative practices, typically applied within the context of an intentional community but also, at times, to be pursued in a solitary setting. Although śramaṇa groups were numerous and disparate in the late first millennium BCE, a thousand years later the only two that survived in any significant institutional form were Jainism and Buddhism, which concurred in rejecting Hindu traditions, adhering to their own scriptural canon, and practicing within their own distinct communities but differed significantly on various points of metaphysics, cosmology, and religious practice. Thus, for instance, Jains accepted the existence of a permanent "soul" (*jīva*), while Buddhists did not; Jains accepted the sentience (in some sense) of plants and physical elements, while Buddhists did not; and Jains promoted a strong form of asceticism, which Buddhists regarded as extreme and in contravention of the middle way between austerity and indulgence preached by the Buddha at the outset of his career. More to the point, perhaps, Jains and Buddhists vied throughout the medieval period—as they had for a millennium—for the support of monarchs and merchants, as part of a three-way competition in which various Hindu groups assumed an ever-more-influential role.

Although Hindu, Jain, and Buddhist traditions were to be found everywhere in the subcontinent during the medieval period, different dynasties tended to favor one or more of the great traditions, often at the expense of the others. The Prātīharas and Rāṣṭrakūṭas of the west were especially munificent toward Hindus and Jains, while in the east, the Pālas, without ignoring these two groups, were especially partial to Buddhism. It should be added, though, that the general trend in this period—as had been the case since early in the first millennium CE—was toward the "Hinduization" of the entire subcontinent, with Jain and Buddhist groups maintaining a strong presence in certain regions (the Jains in the Deccan and west, the Buddhists, as noted, in the northwest and northeast) but presenting a less robust profile in the others. There were many reasons for this trend, perhaps the most salient being the success of Hindus (of whatever stripe), over many centuries, in simultaneously ingratiating themselves to monarchs and merchants on the one hand and to ordinary town and village folk on the other, through an appealing combination of ideology, sacred narratives, social organization, and religious rituals that ranged from pilgrimage to pūjā to spirit possession to various forms of divination. Jains and Buddhists, on the other hand, occasionally did find support with monarchs and (especially) merchants, but their ingrained emphasis on nonviolence (even if unevenly applied) did not easily find favor with kings, while their rootedness in monastic institutions that were often removed from major population centers and worldly concerns[60] gave them less purchase among ordinary people, who looked for most of their ritual needs to brahmins and other representative Hindus.

As the perusal of any survey of Indian religion makes clear,[61] the various ideas, practices, institutions, and identities that constituted religious life on the subcontinent were in constant flux from the very beginning. Hindu traditions shifted from polytheistic ritualism evident in the second-millennium BCE *Ṛg Veda*, to the ascetic, contemplative, and metaphysical preoccupations of the first-millennium BCE Upaniṣads, to the devotionalism of various groups dedicated to the worship of one or another god or goddess that arose late in the first millennium BCE and—without ever entirely superseding earlier approaches—came increasingly to dominate Hindu culture from that time on. Jainism began as an ascetic, monastic tradition in the mid-first millennium BCE, and by the third century BCE had split into competing sects: the more radical "sky-clad" Digambaras, whose male monastics went naked, and the more moderate "white-clad" Śvetāmbaras, who might be monastics, too, but also drew in significant numbers of laypeople, who followed Jain ascetic rules in a modified form. Buddhism seems to have begun only slightly later than Jainism, and in the course of its own development, divided into a multitude of philosophical and monastic traditions, each claiming fealty to the Buddha's teaching, yet each distinct from the others in both obvious and subtle ways. By the turn of the first millennium, the early Buddhist movement had begun to undergo a more dramatic shift, as texts began to appear—the Mahāyāna sūtras—that were not found in the early canons and sometimes taught philosophical doctrines, religious practices, ethical principles, and spiritual ideals different in certain respects from those of the older traditions. The Great Vehicle was slow to gain a foothold in Buddhist monasteries, but its literary and spiritual influence grew over the course of the first millennium CE, so that by the dawn of the medieval period, most Buddhist institutions housed adherents of both the early traditions and the Mahāyāna.

Tantric Contexts

If there was a single religious development that most characterized the seventh to twelfth centuries in India it was the rise of movements that fall under the aegis of the term *Tantra* or *Tantrism*. Quite apart from being a Western (and colonial) scholarly construct rather than an indigenous category, *Tantra*, as David Lorenzen notes, admits of narrower as well as broader definitions: narrowly, it refers to "cults directly associated with the Sanskrit texts known as Tantras, Saṃhitās and Āgamas" (and equivalent writings in Jainism and Buddhism), while broadly it connotes "a wide range of 'popular' religious phenomena that can be broadly characterized as being 'magical' in character."[62] Many scholars, both traditional and modern, have sought to provide simple, single-sentence definitions of Tantra. The Tibetan master Tsongkhapa (1357–1419) describes the common denominator of all tantric traditions—or, at least, the Buddhist ones—as "deity yoga" (T. *lhai neljor*; S. *devayoga*), the process of identifying oneself here and now with the body, speech, and mind of the buddha-deity one someday will become and seeing one's environment as a pure land or divine palace-complex—a maṇḍala.[63] Working from a more Hindu-centered perspective, the modern scholar David Gordon White defines Tantra as

> that Asian body of beliefs and practices which, working from the principle that the universe we experience is nothing other than the concrete manifestation of the divine energy of the godhead that creates and maintains the universe, seeks to rit-

ually appropriate and channel that energy within the human microcosm, in creative and emancipating ways.[64]

Finally, for all too many modern scholars (and some ancients, as well), both in India and elsewhere, Tantra is simply a religion of sex and violence, or sex and violence masquerading as religion. In this view, it is a set of transgressive and antinomian attitudes and practices that are the very antithesis of true spirituality, a "disease"[65] that when introduced into the great Indian traditions did much to debase them and, in the case of Buddhism, helped to kill it off. This negative Orientalist view contrasts with another interpretation, no less Orientalist for its positive evaluation of Tantra, which regards these practices, especially those related to sex, as a refreshing departure from the puritanism besetting most religious traditions and a celebration of natural, "body-positive" human urges that, harnessed properly, may lead to states of surpassing wisdom and joy.[66]

Each of these definitions is open to critique from various perspectives,[67] and despite the efforts of both traditional and modern commentators to define Tantra in a simple manner, most scholars nowadays agree that it cannot and should not be given a single, essentialist definition but is probably best understood through applying Ludwig Wittgenstein's notion of "family resemblances."[68] With this proviso in mind, we may cautiously affirm that, each in their own way, Hinduism and Buddhism (and, in certain instances, Jainism) incorporated into their mainstream a variety of theories and practices that typically included—in various combinations and with differing emphases—such features as the following:

1. A metaphysics that skewed toward nonduality or unity, with a concomitant sense that the physical cosmos is in some sense a manifestation, or expression, of a fundamental spiritual principle, or reality

2. A powerful sense of the homology between macrocosm and microcosm, usually expressed through complex and oftentimes symbolic sets of correspondences—including that between one's body and the cosmos at large—and employment of a governing "imperial metaphor" in which tantric consecrations, deity-yoga practice, and maṇḍalas mimic aspects of medieval Indian "feudal" polity
3. Adherence to an ideal of transformation, seen specifically as the sublimation of the body and mind from coarse to subtle, as in arts like alchemy—whose terminology sometimes was employed
4. The requirement for consecration or initiation (*abhiśeka* or *dīkṣā*) by a qualified guru, which empowers one to assume a divine identity entailing both magical powers and spiritual attainments, including full liberation
5. One's entrance into an esoteric community of initiates sworn to secrecy about key elements of their rites and practices
6. Through the practice of a ritual and contemplative sādhana (means of achievement), the reinforcement of one's divine identity through one, or some, or all, of the following:

    a. Self-visualization as a deity
    b. Employment of special body-postures (*āsanas*) and/or hand gestures (*mudrās*)
    c. Imaginative placement of deities within one's body (*nyāsa*)
    d. Self-location within a visualized sacred space such as a *yantra* or *maṇḍala*
    e. Divinization of one's speech as mantra in order to affect and effect events in oneself and the world
    f. Identification of one's mind with ultimate reality, however conceived

7. At least on the rhetorical level, the celebration of the body, senses, and pleasure, as opposed to the more traditional focus on ascetic transcendence of these "worldly" aspects of ourselves
8. Manipulation of vital winds (*prāṇa*), biotic drops (*bindu*), and states of mind within the subtle body (*sukṣmaśarīra*) of channels (*nāḍī*) and energy centers (*cakra*s) that interpenetrates—and is the source of—our coarse physical body, thereby inducing gnostic awareness, supernal bliss, and magical power
9. A strong propensity to the worship of wrathful and female deities
10. Cultivation of attitudes and actions considered impure or polluted within a Brahmanical or broadly ascetic context, including the exercise of magical powers for coercive or persuasive purposes, ritual consumption of forbidden substances, participation in collective rituals involving song, dance, and sexual yoga, and residence in such "polluted" places as cremation grounds or the neighborhoods of untouchables[69]

It is important to note that many of the characteristics of Tantra listed here—for instance, use of visualization, sacred diagrams, and mantras for magical or soteriological purposes; worship of wrathful or female deities; utilization of the subtle body; and contemplation of cosmic correspondences—may also be found elsewhere in Indian religious traditions that long predate Tantra and, conversely, that not all of the characteristics listed here will be found in every tantric tradition. For instance, while worship of wrathful or female deities is significant, it is not by any means found in every tantric setting, and while the transgressive elements of tantric traditions may be their most sensational and notorious features, they are far from all-pervasive in Tantra, however narrowly or broadly the term is conceived.

The precise origins of Tantra, whether in terms of date, region, or cultural location, have been much debated, although most scholars place it somewhere around the middle of the first millennium CE in various parts of the subcontinent. The question of Tantra's cultural location has been among the most contentious, with some scholars seeing Tantra as a natural development from ideas and practices (including magical ones) already found within the "great" traditions of Hinduism, Jainism, and Buddhism, others suggesting that it was adopted and adapted by the mainstream traditions from the practices of "outsider" tribal or low-caste groups, and still others—the majority nowadays—asserting that it was probably a combination of both mainstream and outside influences.[70] In its patterns of development and practice, Tantra was quite varied, but we might observe generally that the tendency was for the more popular, magical, and antinomian elements associated with the tradition to meet at first with rejection by the guardians of the mainline religions, but eventually to gain a certain degree of acceptance and, importantly, royal support[71]—often at the cost of a degree of domestication, for instance, through the subsumption of tantric concepts and practices under the normative ideologies and practices of this or that mainstream tradition by stressing Tantra's symbolic, internal, and "spiritual" elements. Such domestication was not appreciated by all tantric thinkers or practitioners, and in many cases, the normalization of the tradition was resisted by those who wanted to maintain Tantra's transgressive outlook. In this way, there arose within Tantra something of a dialectic between two polar tendencies: (1) Mainline Tantra, which was closely associated with the standard mythology, doctrines, practices, and institutions of normative Hinduism, Jainism, or Buddhism, and (2) Transgressive Tantra, which might subsist within the mainline institutions (monasteries, ashrams, and the like) and draw on elements of the standard tradition but whose practitioners were most at home at the margins of society or in their own, more intimate institutional settings (such as "clan circles," *gaṇacakras*), where they were free to pursue their ideas and practices unfettered, at least for a time, by convention. The contrast between the Mainline and Transgressive styles of Tantra was far from absolute: there was concord as often as there was conflict, but even when the two strands seemed seamlessly woven together, there remained a certain tension, which has persisted into modern times. These two are not the only options: there is a third way, articulated by poets, philosophers, and adepts of many traditions, that seeks to transcend all dichotomies and distinctions, all rituals and institutions, in a direct, blissful, gnostic encounter with ultimate reality—an approach we might call Radical Tantra.

Non-Buddhist Tantric Contexts

Before focusing in on Buddhist Tantra—also referred to as the Mantra Way (*mantranaya*), the Secret Mantra Way (*guhyamantranaya*), or the Vajrayāna (I will typically use the last term)—we will touch briefly on Jain and Hindu tantric traditions, for regardless of whether Tantra ever was a presectarian or transsectarian religious movement, its Buddhist version cannot be fully understood without reference to the traditions of its competitors in the medieval Indian spiritual marketplace, especially Hinduism. Because it is less obviously interwoven with Buddhist Tantra than Hindu Tantra, the Jain version need not detain us long. As Olle Qvarnström notes, "Tantra was regarded neither as an essential part of Jain theory nor as the principal means of attaining liberation. . . . [H]owever, it did penetrate into mendicant divinatory and meditative practice, and promised mundane as well as soteriological results."[72] The aspects of Tantra that penetrated into Jain practice were primarily in the realm of ritual, for instance the utilization, by both Digambaras and Śvetāmbaras, of certain idiosyncratically Jain mantras for the attainment of worldly goals such as health, wealth, and power and the worship of certain fierce female divinities; and the propitiation, by Śvetāmbaras, of Ghaṇṭākarṇa Mahāvīra, the "Bell-Eared Great Hero," one of a class of powerful male deities known to be protectors of the religion.[73] Given the tradition's ascetic orientation, there never seems to have been a question of its adopting the more transgressive elements of Tantra; as Paul Dundas observes, we do not find among Jains "any serious claim that conventional social and moral values should be turned upside down by engaging in antinomian and sexual and ritual practices" or any particular interest in nondualist or monist metaphysics.[74] Nor, for that matter, does the nondual metaphysics prominent in Hindu and Buddhist Tantra or the consecrations and contemplative self-identification with "deity" found in so many Hindu and Buddhist tantric traditions seem to have taken hold in Jainism.

The world of Hindu Tantra is far more complex and important, and here, we can indicate only its main features in a cursory manner.[75] Although tantric theories and practices are perhaps most closely identified with Bengal, Kashmir, and parts of the south, they eventually made their way into Hinduism everywhere in the subcontinent. Although Hindu tāntrikas often paid lip service to the classics of the mainstream Brahmanical tradition, they mostly concerned themselves with a variety of late-appearing texts designated as āgamas and tantras, which detailed the ideology and techniques that governed their religious lives. Given the eventual ubiquity of Tantra in Hinduism, tantric elements did find their way into Vaiṣṇava traditions,[76] but the original and natural home of Hindu Tantra was in Śaiva and goddess-worship circles, in part, perhaps, because Śiva and such wrathful goddesses as Durgā and Kālī were themselves at one time outsiders to the mainstream tradition who, as it were, worked their way from the periphery to the center of the Hindu imagination.

Some of the earliest identifiably tantric groups include such Śaiva fraternities as the Paśupatas of the mid-first-millennium CE and the somewhat later Kāpālikas and Kālāmukhas,[77] who turned their backs on conventional lay life but did not opt for celibate monasticism, choosing instead to form communities that worshipped Śiva in his various forms, along with dynamic and powerful devīs or yoginīs associated with him,[78] through countercultural and sometimes antinomian practices. The Paśupatas, for instance, adopted the dress and accoutrements of Śiva, such as ashes and a trident; publicly behaved as if mad so as to cultivate ridicule; dwelled in empty caves or cremation grounds; and in the end absorbed into themselves the grace of Śiva, thereby attaining liberation.[79] The Kāpālikas adopted similar practices and were notorious, as well, for ritually consuming liquor, performing sexual rites, and carrying everywhere a skull-cup (*kāpāla*) from which they ate and drank, in imitation of the wrathful form of Śiva known as Bhairava, "the Terrifier."[80] Members of these groups eventually were referred to as *siddhas*, "perfected ones," a term that came to identify tantric adepts of many types during the medieval period and beyond.[81] Such a countercultural lifestyle was not entirely novel. There is evidence as far back as the *Ṛg Veda* of silent sages (*munis*) and vow keepers (*vrātins*) who lived at the margins of society and were regarded with a combination of fascination and fear, and the figure of the potent but problematic *sādhu* or *ṛṣi* has been a fixture in Hindu society and literature throughout its history. With the tantric practitioners' deliberate inversion of Brahmanical notions of purity and pollution, however, the challenge to tradition had become much more overt.

Around the same time, other Śaiva tantric groups, especially, but not only, in Bengal and elsewhere in the east, oriented themselves more toward the union—or reunion—of Śiva with his consort

Parvatī, known in this context as Śakti, his manifest power in female form.[82] Śakta groups, as they are most often known, varied in the degree to which their worship was focused on Śiva or Śakti, with some remaining devoted to the passive, spiritualized male god, others to Śiva's more wrathful manifestations, such as Bhairava, and still others to the active, energetic goddess in one or the other of her forms. In either case, typically the goal of Śakta practice was the attainment of both worldly powers and final liberation. One of many ways in which the attainment of liberation was imagined was as the ascent of Śakti, through subtle-body yogic techniques, from the lowest, or "root," cakra near the base of the spine up through the central channel until it united with Śiva at the thousand-petaled lotus at the cakra at the crown of the head. Over the course of time, Śakta groups divided into two distinct paths. The left-hand way (*vāmācāra*) entailed transgressive practices, often performed in group settings, of which the most notable were the "Five Ms" (*pañcamakāra*): drinking liquor (*madya*), eating meat (*maṃsa*), eating fish (*matsya*), consuming a forbidden parched grain (*mudrā*); and engaging in ritual sexual intercourse (*maithuna*). The right-hand way (*dākṣinācāra*), although committed to many tantric principles and practices, preserved a certain emphasis on Brahmanical purity and tended to find the locus of religious practice not in external transgressive rituals but in inward-oriented transformational yogic practices.

A third and still later medieval Hindu tantric movement of importance is Kashmir (or Trika, "threefold") Śaivism,[83] a nondualist tradition of theory and practice that originated in the mountainous northwest but also flourished in parts of what are now Maharashtra and Odisha and strongly influenced the south Indian tradition of Śrī Vidyā, which focused more on Śakti than Śiva but subscribed to a similar set of ideas and practices. Trika drew on a wide range of earlier Hindu tantric traditions, including those just mentioned and also the mind-only (*cittamātra*) perspective of Yogācāra Buddhism. The Kashmiri masters, who followed a distinctive set of sūtras and tantras, included some of the great philosopher-adepts of Hinduism, most notably Utpaladeva (ninth century) and Abhinavagupta (ninth–tenth centuries). The central doctrine of Kashmir Śaivism is that of "recognition" (*pratyabijñā*), which maintains that our central spiritual obligation is to recognize what we have forgotten: that we ourselves are of the nature of Śiva, and that Śiva, in turn, is best understood as the nondual, blissful source and substance of all that is, described in terms of consciousness and its vibrations or, in threefold terms, as Śiva, Śakti, and physical atoms (*aṇu*), or the epistemic subject, means of knowledge, and objects—with the understanding that the members of any "trinity" all partake of the single spiritual substance that is Śiva. Kashmir Śaiva practices range from standard yogic techniques, to work within the subtle body, to contemplative exercises in which one identifies oneself with Śiva strictly at the level of transcendent awareness. Left-handed practices are described in some texts, but they do not seem to be a key element of the tradition—which, if anything, points the way toward a mode of liberation that is knowledge based and immediate—what I call "Radical Tantra."

Finally, brief mention should be made of the Nāth (protector) Siddha tradition,[84] which seems to have originated in the Deccan in the ninth century CE but is rooted in much older yogic and Śaiva traditions. The Nāth cult, which became especially prominent in the early part of the second millennium, sees Śiva as its *adināth*, or primordial protector and guru, and recognizes a lineage of siddhas who followed in his wake, the most notable being Matsyendranāth (ninth century) and then Gorakhnāth (twelfth century), who organized his followers into an ascetic order that became especially influential in north India and Nepal. In the manner of many other Hindu ascetics, the Nāths typically were itinerant yogins and teachers, and while they may at times have presented an outlandish image and were famed for their interest in alchemy, their acquisition of magical powers, and their collective residence in a heavenly realm known as the *siddhaloka*, their practices were generally less transgressive than those of some earlier tantric groups, being oriented more toward internal contemplation than external ritual. The Nāth lineages have been likened to those described in late Indian, and Tibetan, Buddhist texts, and there may be some historical affinity between the Nāth siddhas and the Buddhist mahāsiddhas, at least to the degree that there is some overlap in lineage lists, with Matsyendranāth (sometimes under other names) finding his way into some Buddhist lineages and figures with well-known Buddhist names like Nāgārjuna and Kṛṣṇācārya (but not Saraha) appearing in some Nāth enumerations.

The picture presented here of Hindu Tantra is vastly oversimplified: the groups mentioned were far more complex than I have indicated, and many groups have gone unmentioned. Nevertheless, two points are worth noting. First, over the course of the development of Hindu Tantra in the medieval period, it seems that the more transgressive and antinomian ("left-handed") practices were most prominent at an early stage, and that as tantric ideas and practices began to be assimilated into (or at least tolerated by) mainline Brahmanical Hinduism, such practices were domesticated and sublimated through a process of internalizing and spiritualizing what had been external and ritualistic, making them "right-handed." Second, however, even as such domestication allowed tantric ideas and practices to become a legitimate part of Hindu tradition, the antinomian elements that marked Tantra's initial appearance never fully disappeared and have continued among certain groups, both in ideology and practice, up to the present day. Even now, the relation between the so-called left-handed, or Transgressive, and right-handed, or Mainline, ways persists as an ongoing structural dialectic within Hinduism that never has been, and perhaps cannot be, fully resolved—except, perhaps, by recourse to the approach of Radical Tantra, which somehow both transcends and subsumes the Mainline and Transgressive traditions.

Buddhist Tantric Contexts

Although Hinduism, Jainism, and Buddhism formed distinct religious communities in medieval India, with their own mythologies, scriptures, institutions, ideologies, practices, and sense of historical and social identity, we should not fall into the trap of thinking of them solely in denominational terms. Wherever they might be found, members of each group shared a common physical environment, a common social milieu, a common culture and language, a common cosmology centered on notions of saṃsāra, karma, and liberation, and a common pattern of religious practice. They also competed with one other, influenced one other, and stole from one other, such that we can never write the history of one tradition without reference to the others. This certainly is the case when it comes to Vajrayāna, but ascertaining the degree to which non-Buddhist—basically, Hindu—ideas and practices influenced Buddhist traditions and precisely when those influences were brought to bear is no simple matter. Were such influences evident from the beginning, even in relatively nontransgressive, mainline tantric paths, or do they apply only to the more transgressive discourses and practices of the later tantras? And in the case of the more transgressive tantras, did the Buddhists simply assimilate ideas and practices from such Hindu groups as the Paśupatas, Kāpālikas, and Śaktas, or were the Hindu groups more beholden to the Buddhists? Scholarly opinion varies on all these points, but the evidence suggests that there was no unidirectional flow and that Buddhists and Hindus interacted with, and influenced, each other in both the earlier, Mainline phase and the later, Transgressive phase of the development of Vajrayāna.[85]

As with tantric traditions more broadly, the exact point at which Vajrayāna begins is impossible to ascertain. Many of the features that would eventually infuse the tantric tradition—such as accounts of visionary meetings with buddhas, the practice of contemplative visualization, the ritual use of protective mantras and *dhāraṇīs*, and a fascination with magical powers—were evident even in the authoritative texts of Mainstream Buddhism, including the Pāli canon.[86] With the appearance of Mahāyāna sūtras, and then treatises, starting around the beginning of the first millennium CE, such features gained even greater prominence, and other prototantric elements were added. These included

- accounts of practitioners—bodhisattvas, or buddhas-to-be—being assisted on the path by the blessings or sustaining power (*adhiṣṭāna*) of not just Śākyamuni Buddha but multiple buddhas, who are ubiquitous throughout the cosmos;
- descriptions of the buddha fields and pure lands inhabited by these buddhas, which in many respects foreshadow tantric maṇḍalas;
- the articulation of philosophical doctrines, such as emptiness (*śūnyatā*), which stressed the metaphysical insubstantiality of all things; mind-only (*cittamātra*), which asserted the fundamentally mental nature of all things and the consequent malleability of reality through the transformation of the mind; and buddha-nature (*buddhadhātu*) or the *tathāgata* matrix (*tathāgatagarbha*), which gave assurance that all beings had awakening as their basic nature and ultimate destiny; and
- the development of the principle of skillful means (*upāya-kauśalya*), which served to explain the Buddha's pedagogical prowess and, importantly, provided an approach to ethics

> that was less rule based and more situational than that of mainstream traditions, specifying that in certain circumstances buddhas and advanced bodhisattvas may transgress standard moral rules if they are certain that doing so will benefit one or more sentient beings.[87]

Precisely how the ideas and practices of "standard" Mahāyāna developed into those of Buddhist Tantra, or Vajrayāna, remains something of a mystery, with some scholars suggesting that the dhāranī (or spell) texts that proliferated in the mid-first-millennium are evidence of a transitional phase between standard and tantric Mahāyāna, and others pointing out, as well, that many of the earliest texts labeled as tantras share as many features with Mahāyāna ritual literature as with full-blown Vajrayāna.[88] Thus, although their outlook and practices may seem at times to reflect a sudden break in the tradition, the Buddhist tantras probably did not appear overnight but gradually, and in various parts of the subcontinent, including, notably, though not exclusively, both the south and the northwest.[89] The earliest such texts—which resemble standard Mahāyāna literature in their claim to be the word of the Buddha but differ in their insistence that practice requires prior ritual consecration by a guru—began to circulate sometime around the seventh century, and they continued to appear throughout the medieval period, as the tradition grew, changed, and came increasingly to dominate Buddhist intellectual and religious life in the subcontinent. Later scholars, both in India and Tibet, would divide the tantras that appeared (each claiming to be the word of the Buddha) into various "classes" or "sets"—variously enumerated as three-, four-, five-, or sixfold. Perhaps the most useful enumeration is the fivefold, which divides the literature (and the practices they describe) into action (*kriyā*), performance (*caryā*), yoga, mahāyoga, and yoginī tantras.[90] Although these five types of tantras do not form a strictly chronological sequence, such that when one type was exhausted the next one arose, it is generally accepted, by both traditional and modern scholars, that most of the action and performance tantras were written down in the sixth and seventh centuries, the yoga tantras in the seventh and eighth centuries, the mahāyoga tantras in the eighth and ninth centuries, and the yoginī tantras between the late eighth and the eleventh centuries. In this sense, to describe each of the sets in their usual order allows us to arrive at some sense of the development of the tradition over the course of the medieval period.

The action tantra class is the largest and most heterogeneous,[91] comprising 469 works in the Tibetan collection of "Buddha-word," the Kangyur, and consisting of a range of ritual and philosophical texts (the latter including some well-known sūtras) composed in the early-to-mid-first-millennium CE. The ritual texts are dedicated to the visualization and worship of a multitude of Buddhist deities, divided by later analysts into three families, the Tathāgata, Lotus, and Vajra, which may be subdivided still further. The longest and best-known action tantra is a sprawling work known as *The Basic Ordinance of Mañjuśrī* (*Mañjuśrīmūlakalpa*), but numerous other buddha or bodhisattva figures—male and female, peaceful and wrathful—including Avalokiteśvara, Tārā, Mārīcī, and a set of five protectresses are included, as well. Although action tantras typically (but not uniformly) require a disciple to receive, from a guru, consecrations (those of the garland, water, and the crown) and to observe numerous vows and pledges related to practicing secrecy, purity, and service to the deity,[92] they do not always prescribe deity yoga, the initiate's self-visualization as the deity at the center of a maṇḍala. They are generally divisible into a yoga with signs, involving visualization, and a yoga without signs, which is the contemplation of emptiness. They are seldom overtly preoccupied with soteriology, being more often focused on ritual service to the deity and to effecting worldly goals through visualization and mantra.

Therefore, later commentators, in both India and Tibet, considered action tantras to be the most externalized, and thus the "lowest," of the tantric classes. At the same time, however, precisely because they were less "advanced" or esoteric, action tantra practices were widely popular among Buddhists in both South Asia and Tibet. The first great commentator on this class of texts was the eighth-century scholar Buddhaguhya.

If the action tantra class is the largest, the closely related but generally somewhat later performance tantra class is the smallest,[93] consisting of only eight texts in the Tibetan Kangyur. Like the action tantras, the performance tantras are divided into the Tathāgata, Lotus, and Vajra "families." The best-known performance tantra is the *Sūtra of Great Vairocana* (*Mahāvairocana Sūtra*) or, alternatively, the *Tantra of Mahāvairocana's Awakening* (*Mahāvairocanābhisaṃbodhi Tantra*); other texts of the class are focused on such deities as Vajrapāṇi and a set of eight goddesses. In addition to the garland, water, and crown consecrations, tantras in this class require three further consecrations, those of the vajra, bell, and name, which enjoin initiates to observe vows and pledges much like those of the action tantras. Further, as in the action tantras, their practices are divisible into a yoga with signs and a yoga without signs, but they are oriented more than tantras of the earlier class toward the practice of deity yoga. Furthermore, while their preoccupation remains primarily external, ritual, and magical, a concern with internal practices and the soteriological goal of buddhahood (imagined as Mahāvairocana) are also evident. In this sense, the performance tantras may be seen as a "bridge" between the largely ritualistic action tantras and the more interior and contemplative yoga tantras. As with the action tantras, the first great commentator on the performance tantras was the eighth-century master Buddhaguhya.

If the action and performance tantras mark a transitional phase between standard Mahāyāna ideas and practices and those of full-fledged Vajrayāna, with the appearance of yoga tantras in the eighth century,[94] the transition to esoteric Buddhism is complete—though far from final. This class of tantras is slightly larger than performance tantra, consisting of fifteen texts in the Tibetan Kangyur. The yoga tantras are divided into five families: the Buddha (headed by the tathāgata Vairocana), the Vajra (headed by Akṣobhya), the Jewel (headed by Ratnasambhava), the Lotus (headed by Amitābha), and the Karma (headed by Amoghasiddhi). Each of the tathāgatas is related to various fivefold classifications, such as the five directions of a maṇḍala (the center, east, south, west, and north, respectively), the five elements (space, water, earth, fire, and wind), and the five kinds of buddha gnosis (the dharma-sphere, mirrorlike, equalizing, discerning, and all-accomplishing gnoses), as well as further fivefold sets of colors, hand gestures, thrones, seed mantras, and offering goddesses, and variously numbered sets of bodhisattvas and protector deities.[95] The "root" (*mūla*) yoga tantra is the *Compendium of Principles of All the Tathāgatas* (*Sarvatathāgatatattvasaṃgraha*);[96] "explanatory" (*ākhya*) or secondary tantras include the *Vajra Peak* (*Vajraśekhara*), *Primal Supreme* (*Paramādya*), *Conquest of the Three Worlds* (*Traokyavijaya*), and the highly influential *Litany of the Names of Mañjuśrī* (*Mañjuśrīnāmasaṃgīti*).[97] Just as the performance tantras required more consecrations than the action tantras, so the yoga tantras further expanded the requirements, so that there are now six: the garland, water, crown, vajra, bell, and name. Some scholars assert that there is a seventh and final consecration in yoga tantra, that of the vajra master (*vajrācārya*), but the question is disputed.[98] The vows and pledges to be observed by initiates are similar to those of the action and performance tantras.

Like those of the action and performance tantras, yoga tantra practices are divisible into a yoga with signs (involving visualization, mantras, maṇḍalas, and so forth) and a yoga without signs that is focused on emptiness. Ritual and magic figure into the yoga tantras as surely as in the lower classes, but the orientation here is primarily soteriological: the goal is the attainment of buddhahood through the sacralization of self and cosmos entailed by deity yoga, with one or another form of Buddha the object of focus but, as in performance tantra, with Mahāvairocana as the most important. One key set of terms developed in the yoga tantras is that of the four seals (*mudrā*): the action seal (*karmamudrā*), pledge seal (*samayamudrā*), great seal (*mahāmudrā*), and dharma seal (*dharmamudrā*), which may relate to hand gestures but are more significant as "confirmations" of various contemplative achievements. Among the commentators on the yoga tantras, the most important are, again, Buddhaguhya, along with other eighth-century figures like Mañjuśrīkīrti and Vilasavajra, and the ninth-century master Ānandagarbha. The yoga tantras comprised the vast majority of the esoteric texts that were transmitted to East Asia during the eighth century CE, so such traditions as Chinese Zhenyan and Japanese Shingon reflect this particular stage of Indian Vajrayāna. The yoga tantras were also highly influential in Tibet during the earlier spread of the teachings there (ca. 650–850 CE). In both cases, the "imperial metaphor," drawn from medieval Indian political structures and practices for the spiritual enhancement of the individual, proved popular among actual imperial figures—the emperors of China, Japan, and Tibet—thereby enhancing the fortunes of Buddhist institutions in those far-flung settings. Like the action and performance tantras, the yoga tantras are typically nontransgressive in their rhetoric and practices, but antinomian elements do appear at times,[99] indicating the influence of early examples of the two final classes of tantra to develop on the subcontinent, the mahāyoga and yoginī tantras, to which we turn next.

Mahāyoga and Yoginī Tantra Contexts

The mahāyoga and yoginī tantras—which were designated by Tibetan scholars of the renaissance period as the "father" (or "method") and "mother" (or "wisdom") tantras, respectively, within the larger class known as the unexcelled yoga-tantras[100]—were written down as early as the eighth century and continued to appear until at least the eleventh century. In the Tibetan Kangyur, they comprise slightly over one hundred texts. Most scholars believe that the mahāyoga tantras generally appeared earlier and the yoginī tantras somewhat later, but there is much temporal overlap between the two and, despite some differences that will be laid out below, they have many features in common, and these will be described first. Both sets of tantras are rooted in the structures, ideas, and practices found in the yoga tantras, but they differ from those in the earlier class in many ways, the most obvious being the way in which they give Vajrayāna a decidedly transgressive turn. They are also, at least in theory, the most interiorized and soteriologically oriented of the tantric systems, hence later scholars' insistence that the action, performance, and yoga tantras are the "lower tantras," and the mahāyoga and yoginī tantras alone are the "higher" classes. Despite their purported emphasis on interiority, the tantras themselves, and much of the literature surrounding them, are replete with ritual and magical elements—indeed it is rare (rhetoric notwithstanding) to find a Vajrayāna text or tradition that completely eschews such elements. They almost certainly were influenced to some degree by earlier or contemporaneous Hindu tantric traditions, such as those of the Paśupatas, Kāpālikas, Śaktas, and Kashmir Śaivites, but the influence, as noted, was likely mutual, and in any case, the Buddhists recast theories and techniques drawn from outside the fold in decidedly Buddhist terms—and sometimes in an overtly triumphalist manner, as in stories about the subjugation of Maheśvara (Śiva) by the wrathful buddha Heruka—a generic term for wrathful male deities of the mahāyoga and, especially, the yoginī tantra class.[101]

As in the yoga tantras, mahāyoga and yoginī-tantra practices are usually subsumed under five buddha families, with their appropriate correspondences to colors, directions, elements, parts of the body, goddesses, seed mantras, bodhisattvas, protector deities, and buddha gnoses. There are some changes, however: Akṣobhya sometimes switches places with Vairocana and becomes the central tathāgata of the maṇḍala; the tathāgatas are often depicted in sexual union with a female consort; and additional correspondences are introduced—for instance, by seeing the five aggregates (consciousness, form, sensation, conception, and formations), the five basic defilements (ignorance, anger, pride, desire, and envy), and the five main cakras of the subtle body (heart, crown, throat, navel, and sex organ) as part of the symbolic equivalency scheme.[102] In addition, there is a clear sense in both sets of tantras that there are buddhas who in some sense preside over the tantras, such as Vajradhara and Vajrasattva, as well as a bodhisattva especially assigned to guard the tradition, Vajrapāṇi, also known as the Lord of Secrets (Guhyapati). The consecrations required in mahāyoga tantra mark a dramatic departure from those found in the lower tantras. The water, crown, vajra, and bell consecrations are subsumed under a single category as elements of the "vase" consecration, and three higher consecrations are introduced: the secret consecration, in which the initiating guru joins in sexual union with a consort and has the initiate taste the mingled sexual fluids, thereby inducing great bliss; the wisdom-gnosis consecration, in which the initiate enters into union with the consort and experiences a blissful, empty gnosis within the body; and the fourth, or word initiation, which entails instruction on the true soteriological significance of the consecrations and the practices they empower the initiate to perform. As with the lower tantras, consecration into a mahāyoga-tantra system empowers the disciple to practice deity yoga, and, in this particular case, it plants the seeds for attaining the four bodies of a buddha: the reality, enjoyment, emanation, and essence bodies. As before, it also entails the observance of vows and pledges by an initiate, but here, the category is expanded to include a specific vajra-master (*vajrācārya*) pledge requiring obedience to the guru and often to impose an enumerated set of root and auxiliary tantric vows, enjoining, for instance, guru devotion, respect for one's fellow initiates, maintenance of *bodhicitta*, contemplation of emptiness, and respect for women.

Mahāyoga and yoginī tantra practices are divided quite differently than those of the lower tantras. Although ritual and magic are present in the higher tantras as in the lower, the strongly soteriological orientation of the later systems, flavored by an infusion of transgressive elements, makes them distinctive. As in yoga tantra, the goal remains the attainment of buddhahood through the sacralization of self and cosmos entailed by deity yoga, but the buddha form with which the practitioner identifies is typically wrathful or semiwrathful in countenance, possessed of multiple heads, arms, and legs, and often depicted in sexual union with a consort. Later analysts eventually identified two major stages, or processes, in the higher tantras: the generation, or creation, stage (*utpattikrama*) and the completion, or perfection, stage (*sampannakrama*).

The generation stage,[103] which is centrally concerned with changing our way of seeing ourselves and the cosmos, follows the same basic procedures as the sādhanas of the lower tantras but in a far more elaborate form. Complex mahāyoga and yoginī tantra sādhanas often begin with the creation, out of emptiness, of a magical protection circle, within which reside wrathful deities who, when they receive appropriate offerings, go forth to dispel obstacles. After the reduction of the protection circle to emptiness, the physical elements emerge and are arranged into the maṇḍala—

the palace—of the buddha-deity to whom the sādhana is devoted. One then dissolves into emptiness, and from emptiness, then from a seed syllable, one arises as the deity himself or herself. Later traditions would equate emptiness, the seed syllable, and the deity body with, respectively, transcendence of the samsaric processes of death, intermediate existence, and rebirth, and with attainment of the reality body, enjoyment body, and emanation body of a buddha. From the deity's union with a consort (who is imagined either in bodily form or symbolically) other deities—buddhas, bodhisattvas, protectors, offering goddesses, and so forth—are generated and placed in various parts of the maṇḍala. The whole process is then divinized by the ritual invocation of the actual deities (the gnosis beings, *jñānasattva*), who descend into the visualized deities (the pledge beings, *samayasattva*). In particularly complex sādhanas, one will generate a maṇḍala *within* the body, visualizing various divine beings at various parts of it, thereby anticipating the divine body one eventually will obtain. After goddesses make offerings to all the maṇḍala deities, one utters mantras appropriate to each one while sending forth light-rays throughout the cosmos to benefit beings and achieve various mundane purposes, which may include exercise of such tantric powers as pacification, increase, coercion, and destruction. One then reabsorbs everything into oneself—the cosmos, the maṇḍala, and its deities—and dissolves one's self-visualization from top and bottom into a seed syllable at the heart cakra, which itself dissolves into emptiness—an emptiness from which one then reemerges as the deity in simple form. In such a form, one may go on to make sacrificial offerings to wrathful deities or reenter everyday life with the "divine pride" that one is enacting one's own future buddhahood, seeing oneself and others as deities, hearing and uttering all speech as mantra, and identifying one's mind with the nondual gnosis possessed by all buddhas.

Entry into the completion stage typically requires complete mastery of the generation stage in all its details, which requires in turn immense powers of concentration.[104] Although completion-stage practices are carried out within the general context of one's self-visualization as a buddha-deity, most of the work is performed within the subtle body (or vajra body), consisting of channels, cakras, vital winds, and biotic drops. Through the application of various bodily postures, forceful breathing exercises, and (sometimes) sexual yoga practices with a consort, referred to, variously, as the seal (*mudrā*), the great seal (*mahāmudrā*), or the action seal (*karmamudrā*), the vital winds are drawn from the outer channels—most notably those on the left and right—into the central channel of the subtle body. There they are mentally directed in such a way as to open up previously constricted cakras and move drops located at various cakras up and down, inducing progressively more intense experiences of emptiness or joy or both. Although, as with all tantric practices, there are variations, typically (and sometimes with the aid of sexual yoga practices) one will further concentrate the mind within the heart cakra, said to be the seat of the "indestructible drop" in which our subtlest mentality (our basic awareness) and physicality (the essential vital wind) reside. There one passes through visions akin to those at the time of death, experiences a blissful, nondualistic gnosis fully realizing the empty and luminous nature of mind/reality, recreates one's body as a divine body, and then, having completed the path, arises as a fully awakened buddha, who has overcome all defilement, transcended death, possesses a buddha's four bodies, and is ready to work spontaneously, effectively, and endlessly to effect the aims of sentient beings from the perfected state of the mahāmudrā attainment (*mahāmudrāsiddhi*).

This synoptic account of the higher tantras, drawn as it is from later scholastic analyses produced in India and Tibet, is, of course, vastly oversimplified, for it fails to account either for the differences between the two broad classes of higher tantra, or among the various tantra systems of a given class, or among the various ideas and practices promulgated within a given tantric system—not to mention the ways in which all of those elements of Vajrayāna played out in historical time. It also fails to account for a whole set of tantras, originating in northwest India in the late first millennium CE, that were accepted only by scholars of the "old," or Nyingma, tradition of Tibetan Buddhism but were generally either rejected or ignored by masters of such "new" Tibetan renaissance orders as the Kadam, Sakya, Kagyu, and Geluk. I cannot enter here into all the details and nuances of the various tantric systems but will indicate at least briefly some of the key features of the mahāyoga and yoginī tantras and the ways in which they differ.

The mahāyoga (or "father") tantras[105]—many of which were transmitted to Tibet during the early, imperial-period spread of Buddhism but were important there as well during the later-transmission period—consist of around thirty-three texts in the Tibetan Kangyur. The most important of the mahāyoga tantras—it was dubbed by later scholars as the "king of tantras"—is the *Guhyasamāja* (*Secret Assembly*);[106] other important texts of this class include the *Māyājāla* (*Net of Illusion*), *Kṛṣṇayamāri* (*Black Yamāri*), and *Vajrabhairava* (*Vajra-Terrifier*) tantras. All of these, and others, were clarified (purportedly by the Buddha himself) in commentarial tantras (*ākhyatantras*) like the Guhyasamāja-related *Vajra Garland* (*Vajramālā*),[107] and then in further treatises and commentaries composed by various masters of the late first millennium. The most important system, the Guhyasamāja, has 133 separate works devoted to it in the Tibetan collection of Indian commentaries and treatises, the Tengyur. The authors of these commentaries and treatises include such luminaries as Padmavajra, Buddhaśrījñāna, Virūpa, Śāntipa, and the Guhyasamāja commentators who went under the names of Nāgārjuna, Āryadeva, and Candrakīrti.[108] As noted, on the whole, though not in every case, the mahāyoga tantras probably appeared slightly earlier than the yoginī tantras, and for all the similarities in outlook and practices from one class to the other, the Guhyasamāja and other mahāyoga systems display certain features that, according to later analysts, separate them from the yoginī systems. The most notable, perhaps, are (a) their greater tendency to populate their maṇḍalas with, and to worship, male deities, while paying due respect to female deities (b) their special focus on completion-stage techniques for harnessing the vital winds and leading the practitioner through five stages to a culminating series of experiences of emptiness—the empty, the very empty, the great empty, and the all-empty—which correspond to experiences occurring at the end of a normal death process: the white, red, black, and clear-light (or luminous) visions, respectively.

The yoginī (or "mother") tantras[109]—a few of which were transmitted to Tibet during the early period of the teaching but that were most influential during the later, "renaissance" period—consists of over seventy texts in the Tibetan Kangyur. The most important of the tantras are the *Union of All the Buddhas* (*Sarvabuddhasamāyoga*), often considered the earliest of the class, *Cakrasaṃvara*,[110] *Hevajra*,[111] *Buddhakapāla*, *Mahāmāyā* (*Great Illusion*), and *Kālacakra* (*Wheel of Time*), which is usually considered the last of the class to appear.[112] As with the mahāyoga tantras, these basic yoginī tantras were clarified in commentarial tantras, such as the Hevajra-related *Drop of Mahāmudrā* (*Mahāmudrāṭilaka*), and then in hundreds of further treatises and commentaries composed by late first millennium masters. The Tibetan Tengyur contains over two hundred works devoted to the Cakrasaṃvara system and around 165 on the Hevajra. Authors of yoginī-tantra commentaries and treatises include such notables as Saraha, Lūyipa, Kṛṣṇācārya, Puṇḍarīka, and Nāropa.[113] Among the features that distinguish the yoginī tantras from those of the mahāyoga class, the most important are

- their tendency to populate their maṇḍalas primarily with female deities, usually identified as yoginīs, *ḍākinī*s, or devīs, even when the central deity of the maṇḍala is male;
- the way in which they gave rise to important meditational deities to whom no specific tantra is devoted, most notably the female buddha Vajrayoginī,[114] who seems to have been derived from the consorts of Cakrasaṃvara and Hevajra, Vajravārāhī and Nairātmyā, respectively;
- their special focus on completion-stage techniques for generating four progressively more intense states of joy (*ānanda*), which are inseparably conjoined with a gnostic realization of the emptiness that is the true nature of mind/reality, namely, joy (*ānanda*), supreme joy (*paramānanada*), cessative joy (*viramānanda*), and connate joy (*sahajānanda*); and
- their focus on various tantric "terms of art" to refer to the ultimate reality/experience, most notably
  - "the connate" (*sahaja*), which designates the ultimate, transrational gnostic state in which, for instance, saṃsāra and *nirvāṇa*, conventional and ultimate truth, bliss and emptiness, and other pairings are experienced nondually as "coemergent" or "born together," that is, possessed of a single taste (*ekarasa*) or the same nature;[115]
  - the primordial nature (*nijasvabhāva*), which refers to the fundamental emptiness, luminosity, and bliss that have been the inborn nature of mind (*citta*) or mind-itself (*cittatvā*) from beginningless time, and which only advanced tantric techniques can uncover;
  - the great seal (*mahāmudrā*), which gains greater importance than in the yoga tantras and refers, among other things, to a female sexual consort, the gnosis of connate emptiness and bliss, the emptiness that "seals" the nature of all phenomena, a technique for contemplating the

true nature of mind, and the buddhahood in which the tantric path issues;[116] and

- the adamantine, or diamond-like (*vajra*) body, speech, and mind that are explored, mastered, and utilized by advanced tantric practitioners such as the mahāsiddhas, for whom they are equivalent to the bodies (*kāya*) of a buddha.

As should be evident, the path to buddhahood described in the mahāyoga and yoginī tantras is complex and difficult: although often promoted as the quick and natural way to awakening, it requires of the initiate an extraordinary amount of discipline, compassion, wisdom, and ritual and meditative prowess. It is unsurprising, therefore, that there emerged within the various higher-tantra systems an alternate discourse, which insisted on dropping all ritual and contemplative elaboration and simply, directly realizing the primordially pure, luminous, blissful, and empty nature of the mind—thereby attaining buddhahood in an instant. Within the mahāyoga and, especially, the yoginī tantra practice-communities, this direct approach—a Buddhist instance of what I have called Radical Tantra—was articulated in terms of the great seal (*mahāmudrā*), the connate nature (*sahaja*), or the primordial mind (*nijacitta*), while within communities oriented toward what later would be called the Nyingma tantras, it was described as the great perfection (S. *mahāsandhi*; T. *dzokpa chenpo*, or *dzokchen*) or the yoga of transcendence (S. *atiyoga*). The rhetoric of the direct approach may be gleaned from passages in the higher tantras themselves, but it is more readily apparent in later commentaries and treatises, and most especially in the songs of the mahāsiddhas, the great adepts who were the most charismatic exponents of the higher tantras, and whose contributions we will examine in the next section.

Mahāsiddha Contexts

The mahāsiddhas—the great perfected ones, or great adepts—are the exemplary practitioners of the Buddhist higher tantras.[117] Very few can be dated with certainty, and some may be literary inventions, but like their counterparts, the siddhas of Hindu traditions, they were at once admired, loathed, feared, and emulated in medieval India and were a source of endless inspiration in the Tibetan and other inner Asian Buddhist traditions that inherited the literature, lore, and teachings of late Indian Buddhism—for many of these traditions, they were important members of practice lineages that gave coherence and justification to Tibetan Buddhist orders. The mahāsiddhas are grouped and enumerated in various ways, but the most famous account, that of an eleventh-century author,[118] purportedly Indian, named Abhayadatta, counts eighty-four,[119] which include major figures like Indrabhūti, Lakṣmīṅkarā, Saraha, Nāgārjuna, Āryadeva, Lūyipa, Śavaripa, Virūpa, Kṛṣṇācārya, Tilopa, and Nāropa but also many more masters about whom little is known, and it excludes many figures classified elsewhere as mahāsiddhas, such as Padmavajra, Maitrīpa, Abhayākaragupta, and Padampa Sangyé, as well as the masters of the great perfection recognized in the Nyingma tradition of Tibetan Buddhism, such as Mañjuśrīkīrti, Śrī Siṃha, Padmasambhava, Vimalamitra, and Vairocana.[120]

A brief demographic survey of these masters reveals the following:[121]

- Eighty of the mahāsiddhas are male and four female, and the adepts' gurus are also primarily males (whether human or divine), although eleven were initiated and instructed by female deities such as Vajravārāhī, Tārā, or one or another (usually unnamed) ḍākinī.
- Although their birthplaces are not always identifiable (and,

as in the case of Saraha, alternate sources sometimes differ on their locale), at least three hailed from the northwest of the subcontinent, seven from the south, and two from the west, while the vast majority—well over fifty—are associated with the domains of the Pāla empire.

- In terms of social status, nine are identified as brahmins, seventeen as princes or rulers, four as merchants, nine as monastics, and over half as low caste, either as unspecified śūdras or as involved in occupations such as farming, hunting, fishing, cobbling, wine selling, bird catching, cremation-ground supervision, or pottery.
- The tantric systems in which they specialized go unmentioned in more than half the cases, but of those that are described, six practiced Guhyasamāja, eighteen Hevajra, and sixteen Cakrasaṃvara.

Although Abhayadatta's text is far from our only source for biographies of the mahāsiddhas,[122] it is among the earliest and most detailed, and even if we allow for considerable fictionalization on the author's part, we still emerge with a general sense of who these figures were: they were overwhelmingly, but not exclusively, male, as were their teachers; most of them were born and lived in the northeastern regions usually controlled by the Pālas in the medieval period; their social status and occupation varied widely, but at least half were born in—or adopted—"lower" professions; and of the masters whose tantric system is identified, a minority focused on the mahāyoga tantras (specifically, the Guhyasamāja), while the vast majority practiced the yoginī tantras (Hevajra and Cakrasaṃvara in roughly equal measure).

Of the mahāsiddhas described by Abhayadatta, all but four have at least one work ascribed to them in the Tibetan Tengyur, and many of the major figures are credited with a dozen, a score, or more writings.[123] Particularly among the more prolific, the genres in which they wrote range widely: countless sādhanas and other ritual texts connected to tantric deities; commentaries on important tantras like the Hevajra (Kṛṣṇācārya), Buddhakapāla (Saraha), and Kālacakra (Nāropa); prose or verse treatises on tantric themes such as Lakṣmīṅkarā's *Connate Attainment* (*Sahajasiddhi*) and Nāgārjuna's *Five Stages* (*Pañcakrama*); and a huge trove of tantric songs—some of them quite personal in nature—which are typically written in one of three main poetic genres: dohās, performance songs (*caryāgīti*), and vajra songs (*vajragīti*).[124] The term *dohā* properly refers to a didactic couplet (sometimes part of a quatrain) that, in the Indic-language specimens available to us (for example, in Apabhraṃśa or, in the post-Buddhist era, Hindi or another north Indian vernacular language), typically involves a specific meter and an end rhyme; however, the term is also used to describe a collection of such verses into a "treasury" (*kośa*) and the themes found in such collections, mainly instructions on yogic practice, peppered with occasional reports of the author's spiritual experiences.[125] Performance songs also display regular meters and end rhymes in their Indic-language versions (for example, in Apabhraṃśa or Old Bengali) but are distinguishable from dohās by virtue of their being self-contained short songs that typically express the author's experiences and ideas using highly symbolic, idiosyncratically tantric imagery.[126] Vajra songs utilize similar poetic forms in their Indic-language versions (typically in Apabhraṃśa) and are distinctive because of their function: they were meant to be sung at tantric ritual feasts (*gaṇacakra*).[127] None of these categories is hard and fast: there are, for instance, "dohā treasuries" (like the several attributed to Saraha) that include verses in meters other than the dohā and vajra songs (like Saraha's *Body*, *Speech*, and *Mind Treasuries*) that are highly didactic. The more important point is that these songs—many of which may have originally been oral compositions—are among the most striking examples of medieval Indian Buddhist literature, and they undoubtedly proved as appealing, and mystifying, to their listeners or readers a millennium ago as they do to modern readers, whether in Asia or elsewhere.

Given their numbers and diversity and the breadth of their writings, we must be cautious about identifying a central teaching of the mahāsiddhas, for there inevitably will be exceptions to any generalization. With that caveat in mind, however, we may note that many but not all the great adepts would agree on the following—at least on a rhetorical level:[128]

- The standard "Hindu"-based system of caste hierarchy, rooted in concerns about purity and pollution, is not the social exemplification of a divine order but an arbitrary human convention, and its rules—including those prohibiting contact with low-caste people and engaging in low-caste occupations—are subject to abrogation.
- Whether non-Buddhist or Buddhist, nontantric or tantric, conventional religion—with its formulaic ideas, elaborate rituals, ascetic practices, and complex meditations, not to mention the hypocrisy and corruption of many of its proponents—is more likely to lead people away from spiritual freedom than toward it and must be eschewed if liberation is to be attained.
- Scholarly study, philosophical analysis, and metaphysical speculation—indeed all conceptual and mental elaboration—divide up mind and the world in ways that have nothing to do with their actual nature and must be transcended on the path to awakening.
- In more positive terms, the surest way to attain freedom is to see, in a direct and unmediated way, the nature of one's mind, which is pure, luminous, blissful, empty, and aware—

and is available only to those who have received blessings and instruction at the feet of a qualified guru.

- Along with realizing the nature of the mind, the disciple must be willing to utilize the senses and the body on the spiritual path, transmuting ordinary sensory experience into divine delectation and working within the vajra body to transform mind and body into those of a buddha.
- The disciple must be willing, when necessary, to embrace overtly transgressive practices, from ingesting the "five nectars" (also referred to as "lamps")—urine, feces, semen, blood, and marrow—and the "five meats" (also referred to as "goads")—those of a bull, dog, elephant, horse, and human—so as to overcome dualistic ideas about pure and impure or pleasant and repellant, to cultivating sexual yoga so as to manipulate energies within the subtle body and generate transcendent bliss, to evoking and mastering wrathful forces so as to dispel obstacles to one's own practice and the welfare of beings, to developing yogic powers that effect good for oneself and the world on both the mundane and transmundane levels.

No doubt, other common teachings might be cited, but these are the ones that appear most often in the mahāsiddhas' writings, especially their spiritual songs.

Although the mahāsiddhas sometimes seem like "lone wolf" iconoclasts, they were denizens of medieval Indian society, where they interacted with people of all castes, occupations, and religious persuasions, and themselves often belonged to formal or informal communities of kindred spirits. Although the places they frequented included cremation grounds, low-caste settlements, and out-of-the-way jungles or mountains, they also dwelled in towns and cities—and not infrequently in Buddhist monasteries, where their presence was often regarded with a combination of fascination and suspicion.

This is quite understandable, given that monasteries were, at least in theory, bastions of celibacy, whose denizens were committed to following one or another set of *pratimokṣa* (individual liberation) vows incumbent on all monastics. Mahāsiddha practices, on the other hand, could include any number of transgressive elements, including sexual yoga, the ingestion of various types of forbidden or disgusting bodily flesh and fluids, consumption of alcohol, and evocation of wrathful deities and energies. Although on a day-to-day basis, the sādhana practice through which an adept identified with a particular buddha-deity might be carried out alone, key elements of tantric ritual were collective in nature, especially the consecrations that laid the basis for sādhana practice (described in the previous section) and the ritual feasts (*gaṇacakra*), in which practitioners—assuming the identity and accoutrements of the wrathful buddha Heruka if male and one or another yoginī if female—came together to sing, dance, offer, and consume various "impure" substances and engage in sexual yoga. An evocative description of the ritual feast is given in the *Hevajra Tantra*:

> The [male organ] is located at Kollagīri, the [female organ] at Mummuṇi.
> The hand drum is sounded forcefully. Compassion is practiced, not discord.
> Here we eat meat and drink liquor in great quantities.
> Hey! The worthy enter here, the unworthy are barred.
> We bring feces, [urine, semen, menstrual blood, and marrow]. Here we eat herbs and human flesh with relish.
> We move to and fro without thought of pure and impure.
> Adorning our limbs with bone ornaments, here we enter the corpse.
> In the meeting we perform the sexual union; the untouchable is not rejected here.[129]

The passage goes on to describe songs, dances, offerings, and sexual practices in considerable detail. Needless to say—especially when taken at face value—this is not standard ritual fare in Indian towns or villages, let alone in Buddhist monasteries, yet the four consecrations and the clan-circle feast were arguably the key social rites for practitioners of the mahāyoga and yoginī tantras, so they could hardly be ignored. At other times, however, the very same mahāsiddhas might decry both Mainstream and Transgressive tantric practices and insist that freedom lies only in a direct, nonconceptual realization of the nature of mind—the way of Radical Tantra.

What to make of all this is a problem that has preoccupied scholars both in medieval India and in the modern academy. Two main questions have been debated; we can answer neither definitively here but will mention, and reflect upon, each one briefly.

The first question is interpretive: To what degree should the transgressive practices described in the *Hevajra* and other mahāyoga or yoginī tantras, as well as in the songs of many of the mahāsiddhas, be taken at face value? The options here range from literalism, to symbolism, to "multilevelism." Literalism is marked by an incapacity or unwillingness to read such passages anything but literally. Interestingly, it is the outlook both of puritans—who declare on the basis of a literal reading that Vajrayāna is a completely degenerate form of Buddhism—and of libertines—who declare on the basis of the same reading that Vajrayāna is the one known form of religious thought and practice that allows us to fully engage our senses and sexuality. Yet as we know, tantric discourse at any level is awash in symbolism, so literalism seems a rather superficial interpretive tool, reflective of cultural prejudice or personal predilection rather than serious scholarly investigation. Recognition of symbolism, however, may also result in its own puritanical interpretations, whereby *nothing* is taken literally and discussions of sexual and other transgressive themes are read as merely colorful ways of invoking either standard Buddhist tropes—as when references to sexual yoga are read solely in terms of the union of compassion and wisdom required for buddhahood—or as connoting elements of our psychophysical being or our subtle body, as in Kṛṣṇācārya's commentary to the *Hevajra* passage above or Munidatta's commentary to the *Treasury of Performance Songs*.[130] These are not the only interpretive options, however: a multilevel reading that affirms the symbolic complexity and richness of tantric practices without denying that such practices were (and sometimes still are) enacted in a bodily manner may come closest to capturing the multifarious ways in which Vajrayāna practitioners participated actively—even "transgressively"—in their physical and social world while at the same time appreciating the many layers of meaning—and spiritual achievement—implied by their actions and the language used to describe them.[131]

The second question is social: To what degree were the mahāsiddhas countercultural rebels who thumbed their noses at the medieval Indian social, cultural, and religious establishment, including that of Buddhist monasticism? In other words, did they practice Mainstream Tantra, Transgressive Tantra, or perhaps some combination? Once again, a straightforward reading of the rhetoric of the mahāsiddhas can easily give the impression that, in the evocative words of Stephan Beyer,

> they sang of wisdom as the great Whore, for she opens herself to every man who seeks her. They sang in puns and riddles, made love to the spontaneous woman within them, and preached a world turned upside down: they slept in bliss and drowned in emptiness, and were altogether quite outrageous and shocking to all good and sober citizens, and from them sprang all the traditions of the Spontaneous Way.[132]

In this somewhat romanticized view of the mahāsiddhas—propounded in a qualified way, too, by Ronald Davidson[133]—their rejection of monasticism and scholasticism, their decision to dwell in marginal or out-of-the-way places, and their enactment of transgressive rituals all signify a complete break with the conventions of their time—and may, incidentally, serve to inspire the downtrodden or the culturally disaffected in any place or time. An alternate view, promoted by Christian Wedemeyer, suggests that tantric "performances" (*caryā*)—a general term for the transgressive practices we have noted—are not "rituals of rebellion" so much as they are a "carnivalesque" phase in the career of a Buddhist monk, a part of the "common repertoire of Buddhist professionals" that is marked by a period in which one temporarily leaves behind the monastery and monastic vows, dwells in "impure" places such cremation grounds, consorts with low-caste and other marginal people, and indulges in transgressive practices—all for the specific purpose of cultivating viscerally rather than just theoretically an appreciation for nonduality and the pure gnosis that lies at the heart of ourselves, all other beings, and perhaps the cosmos itself.[134] There certainly is evidence for such a view of the mahāsiddhas in the texts cited by Wedemeyer, but it is open to question whether this suffices to explain every instance of transgressive rhetoric and practice in the vast literature of the Buddhist tantras, let alone account for the well-documented tensions between monastic abbots and disciplinarians on the one hand and at least some tantric practitioners residing within the monastery walls on the other.[135] As with the first question, a more promising answer to the second one may be found in a both/and position: recognizing that in some cases Vajrayāna practitioners were operating within the domesticating compass of monastic life, while in others they evaded it entirely: that there were some monks who underwent a time of "wilding" as an institutionally recognized part of their career and some Buddhists who left the monastery never to return, or never entered it in the first place, disdaining the restrictions on life and thought typically enforced there, and finding genuine freedom and happiness through the pursuit of their own "spontaneous way," which might be associated with Transgressive Tantra but also at times seemed sympathetic to the more uncompromising approach of Radical Tantra.

Just where Saraha might fit within such discussions is a question to which we will return in detail later. For now, let us simply affirm that the context in which he (if indeed he was a single individual) lived was that of medieval India, probably the north and possibly the east, with its political instability, its social and economic changes, its linguistic variety, and its profusion of competing religious traditions, all of them influenced to one degree or another by tantric ideas and practices. In a specifically religious sense, Saraha's context was almost certainly Buddhist—perhaps monastic, perhaps nonmonastic, or perhaps each at different times—and within Buddhism his primary interests seem related in one way or another to the "higher tantras," especially the yoginī tantras, with their varying rhetorics of both Transgressive and Radical approaches to Tantra, while his primary religious identity, at least from the perspective of later tradition in India and Tibet, is that of a mahāsiddha. To flesh out these suggestions and to see whether anything more can be said with certainty about Saraha as a historical individual, we will turn, at last, in chapter 1, to his life, or lives, as revealed through hints from his own writings and through later hagiographies.

Life

CHAPTER 1

Versions of Saraha's Life

Sources and Problems

In attempting to discern from a historical point of view who Saraha might have been and how his life unfolded, we have an abundance of sources, almost none of them very reliable. There are two basic kinds of texts to which we can turn in attempting to glean information: writings attributed to Saraha in which he speaks from a first-person perspective and hagiographies devoted to him produced by Indian and—especially—Tibetan writers of the eleventh and later centuries. We will treat each of these types of sources in turn—the first rather briefly, the second in greater detail.

Among the more striking literary features of the songs of the mahāsiddhas is the self-referentiality of their authors. Whether in dohās, vajra songs, or performance songs, the masters who sang them will, on occasion, speak of themselves, either using the first-person pronoun or referring to themselves by name, most often by employing the formula, "X said." From a survey of his songs, we see that Saraha uses the first-person pronoun infrequently but in a variety of ways, sometimes simply to identify himself in conjunction with his name, "Saraha," or "the Archer";[136] sometimes to tout his own wisdom or experience,[137] or, more rarely, to suggest his possible shortcomings;[138] sometimes to indicate his relation to his guru or a particular deity;[139] and sometimes to show his connection to a female figure, such as a consort or a yoginī.[140] Among the most intriguing uses of the first-person is in a short, erotic song called *Ornament of Springtime*, where he adopts the voice of a youth—presumably but not overtly female—who longs for the arrival of her lover, Heruka.[141] The self-identifying third-person pronoun—"Saraha" or "the Archer" is most often encountered in reference to statements he has made, as in passages like "Saraha has taught and gone away," or "the Archer takes up this song," or "Saraha, who knows for himself, declares this."[142] It should be evident from just these few examples that although there are explicitly "autobiographical" passages in some of Saraha's songs, they reveal very little specific information about the author—only, really, that he may have had some connection to archery (or perhaps arrow making), that he considered himself a singer and a sage who spoke the truth, and that he was devoted, in various ways, to his guru and various deities, both male and female. The passages do not provide even a glimpse of a connected biography of Saraha, and for instances of that, we must turn to the hagiographical tradition of late medieval India and of Tibet.

That tradition yields a rich lore about Saraha but very little in the way of biographical information. The stories that we have appeared in the greatest profusion between the eleventh and sixteenth centuries. Some Indic sources are traceable to the early part of this span, but most texts, both earlier and later, are Tibetan. The few incontestably Indic texts we possess outside Saraha's literary corpus likely postdate the Great Brahmin by a century or more and give only the sketchiest details about his life. A commentary on the *King Dohā* by the eleventh-century Nepalese master Balpo Asu specifies that Saraha was a brahmin, was blessed by a ḍākinī, practiced tantra, understood reality, and appeared in various guises to a king: as a brahmin, a scholar, a yogin, and a low-caste person.[143] A commentary on the *Dohā Treasury* by Advaya Avadhūtipa (eleventh–thirteenth century?) notes only that he consorted with a "realized fletcheress,"[144] providing thereby an early suggestion of one of the main storylines about Saraha, what Kurtis Schaeffer has called the "fletcheress narrative." As noted earlier, an early second-millennium lineage text from Nepal lists him as a disciple of Nāgārjuna and an important transmission-holder but says nothing about his life or deeds.[145] The most important early "Indic" life of Saraha is that contained in the *Lives of the Eighty-Four Mahāsiddhas*, attributed to the eleventh- or twelfth-century master Abhayadatta, but modern scholars have suggested that this work may belong to the category of "gray texts": purportedly Indic writings that were created in Tibet and may be of Tibetan rather than South Asian provenance or, at the very least, are "intercultural creative efforts[s]."[146] It is, however, the only text containing a substantial hagiography of Saraha that found its way into a Tibetan Tengyur,[147] so it clearly was regarded as a genuinely Indian work by many scholars of the Tibetan renaissance period. As the earliest source of the "radish-girl narrative," another important storyline of Saraha's life identified by Schaeffer, it is quite significant and will be translated in the next section.

Perhaps the earliest indisputably Tibetan author to say something about Saraha's life was the twelfth-century Kadampa master Pharpuwa Lodrö Sengé, who writes in his commentary on the first verse of the *King Dohā*, "King Mahāpāla saw Saraha appear as a brahmin reciting the Vedas, as a monk preserving the teachings, and [as] cavorting with the fletcheress."[148] A century later, Chomden Raldri notes in the introduction to his commentary on the *Dohā Treasury Song*, or *People Dohā*, that Saraha was a brahmin from south India who learned Buddhism from the tantric bodhisattva Vajrapāṇi and the gnosis-ḍākinī Sukhasiddhī and taught his great song to Padmavajra, Nāgārjuna, and Śabareśvara (that is, Śavaripa).[149] Around the same time, an unknown Tibetan scholar composed a text entitled *Stages of the Guru Transmission* (*Lama Gyupai Rimpa*), which provides accounts of the lives of members of the Indian mahāmudrā linage, including Saraha. The life story of Saraha in this text provides the first extended version of the "fletcheress narrative" and, preceding it, another important storyline, the related but distinguishable narrative of five brahmin brothers, of whom Saraha is the youngest, and their encounters with ḍākinīs, four of whom are disguised as brahmin girls.[150] Like Abhayadatta's account, the *Stages* version will be translated in the following section.

Translations of Two Early Hagiographies

Abhayadatta's account,[151] which may be the earliest extended hagiography of Saraha, is, as noted, the first to focus on the radish-girl narrative:

> [29] The story of Guru Saraha:
>
> Saraha was of the brahmin caste and was from Roli, which was part of the city-state of Rajñi in eastern Iṇdia. He was the son of a ḍākinī. Although he was a brahmin, he had faith in the Buddhadharma, and through hearing the Dharma from countless masters, he [developed] confidence in the Secret Mantra Dharma. He upheld both Brahmanical and Buddhist vows, practicing the Brahmanical religion by day and practicing the Buddhist religion at night.
>
> When he resorted to liquor, every brahmin heard of this and they all assembled in order to have him exiled. They said to King Ratnapāla, [30] "You are the king. Is it proper to engage in a perverted religion in this land? Saraha, the Archer, may be the chieftain of fifteen thousand households in Roli, but by drinking liquor he has undermined his caste [status], and must be exiled." The king said, "I don't want to exile someone who controls fifteen thousand households."
>
> The king then approached Saraha and said, "You are a brahmin, and it's not proper for you to drink liquor." Saraha said, "I didn't drink liquor and will swear an oath [to that effect], so assemble every brahmin and all the people." They

all assembled, and Saraha declared, "If I have drunk liquor, let my hand burn; if I have not drunk it, may it not burn." He plunged his hand into boiling butter, and it was not burned. The king said, "So in truth, did he drink liquor or not?" [31] The brahmins said, "In truth, he drank."

Repeating his [statement, Saraha] drank molten copper and was not burned, but [the brahmins] said, "Nevertheless, he drank." "Well, [said Saraha,] if someone goes into the water and sinks, then they drank, but if they don't sink, then they didn't drink." The other brahmins went into the water singly or in pairs. [When he went in,] Saraha did not sink, while the others did. "Saraha did not drink," [everyone] declared. Saraha further said, "Let's get weighed on a scale; the one who is heavier did not drink, and the one who is lighter drank." When this was done, Saraha was heavier, and he declared, "I did not drink." Likewise, even when they loaded [onto the scale] three iron boulders, each weighing the same as a man, Saraha was heavier—and he was heavier even than six [boulders], Saraha was. The king declared, "If someone who has such abilities drinks, let them drink!"

All [32] the brahmins, and the king as well, bowed down to Saraha and requested instruction. He sang songs to the king, queens, and all the people; these are known as the Dohā Trilogy. The brahmins abandoned their own religion and entered the Buddhist teaching.

After that, Saraha took on a fifteen-year-old servant girl, instructed her, and led her to another land. They lived in a remote place. He engaged in practice, while the girl served him and cared for him. One day, he said, "I want to eat radishes," so the girl added radishes to buffalo yogurt and took it to him. He was sitting in concentration, though, and wouldn't get up.

Saraha did not rise from that concentration for twelve years. When he [finally] got up, [33] he asked, "Where are the radishes?" The servant girl replied, "You've been in concentration for twelve years without getting up, so now where are they? Springtime has passed, and there are none." Saraha said to the girl, "Now I will go to the mountains to practice." The girl said, "Isolating the body is not isolation; isolating the mind from signs and concepts is supreme isolation. You sat in concentration for twelve years, but you couldn't sever a tiny sign, the thought of radishes. What's the good of going to the mountains?" When she said this, Saraha thought, "That's true," and he abandoned signs and concepts, took to heart the primordial meaning, obtained the special attainment of supreme mahāmudrā, and worked limitlessly for the aims of beings. He and the girl [eventually] went to the land of the ḍākinīs.

This completes the story of Guru Saraha.

The second early extended narrative is that of the anonymous thirteenth-century *Stages of the Guru Transmission*,[152] which provides the first detailed version of both the narrative of the brahmin brothers and the disguised ḍākinīs and the so-called fletcheress narrative:

[451] When he arrived from Śrī Parvata in the south, Jñānāvalokita[153] saw that the youngest of [five] brahmin brothers who were court chaplains of the king of Vārāṇasī was a candidate for the instantaneous instruction. Seeing that he could be trained by certain methods and seeing that he could be trained by someone appearing as a female, [Jñānāvalokita] emanated in the form of five gnosis ḍākinīs: four brahmin girls and a fletcheress.

[452] Then, the five brahmin brothers who were the king's

court chaplains went to relax across from a bathing tank and saw there four brahmin girls, youthful in form, in the fullness of youth, [wearing] beautiful ornaments, and endowed with [auspicious] signs. The five brothers desired them, and asked, "Where do you originally come from? Where are you going now? What are you doing at present? Who are you?" They said, "We originally come from nowhere, we're going nowhere now, we're doing nothing at present, and who we are, are brahmin girls." Then they brought forth the Vedas, and when they fluently recited the four [collections]—the *Sama Veda*, the *Yajur Veda*, the *Atharva Veda*, and the *Ṛg Veda*—[the brothers] were confident that they were indeed brahmin girls.

[The brothers then asked,] "Do you not have husbands?" [They replied,] "We have no husbands."[154] [The brothers asked,] "Well, would we be suitable marriage partners for you?" [They replied,] "That would be suitable." Then, the four elder brothers married them. The youngest [brother] thought, "The four brahmin girls I met have married my four older brothers, and now that the four women have become the brides of my elder brothers, I don't need to get married, so I should become a Buddhist, take monastic vows, and act solely [according to] the sublime Dharma." He first took novice vows from the Mahāyāna master Śrīkīrti, then learned everything [taught] in the Definitional Vehicle and the Fruitional Secret-Mantra Vajra Vehicle and became a great scholar. Then, when he came before the king in his palace, he was appointed court chaplain.

One day, when he had gone to relax in the royal walled garden, he saw right there in the garden the four brides [453] of his older brothers—the very same. Each one was pouring liquor into a skull-cup she held and then drinking it. The master thought, "When brahmins hold skull-cups and drink liquor, one shouldn't go near them. These four brahmin brides must be either yoginīs or ḍākinīs who have come [in disguise]."

Each showing a symbolic gesture, the four said to the monk, "Come, come! Even though we are brahmin girls, we drink secretly. Even though you are a monk, it is permissible for you to come here when requested, and we so request." They held up in their hands the skull-cups [filled with] liquor, and the master thought, "If it's permitted for a brahmin to drink liquor, then although I have entered the door of the insider Buddhists in general, there are Secret–Mantra Great Vehicle practitioners among them who are permitted to drink. These brahmin girls all are emanations of either yoginīs or ḍākinīs, and if [I drink] it's possible that special attainments will emerge."

Thinking thus, he took in hand the skull-cups full of liquor and consumed them [one by one]. There were four different liquors: rice liquor, safflower liquor, grape liquor, and honey liquor, which [induce] understanding of the method for indicating the primordial connate [nature] through the sublime guru's special instruction on the four joys.[155] When he drank them, [the liquors] resolved into a single taste. When the four joys[156] [described by] the sublime guru were indicated to him and pointed out to him, then he realized them. He understood the signs of the essential single taste of all dharmas, which is the primordial connate [nature], the connate mahāmudrā. [Among] a multitude of tastes, he experienced supreme bliss, he realized the primordial connate [nature], and when he had inner experience, he understood the signs of disconnection [entailed by] the great untainted bliss and realized [that state].

In that [454] way, he drank the liquors that brought on signs of special attainments. His body became drunk with the liquor, while his mind became drunk with reality. At that time the four ḍākinīs conferred [the four] consecrations [upon him], and at that point, [he] saw directly before him the bodhisattva Sukhanātha [and] Śrī Hayagrīva, and then instantaneously took to heart, exactly as it is, the special instruction on, and the realization of, the essential meaning of the great seal of buddhahood. He became free from all concepts, whether worldly or transworldly, and [proclaimed]: "I am a brahmin, yet they think I am not; I am a monk, yet they think I am not; I am a yogin, yet they think I am not. I am free from all concepts." Thus, he was freed instantaneously through being blessed in the presence of the sublime guru, without depending on a meditative path, and so was known as an "instantaneous person."

Then, [after] engaging in incalculable practices, he arrived in a great marketplace, known [in Sanskrit] as the *haṭṭa*. In the middle of that marketplace—whose shops sold various kinds of gold, silver, pearls, horses, cattle, and grains—a fletcheress had stacked up many bamboo shafts. Picking out one bamboo shaft, she heated it in a fire and, having straightened it well, she closed [one] eye—that of apprehending a self in consciousness—while keeping open [the other]: the stainless eye of gnosis. She made the arrow without wavering either right or left.

Seeing this, [the monk] [455] said to the fletcheress, "Where do you originally come from, woman? Where are you going now? What are you doing with this arrow?" The woman said, "I originally come from nowhere, I'm going nowhere now, and I'll shoot this arrow into a heart." "Well," [he asked], "into whose heart will you shoot an arrow?"

"I will shoot it into the heart of this very monk," [she replied]. He said, "You're not a woman who makes arrows; you're a maker of symbols." She asked, "Do you understand, monk?"

He said, "I understand the symbolism. I understand that the bamboo is a symbol of knowing the uncontrived primordial [nature] that is the essential meaning of the thought of the Buddha. I understand that making one arrow is a symbol of my being among the very few fortunate enough to [penetrate] the essential meaning instantaneously. I understand that heating [the arrow] is a symbol of the need to rely first on the heat of the special symbolic instructions—as well as the blessing—of the guru. I understand that straightening [the arrow] without ever wavering is a symbol of the need to act, without ever wavering, on the primordial, essential meaning taught by the sublime guru. I understand that the [arrow's] four feathers are a symbol indicating [how] we exaggerate [the reality] of all dharmas, which are [merely] designated by conventional labels and other [signs]. I understand that [the arrow] having two notches is a symbol[157] of realizing the inseparable union of both method and wisdom, [both] emptiness and compassion. I understand that affixing the arrowhead is a symbol of the primordial [nature], the connate [nature], suchness, the unchanging reality-body. I understand that coming from nowhere and going nowhere are a symbol of [how] the primordial connate [nature], suchness, neither comes nor goes."

Having thus displayed his understanding of the symbolic teaching, he said to the woman, "Aha! Woman, you [have conveyed] instantaneously by way of symbols the single teaching that ascertains the essential meaning of Buddhism, the thought of the buddhas of the three times." The woman replied, "Aha! The essential meaning of the thought of the buddhas of the three times is realized only through the guru's blessing or through symbols, and not through words, designations, or syllables. Since you have understood the symbols exactly as they are, you are a realized yogin. Now, [456] take this arrow." Saying this, she put the arrow in his hand. [Henceforth,] he was labeled " the Archer" [Saraha]. He was called "the Archer" because with his own mind he shot to the core of the profound symbols [shown] by the sublime guru, and he was called "the Archer" because he shot the arrow of nondual gnosis into dualistic thought. Thus, when he went off with the fletcheress to [engage in tantric] practice, he became widely known as Saraha.

Then, when Dārikapa, who for twelve years had served a prostitute in [ways] both exalted and debased, assembled the cemetery yogins for a ritual feast, [Saraha], adorned by the eight kinds of ornaments,[158] sang the "Song of the Vajra Skull" in response to questions. [Then,] to the king, he sang forty verses; to the queens, he sang eighty verses; to the people in general, he sang 160 verses; to the yogins, he sang songs in twenty verses and twelve verses; and he also sang many songs on the six dharmas for contemplation, and so forth.

Then, the Great Brahmin's mind transformed into the reality body and his body transformed into the complete enjoyment-body, and together with the gnosis ḍākinī, he playfully disappeared into the sky, becoming a buddha without any aggregates remaining. It is said that the impure will not see him appear, while the pure will see him appear directly before them. Those are the transmissions of the instantaneous [way].

Although this is not the place for a detailed comparative textual analysis, suffice it to say that story elements, and even phrases, found in the two early texts translated above made their way into most later Saraha narratives, as will be evident from the next section.

Themes and Later Variations

As noted, there are really three separate narratives at work in these earliest extended hagiographies of Saraha: the radish-girl story, the brahmin-brothers-and-girls story, and the fletcheress story. In later hagiographies, the three narratives were combined in various ways. The anonymous *Tales of Dohā Lineages* (presixteenth century) includes mention of the brahmin girls (though not the brothers) and gives a version of the fletcheress narrative.[159] In his *Blue Annals*, Gö Lotsawa Zhönupal (1392–1481) mentions a set of five ḍākinīs who taught mahāmudrā to Saraha in Oḍiyāna but does not mention either the radish girl or the fletcheress.[160] Kunga Rinchen (1475–1527) focuses on the radish-girl narrative, while also mentioning the five brahmin brothers (but not the brahmin girls) and presenting a brief version of the fletcheress narrative.[161] Pawo Tsuklak Trengwa (1504–66) mentions five brahmin brothers and four brahmin girls and gives a brief account of Saraha's encounter with the fletcheress.[162] In one of the best-known accounts, Karma Trinlepa (1507–54) sees Saraha as one of five brothers, but the only female mentioned is the fletcheress, whose arrow-making instructions to Saraha are related in great detail.[163] In his influential *Moonbeams of Mahāmudrā*, Dakpo Tashi Namgyal (1512–87) mentions none of the three accounts, specifying only that Saraha was taught by two bodhisattvas who were themselves emanations of Avalokiteśvara and Mañjuśrī, respectively.[164] Reporting an "oral tradition of Vajrāsana" (that is, Bodh Gaya), Pema Karpo (1527–92) tells a quite different story, in which Saraha is one of two brahmin brothers who worship and then reject the Hindu Śaiva deities Maheśvara and Umā and then become Buddhist monks who founded important monasteries—after which Saraha became a tantric practitioner, taking on a yoginī as consort.[165] Finally, Tāranātha (1575–1634) focuses on Saraha's encounter early in life with a yoginī who offers him liquor and corrupts his Brahmanical status, then describes his subsequent time as a Buddhist monk and his later encounter with the fletcheress, whose instruction leads to his final realization.[166]

The stories surrounding the radish girl, the brahmin brothers and brahmin girls, and the fletcheress are only a few of the many narrative elements that appear (or don't), in one form or another, in the later hagiographies. Within the broad frame of the three main narratives, other plotlines that appear with some regularity include

- Saraha's passage through three distinct stages of life, as a brahmin, Buddhist monk, and tantric yogin;[167]
- his attainment of ultimate realization as a result of instruction by one or more yoginīs or ḍākinīs, typically disguised as either brahmin or low-caste women;
- his consumption of liquor offered by one or more ḍākinīs;
- his being reviled by other brahmins and threatened with loss of his caste status, for either drinking liquor or consorting with a low-caste woman, or both;
- his subjection to trials to demonstrate that, despite all appearances, he is pure;
- his singing of dohā verses for the king, queens, and people of whatever land he is said to inhabit;[168] and
- his final apotheosis, usually in the company of his ḍākinī consort.

There are many other details, however, on which the hagiographic tradition differs significantly, for instance:

- The texts variously locate Saraha's birthplace in Oḍiyāna, Vārāṇasī, Rādhā (perhaps Vṛndāvana?), Odisha, or Rajñi (all in north India) or somewhere in the south, such as Vidarbha.
- The monarch with whom he interacted is most often listed as Mahāpāla, but kings by the name of Ratnapāla, Candanapāla, and Lahalya also are mentioned.
- Although there is general agreement that he was instructed by one or more yoginīs or ḍākinīs (often unnamed but sometimes identified as Hedharmā, Sukhasiddhī, or Vajrayoginī), he is also said to have learned from such humans as the Buddha's son Rāhula; Rāhula's disciple Mahāyāna Śrīkīrti; the early Perfection of Wisdom master Rāhulabhadra;[169] the great poet Aśvaghoṣa; the *sthavira*s Kāla and Kāṅha;[170] such bodhisattvas as Avalokiteśvara, Mañjuśrī, Vajrapāṇi, Ratnamati, and Sukhanātha; and the tantric buddhas Heruka, Guhyasamāja, and Hayagrīva.
- His students are said to have included Mitra, Padmavajra, Nāgārjuna, and Śavaripa, although the latter is often regarded as a granddisciple, and Nāgārjuna is the direct disciple most often named by later tradition.
- Although generally (if not universally) credited with the *King*, *Queen*, and *People Dohās*, he is also said, in one biographical source or the other, to have composed the *Alphabetical Dohās*, the *Body*, *Speech*, and *Mind Treasuries*, the commentary on the *Buddhakapāla Tantra*, and various vajra songs—although as noted, there are many more works attributed to him in the Tibetan Tengyur and other noncanonical collections.
- Finally, at the end of his earthly teaching career, he is variously said to have dissolved into the reality body, gone to "another realm," departed for the heavenly realm of the ḍākinīs, or traveled to Śrī Parvata in southern India, where he resides to this day.

Although in this welter of hagiographic storylines and details there are clearly some themes that are more common and some that appear only briefly or occasionally, there really is not much of a "common core" to the accounts. We might affirm that Saraha *typically* was said to be a brahmin who may have ordained as a monk and may at some point have become a tantric practitioner; to have been instructed by, and consorted with, yoginīs or ḍākinīs; and to have sung instructional songs to the king and others whom he encountered. Even if this is something like a lowest common denominator in the lore surrounding Saraha, it really tells us little or nothing about what his actual life may have been like—only how later tradition, some of it Indic but most of it Tibetan, *imagined* his life. In reality, the tellers of these tales probably had little to go on but a name with a particular meaning ("archer"), certain texts attributed to an author by that name, and a few basic narrative elements, handed down either orally or in writing, that became associated with that name and those works. Those elements then were combined and recombined in various ways by different hagiographers to provide listeners or readers with an inspiring and coherent sense of the life of a key late Indian Buddhist master, who was constructed *ex post facto* as a mahāsiddha, a prolific author, and the forefather of one of the most important of all Indo-Tibetan lineages of teaching and practice, that of mahāmudrā.

Saraha in Lineage, Dream, Vision, Image, and Panegyric

In his *Blue Annals*, Gö Lotsawa articulates the well-nigh universal Tibetan belief that "Saraha was the first to introduce mahāmudrā as the chief of all paths."[171] Although, as noted, the undated Nepalese lineage text discovered by Tucci makes Saraha subordinate to Nāgārjuna, and the early twelfth-century account of the eighty-four mahāsiddhas by Abhayadatta neither specifies Saraha's disciples nor mentions his connection to a mahāmudrā teaching (as opposed to a mahāmudrā attainment), a consensus seems to have developed fairly early in Tibet that he was indeed the forefather of the mahāmudrā practice lineage, with his Dohā Trilogy serving as key root texts for understanding and practicing the great seal. He also was seen in Tibet as a founding human member of numerous Vajrayāna lineages, especially but not solely those related to the yoginī tantras.[172] The lineages with which Saraha became associated were almost certainly Tibetan concoctions, but they are no less important for their "historical" unreliability, for lineage creation is, everywhere in the Indic and the Buddhist world, a vital activity that helps to assure spiritual legitimacy and continuity, hence institutional prestige and authority. To the degree that Saraha could be said to be part of an unbroken lineage of masters traceable back to one or another buddha figure, the teaching he represented (for instance, that of mahāmudrā) was thereby legitimated, as was the religious order (such as the Kagyu, Jonang, or Geluk) that had "inherited" the lineage.

The process whereby lineages involving Saraha were created in renaissance Tibet—especially within the Kagyu orders—still awaits detailed scholarly study.[173] It is clear, however, that by the sixteenth century, the heyday of Kagyu scholastic analysis of mahāmudrā, a rough consensus had emerged on the constituents of the lineage of which Saraha was the founder. Thus, for instance, Dakpo Tashi Namgyal describes a mahāmudrā lineage that follows the sequence of the primordial buddha Vajradhara, the bodhisattvas Ratnapāla and Sukhanātha, Saraha, Nāgārjuna, Śavaripa, Maitrīpa (who meets Śavaripa in a vision), and Maitrīpa's disciple Vajrapāṇi—who spread the transmission in Tibet. An alternate version of the lineage focuses on the mahāsiddha Tilopa, who is sometimes said to have had only Vajradhara as his teacher but is also reputed to have studied with many human figures, both male and female, of whom one was Nāgārjuna—himself, of course, regarded by then as a direct disciple of Saraha. Tilopa famously transmitted various teachings to Nāropa, who passed them on to Marpa the Translator (eleventh century), the founder of the main line of Tibetan Kagyu traditions.[174] Similarly, the Jonang scholar Tāranātha devotes the very first chapter of his *Seven Instruction Lineages* to mahāmudrā, laying out a transmission that runs as follows: Vajrayoginī, Rāhula (that is, Saraha), Nāgārjuna, Śavaripa, Lūyipa, Dārikapa and Deṅgipa, Tilopa, and Nāropa (thence to Marpa). In an alternate version mentioned by Tāranātha, Maitrīpa directly learns mahāmudrā from Śavaripa in a visionary encounter and passes on his teaching to numerous disciples, including Vajrapāṇi—who, again, transmits the lineage to Tibet.[175] Finally, we might note that Yeshé Gyaltsen (1713–93), a later Geluk scholar, in the course of articulating a "long" or "distant" mahāmudrā lineage within his tradition, describes a transmission that includes Vajradhara and then proceeds through the bodhisattva Vajrapāṇi to Saraha, who teaches both Nāgārjuna and Śavaripa. The line running through Nāgārjuna then goes to Lūyipa, Dārikapa, Diṅkampa (Deṅgipa), Tilopa, and Nāropa, thence to Marpa and his Kagyu successors in Tibet, until it is transmitted to the founder of the Geluk, Tsongkhapa (1357–1419). The line from Śavaripa goes directly to Maitrīpa, who in turn teaches Marpa, and the Kagyu lineage proceeds down to Tsongkhapa as before.[176]

Although there are differences among these three representative lineages (each from a different Tibetan order)—and further variations that are evident in the hagiographical literature—an overall consistency is evident, with the core transmission consisting, on the Indian side, of one or another form of buddha, Saraha, Nāgārjuna, Śavaripa, and Maitrīpa, with other masters (for example, Lūyipa, Tilopa, Nāropa) included in various ways. As with the hagiographies, the lineage lists tell us little of the actual religious history of which Saraha may have been a part; they do, however, tell us much about how Tibetans conceived of late Indian Buddhism and sought to legitimize traditions of thought and practice through the invention (mostly, if not entirely, out of whole cloth) of histories that served both spiritual and institutional purposes.

It was not just in teaching lineages that Tibetans came to include Saraha: after the development of the system of "succession by reincarnation," also known as the "tulku system," in the thirteenth century, Saraha came to be incorporated into the "long" incarnation lineages of a number of orders or suborders. Thus, the Karmapa hierarchs of the Kagyu order (who are generally credited with originating the tulku system) came eventually to be seen not only as heirs to Saraha's mahāmudrā instruction lineage but also in some sense to *be* Saraha, in that they partook (and still partake) of a rebirth lineage that begins with the ancient buddha Paropakāravikrīḍita (T. Shenpen Namröl) and includes, among others, the bodhisattva Avalokiteśvara, the Oḍiyāna master Padmasambhava, and Saraha himself.[177] Nor was the Karmapa the only order to incorporate Saraha into its incarnation lineage: he also was (and is) regarded as an Indian predecessor of the Dudjom incarnates, who since the nineteenth century have provided a series of masters revered for their presentation of the Nyingma great perfection.

Quite apart from retrospectively identifying Saraha as a key but distant member of a long lineage of Buddhist masters or a series of incarnations, Tibetans also sometimes found themselves in his presence far more immediately, through dreams and visions—two types of marvels that are not always sharply distinguished within the tradition. Thus, in a text attributed to Marpa—who helped bring the dohā tradition to Tibet in the eleventh century—the great translator reports that while being detained by tax collectors in Nepal he had a dream one night in which two brahmin girls conveyed him on a palanquin to Śrī Parvata in south India, where in a fig-tree grove he met Saraha, who was seated on a corpse, flanked by two queens and wearing cremation-ground attire. After circumambulating and prostrating to Saraha, Marpa requested blessings, and the Great Brahmin did so:

> He blessed my body. . . . The moment he placed his hand upon my head, my body, like that of a drunken elephant, was intoxicated with uncontaminated bliss and an experience of immutability dawned within me. . . . He blessed my speech. . . . He unveiled the meaning of the four syllables,[178] the lion's roar of emptiness, and, like the dream of a mute, an experience beyond words dawned in me. . . . He blessed my mind . . . and I realized the [reality body], that which neither comes nor goes, and within me dawned the experience of having no thoughts, like that of a corpse in a cremation ground.[179]

Saraha then sings a vajra song of the nature of reality, which advises Marpa to "follow the behavior of savages, be carefree, eat flesh, be a madman, be like a fearless lion, [letting] your elephant mind wander free," and concludes:

> As the bee hovers over flowers,
> Do not view samsara as defiled;
> There is no nirvana to attain.
> This is the way of the natural state:
> Rest in uncontrived freshness.
> Do not think of activities and do not be partial;
> Look toward the center of the sky—utter simplicity.
> To go beyond the exhaustion of phenomena

Is essential;
This is the summit of views, mahāmudrā.[180]

Waking from his dream, Marpa feels that his mental confusion has been dispelled, such that "even if I were to meet the buddhas of the three times, I would have nothing to ask them. This was the decisive experience of mind-itself." He goes on to admit that such visions should not be spoken of but "I could not help myself," and he gives a brief exposition of the various symbols contained in Saraha's song.[181]

Other early Kagyu masters to report or imply a dream or visionary encounter with Saraha include, notably, the first three Karma Kagyu hierarchs. The first Karmapa, Dusum Khyenpa (1110–93), recounts meeting him at Paltri, in Tibet.[182] The second Karmapa, Karma Pakshi (1204–83), is credited with an inspired vajra song that, except in its opening and closing verses, conveys a brief but complete mahāmudrā teaching through the voice of a master variously identified as Saraha and Śabareśvara.[183] The third Karmapa, Rangjung Dorjé (1283–1339), reports encountering Saraha in a dream at the age of twelve, near Tsurphu Monastery in central Tibet. Like Marpa in the dream described above, Rangjung Dorjé travels to Śrī Parvata in south India to meet Saraha, in this case accompanied by friends rather than brahmin girls. While his companions search the southern side of the mountain, Rangjung Dorjé sits in meditation on the eastern slope. When flower petals fall around him, he collects them and makes an offering cairn, at which point a "small, sweet voice" proclaims from the sky, "The guru, the Great Brahman [Saraha], / Is your mind's nature— / It is a grave mistake to look for him elsewhere."[184] Rangjung Dorjé replies in verse, expressing appreciation that he has been granted a sign, and the voice of Saraha himself then sings from the sky "a dohā beyond speech," affirming that he is indeed the nature of Rangjung Dorjé's mind and imparting advice to him:

> Hey child! Mahāmudrā is the essence of
> All past, present, and future buddhas.
> Stay uncomplicated!
> . . . .
> *E ma ho*! Mind's nature is simplicity;
> It comes from nowhere and has
> Nowhere to go, just like a crazy person.
>
> Hey child! Like a river dissolving into the sea,
> It has no creation and no cessation;
> So stay in mahāmudrā![185]

At that point, Rangjung Dorjé sees the flower cairn, the rocks, and the mountain all taking on the nature of Saraha, and he settles into a relaxed, natural, and joyous state of mind, which he recalls as he sings of his encounter and encourages his disciples to practice the great seal.[186]

Lest we think that only Kagyu masters were associated with Saraha, it is worth noting that the Great Brahmin appeared, too, to figures as disparate as the itinerant Indian yogin Padampa Sangyé (d. 1117)—who founded the Shijé (Pacification) tradition and transmitted numerous canonical and paracanonical works by Saraha to Tibet—and the founder of the Geluk order, Tsongkhapa.[187]

Further evidence of Saraha's importance in Tibetan culture is provided by the numerous commentaries on his *King*, *Queen*, and *People Dohās* composed on the plateau; the many quotations from his works deployed by masters of every tradition; the countless Tibetan depictions of him (almost always as an arrow-wielding yogin) in

Tibetan thangka paintings, woodblock prints, and iconographic guides; and devotional songs composed in his honor, of which perhaps the most notable is that of the controversial Sakyapa master Shakya Chokden (1428–1507), who celebrates the Great Brahmin as "the supreme second Teacher . . . / the first of all those who have reached the ground of perfection . . . / [dwelling] on the mahāmudrā ground . . . / [seeing all things] as the mind as such, the wishing jewel." Furthermore,

> Acting out straightening arrow and reed
> You saw that there's nothing
> Other than your own primordial awareness.
> Then in this way all things
> Became a single taste in great bliss.
> . . . .
> With a single arrow, ablaze with emptiness and primordial awareness,
> You put hordes of demons—collected thoughts—
> To sleep in a place where all is dark.
> Fulfillment of primordial awareness, such virtue there is in you![188]

Where This Leaves Us

This chapter has touched upon a wide variety of sources that might fill out our sense of who Saraha "really" was, from hagiographies, to lineage texts, to reports of dreams and visions, to artistic representations, to songs of praise. Yet because the sources are overwhelmingly Tibetan—and mostly of later Tibetan vintage at that—virtually nothing we have surveyed provides reliable information about the life and times of Saraha as the Indian Buddhist master he presumably was; it tells us only what Tibetans made of him. And as we push back in time through Tibetan tradition, the closer we come to Indic sources, the less information we have—to the point where we arrive at a sort of biographical event-horizon, beyond which all illumination collapses into an informational black hole and Saraha simply disappears. In that sense, our attempt to limn the life of the Great Brahmin has landed us back where we began, able to affirm only that "Saraha" was likely the name of a Buddhist master who lived somewhere on the Indian subcontinent; who flourished sometime between the eighth and eleventh centuries; who wrote in a variety of literary genres, most notably various types of poetry; and who was an exponent of—among other things—Vajrayāna traditions, especially those of the yoginī tantras. Perhaps, then, it is better to leave aside "biographical" sources and seek to understand who Saraha was from a different angle—namely, from the original texts attributed to him that are extant in either an Indic language or in Tibetan translation—in other words, to approach him less as a biographical subject than as a corpus of writings, or, as Klaus-Dieter Mathes and Péter-Dániel Szántó put it, "not [as] as an actual, singular author but [as] a literary event."[189] It is to such an approach that we will turn in the next chapter.

Teachings

CHAPTER 2

The Saraha Corpus

A Survey

As I SUGGESTED at the end of the previous chapter, Saraha is exceedingly elusive when sought through "biographical" sources—to the point where it may be that we really don't have any "Saraha" beyond the corpus of texts ascribed to him in Indian and Tibetan tradition. Thus, it seems worthwhile to survey that corpus, to see if there emerges from it anything like a coherent sense of the Great Brahmin's take on life and liberation, and hence of who he might have been. I will divide my discussion most broadly by the language—almost always Apabhraṃśa or Tibetan—in which a text is available, with the longer section on Tibetan versions subdivided according to whether a text is found in the Tengyur or outside the canon.[190] I will conclude the chapter with some reflections on what such a survey does or does not reveal about Saraha.

Texts Available in Indic Languages

The vast majority of Saraha's corpus is extant only in Tibetan, but over the past century-plus a significant number of texts in Apabhraṃśa or (occasionally) Sanskrit have come to light.

TEXT 1: *DOHĀ TREASURY*[191]

As already noted, Saraha's most famous, important, and oft-cited text is the *Dohā Treasury* (*Dohākoṣa*), typically referred to in the Tibetan tradition as the *People Dohā* (*Mang Doha*), because it was supposedly addressed to the general populace of the kingdom the Great Brahmin frequented.[192] To describe it, however, as a "text"—singular—is misleading, for there are, rather, multiple works with that title (or a slight variation of it) extant in both Apabhraṃśa and Tibetan—found either as independent texts or incorporated into commentaries. In no case does one text exactly correspond to another: the extant Apabhraṃśa *Treasuries* often differ markedly among themselves, while the two main Tibetan versions—what I call the Canonical Tibetan *Treasury* and the Long Tibetan *Treasury*, to be described in the next part of the chapter—overlap only in part, with neither corresponding exactly to any *Treasury* found in Apabhraṃśa. Indeed, the longer *Treasuries* extant in either Apabhraṃśa or Tibetan share fewer than seventy verses among themselves, with many more verses occurring in just one or two texts.[193] At the same time, we should not assume that the common verses form some sort of urtext of the *Dohā Treasury*, for, despite scholars' best attempts at reconstruction,[194] we do not know how, or by whom, one or another version was redacted a millennium ago, hence what verses were included or excluded (or why) by this or that editor. Indeed, we should not expect uniformity in texts entitled *Dohā Treasury*, even by the same author, for the term *dohākoṣa* is really a generic one, applicable to any collection of verses in the dohā style, such that there are texts with the title *Dohā Treasury* attributed not only to Saraha but also to other masters as well, including Tilopa, Kāṅha/Kṛṣṇācārya, Virūpa, Lūyipa, and Kaṅkana.

That said, we will briefly describe here the contents of three significant and quite distinct Apabhraṃśa texts entitled *Dohā Treasury*. The first, which I call the Short Apabhraṃśa *Treasury*, was discovered by Prabodh Chandra Bagchi in 1929 in the Darbar Library in Kathmandu. It is a text of only twelve verses,[195] only one of which is common to other versions, whether in Apabhraṃśa or Tibetan. The manuscript discovered by Bagchi is, however, clearly dated to the equivalent of 1101 CE, making it one of the few Indic tantric writings for which we have an unambiguous *terminus ante quem*, if not a date of composition. The second, which we might call the Standard Apabhraṃśa *Treasury*, was found in Kathmandu in 1909 by Haraprasād Śāstrī, who extracted Saraha's Apabhraṃśa dohās from a copy of a Sanskrit commentary upon them composed by Advayavajra.[196] Śāstrī published the dohās, unedited, in 1916; his work was filled out and corrected with the help of other texts (both Indic and Tibetan) by Muhammad Shahidullah (1928) and Bagchi (1938).[197] In that sense, the Standard Apabhraṃśa *Treasury* is really a set of three closely related versions—plural. The third text is the Long Apabhraṃśa *Treasury*, discovered by Rāhula Sāṃkṛtyāyana in 1934 at Sakya Monastery in Tibet. It was published in 1957 and revised (and translated into Sanskrit and English) by H. C. Bhayani in 1997. In 2024, Klaus-Dieter Mathes and Péter-Dániel Szántó edited and analyzed two more recently discovered manuscripts: the Tokyo manuscript, which may be an early specimen from India proper and consists of fifty-six verses; and the Göttingen manuscript, which is from Nepal and consists of 110 verses—hence is quite similar in content to the Standard Apabhraṃśa Version.[198] These works add still more evidence of the plurality of the *Dohā Treasury*.

The Short Apabhraṃśa *Treasury*,[199] which is, as noted, the earliest datable extant text attributed to Saraha, consists of just twelve sometimes-obscure verses, which follow no obvious sequence, though they are framed by an author's "promise to compose" and an editor's afterword, giving them the feel of a short but more or less complete work. At the outset (verses 1–3), Saraha (or his editor) states that he will speak of true reality, or thatness (*tattva*), which when known through the words of the guru, allows one to see through the net of delusion and cut attachment. This reality, however, is elusive (verses 4–7a): it is unmoved by wind, unburnt by fire, and unsoaked by rain; it cannot be entered or abandoned; it is undecaying; not existent in the usual sense; unmoving; and it cannot be indicated—yet it is to be known as the taste of sameness (*samarasa*), the connate joy (*sahajānanda*), the supreme lord (*parameśvara*). Saraha goes on to reiterate the importance of the guru (verses 7b–9), stating that if he is worshipped as Vajradhara and one hears him proclaim "ha, ha, ha," one won't enter saṃsāra, but adding, paradoxically, that although the whole world tastes of the connate nectar of immortality, the guru does not teach this in words, nor can the student really comprehend it, asking, "Who teaches this to whom?"[200] Saraha further asserts (verses 10–11) that the fruition of thatness (*tattva*) is beyond the sphere of cognition (*manas*) and to be understood only through one's own reflexive awareness (*svasaṃvedyaṃ*), while thatness itself is not existent yet can be described as indestructible, motionless, the highest step, sky-like, and greatly blissful—in short, the sole reality, which is beyond mind yet must be seen. Finally (verse 12) the editor of the text specifies that he has brought together these verses on essential meaning (*hṛdayārtha*) from three dohā collections composed by Saraha—a statement that, as observed by Schaeffer (2005, 104), gives us a rare glimpse into the process by which a dohā treasury like Saraha's was compiled. A final note: despite its brevity, the Short Apabhraṃśa Version of the *Dohā Treasury* provides a remarkably concise statement of many of Saraha's major themes, including the importance of the guru, the ineffability of the blissful, connate ultimate reality, and the need to recognize it, in the end, through one's own inner perception.

The Standard Apabhraṃśa *Treasury*,[201] which is the best known and most often translated of the Apabhraṃśa *Treasuries* (and which overlaps significantly, but not completely, with the Canonical Tibetan *Treasury*), contains 114 verses in Shahidullah's edition and

112 in Bagchi's.[202] As noted, the Apabhraṃśa text was discovered by Śāstrī embedded in the Sanskrit commentary by Advayavajra, which remains the only commentary on the text extant in an Indic language. Advayavajra and other Indic (and, later, Tibetan) scholars understood the text in quite different ways,[203] yet it might be argued that it is a work that defies rational organization—in part because it is, like the Short Apabhraṃśa *Treasury*, itself the product of an editorial process whereby various dohās, in many cases originally unrelated, were collected together under a single "cover" according to editorial principles obscure to us. It is true that the first dozen or so verses (which are found in virtually every known longer version of the *Dohā Treasury*, whether Indic or Tibetan) constitute a wide-ranging critique of Indic religious traditions, whether Hindu, Jain, or Buddhist, and true, too, that later on there are thematically connected sets of verses related, respectively, to yoginīs and the "great tree of emptiness," but the rest of the text—in far greater detail than the Short Apabhraṃśa *Treasury*—weaves rather unsystematically in and out of numerous key themes that are emblematic of Saraha's thought, including

- the critical dismissal of mainstream social ideas like caste purity and standard religious practices such as devotional worship, pilgrimage, asceticism, meditation, and ritual;[204]
- an equally vehement rejection of scholarship, philosophical analysis, and indeed any sort of dichotomous or dualistic thinking, even in the realm of ethics;[205]
- a positive focus on the direct, immediate, and transrational realization of the true nature of one's mind, most often referred to as the connate (*sahaja*), which is the untraceable source and empty substance of everything—and also referred to as gnosis (*jñāna*), mind (*citta*), nonmind (*acitta*), the nondual (*advaya*), the primordial nature (*nijasvabhāva*), the pure

(*viśuddha*), the stainless (*nirmala*), the ultimate (*paramārtha*), awakening (*bodhi*), buddha, the bodiless (*aśarīra*), great bliss (*mahāsukha*), great passion (*mahārāga*), the lord (*īśvara*), the single god (*ekadeva*), the self (*ātman*), emptiness (*śūnyatā*), the profound (*gambhīra*), thatness or true reality (*tattva*), suchness (*tathatā*), or just "it" or "that" (*tat*);[206]

- despite its ineffability, an attempt to approach the connate through the deployment of similes and metaphors, such as sky or space, a jewel, the ocean, water, a virgin's first experience of sex, a seed, the root, a yoginī, a moonstone, an elephant, and a great tree;[207]
- a celebration of the body, the senses, and sexuality, interwoven with a penchant for the worship of yoginīs and the practice of subtle-body yogas like those described in the later Buddhist tantras;[208] and
- an insistence on the absolute indispensability of relying upon the guru in pursuit of one's spiritual goals.[209]

It should be added that despite his critical, subitist, transgressive, and radically gnostic rhetoric, Saraha lifts the curtain now and again to reveal that he is still working within the bounds of standard Mahāyāna ethics and soteriology, insisting, for instance, that success on the path requires a proper balance between realization of emptiness and the practice of compassion, and concluding his text with the traditional observation that not to work for others' benefit or give gifts to the needy is "the fruit of saṃsāra" and that it is best to toss aside the self.[210] Finally, we might observe that Saraha is very much present in his own verses, naming himself on more than a dozen occasions, and frequently addressing his listener/reader directly. Sometimes he addresses him or her as "friend" or "child," but more often he uses the dismissive "fool," perhaps because, like the Buddha himself after his awakening, he doubts that—despite all his efforts and the fact that he keeps no secrets—anything he wishes to say can truly be expressed or understood.[211]

The Long Apabhraṃśa *Treasury* is the less studied of the two longer Indic-language versions,[212] perhaps because (a) Sāṃkṛtyāyana's edition was published two decades after the pioneering works of Śāstrī, Shahidullah, and Bagchi; (b) its scholarly apparatus, including translations, is in Hindi rather than a Western language; and (c) it corresponds less closely to the Canonical Tibetan *Treasury* than does the Short Apabhraṃśa *Treasury*. It is, however, considerably larger than any edition of the Standard Apabhraṃśa *Treasury*, containing 165 verses by Sāṃkṛtyāyana's count and 163 by Bhayani's. It contains most of the verses found in the Standard Apabhraṃśa *Treasury* and the Canonical Tibetan *Treasury*, but it also includes around a half dozen verses found in the Canonical Tibetan *Treasury* but not in the Standard Apabhraṃśa *Treasury*, as well as eighty or so verses found nowhere else.[213] Because the Long Apabhraṃśa *Treasury* includes most of the dohās found in the Standard Apabhraṃśa *Treasury*—though often in a different order—my remarks above about Saraha's themes hold here, as well. I cannot detail the many interesting verses unique to the Long Apabhraṃśa *Treasury* but simply note the following:

- The critical spirit present in all longer versions of the text is much in evidence, with passages that reject notions of caste purity; the worship of deities, especially those given shape and form; the practice of meditation; and intellectual activity.[214]
- The strong emphasis on the ultimacy and realization of the connate (*sahaja*) is equally evident. Although often described apophatically as ineffable, unthinkable (*acintya*), unexcelled (*anuttara*), nondual (*advaya*), and empty (*śūnya*),[215] it also is affirmed as synonymous with the supreme lord, brahman,

thatness (*tattva*), the ultimate (*paramārtha*), the beyond (*para*), and, above all, the mind (*citta*), which is both the self-aware (*svasaṃvitti*, *svasaṃvedanā*) source of all things and itself utterly free and unbound, even amid the world of concepts and delusions.[216]

- To realize the nature of mind, or the connate, is, as elsewhere in Saraha, the prime directive. The mind may be naturally free and unified, but it is besieged by thoughts, emotions, and doubts, behaving like a wild elephant, and we must reacquaint ourselves with its true nature.[217] In some sense, only the connate can realize the connate, but through the guidance of a guru, one may extract it from its attendant delusions as a swan draws out milk mixed with water by, for instance, utilizing various yogic techniques involving breath control and working within the subtle body; or making "sameness" one's wife, dwelling in the soundless, clothing oneself in space, and eating the food of the single taste of reality; or simply reducing all things to emptiness, establishing the mind in sky-like vacuity, and turning mind into nonmind.[218]
- Also, as elsewhere in Saraha, the ethical implications of realizing the connate are complex. Although the connate nature involves none of the delusions, dualities, or distinctions posited by the intellect, at times Saraha utilizes the conventional language of Buddhist cosmology, metaphysics, and psychology—for instance, by describing how one's habit patterns are the noose of saṃsāra, killing leads to hell after death but mercy to heaven, passion must be quieted like a restless bird in the mouth of a cat, and the senses must be kept from wandering afar, lest one's cattle be stolen from home. He also insists that the connate cannot be attained through sensuous desire and describes a scenario in which

he chastely gazes upon his beloved throughout the night, and "the dawn breaks most clearly."[219]

- Elsewhere, however, he speaks of transcending both evil and good and of the need to enjoy sense pleasures. He likens attainment of the connate—often described as supreme great bliss (*paramamahāsukha*) or natural bliss (*sukhasvabbāva*)—to the experience of real sex after one has only dreamed of it, insisting at one point that sexual yoga practice may induce self-aware nirvāṇa, and he speaks more generally of how when one is filled with the joy attendant upon realization of the connate, "you dance, sing, and play as you like." Yet, as on other occasions, he insists upon the centrality of compassion to the yogin's life, reminding practitioners that even if they have realized emptiness, if they do not combine it with compassion, they will not attain the translinguistic reality.[220]
- Finally, Saraha adds a few more personal comments to those found in the Standard Apabhraṃśa *Treasury*, remarking, for instance, that he is uninterested in wealth or power (*ṛddhi-siddhi*). He speaks of himself as the author of this collection of dohās, which is based on understanding what the treatise tradition has to say about Dharma and saṃsāra, and through which reality may be known. Finally, although he does not specifically identify himself as an archer or arrow maker, he does employ the fletcher's language, contrasting a headless arrow, which will not pierce its target, with a proper arrow, which will reach its target when emptiness is aimed at within emptiness.[221]

Text 2: *Performance Songs*[222]

The *Treasury of Performance Songs* is an anthology of fifty or so Apabhraṃśa[223] song-poems about tantric conduct, practice, or performance (*caryāgīti*) that were selected and commented upon, in Sanskrit, by the thirteenth- or fourteenth-century scholar Munidatta. Since their discovery and publication by Haraprasād Śāstrī over a century ago, they have been edited and translated numerous times and have become an important source for our understanding of medieval Indian Buddhist literature. Munidatta's commentary was also translated into Tibetan, probably from a slightly different edition than that extant in Sanskrit. The songs discussed by Munidatta are attributed to twenty different mahāsiddhas, most of whom are among the commonly listed pantheon of eighty-four. Thirteen of the songs are attributed to Kāṅha (or Kṛṣṇācārya), eight to Bhusuku, four to Saraha, three to Kukkuripa, two each to Śāntipa (or Ratnākaraśanti) and Śabari (or Śavaripa), and one each to fourteen others. Among the notable features of the songs are (a) their often highly personal way of speaking, (b) their employment of extended metaphors and symbolic language redolent of advanced tantric theories and subtle-body practices, (c) their frequent celebration of apparently transgressive behavior, and (d) the identification of each song with a particular tune or melody (*rāga*), which may well reflect a later interpretive addition rather than a song's "original" performative setting—assuming it was performed before it was written down.

The four performance songs attributed to Saraha[224] are less transgressive than those of some other mahāsiddhas included in the *Treasury*, most notably Kṛṣṇācārya,[225] but in other respects they are typical of the genre, with each being a collection of more or less thematically linked rhyming couplets that together make up a "song."

Saraha begins song 1 by lamenting how worldly beings bind themselves to saṃsāra and nirvāṇa through wrong views, and declaring himself the "inconceivable yogin," who wonders how birth and death could really exist, since in reality birth and death, like the living and dead, can't be distinguished. Those concerned with birth and death, he notes, play with alchemical elixirs but cannot escape aging and death. He concludes by posing an "unthinkable" question: whether karma or birth comes first.

Song 2 begins with an assertion of the essential freedom of the mind, where the elements of tantric seed syllables do not apply. Saraha goes on to insist that we should take neither the "straight" path nor some other, nor go away "to Laṅkā," for awakening is near and the self is known by the self; on the other hand, those who proceed along "this or the farther shore" and associate with evil people will perish spiritually. He concludes by lamenting those who think the straight path is to be found in "the trench on the left and the abyss on the right"—that is, in extremes.

Song 3 begins by likening the body to a boat and cognition to an oar and asserts that it is the guru who hands one the oar; when the oar of mind-itself is steady, the passengers will reach the farther shore. Yet while the boatman's guidance is important, in the end one may have to abandon ship, and by letting go and entering the connate nature, reach the far shore. When one's crossing is imperiled by obstacles, fierce currents, and "the waves of existence," Saraha concludes, it's best to practice "sky concentration."

Song 4 begins with the image of tearing apart one's own cognitive flaws "with the hands of emptiness" and with encouragement not to abandon the guru's word. Saraha goes on to observe that, in "the sky born from *hūṃ*," one takes a wife and, conquering illusion, proceeds to the farther shore. Illusion is conquered by seeing that within connate emptiness such confused constructs as self and other cannot stand. Saraha laments those who, although nectar is available, swallow poison and place the mind under others' sway, saying that he himself knows what he has drunk, and will consume instead his "vile relatives"—the defilements. He concludes by remarking, "Better an empty cowshed than the vile ox" of selfhood, which ruins beings, and asserting, "I behave as I like."

Text 3: *A Dohā Collection*[226]

Along with the Short Apabhraṃśa *Treasury* and a more complete edition of the Standard Apabhraṃśa *Treasury*, Bagchi discovered in Nepal in 1929 a collection of twenty untitled dohās attributed to Saraha, some incomplete, which he presented as *Dohās of Sarahapāda*. This text, which is likely fragmentary, echoes many of the themes already noted. Thus, for example, Saraha advises us neither to be unmoving nor to desire the self, and observes that just as salt dissolves in water, so even a false Dharma turns into great bliss (verses 1b–2). Elsewhere, he instructs us to cut off breath through the power of "primordial cognition" (*nijamanas*) (verse 4b), and, inspired by the words of the guru, to go from mind to nonmind (verse 5). Mantras, he notes, do not bring peace (verse 6a), nor does seeing a tree bearing fruit allow us to smell it, nor does the mere sight of a physician cure illness; so long as we do not know the self, we cannot train on the path (verses 7–8a). When we stumble along blindly, we will fall into a hole, but when understanding, or awareness (*saṃvitti*), enters the heart, duality will be destroyed (verses 8b–9). Indeed, when self-awareness grasps the essential, awakening is not far off, and through reflection on emptiness, mind will flow unimpededly, its pollution swept away, while if we are mindful of the floods of passion, all senses will taste the same, and we will free beings and attain nirvāṇa: accruing good qualities through yoga, we will enjoy bliss and be unbound from becoming (verses 10–13). Saraha advises us not to be bound by indulging in poisonous vices (verse 14) and, addressing his listener as "fool," advises them not to make worldly distinctions but instead to make the mind "replete with sky" (verse 16). Self-awareness, he adds, destroys desire, as the risen moon illuminates the night (verse 17). In the last full verse (verse 18; verses 19 and 20 are fragmentary and obscure), Saraha notes that when we are in harmony with all the elements and the senses and furnished with the qualities of the five conquerors, or buddhas, we may do as we please.

Text 4: Two Sādhanas of Lokeśvara Who Subdues the Three Worlds[227]

The Tibetan Tengyur contains six sādhanas—deity-meditation manuals—devoted to Trailokyavaśaṃkaralokeśvara, that is, Lokeśvara (or Avalokiteśvara) Who Subdues the Three Worlds. Of these, five are attributed to Saraha, and two of them have been preserved in Sanskrit in the twelfth-century anthology known as the *Garland of Sādhanas* (*Sādhanamālā*). These may be the only complete texts attributed to Saraha extant in Sanskrit.[228] As Benoytosh Bhattacharyya notes, "This form of Lokeśvara does not appear to have been very widely represented," with only one extant sculpture of it having been identified, in Nepal. Although the deity is also known as Oḍiyāna Lokeśvara, he is said by Bhattacharyya to have been worshipped primarily in what is now Odisha; both, as we know, are possible locations of Saraha's homeland. It should be noted that although Avalokiteśvara is typically regarded as a peaceful deity, his traditionally enumerated 108 forms adopt various guises. The Subduer of the Three Worlds is one of the more wrathful and tantrically inflected forms: he is described in the sādhana as red in color, sitting in vajra posture, having three eyes, and holding in his hands a noose and a goad; additionally, he is associated with various yoginīs. The two sādhanas are of similar brevity (1–2 folio sides) and similar in content. Essentially, they instruct the practitioner to set before them a scroll painting of the deity and establish in front of that an earth maṇḍala in which a saffron moon-maṇḍala is placed. Then, through specific mantras, one activates the deity and invites him to reside in the maṇḍala. That done, one establishes a sun disk and an *oṃ* syllable at one's heart, from which light-rays emanate, making offerings, confessing evil, and performing other rituals. The light-rays are reabsorbed, and one then imagines oneself as the Subduer of the Three Worlds, as described above. Emanated deities stream forth from one's heart, making offerings and requesting consecration from the yoginīs, who dance and sing and grant consecration. One then concentrates on a sun disk at one's navel and confirms one's own natural purity through one or more mantras. At this point, some versions of the sādhana describe the benefits of the practice: the attainment of physical stability, nondual gnosis, the union of the five buddha-awarenesses, and freedom from passion and anger. The sādhana typically concludes with offering mantras directed to various worldly deities.

Uncollected Fragments

Finally, a variety of isolated Indic-language dohās (or portions of dohās) attributed to Saraha have been found scattered among several medieval Indian texts, most notably Munidatta's commentary on the *Treasury of Performance Songs*, which cites him twenty-one times, including eight times in Sanskrit rather than Apabhraṃśa, and the *Compendium of Good Sayings,* which cites him around a dozen times, always in Apabhraṃśa. Some of the citations are from texts found elsewhere (most often in the *Dohā Treasury*), while others are unattested in other extant texts.[229] Located as they are in disparate sources, the whole or partial dohās not attested elsewhere do not, of course, form any sort of collection, let alone a coherent sequence, and here we will only remark that they touch on many of the same themes articulated in the other Apabhraṃśa works we have surveyed, including the stupidity of some who espouse buddhahood, the importance of the guru's word, the supremacy of the connate, exaltation of the mind, control of the breath, alignment of the senses and mind with the ultimate, the worship of yoginīs, a concern with freedom from bodily decay and death, and the attainment of bliss through the union of vajra and lotus and the ensuing descent of "nectar" through the central channel of the subtle body.

Texts Available Only in Tibetan

The works attributed to Saraha available in Apabhraṃśa or some other Indic language are significant and influential historical documents, but they constitute only a small percentage of the output credited to him by the tradition on which he had the greatest impact, that of Tibet. Indeed, a large majority of Saraha's works are found only in Tibetan translation. I will defer discussion of the problems they pose for the literary or religious historian until the end of this chapter, only remarking here that (a) they vary widely in terms of style, substance, and terminology, and (b) their authenticity in some cases has been questioned by traditional Tibetan scholars, not to mention modern ones, such that they may not represent a unified body of work produced by a single individual in Pāla-era India. For the moment, I will simply treat them as part of our survey of the Indo-Tibetan Saraha corpus, giving a brief précis of each. I will first summarize those texts found in one or another recension of the Tibetan Tengyur, in their order of appearance in the Dergé edition—with one song of praise found only in the Peking and Narthang editions noted at the end. A brief section on noncanonical works found in Tibetan translation will complete the survey.

Canonical Texts

Text 5: *Sādhana of the Glorious Vajrayoginī*[230]

Found in all three major recensions of the Tengyur, this text is attributed not to Saraha but to Trisaraha—the third or triple Saraha. Its authorship is quite murky: according to the colophon, it was transmitted from Vajrayoginī to Nāgārjuna to Trisaraha, who passed it on to Karopa, who wrote it down. Karopa is the name of a disciple of Maitrīpa, so it is possible that Trisaraha refers to Maitrīpa himself, either as third in a lineage that begins with Saraha and Śavaripa or simply as third in the lineage of this text. Alternatively, Trisaraha could be an otherwise unattested name for "our" Saraha (serving here as the disciple rather than teacher of Nāgārjuna) or simply the name of a figure about whom nothing else is known. In any case, the text itself identifies the practice tradition with Oḍiyāna, the northwestern region of the subcontinent that, according to some Tibetan traditions, was Saraha's homeland.

The text is a versified sādhana devoted to a version of Vajrayoginī that is red in color, naked but for bone ornaments, her face semi-wrathful in countenance, (with a small sow's head protruding to the right), standing in a familiar half-dance pose, with her left leg extended and her right leg bent so that her right toe touches her left calf, holding a skull-cup in her left hand and a chopper in her right, with a *khaṭvāṅga* held in the crook of her left elbow. The text leads the practitioner from preparatory visualizations, prayers, and rituals to their instantaneous self-visualization as Vajrayoginī, followed by various offerings, mantras, and the emission and reabsorption of light-rays—at which point the actual Vajrayoginī (described in detail) appears at their navel cakra and dissolves into them, purifying body, speech, and mind. The practitioner visualizes armored goddesses at various cakras, emanates various maṇḍala goddesses and offering goddesses, sings an eight-line song of praise to Vajrayoginī, joins gnosis and bliss within the subtle body, and finally utters a long series of mantras. The sādhana goes on to give instructions on ritual service to Vajrayoginī: the use of the left hand, the preparation of various offering substances, the timing of ritual feasts, and other elements of practice well known from yoginī-tantra literature. It also celebrates the benefits of proper practice, warns of the woes awaiting those who break their pledges, and ends with the hope that those who practice sādhana will see the face of the Noble Lady.

TEXT 6: *THE GNOSTIC: A COMMENTARY ON THE "BUDDHAKAPĀLA TANTRA"*[231]

The *Buddhakapāla* (*Buddha Skull*) *Tantra*[232] is a ninth-century (or later) yoginī tantra—extant in both Sanskrit[233] and Tibetan—that is related to the older and more foundational *Cakrasaṃvara Tantra*. Its maṇḍala is regarded as a near-mirror image of the Cakrasaṃvara maṇḍala, and its practices are sometimes said to make explicit the completion-stage instructions only implied in the early Cakrasaṃvara literature.[234] The central deities of the tantra's maṇḍala are Buddhakapāla and his consort Citrasenā, who are regarded as inseparable from twenty-four surrounding yoginīs produced by their union. The text, in a mixture of prose and verse, consists primarily of a teaching by Citrasenā and is divided into fourteen chapters, which cover such common tantric topics as the origins of the teaching (chapter 1),[235] taking a proper perspective on tantric practice (chapter 2), generating deities (chapters 3, 7), receiving consecrations (chapters 3, 14), preparing tantric substances (chapters 4, 12), concocting medicinal preparations (chapters 5, 10), generating maṇḍalas (chapters 6, 7), making effigies (chapter 6), presenting burnt offerings (chapter 8), performing the tantric "lifestyle" (*caryā*) (chapter 9),[236] practicing fertility rituals (chapter 10), learning magical herbs (chapter 10), becoming a spell holder (*vidyādhara*) (chapter 11), deploying mantras (chapters 12, 14), engaging in sexual yoga (chapters 12, 13), transforming aspects of one's ordinary being into yoginīs (chapter 13), and appealing to the yoginī for liberation from saṃsāra (chapter 14).

Saraha's *The Gnostic*, one of three commentaries on the *Buddhakapāla* in the Tengyur (the others are by Padmavajra and Abhayākaragupta), covers forty-six folios, making it by far the longest text attributed to him, comprising over a third of his total output. In style, it is what Tibetans call a "word commentary" (*tsikdrel*), which explains a text word by word, or phrase by phrase—an approach that has the advantage of being thorough and the disadvantage (at least to the modern reader) of sometimes seeming pedantic. Because it is the only extant tantric commentary by Saraha, it represents his most detailed exposition of a tantric system, and the fact that at least three other texts attributed to him also focus on Buddhakapāla indicates that this was a yoginī tantra of particular importance to him—a key, perhaps, to understanding the less systematic references to tantric ideas and practices scattered throughout his poetic oeuvre. At the very least, his works on Buddhakapāla deserve more scholarly scrutiny than they have received to date, and of these, *The Gnostic* is by far the most important.

Text 7: *Sādhana of the Glorious Buddhakapāla*[237]

Saraha's Buddhakapāla sādhana is a work primarily in prose, with occasional verses of exhortation, supplication, or celebration interspersed. It follows the blueprint of most other sādhanas. It starts with the author's homage to the blood-drinking deities who delight in aiding beings and his promise to convey the teaching received through the guru transmission. One is instructed to emanate, from the heart, goddesses who make offerings to Buddhakapāla and his consort Citrasenā—who are surrounded by twenty-four yoginīs—then to take refuge, offer confession, and contemplate the four immeasurable qualities: love, compassion, joy, and equanimity. Then, through various transformations of syllables and symbols, one surrounds oneself with the mansion of the deity, and then, through further transformations, generates oneself as Buddhakapāla and Citrasenā and visualizes around oneself three concentric circles, in each of which—on lotuses at the cardinal and intermediate directions—are eight yoginīs; four female door-guardians stand at the entrances to the palace. The yoginīs make offerings and drink the five nectars from a skull-cup, and at that point, the union of Buddhakapāla and Citrasenā issues in sexual substances, which rouse the yoginīs to passionate song and then transform into the actual Buddhakapāla and Citrasenā, who upon request dissolve into one. Then, the tathāgatas bless the yoginīs with sexual fluids, and the yoginīs bestow the three higher consecrations: the secret, wisdom-gnosis, and nonarising (or fourth/word). The consecrations complete, the yoginīs dissolve into the root cakra, the maṇḍala circles are sealed, and one offers songs of praise, along with the five nectars. From various syllables and elements, one next generates a skull-cup brimming with the five nectars and the five meats, which are cooled by a descending stream of nectar. One then sings verses celebrating breath-related subtle-body practices that generate the four joys and issue in a state of great bliss. The sādhana concludes with advice on mantras to recite and practices to follow throughout four daily sessions and a promise that if practiced assiduously, the sādhana will bring buddhahood within six months.

Text 8: *Offering Rite for All Elemental Spirits*[238]

This short ritual text is set within the context of Buddhakapāla tantric practice. It instructs the practitioner to begin by reciting mantras expressing the defects of the ordinary world, then reducing it to emptiness. Within this emptiness, on a sun disk, a *hūṃ* syllable becomes a double vajra, which transforms into the base and walls of a maṇḍala palace, on which instantly appear the twenty-four deities of the three maṇḍala circles, sentient beings of the three spheres, and direction protectors. One is then instructed to visualize oneself as Heruka, armored at various parts of the body. Then, atop a wind maṇḍala atop a fire maṇḍala, one generates a skull-cup containing the five nectars and the five goads (that is, meats); when the wind blows on the fire, the contents of the skull-cup melt and boil and then are cooled by nectar generated from a moon disk. At that point, through repetition of a mantra and the playing of music, one invokes the gnosis beings corresponding to the visualized deities, and each dissolves into its counterpart, thereby divinizing it. One then utters further mantras through which the substances in the skull-cup are offered to the maṇḍala deities and the field protectors, and when they have drunk and eaten to their satisfaction, one recites verses that reflect on the essencelessness and purity of all things and express wishes for the happiness of beings; one concludes by snapping one's fingers three times, sounding the bell, and dismissing the invited guests.

Text 9: *Illumining the Stages of the Maṇḍala Rite of the Glorious Buddhakapāla*[239]

Covering fourteen folios in the Dergé edition of the Tengyur, this ritual manual, written mostly in verse, is the second-longest extant work credited to Saraha. It focuses in detail on the Buddhakapāla maṇḍala and the deities that inhabit it, providing prayers, ritual instructions, iconographic descriptions, mantras, an account of the consecrations conferred within the maṇḍala, explanations of certain symbols and their correspondences, and occasional reflections on the nature of reality. Like Saraha's other Buddhakapāla-related works, including his lengthy commentary on the tantra itself, *Illumining the Stages of the Maṇḍala Rite* is of interest mostly because it gives readers a perspective on a tantric system that (if we are talking about a single Saraha) seems to have appealed to him—but like the other works, too, it reveals more about the Buddhakapāla system than about Saraha, who remains well hidden behind the standard conventions of the ritual-related genre.

Text 10: *Dohā Treasury Song* (*People Dohā*)[240]

As noted earlier, Saraha's best-known work, the *Dohā Treasury*, is found in multiple editions in Apabhraṃśa and Tibetan, with the two significant Tibetan editions being what I call the Canonical Tibetan *Treasury* and the Long Tibetan *Treasury*. The Canonical Tibetan

Treasury is actually entitled *Dohā Treasury Song* (S. *Dohākoṣagīti*), but I will generally refer to it by the name most commonly used by Tibetans, the *People Dohā*, which, as we know, indicates its inclusion in a trilogy (the *Doha Korsum*) with two other dohā collections designated by Saraha's purported audience, the *King Dohā* and *Queen Dohā*, which will be summarized shortly.

The *People Dohā* is similar in many respects to the Standard Apabhraṃśa *Treasury* first discovered by Śāstrī, then edited by Shahidullah, Bagchi, and Mathes and Szántó, and translated by Shahidullah, Snellgrove, myself, and Mathes and Szántó. Only a handful of the 112 or 114 verses in the Standard Apabhraṃśa *Treasury* lack recognizable counterparts in the *People Dohā*, while the Canonical Tibetan version adds more than two dozen full or partial verses—interspersed at various junctures—that are not found in the Standard Apabhraṃśa version, although as mentioned, a few of them are found in the Long Apabhraṃśa *Treasury*. Despite the considerable overlap between the Standard Apabhraṃśa *Treasury* and the Canonical Tibetan *Treasury*, the latter cannot simply be regarded as a translation of the former, for not only does the Tibetan version include 20 percent more verses than the Apabhraṃśa but many of the verses shared by the two versions have differences significant enough that it is hard to see how the Tibetan could be a direct translation of the Apabhraṃśa of the Standard version.[241] Given these facts, it is possible that the *People Dohā* is, in fact, a Tibetan translation of a lost Apabhraṃśa version of the *Dohā Treasury* that has both commonalities with, and significant differences from, the Standard Apabhraṃśa version. It should be noted, too, that, as is the case with virtually any text translated from an Indic language into Tibetan, there are several different Tibetan recensions of the *People Dohā*. The Dergé, Peking, and Narthang editions of the Tengyur include numerous variant readings, and Tibetan scholars—including most notably the seventh Karmapa, Chödrak Gyatso (1454–1506), and

Karma Trinlepa (1456–1539)[242]—sometimes present readings (their sources unclear to us) that are not found in any of the canonical recensions. Nevertheless, the Canonical Tibetan *Treasury* has as much coherence and consistency as any other Tibetan translation and may rightly be treated as a single text.

The themes covered in the *People Dohā* are those outlined earlier, in the account of the Standard Apabhraṃśa *Treasury*, including critiques of nearly all forms of ritual, meditation, asceticism, philosophy, and social conventions; exaltation of the guru; celebration of the body and the senses; the worship of yoginīs; and, above all, focus on attaining an immediate, gnostic apprehension of the nature of one's own mind—which is connately pure, blissful, luminous, and empty. The additional verses (some complete, some partial) found in the *People Dohā* but not in the Standard Apabhraṃśa *Treasury* cover such topics as the viciousness of "the unfortunate," who laugh at sublime beings (my verse 1), the myopia involved in seeing everything in terms of emptiness (verse 13), the importance of making the mind "like sky," thereby dissolving the vital winds into mind and letting great bliss overflow (verses 45–47), the way in which gnosis transcends thought through its realization of thatness (verse 49), the inability of ordinary beings to fulfill their aims (verse 50), the obliteration of action and inaction, bondage and freedom in the face of realization (verse 51), the importance of relaxing the mind (verse 52), the irrelevance of scholarly analysis and the importance of the yogin's ability to abide in nirvāṇa but "beautify existence" (verse 70), the traps of misperception into which even "a person who's sublime" can fall (verse 85), the lack of difference between meditation and nonmeditation (verse 95), the stability induced when mind sees its own nature and dissolves into it (verse 96), the wondrousness of the yoginī (verse 105), the pointlessness of Vedic recitation over against the recognition of the sublime mind where all things rise and set (verse 108), the importance of the "single syllable" that connotes the ultimate (verse 112), and the pointlessness of referential thinking or meditation (verses 122–23).

Finally, it should be noted that, in one form or another, the *People Dohā* also is contained within Tibetan translations of the Indian commentaries found in the Tengyur, those of Advayavajra, Mokṣākaragupta, and Advaya Avadhūtipa, and that these commentaries sometimes present variant ways of reading or dividing verses.

Advayavajra's *Scriptural Commentary on the "Dohā Treasury"*[243] is, as noted, the one commentary on Saraha's *Treasury* extant in Sanskrit—indeed, it was in a copy of this text that the standard collection of Saraha's Apabhraṃśa dohās was first discovered. The Sanskrit version is keyed to the 112 or 114 verses in the Standard Apabhraṃśa *Treasury*, while the Tibetan translation, with minor exceptions, also includes commentary on the two dozen or so additional verses included in the Canonical Tibetan *Treasury*, bringing the total number of verses (depending on how one divides them) to somewhere between 134 and 145—indicating either that the Tibetan version was based on an alternate Indic-language text available to the translator but now lost or that the standard Sanskrit version was translated into Tibetan but edited on the plateau so as to incorporate the additional verses found in the canonical version of the *Treasury*—or perhaps in the commentary of Mokṣākaragupta, to be discussed momentarily. The Advayavajra commentary was not uniformly revered by Tibetan scholars, some of whom considered it quite pedestrian, and certainly not composed by the great Maitrīpa, of whom Advayavajra is a well-known alias.[244] As analyzed by Brunnhölzl, the commentary follows this thematic sequence: a critique of non-Buddhist and Buddhist approaches to theory and practice (my verses 1–26); the instructions of the guru (verses 27–41); the procedure, purpose, features, and benefits of purifying the mind (verses 42–63); knowing true reality (verses 64–65); the importance of following the guru's instructions (verses 66–101);

celebration of the yoginī (verses 102–17); and the yogin's skill and compassionate activity (verses 118–34).[245]

Mokṣākaragupta's *Scriptural Commentary on the "Dohā Treasury"*[246] adheres closely to the Canonical Tibetan *Treasury*. The name of its author is also that of a well-known eleventh-century (or later) Buddhist philosopher, whose *Discourse on Reasoning* (*Tarkābhāṣa*) is a classic introduction to Indian Buddhist thought,[247] but questions remain as to whether Mokṣākaragupta the commentator is the same as Mokṣākaragupta the philosopher, and whether, indeed, the *Dohā Treasury* commentary attributed to Mokṣākaragupta was created in India or Tibet—although Tibetan scholars universally accepted it as authentically Indian.[248] According to Brunnhölzl, the commentary focuses on the following themes: critique of other approaches (my verses 2–16); the connate in general (verses 17–23); the causal connate in detail (verses 24–43); the path connate (verses 44–128b); and the fruitional connate (verses 128c–38)—with the long section on the path connate divisible into discussions of dissolving mind and breath (verses 44–53), methods of freeing and binding the mind (verses 54–57), the connate's presence and qualities (verses 58–63), ways of cutting through concepts (verses 64–73), the importance of the guru (verses 74–77), settling the mind (verses 78–83), leaving the mind uncontrived (verses 84–91), focusing on emptiness (verses 92–106), the inseparability of bliss and emptiness (verses 107–20), and settling the mind in nonduality (verses 121–28b).[249]

Advaya Avadhūtipa's *Commentary on the Essential Meaning of the "Dohā Treasury"*[250] also adheres fairly closely to the Canonical Tibetan *Treasury*. Despite its attribution to Advaya Avadhūtipa—like Advayavajra, an epithet of Maitrīpa—both traditional and modern scholars have cast doubt not only on its composition by Maitrīpa but on its Indian provenance. The Seventh Karmapa notably excluded it from his anthology of Indian mahāmudrā works, and recently, Karl Brunnhölzl has argued on linguistic and terminological grounds that it likely was composed, in Tibetan, by Balpo Asu, known to Tibetans as Kyemé Dechen (*Ajamahāsukha), a Nepalese disciple of Maitrīpa's student Vajrapāṇi.[251] Whoever the author may have been, his commentary, like most others, broadly divides Saraha's *Treasury* into, on the one hand, a critique of both non-Buddhist and Buddhist theories and practices (my verses 2–17) and, on the other, an exposition of Saraha's own approach to realizing the ultimate (verses 18–134), ingeniously divided according to thirty-five examples—most of them keyed to ultimate reality and the yogin's experience of it—that are drawn from the text, including, notably, treasure in one's palm (verse 21), water poured into water (verses 34, 89), sky (verses 36, 45–47), a camel (verse 53), a small child (verse 71), a maiden's bliss (verse 72), a lotus (verse 78), a trained elephant (verse 82), a ship's raven (verse 84), water and waves (verse 87), a forest fire (verse 90), a wish-fulfilling jewel (verse 92), salt dissolving in water (verse 96), a wife who consumes her husband (verse 103), a mirage (verse 112), a moonstone (verse 116), and bubbles in water (verse 125).[252]

Text 11: *A Song of the Overflowing Inexhaustible Treasury*[253]

A fourth canonical commentary on Saraha's *Dohā Treasury*, also attributed to Advayavajra, the *Extensive Commentary Clearly Teaching the Innate Primordial Thatness*, contains within it the text of what I call the Long Tibetan *Treasury*, entitled *A Song of the Overflowing Inexhaustible Treasury*. At 799 lines (organized by Brunnhölzl into 170 verses), that extracted text forms the longest version of Saraha's essential work extant in either Apabhraṃśa or Tibetan. Some early Tibetan scholars, as well as their modern counterparts, have argued that it was produced in Tibet, based partly on the Canonical Tibetan *Treasury* and partly on either invented Tibetan dohās or dohās for which no Indic originals are known, and that it may have been put together by the text's purported translator, Prajñājñānakīrti, who may be identical to Kor Nirupa, an early second-millennium Indo-Tibetan scholar recognized as a part of the lineage of Maitrīpa and Vairocana.[254] On the basis of the commentary, Brunnhölzl analyzes the *Inexhaustible Treasury* into sections on mistaken ideas and practices (his verses 1–21), the distinctive features of essential reality (verses 21–31), the importance of the guru (verses 32–53), the activity of those who train in the primordial state (verses 54–80), the process of making true reality a living experience (verses 81–142), the state of fruition (verses 143–69), and dedication (verse 170).[255]

The *Inexhaustible Treasury* contains equivalents to virtually every verse of the Canonical Tibetan *Treasury*, interspersed with nearly three dozen full or partial verses found nowhere else. Those verses include references to, for instance: the connate as the body of inseparable bliss and emptiness (verse 1), Saraha's opponents as performing monkey-like practices (verses 5–6), the flaws of the eighteen lower-vehicle schools and the Sautrāntikas (verses 16–18) as well as of tantric practitioners obsessed with the four consecrations (verse 20), the limitations of an analytical focus on emptiness (verses 21–24), the pervasiveness of great bliss, which should be celebrated with dance and song (verse 47), the absence of waxing and waning in the natural mind (verse 79), the realization that self and no-self, which are unestablished, are themselves the guru's body (verse 96), the capacity of the vajra mind to be free from harm and capable of miraculous displays (verse 109), the virtues of resting and relaxing the mind in a natural state (verses 122–23, 133), the identification of the unexamined state with the deities Vajrasattva and Samantabhadra (verse 147), the identity of deluded notions with the pure nature of mind (verse 150), the importance of leaving behind the "home of the mind" and its fixations (verses 157–58), the all-pervasiveness of the "tree" of true reality (verses 162–63), the lack of difference between realization and nonrealization (verse 164), the meaning of the expression *e-ma* (verse 169), and encouragement to beings to sing the song of reality within themselves (verse 170).

TEXT 12: *DOHĀ TREASURY: A PERFORMANCE SONG* (*KING DOHĀ*)[256]

Apart from the Standard Apabhraṃśa and Canonical Tibetan versions of the *Dohā Treasury*, Saraha's *Dohā Treasury: A Performance Song*, or *King Dohā*, is probably his best-known and most commented-upon work. Purportedly taught to the king of the country in which he lived, it forms part of Saraha's most celebrated textual cycle, the Dohā (or Essential) Trilogy, along with the *People Dohā* and the *Queen Dohā*. No Indic-language version of either the *King* or *Queen Dohā* is extant—nor, apparently, was either available in an Indic language even in the twelfth century, nor has any Indic-language commentary of either been found, although a Tibetan translation of an Indic commentary on the *King Dohā*, by Balpo Asu, is included in the standard versions of the Tengyur.[257] This led to suggestions by some Tibetan scholars that the texts are in fact forgeries, composed in Tibetan by the Nepalese scholar Balpo Asu or the Tibetan commentator Pharpuwa Lodrö Sengé.[258] Nevertheless, the texts were included in the standard editions of the Tengyur and commented upon by a variety of Tibetan masters (especially in Kagyu tradition), for most of whom their authenticity was beyond question.

The *King Dohā* consists of forty verses, which, according to the Tibetan commentator Karma Trinlepa (who in turn cites Balpo Asu's Indic commentary), is divisible into first a brief presentation of the ground, path, and fruition of mahāmudrā (a term that does not appear in the text) (verses 1–6), followed by detailed expositions of the ground great seal (verses 7–20), path great seal (verses 21–36), and fruitional great seal (verses 37–39), followed by a conclusion (verse 40).[259] Perhaps the most notable feature of the *King Dohā* is its liberal use of examples illustrating both deluded and awakened ways of understanding the world. Thus, confusion and dualistic thought are exemplified by, for instance, seeing waves as different from water (verse 1), seeing a single lamp as two (verse 2), blindness (verse 3), errant bees (verse 7), beasts (verse 8), insects wallowing in excrement (verse 9), those fooled by mirror images (verse 15), water turned to ice in winter (verse 17), a jewel buried in mud (verse 18), the seeds and sprouts of ignorance (verse 19), attachment to sexual pleasure (verse 21), ritualism and pseudoyogic practices (verses 23–25), confusing brass for gold (verse 26), deer deluded by a mirage (verse 28), and a pig "obsessed with worldly muck" (verse 40). Conversely, the ultimate—bliss, the connate, the inherent nature, gnosis—is exemplified by, for instance, the oneness of waves and water (verse 1), the singleness of rivers in the sea (verse 4), the brilliance of the sun (verse 4), the undiminishing ocean (verse 5), the taste of sky nectar (verse 8), the dried-up footprint of an ox (verse 10), the sweetness of seawater in clouds (verse 11), crop-ripening rain (verse 12), honey within a flower (verse 14), the formlessness of a flower's scent (verse 16), a lotus unstained by mud (verse 30), a lamp blazing in darkness (verse 34), and the seeds and sprouts of joy (verse 38).

Text 13: *The Inexhaustible Treasury: A Song of Instruction* (*Queen Dohā*)[260]

With the *People* and *King Dohā*, the *Queen Dohā* is part of Saraha's Essential Trilogy. No Indic-language version is extant, nor is there any known Indian commentary on the text, so the *Queen Dohā*, like the *King*, has been regarded by some scholars as a Tibetan rather than an Indian text. Like the *King Dohā*, however, it was incorporated into the various recensions of the Tengyur and has been commented upon by numerous Tibetan scholars, most notably Rangjung Dorjé and Karma Trinlepa. Like the other two texts in the trilogy, it has been cited with some frequency in scholastic literature—about as often as the *King Dohā* but far less than the *People Dohā*. The *Queen Dohā* consists of eighty verses, divided into eight sections containing ten verses each. Each section begins with the exclamation, "Amazing, the secret language of the ḍākinīs!" The sections are entitled, respectively: (1) "the natural state," that is, the basic nature of reality, "nondual mahāmudrā"; (2) "pitfalls," which are encountered on the path by those who think dualistically, lack consecration, break their vows, or ignore the guru; (3) "contemplation," in which, through the word of the guru and the embrace of a consort, the mind is settled in a luminous state beyond duality, distraction, or perturbation; (4) "encounter," in which, at the guru's prompting, one identifies solely with primordial gnosis; (5) "connection," in which the yogin identifies a female consort (*mahāmudrā*) and engages in transgressive tantric performance (*caryā*); (6) "commitment," in which the importance and benefits of guru devotion are described; (7) "fruition," in which the reality body, enjoyment body, emanation body, and essence body of buddhahood are celebrated; and (8) "instruction," in which the practitioner is encouraged to let the freed mind, the great gnosis, settle into its own nature, without need of cogitation, contemplation, complication—or even devotion or deeds. It is worth noting that although Saraha's Essential Trilogy is regarded by all Tibetan traditions as a seminal source for understanding mahāmudrā, it is only the *Queen Dohā* that mentions the term, using it to refer both to a female consort and the actual nature of mind/reality. The *People* and *King Dohās*, by contrast, focus more on such notions as the connate and the primordial nature. All the texts, however, agree on the need to transcend intellect, contrivance, and ritual so as to identify—and identify with—the natural mind, the pure, luminous gnosis that is the ground, path, and goal of all our spiritual efforts.

Text 14: *Alphabetical Dohās*[261] and *Explanatory Notes on the "Alphabetical Dohās"*[262]

Although not extant in its Indic-language original, Saraha's *Alphabetical Dohās* is an intriguing instance of a poetic genre that requires the author to divide the work into verses sequenced according to the syllables of the alphabet, such that each line of a given verse begins with a word starting with the syllable appropriate to that verse. Thus, in the first verse, each line would begin with a word starting with *ka*, in the second verse a word starting with *kha*, and so forth. Such an approach cannot easily be replicated in translation, and the scholar credited with translating both the root text and commentary into Tibetan, Vairocanavajra, does not attempt the feat. Saraha's root text includes verses and lines that begin with consonants (thirty-three in all) but no vowels; it appears to have been composed in either Apabhraṃśa or an unidentified Prakrit.[263] The original language of the commentarial *Explanatory Notes*, also attributed to Saraha, is uncertain: it may have been composed in Sanskrit, but it also shows signs of redaction by someone familiar with the Tibetan translation—perhaps the translator himself, Vairocanavajra. Either way, it serves as a helpful gloss on the original verses, providing in transliterated form the Indic-language word that starts each line. At the same time, it does not explain in much detail the practices alluded to in the verses.

In terms of content, the *Alphabetical Dohās* is one of Saraha's most explicitly tantric texts, replete with richly symbolic language evocative of the subtle-body practices and transgressive behavior associated with the completion stage of unexcelled yoga-tantra, especially the yoginī tantras. There are many references, both veiled and obvious, to—for instance—the downward dripping of nectar (bodhicitta, or semen) from the crown cakra, to sexual yoga practices, to the antinomian behavior of yogins and yoginīs, to drying up the vital winds that course through the channels, to identifying with the sky—all in service of attaining freedom in and through the connate mind of bliss and emptiness. For instance, the verse beginning with the syllable *ka* speaks of the embrace of a low-caste *ḍombī* maiden, the placement of the vajra within the "mother's" lotus, and the downward dripping of nectar, or camphor (verse 1). Other verses evoke such images and practices as resting in nirvāṇa while eating and drinking (verse 2), milking the sky (verses 3, 29), changing the "house mistress" into primordial cognition (verse 4), experiencing the four joys, moments, and drops within the subtle body (verse 6), sipping nectar like a bee (verse 9), relying upon the guru (verses 10–11), lighting the inner fire through chanting mantras and embracing the ḍombī (verse 12), looking to the moon in the sky (verse 16), bathing in supreme bliss (verse 17), projecting maṇḍalas into the sky (verse 21), a yoginī singing and dancing, (verses 22, 25), combining sun and moon in "the alchemist's way" (verse 26), Vajrayoginī delighting in the connate (verse 28), binding the "supreme colorless lord" to the body (verse 32), and drying up the oceans with the sound of *kṣa* (destruction) (verse 33).

TEXT 15: *BODY TREASURY: AN IMMORTAL VAJRA SONG*[264]

The *Body Treasury* is, with the *Speech Treasury* and *Mind Treasury*, one of a triad of so-called vajra songs attributed to Saraha.[265] Another text, *Cognitive Disengagement from Body, Speech, and Mind*, is often added to the three to form a tetralogy.[266] The four are said by the fourteenth-century historian Gö Lotsawa to be part of a collection of ten mahāmudrā texts (others include Saraha's *People* and *King Dohās*) transmitted to the Tibetan scholar Nakpo Sherdé by Maitrīpa's student Vajrapāṇi—who might also have transmitted them earlier to Balpo Asu.[267] The four texts are important works, but no Indian or Tibetan commentary on any of them is extant, and they were rarely discussed by Indian or Tibetan scholars. Still, if they truly were composed by Saraha, they contain his most detailed discussions of mahāmudrā, both as it relates to the other seals of tantric practice (the action, pledge, and dharma seals) and as an index of ultimacy that transcends all categories. The texts also utilize a distinctive fourfold scheme of symbolic realizations within the practice of mahāmudrā—namely, recollection (*drenpa*), nonrecollection (*drenmé*), nonarising (*kyemé*), and beyond thought (*lodé*). These terms also are employed in Vajrapāṇi's commentary on the *Heart Sūtra*, as well as in his disciple Balpo Asu's commentaries on the *People* and *King Dohās*, mentioned above.[268] This might suggest that if Asu was suspected by some Tibetans to be the true author of the *King* and *Queen Dohās*, he might just as reasonably be taken as the author of the quartet, as well. However, because the four texts seem to have dropped with barely a ripple into the pond of Tibetan scholarship, debates as to their authorship apparently never occurred.

Divisible into just under 120 verses, the *Body Treasury* is the longest of the quartet. Like any major poetic work attributed to Saraha, it covers a variety of important themes, including the nature of mind, emptiness and compassion, mahāmudrā, the connate, great bliss, tantric subtle-body practices and experiences like the four joys, the realizations attained on the path to freedom, and the bodies of a buddha as seen from a tantric perspective. Like most other dohā collections, it lays out these themes in a rather unsystematic fashion. Nevertheless, Lara Braitstein, the first modern scholar to study the three vajra songs, has organized the topics of the *Body Treasury* as follows: a broad critique of religious and philosophical systems (my verses 1–2), a description of the nondual nature of the connate, and the inseparability of aspects by which it is described (verses 3–13), practical instructions, with a focus on cognizing nonduality (verses 14–26), a critique of conventional meditation techniques, along with practice instructions on mahāmudrā (verses 27–30), discussion of the mahāmudrā teaching as transcending Mahāyāna and Tantra, along with an analysis of the four symbolic realizations and the four seals (verses 31–38), aspects of nonduality and self-awareness (verses 39–52), the nonduality of mahāmudrā (verses 53–66), a presentation through the metaphors of ocean and sky (verses 67–71), descriptions of the great seal and instructions on its practice (verses 72–88), a comparison between conventional paths and the mahāmudrā approach (verses 89–100), a presentation of various tantric themes through further metaphors, such as ice melting into water, an untied knot, the flight of a ship's raven, a tamed elephant, salt in water, a wildfire, a flowing stream, a lamp, and the best of medicines (verses 101–10), attainment of the goal through the four mahāmudrā symbolic realizations (verses 111–17), and a final aspirational prayer (verse 118).[269]

TEXT 16: *SPEECH TREASURY: A GENTLE VAJRA SONG*[270]

The *Speech Treasury* contains just under fifty verses and recapitulates many of the themes treated in detail in the *Body Treasury*. The presentation of themes is typically unsystematic, but Braitstein provides at least one possible template, as follows: a condensed summary of the *Body Treasury* (my and Braitstein's verse 1), the importance of compassion to realization of mahāmudrā (verses 2–4), reliance on the guru in order to accomplish mahāmudrā (verses 5–6), outline of traditional tantric assumptions and practices (verses 7–10), Saraha's critique of conventional approaches and instructions on nonduality (verses 11–47), and his final affirmation of mahāmudrā as direct cognition, followed by a concluding aspiration prayer (verse 48).[271] The penultimate section, containing fully two-thirds of Saraha's verses, ranges widely through both critical and constructive perspectives, refuting the views of various non-Buddhist groups and denying the utility of standard tantric categories, of generation-stage "yoga with signs," of tantric pledges applied without skillful means, and of sexual yoga performed with desire, while affirming the importance of hearkening to the guru's word, properly employing the senses, and homing in repeatedly on the real nature of things—suchness, thatness, or emptiness—where awareness, bliss, and all special attainments, including buddhahood, arise.

TEXT 17: *MIND TREASURY: A VAJRA SONG ON NONARISING*[272]

The shortest of the three vajra songs is the *Mind Treasury*, which is typically divided into fewer than thirty verses. Employing a concise and paradoxical mode of expression, Saraha recapitulates many of the major themes found in the *Body* and *Speech Treasuries*, including the inconceivable, nonarising, and the nondual nature of ultimate reality; the equivalency among mahāmudrā, the connate, great bliss, self-awareness, and luminous gnosis; the inadequacy of standard philosophical or tantric methods for attaining realization; the proper enjoyment of the senses; the application of the four symbolic realizations; and the indispensability of the guru. He illustrates his major themes by recourse to several familiar images, including a lamp, the ocean, a lotus, deer deep in a forest, and a sea of jewels. Braitstein again provides a possible way of organizing the text, dividing it into a presentation of the connate through metaphors, especially that of the lamp (my and Braitstein's verses 1–6), instructions on nonduality (verses 7–14), instructions on mahāmudrā (verses 15–23), a critique of dualistic tantric practice (verses 24–25), and reliance on the guru in order to accomplish mahāmudrā, along with a final aspiration prayer (verses 26–27).[273]

TEXT 18: *COGNITIVE DISENGAGEMENT FROM BODY, SPEECH, AND MIND*[274]

As noted above, *Cognitive Disengagement from Body, Speech, and Mind* is often included with the *Body*, *Speech*, and *Mind Treasuries* as part of a quartet of Saraha texts that were transmitted and, it seems, translated together in the eleventh century. Although it focuses on a term familiar from the Maitrīpa corpus but rarely found elsewhere in Saraha's writings—namely, cognitive disengagement (*amansikāra*)—it also, like the three vajra songs just described, refers frequently to mahāmudrā and the four symbolic realizations (recollection, nonrecollection, nonarising, and beyond thought) and does seem of a piece with the *Treasuries* in its overall thematic, terminological, and literary approach. It is one of Saraha's longer poems and, like so much else in his poetic corpus, it is difficult to systematize. Brunnhölzl suggests that it might roughly be divided along the following lines: praising the qualities of the guru's body, speech, and mind (my verses 1–3), realizing (or not) the qualities of mahāmudrā (verses 4–8), description and praise of the expanse of nonreferentiality (verses 9–11), describing those who are and are not able to realize the nature of mind (verses 12–27), descriptions of thatness and what it is not (verses 28–44), how thatness can and cannot be realized (verses 45–57), further descriptions of thatness and mahāmudrā (verses 58–62), the all-inclusiveness and impartiality of mahāmudrā (verses 63–79), and instructions on how to see and act in the context of mahāmudrā, capped off by a final aspiration prayer (verses 80–96).[275] The latter sections include discussions of how mahāmudrā relates to the other tantric seals and to the fruits of the path—namely, the bodies of a buddha. Throughout, as in other works in the tetralogy (and Saraha's works more broadly), it illustrates its "argument" with such familiar examples of ultimate reality and its realization as the sky, the ocean, jewels, and so forth.

Text 19: *The Mahāmudrā Pith-Instruction Called "Dohā Treasury"*[276]

Apart from the *People*, *King*, and *Queen Dohās*, the *Mahāmudrā Pith-Instruction* is the Saraha work most often cited by Tibetan scholars. The colophons to the Tibetan versions typically credit it to Mahāśabara Saraha. As noted earlier, this could conceivably designate the Great Brahmin's disciple or granddisciple Śavaripa,[277] but the prevailing view is that it was composed by "our" Saraha, for it is under one or another of his names (usually "Saraha" or "the Great Brahmin") that it is most often quoted in Tibetan literature. Besides being included in the Seventh Karmapa's mahāmudrā anthology, it is found in another influential collection put together in Tibet, the *Eight Dohā Treasuries*.[278] There are no known Indian or Tibetan commentaries on the text, but the Ladakhi scholar Trulshik Pema Chögyal (1876–1958) provides a useful outline in his edition of the *Eight Dohā Treasuries*, in which he divides it into three main sections: (1) the basic nature of mahāmudrā (my verses 1–17), (2) the mahāmudrā path (verses 18–38), and (3) the fruition of mahāmudrā (verses 39–44). Mahāmudrā's basic nature is explored through a description of what it is and isn't and the defects entailed by not realizing its "mode of being," followed by an expression of Saraha's own realization. Mahāmudrā as path involves (a) gaining a proper understanding ("right view") of mahāmudrā's mode of being; (b) meditating upon that by way of nonmeditation, which is said to be the highest form of meditation and inseparable from ordinary mind; and (c) behaving in a naturally compassionate manner, untainted by concerns with ordinary conventions of good and bad. Mahāmudrā as fruition requires the recognition that there is nothing to abandon or obtain, for mind is pure from the start—and yet when it is revealed through the path, we may speak of it as Vajradhara and assert the power of prayer to fulfill our own and others' aims.[279] Both the terminology and imagery of the *Mahāmudrā Pith-Instruction* are familiar from other texts attributed to Saraha, with the ultimate and its realization described in terms of mahāmudrā, mind, nonduality, the connate, the pure inherent nature, the primordial nature, great bliss, cognitive disengagement, the single taste, suchness, thatness, and so forth, illustrated through images such as the sky, the sun, a lion, the sea, a raven, a jewel, a madman, a child, a lotus, and a wish-granting tree.

TEXT 20: *TWELVE VERSES OF INSTRUCTION*[280]

Despite its title, the *Twelve Verses of Instruction* is not easily divided into a dozen stanzas. Not much cited or discussed in Tibetan literature, it does have an anonymous commentary, purportedly composed in India, that was translated into Tibetan but not included in the Tengyur; it is, however, contained in the Seventh Karmapa's anthology of Indian mahāmudrā texts.[281] The author of the commentary describes the *Twelve Verses* as part of an otherwise unknown collection of five Saraha texts, of which the other four are the Dohā Trilogy and the *Stages of Self-Blessing*.[282] The text itself begins with a description of bodhicitta, which is said to be peaceful and skylike, equivalent to unchanging thatness, nonconceptual gnosis, omniscience, and buddha itself, and which impartially pervades all beings, however different they may seem (my verses 1–5). The heart of the poem is a series of observations about various animals: tigers live in caves, fireflies emit light, camels attract snakes, bees consume poison, vultures recognize gems, ducks know the future, herons' tears capture beings, weevils smell with their eyes, and so forth (verses 6–10). In the final verses, Saraha draws out a lesson: if doing what comes naturally through previous tendencies (*vāsaṇā*) were sufficient for attaining gnosis, then all these animals—and brahmins, with their malice and mantra muttering—would be free, but in both cases, there is only instinct and worldly knowledge (verse 11). Saraha closes with an exhortation to practice the perfect gnosis outlined at the beginning of the poem so as to gain awakening and the special attainments that accompany it (verse 12).

TEXT 21: *STAGES OF SELF-BLESSING*[283]

This panegyric poem is said by the Tibetan scholar Pema Karpo (1527–92) to be an exemplar of the "devotional great seal."[284] It is unusual among works attributed to Saraha in several respects. First, its utilization of an ornate poetic style (*kāvya*) stands in contrast with the less elaborate—though still allusive and sometimes elusive—approach typically found in dohās. Second, although Saraha certainly expresses devotion—whether to buddhas, tantric deities, or the guru—at many points in his writings, the *Stages of Self-Blessing*'s near-exclusive emphasis upon supplication of such figures makes it stand out. Finally, the deities mentioned in the poem are primarily (if not exclusively) connected not to the yoginī tantras most often evoked by Saraha but to the mahāyoga tantra tradition of Guhyasamāja—and indeed, the term *self-blessing* (*svādhiṣṭhāna*) refers, *inter alia*, to the third of the five stages of completion-stage practice in the Guhyasamāja literature. The poem itself, which received no commentary in either India or Tibet, is divisible into sixteen verses. Verses 1–7 sing praises of a variety of deity figures, including the Buddha in his tantric form as "lord of illusory emanations," the buddha Akṣobhya, the "queen marked by vajra words," the goddess with vajra limbs, the buddha Vairocana, and Vajralāsyā and other consorts, whose nature is that of Prajñāpāramitā. The next several verses (7–11) celebrate the guru and sing of the accomplishments that ensue from worshipping and heeding the guru and the sorrows entailed by ignoring the guru's advice. Finally (verses 12–16), Saraha describes the "yoga of effort," free from dualistic fixation, taught by the guru and describes with considerable emotion his show of reverence to the guru through prostration and a flower-garland offering, his enjoyment of the "blissful savor" that accompanies the guru's wisdom, and his amazement at the import of the guru's teaching of emptiness, which leads to bliss and the understanding that "there is not the slightest difference between existence and peace."

Text 22: *The Summit of Instruction on Suchness: A Dohā Song*[285]

This dohā song, which is divisible into around twenty verses, has no known Indian or Tibetan commentaries. It covers many of the major themes of Saraha's mahāmudrā-centered texts: the necessity for realizing the connate nature shared by all (verse 1); the way in which suchness transcends categories, refutations, and proofs (verse 2); how, in mahāmudrā, there are no concepts or entities, and there is nothing to abandon or attain, yet through it the three buddha bodies are attained (verses 3–6); the necessity for freeing the mind from fixation on external objects and settling into the luminosity of mind-itself (verses 7–8); the emptiness and nonarising of all things, whereby they neither exist nor don't exist (verses 9–11); how the inherent nature transcends duality and nonduality, one-pointedness, and the single taste (verse 12); how dancing girls "sway with suchness," without grasping or categorizing (verse 13); the ultimate nonexistence of every element of the path and fruit (verse 16); the need for going beyond duality and distinctions in order to attain blissful connate gnosis, which is constant "like a flowing river or the sky" (verses 17–21); the uselessness of concepts and signs, including nonmeditation (verses 22–23); the celebration of the connate through dances and songs, "as yoginīs circle to the left" (24); and a final exhortation to realize the inherent nature, which is inexpressible, unaspected, and "effortlessly enters everywhere" (verse 25). Incidentally, Pema Karpo finds in the *Summit of Instruction on Suchness* Saraha's clearest foreshadowing of the four stages of mahāmudrā practice commonly described in Kagyu tradition: one-pointedness, nonelaboration, the single taste, and nonmeditation, though he does not lay out the fourfold scheme explicitly.[286]

Text 23: *Dohā Song of View, Meditation, Conduct, and Result*[287]

The title of this brief song refers to a fourfold way of organizing Buddhist practice that arose late in the Indian tradition and became extremely popular in Tibet, whereby one begins by attaining the correct view of reality, meditates one-pointedly upon that view, undertakes conduct appropriate to one's place on the path, and attains the final result, or fruition, of that path—namely, buddhahood. The text has no known Indian or Tibetan commentaries and is not often cited, but in less than twenty verses, it distills, in a quasi-systematic fashion, many of the main points found elsewhere in Saraha's writings, employing many familiar similes to illustrate those points. Thus, the opening verses, composed by "Saraha, an adept of Hayagrīva," focus primarily on the view—that is, one's correct apprehension of the nature of things, which is described as mind-itself; the nonduality of saṃsāra and nirvāṇa and buddhas and sentient beings, like that of water and waves; the "great seal (mahāmudrā) of union," which is "blissful, luminous, and nonconceptual like the sky," all-pervasive and unstained, ineffable, empty like a moon's reflection in water and yet "the essence of compassion"; and the uncontrived primordial mind, beyond concepts, hatred, or desire (verses 1–6). Turning to meditation, Saraha notes that contemplation of one's inherent nature requires knowing that "the body is the supreme abode" and mind-itself "the accomplisher of . . . yoga," then instructs the yogin to bind and release the senses, recognize all things as mind and turn them into deities, loosen conceptualization, abandon action, transcend recollection and nonrecollection, and—like a child, a bee in a garden, a lion in the forest, or wafting breezes—allow mind to dissolve into itself (verses 7–11). Conduct is identified as "mind-itself that's conscientious," and Saraha instructs us to free our inherent nature and "act like a lunatic, without attachment"—yet at the same time adopt "whatever conduct is beneficial" (verse 12). The "nonappearing result" that cannot be sought, the mahāmudrā of "empty suchness and inherent nature," is simply the revelation of mind-itself, emerging within appearance, where everything—outer and inner, and view, meditation, and conduct—is connate and integrated, like currents in a flowing river or like a cloudless sky (verses 13–15).

Text 24: *Ornament of Springtime: A Dohā-Treasury Song*[288]

This short, charming, mysterious song is, on one level, an expression of longing for the tantric buddha Heruka, voiced by a "youth" (*shönu*) whose gender is not specified but would seem to be female. In that sense, the song might be an early instance of an Indian male poet adopting a female persona, a practice also encountered in Hindu devotional poetry (for instance, in the works of Sūrdās), as well as in some poems of the Spanish mystic St. John of the Cross. On another level, however, the song may be a classic instance of tantric symbolic language; as noted by Brunnhölzl, in yoginī-tantra systems, "spring" may refer to the Blessed One, that is, Heruka, or the moon (the white drop); "ornament" to the Blessed Lady, that is, Vajravārāhī, or the sun (the inner fire); and "ornament of springtime" to their blissful union.[289] In any case, the song begins with the "youth" describing her (or his) intoxication by spring flowers, pomegranates, and other delights and calling to Heruka to be her protector and to keep her from dying of passion (verses 1–2). The gnomic third verse expresses the youth's wish to smell *ambhakāruna* flowers and describes how a hunter beats his drum, a fierce, low-caste woman (*caṇḍalī*) carries a lamp, and a master painter descends. In the next verse (4), the youth prays that "the young man will come," and asks again that, "at the beginning of spring," he protect her from dying of passion. She adds that wherever she looks, "I see nothing but you, / and in the fire of my passion, / I don't even think of my own body" (verse 5). The final verse (6) expresses the wish that through prayers to the four transmission yoginīs, the Blessed Heruka may be roused.

Text 25: Two Untitled Songs[290]

Each of these two brief songs, which are found in succession in the Tengyur, is simply designated at the end as *Song of Saraha*, with no further information. They are more "songlike" than many of Saraha's poems in that they are both structured so that there is thematic variation in the first two lines of each verse followed by a (mostly) consistent two-line refrain. Song 1 is composed in the same spirit as many of Saraha's mahāmudrā-oriented poems, addressing the ubiquity of those who talk about "the deep" and the rarity of those who "rejoice in nonarising," the instruction to settle the mind "without reference point," the need for "the guru's unsurpassed blessing," and the importance of *not* seeking either great bliss or "the middle." The first three verses end with the refrain: "Ah! Since the depths of the mind are difficult to know, / when you connect with the connate, [mind] is nonexistent." The final verse concludes differently: "Deep, deep! You may say everything about the world, / but [real] joy resides in nonarising." Song 2 is thematically and stylistically reminiscent of Saraha's *Queen* and *People Dohās*, performance songs, and other more explicitly tantric works, especially in its repeated image of an exemplary yoginī "milking the sky," which may refer to either bringing down the drop of bodhicitta from the crown cakra through completion-stage practices or simply realizing emptiness. Its verses articulate, respectively, how emptiness and compassion are "naturally mixed"; how the yogin should dwell not on the ground of saṃsāra but where "sky joins with sky"; how in such yoga one leaves home and tastes stainless great compassion, and how one should heed Saraha's advice to "milk the sky day and night." The refrain, which completes each of the four verses, is "I see the empty yoginī, / riding through the sky, milking it, drinking it, dwelling in it."

Text 26: *Vajra Secret Song: A Pith Instruction on Mahāmudrā*[291]

Despite its title, this long, versified text is quite unlike other works attributed to Saraha that mention or allude to mahāmudrā. Indeed, it is not a self-evidently religious text or a markedly Buddhist one.

It contains 540 lines, almost all of which are discrete and sometimes gnomic sayings. In Tibetan, each is in the same seven-syllable poetic meter, but read in succession, very few bear obvious thematic relations to one another.[292] As Schaeffer observes of such compositions—which in Tibet were referred to as "symbol-songs" (*dagur*)—"when ten or twenty lines are strung together, the effect is dizzying, with one—seemingly—unrelated 'symbol' or metaphorical expression following another."[293] The transmission of such symbol-songs from India to Tibet is strongly associated with the south Indian master Padampa Sangyé (d. 1117), and not coincidentally, the Indian cotranslator of the *Vajra Secret Song* is identified as Kamalaśīla, Padampa's ordination name. More broadly, the text may also be related to the popular South Asian (and Tibetan) literary genre of "wise sayings" or *bons mots* (S. *subhāṣita*; T. *lekshé*), which when collected, sometimes seem to involve non sequiturs like those apparent in symbol-songs.[294] A few examples should suffice to convey the flavor of the *Vajra Secret Song*: "You can't prevent a crazed bee from drinking nectar. / When you've become wealthy on your own, you don't need a Chinese jacket. / You wander in a ruined castle laced with precious gold. / The guide who leads you to the island is free from doubt. / . . . / The radiance of a jewel will not be disturbed by wind. / The forest-dwelling elephant obtains self-mastery. / At the time of death, a small kingdom must be destroyed. / An untainted golden pot beautifies any place."[295]

Although the text occasionally makes "religious" references—whether to personages like the Buddha, deities, monks, ascetics, or brahmins, or to concepts like the aggregates, suchness, nonconceptuality, and the vajra body, most of the sayings are, on the face of it, secular, speaking of human beings such as mothers, fathers, children, kings, queens, sea captains, merchants, farmers, athletes, doctors, drunkards, and untouchables; human products like castles, shops, boats, plows, chariots, mirrors, and food and drink; human activities such as sailing, trading, farming, herding, building, ruling, and fighting; or aspects of the nonhuman world, such as sky, rainbows, oceans, islands, rivers, mountains, trees, flowers, jewels, fire, and, it seems, nearly every animal known to ancient India. It is not, of course, impossible to give such sayings spiritual interpretations—the religious imagination, after all, knows no bounds, and several of the other "symbol-songs" anthologized by Padampa Sangyé also mention mahāmudrā in their titles[296]—but it is noteworthy, too, that despite its title, its length, its inclusion in the Tengyur, and its attribution to Saraha, the *Vajra Secret Song* was excluded from the Seventh Karmapa's anthology of Indian mahāmudrā texts. And indeed, the text seems to have been completely ignored in Tibetan literature on mahāmudrā. With one exception, discussed immediately below, it remains an intriguing outlier in Saraha's oeuvre, and while it does not live up to its title on the surface, it casts an interesting light on the folk wisdom of India and the ways in which apparently ordinary aphorisms might be thought to convey deep religious significance.

Text 27: *Key Instructions*[297]

This text, which is included in both the Tengyur and the collection of seventeen mahāmudrā-related anthologies transmitted in Tibet by Padampa Sangyé, is a symbol-song much in the vein of the *Vajra Secret Song*, consisting mostly of single-line gnomic sayings. It is said to have been transmitted to Kamalaśīla (that is, Padampa Sangyé) by "the great hunter Saraha" (T. *ngönpawa chenpo saraha*; S. **mahāniṣādasaraha*).[298] Saraha was counted among the fifty-four male teachers (there were fifty-four females, as well) with whom Padampa Sangyé studied—more likely, given issues of chronology, in visionary rather than bodily form. As noted earlier, Mahāśabara Saraha may refer to Saraha or possibly to his granddisciple Śavaripa, and, as before, we will provisionally identify the name with "our" Saraha—while noting that in this case, it is also possible that the true author is Padamapa Sangyé himself. While the *Vajra Secret Song*'s 540 lines are undivided in any way, the 142 lines of the *Key Instruction* are separated into seven distinct sections, ranging in length from fifteen to twenty lines. The sections are said to relate to the view, meditation, conduct, fruition, the path, experiences, and "the key point," respectively. Each is framed by (a) an initial homage to Heruka and the assertion that "the ḍākinī's blessing" is a symbol of the topic covered in that section, and (b) a final acknowledgment that the particular teaching was conveyed to Kamalaśīla by Mahāśabara Saraha. The sayings themselves are quite similar to those in the *Vajra Secret Song*, and despite their "topical" division, it is, at first glance, difficult to see how one string of sayings differs in "content" from another. Nevertheless, symbolic readings are certainly possible, and may—judging from what we know of Padampa Sangyé's style of teaching—have been part of the religious milieu of early-renaissance Tibet, if not of Saraha himself.

Text 28: Five Sādhanas of Lokeśvara Who Subdues the Three Worlds[299]

As observed earlier,[300] five of the six texts in the Tengyur devoted to the semiwrathful tantric form of Avalokiteśvara known as Lokeśvara Who Subdues the Three Worlds (Trailokyavaśaṃkaralokeśvara) are attributed to Saraha.[301] The five sādhanas (two of which, as we know, have been preserved in Sanskrit) are all brief (1–2 folio sides) and are much alike in content. Having summarized their essential content earlier,[302] I will not repeat their descriptions here but merely note that, as in most sādhanas, the worshipper is instructed both to visualize the deity externally and to visualize themselves as the deity, performing various rituals for their own and others' sake, primarily through the emanation and reabsorption of visualized light-rays and the recitation of appropriate mantras. Also as usual, performance of the sādhana is said to result in various mundane and transmundane powers.

Text 29: *Praise of Mahākāla*[303]

This panegyric of the wrathful protector Mahākāla, the Great Black One, is not found in the Dergé Tengyur, but of major editions, it is found in both the Peking and Narthang, where in each case it is attributed to Saraha. The poem essentially is a recitation of the symbolic import of the basic iconography of Mahākāla, who is black in color and terrifying in mien, wears bone ornaments, and has one face, three eyes, six arms, and two feet that trample demons. His single face indicates that he does not move from the reality sphere, his six arms that he has completed the six perfections, and his two feet that he overcomes obstacles. The chopper in his upper right hand symbolizes his severance of the root defilements, the garland in his middle right hand his nonforgetting of sentient beings, and the hand drum in his lower right hand his proclamation of Dharma, while the skull-cup in his upper left hand symbolizes his destruction of conceptuality, the khaṭvāṅga in his middle left hand his uprooting of the three poisons, and the noose in his lower left hand his liberation of beings from their bondage. His fangs indicate that he has overcome corruption, his three fiery eyes that he is free from the three poisons, his straight-up hair that he guides beings in liberating yoga, his bone ornaments that he controls the ḍākinīs, and his having Akṣobhya as his crown ornament that he has mastered the four consecrations. His encomium complete, Saraha concludes by reverently bowing down to Mahākāla, the bestower of blessings.

Miscellaneous Verses

These, then, are the Tibetan canonical texts that, with greater or lesser plausibility, have been credited to Saraha. It should be noted, as well, that individual verses attributed to him are found scattered in various other works in the Tengyur, chiefly anthologies of mahāsiddha songs. The most famous of these is a verse found in *Vīraprakāśa's *Essential Realizations of the Eighty-Four Mahāsiddhas*: "Hey, friends! The connate / is attained in the presence of the guru; it's not attained otherwise; / when you realize the ultimate, the essential, in their presence, / mind is deathless and the body unbreakable."[304] Others may be found in several collections, brought to Tibet by Padampa Sangyé, that eventually made their way into the Tengyur, including the *Secret Songs of the Mind*, which includes this verse: "Hey, friends! The nature of mind is the root of saṃsāra and nirvāṇa. / When you realize it, you relax without fabrication into nonmeditation. / Settled within yourself, if you seek elsewhere—oh, my!—that's error. / There is no 'this is' or 'this isn't'—everything is connate clarity."[305] Also, the *Vajra Songs of the Siddhas* contains this verse of Saraha's: "Formerly, in Bodh Gaya, [I attained] nonrecollection. / My mind overcome, I could not speak. / Luminosity, self-nature without coming or going, / free from duality—that's mahāmudrā."[306]

Paracanonical Texts

The Tengyur, in one or another edition, enjoys the prestige of being the "official" compilation of Indian Buddhist commentaries and treatises in Tibetan translation, but, like canonical collections everywhere, it is the result of a long editorial process involving decisions (historical, textual, and sometimes political) about both inclusion and exclusion, and in Tibet, paracanonical texts purportedly of Indic origin have circulated for centuries, their importance barely diminished by their "unofficial" status. Thus, although most important works by Saraha were included in the Tengyur, there are texts attributed to him that fall outside the canon yet have been regarded as significant by many Tibetan scholars and masters. In the subsection that follows, I will try to briefly convey a sense of what some of these texts are and what they say.

Other Versions of the *People Dohā*

Saraha's most famous work, the *Dohā Treasury*, or *People Dohā*, is found not only in multiple Apabhraṃśa versions and two Tibetan canonical versions but also in noncanonical versions created in Tibet. One of these, the *Song of the Overflowing Inexhaustible Treasury* (which I call the Long Tibetan *Treasury*), is, as noted above,[307] incorporated within the commentary upon it by Advayavajra, the *Extensive Commentary Clearly Teaching the Innate Primordial Thatness*, which is found in the Tengyur. While the root text of the *Song* is not found as a separate item in the Tengyur, it is included in the Seventh Karmapa's *Indian Mahāmudrā Texts*,[308] indicating that, by around 1500, it either had been extracted from the commentary or was circulating as an independent text that did not come to the attention of the redactors of the Tengyur. As we know, the preponderance of scholarly opinion is that the text was composed in either Nepal or Tibet, most likely combining some dohās securely traceable to India (those comprising the Canonical Tibetan *Treasury*) with some that were added on later—and if they were not composed outright in Tibetan, they at least cannot be traced to any Indic original.

The other major Tibetan version of the *People Dohā*, the Canonical Tibetan *Treasury*, has a more-or-less standard form but does admit of variant readings not only among the major recensions of the Tengyur but also as carried over into Tibetan commentaries—for instance, those of Chomden Raldri and Karma Trinlepa.[309] Slightly further afield is a text like the commentary on the *People Dohā* by Lingrepa Pema Dorjé (1128–88), who rather than trying, like most scholars, to provide a coherent outline for an often unruly text, simply rearranges the text to fit into a preconceived outline, whose main categories are (1) rejecting the assertions of non-Buddhists, (2) relying upon the guru, (3) meditative experience, (4) realization, (5) reinforcing one's practice, and (5) the dawning of the result.[310]

Text 30: *Special Mahāmudrā Instruction for Death Time*[311]

In classic Buddhist fashion, this brief song contrasts the transience of the body with what is everlasting—namely, mind-itself, mahāmudrā, the eternal realm—which is realized not through the standard cognitive mode represented by the term *recollection* but through *non*recollection. Although the verses contain little explicit instruction for the time of death, it is quite clear that at that time a practitioner should hew to the pure rather than the impure and the permanent rather than the impermanent, for only thus can liberation come about. The song includes two striking images: that of a house whose owner has died, a symbol both for a dead body and for the absence of permanent self in the body or any of its manifestations; and that of a snake, whose poisonous vapors are noxious but fleeting, just as are the body and its ordinary cognitions, and whose dismembered body is also a reminder of the absence of an owner, a self, within the body, an absence that is described as "a corpse within a corpse."

Text 31: *Melody of the Precious Reality Body beyond Thought*[312]

This song in twenty-four lines is found neither in the Kangyur nor in the Seventh Karmapa's anthology. As with many works linked to Saraha, its authorship is ambiguous. It is included among the collected vajra songs (*dorjé gur*) attributed to the second Karmapa, Karma Pakshi, who frames the text in his own voice but for the most part channels the voice of "a supreme person / beyond thought," who is identified twice as Saraha and once as Śabareśvara (*ritrö wangchuk*)—a name that, as we know, may refer either to Saraha or to his disciple or granddisciple Śavaripa. Given the occurrence of both names, it seems best to identify the voice at the center of the song as that of "our" Saraha, and the text, given its completeness, as a part of Saraha's corpus, at least by extension. The wisdom conveyed to Karma Pakshi by Saraha—identified as a "special instruction [from] the hearing transmission"—is typical of the mahāmudrā literature attributed to the Great Brahmin. He speaks of the unborn nature in which saṃsāra and nirvāṇa are the same; the reality body of one's own mind, where "nondual appearances are a sparkling reflection in mind"; the yogin who remains in the realm of "the gnostic," actionlessly acting in all situations; the unity and perfection of all dharmas, "like rivers merged into the ocean"; and the completion of the yogin's work when they "dwell in the expanse / of nonmeditation [and] realize the essential meaning." In the final verse, Karma Pakshi returns to his own voice and expresses the hope that this "little song" conveying Saraha's thought will be transmitted to "the fortunate."

Miscellaneous Verses

As with canonical texts, numerous Tibetan works outside the Tengyur contain verses attributed to Saraha but untraceable to any Indic source. Several Padampa Sangyé–related noncanonical anthologies of siddha songs, including his *Silver Orb*, *Golden Orb*, and *Crystal Orb*, also include verses credited to Saraha, such as the following:

> Hey, the root of samsara and nirvana is the mind's nature,
> Realizing this, [you] must, without meditation, settle
> [yourself] fully, without artifice.
> Settled in oneself, Oh what a mistake it is to search elsewhere.
> [This is] the natural state, without [talk like] "This is it, this
> isn't."[313]

The *Treasury of Special Instructions* (*Gdams ngag mdzod*), the great nineteenth-century compendium by Jamgön Kongtrul (1813–99), also contains an anthology of siddha songs in which Saraha is represented. There, he sings,

When someone speaks of any phenomenon,
That speech is an act of remembrance,
So is it not also the faculty of remembrance
That speaks even of nirvāṇa?

Whatever appears—earth, water, fire, or wind—
Simultaneously appears within emptiness.
The splendid appearance of gnosis
Occurs in remembrance alone."[314]

Yet another verse attributed to Saraha is found in Tāranātha's *Seven Instruction Lineages*, where the Great Brahmin, in a more autobiographical vein, remarks:

Oh ho! I am a brahmin and I live with a girl who works with bamboo.
I see neither caste nor no caste.
I have taken the disciplines of the shaven-headed monks and yet I wander with this wife of mine.
There is no distinction between attachment and nonattachment.
These impurities are only thoughts. Others don't even know this.
They are just like poisonous snakes.[315]

Also, as we saw in chapter 1, Saraha appears occasionally in the dreams of Tibetan masters—including Marpa, the first and third

Karmapas, and Tsongkhapa—where he typically imparts to them verse-instructions on the nature of reality and how to realize it.

Finally, as we might expect, given his influence on mahāmudrā traditions in Tibet, Saraha is quoted frequently in treatises on the theory and practice of mahāmudrā. The *People Dohā* is undoubtedly the text most often cited, but others are quoted as well. Although it may not be typical, *Moonbeams of Mahāmudrā*, by the Kagyu scholar Dakpo Tashi Namgyal (1512–87), is emblematic of Saraha's importance. In his massive treatise on great-seal theory and practice, he quotes the Great Brahmin almost 130 times, more than he cites any other Buddhist master. He quotes the *People Dohā* fifty-four times, the *Queen Dohā* thirty-five times, the *Mahāmudrā Pith-Instruction Called "Dohā Treasury"* thirty-one times, the *King Dohā* six times, and the commentary on the *Buddhakapāla Tantra* once; one citation is attributed to Saraha but cannot be traced to his known corpus.[316] In a different Tibetan tradition, and on a smaller scale, the Geluk master Losang Chökyi Gyaltsen (1570–1662) cites Saraha around a dozen times in *Lamp So Bright*, his commentary to his own root verses on mahāmudrā practice according to the tradition of Tsongkhapa. He quotes almost exclusively from the *People Dohā*, primarily in the context of his discussion of what he calls "mantra great seal," although he does cite verses as well during his analysis of serenity and insight meditation as two phases of "sūtra great seal" meditation.[317] Many other examples could be adduced, but these citations do not add to our understanding of Saraha's corpus—only of how it was used in Tibet. Indeed, it is reasonable to assume that few Tibetans read Saraha's Tibetan corpus in its entirety, and that for most, their knowledge of the Great Brahmin's words was filtered through the selections in treatises like *Moonbeams of Mahāmudrā* or *Lamp So Bright*, which focus on only a few works—the Dohā Trilogy and the *Mahāmudrā Pith-Instruction*—leaving most of Saraha's works unexplored.

Saraha as Corpus

At the beginning of this chapter, I suggested that if we cannot securely locate Saraha in the biographical material we possess, then perhaps we could regard him as a "corpus," whose written works convey as much about him as we may ever hope to know. In the survey of his works that followed, we identified nearly forty separate works attributed to Saraha. Reading over the contents of his texts, we see how widely divergent they are. In terms of genre, they range from prose works such as a long tantric commentary and multiple sādhanas, to versified songs of praise, ritual instruction-texts, dohā collections, vajra songs, performance songs, and symbol-songs. In terms of style, they range from straightforward commentary to expressions of faith in gurus or deities, practical meditation instruction, gnostic philosophizing, and gnomic symbolism—sometimes articulated in impersonal terms and at other times in Saraha's distinctive, insistent voice, which is at various times sarcastic, dismissive, confrontational, ironic, compassionate, or ecstatic, and never less than self-confident. In terms of theme and terminology, their focus ranges from conventional or symbolic presentations of "gradual" yoginī-tantra theories and practices to radical explorations of the many ways of directly approaching the ultimate—which is variously conceived as the connate, great bliss, mahāmudrā, emptiness, thatness, suchness, mind-itself, the primordial nature, or some other term for highest reality—and is expressed through various only partially overlapping sets of categories, such as the four seals (action, pledge, dharma, and great seals), the four symbolic realizations (recollection, nonrecollection, nonarising, and beyond thought), the four joys (joy, supreme joy, cessative joy, and connate joy), or the four phases of the path (view, meditation, conduct, and result).

More to the point for now, our survey of the Saraha corpus has revealed that many works attributed to him are of uncertain authorship. For instance, the *King* and *Queen Dohās*, which form part of the so-called Essential Trilogy basic to Tibetan conceptions of mahāmudrā, were said by some scholars on the plateau to have been concocted by a figure much later than Saraha, such as the Nepalese master Balpo Asu. The little-discussed trilogy (or tetralogy) on body, speech, and mind, with its distinctive terminological scheme, may similarly be suspected of being a later composition, with Balpo Asu again being a possible author. Several works, including the well-known and oft-cited *Mahāmudrā Pith-Instruction*, are attributed to Mahāśabara Saraha, who may or may not be identical to "our" Saraha. Saraha's autocommentary on his *Alphabetical Dohās*—if not the dohās themselves—are possibly the work of its translator, Vairocanavajra. Saraha's intriguing and gnomic symbol-songs are said to have been transmitted from India to Tibet by Padampa Sangyé, but it is not unreasonable to suspect that he may be their author. Further—and perhaps most importantly—the work for which Saraha is most famed, the *Dohā Treasury* (known to Tibetans as the *People Dohā*), is found in multiple versions in both Apabhraṃśa and Tibetan. While what I have called the Standard Apabhraṃśa Version and the Canonical Tibetan Version are the best-known versions south and north of the Himalayas, respectively, they have no special claim to "authenticity" over competing versions, only to popularity and prestige. We must remember, after all, that *all* versions of Saraha's writings, most especially the *Dohā Treasury*, are composite works to begin with, drawn from oral and written traditions that predate any given text—and well-nigh impossible to trace to any specific historical individual named "Saraha." In this sense, like the biographical tradition, the literary tradition surrounding the Great Brahmin presents us with an image not of singularity but of multiplicity, and with an author, if ever there was such, who long ago may have been scattered among a wide range of texts that bear his name—behind which he hides as surely as he hides amid the stories about his lives.

Saraha does, however, insist, in his *King Dohā*, that "the king sees Saraha appearing / in various guises, although he is one" (verse 1), and in the final two chapters of this section, we will give him—and the traditions that regard him as a unitary author—the benefit of the doubt, as we attempt to summarize what it is that Saraha seems to be saying, how he says it, and what the implications of his life and teachings have been, whether in premodern India, classical Tibet, or the modern world.

CHAPTER 3

The Medium

Saraha as Poet

As I SUGGESTED at the end of the previous chapter, Saraha admits to appearing in multifarious aspects in Indic and Tibetan tradition. In this and the following chapter, I will focus on two major roles: as poet and as religious teacher. Although we know that "Saraha" may be a name that refers to multiple authors who may have lived in various places over the course of multiple centuries, I will treat him in these chapters as a unitary individual, for this is how he has been seen in the tradition for which he has mattered most, that of Tibet. Using this approach, I will, in this chapter, briefly examine Saraha as a poet, poet-singer, or poet-saint, touching in turn on questions of what is oral and what is written in the "songs" of Saraha, elements of his prosody from both an Indic- and a Tibetan-language perspective, and his use of images and symbols.

Oral and Written Literature

From time immemorial, singers of both secular and spiritual songs have wandered through the Indian landscape, imparting through their rhymes, rhythms, and images stories to entertain their listeners and truths to which they might hearken. From the ṛṣis who transmitted the *Ṛg Veda*, to the bards of the *Mahābhārata*, *Rāmāyaṇa*, and other national or regional epics, to the bhakti poets who traversed every part of the subcontinent singing in nascent vernaculars, to the medieval and modern siddhas, *sants*, and other singers of dohās and other didactic verse-styles, the Indic world has been suffused with song, and it is evident that in a culture where written literacy was at a premium, and often restricted, oral composition was among the supreme art forms. Oral composition could be careful and calculated—a singer might compose a song mentally and then revise it repeatedly in their mind before finally singing it to an audience—or it might be quite spontaneous, performed on the spur of the moment as the natural outflow of ecstatic experiences or states of mind. The latter, certainly, is the image of tantric Buddhist poet-saints cultivated in Tibetan Buddhist circles. Great masters of song such as Milarepa are typically depicted as composing their verses on the spot, either in response to questions or comments offered by listeners, or simply prompted by a felt need to sing forth their own insights. By the same token, Tibetan literature describes Indic siddhas like Saraha, Tilopa, and Virūpa as composing their verses on the spur of the moment and delivering them orally to an audience—as, for instance, when Saraha is said to have sung his *People*, *Queen*, and *King Dohā Treasuries* to audiences of commoners or royals in the country he inhabited.

It is entirely possible—perhaps even likely—that Saraha, whoever he originally may have been, did compose verses or songs spontaneously before an audience of amazed listeners, or perhaps he worked them out beforehand in his head and then performed them in a style that suggested spontaneity. He implies as much in several verses.[318] It is, however, undeniable that—with the possible exception of performance songs attributed to Saraha that are sung in ritual contexts by the Newārs of the Kathmandu valley of Nepal[319]—all we have today are *written* artifacts, which may be traces of an originally oral composition or may have been written down to begin with. Most of Saraha's poetic corpus, as we know, is found only in Tibetan "translation." (The scare quotes are a reminder that some texts purported by Tibetan tradition to be Indic may actually have been composed in Tibetan.) Texts translated into Tibetan are, of course, at a considerable remove from their Indic sources, especially in matters of prosody (structure, sound, rhythm, and rhyme) but also in the realm of images and symbols, some of which are carried over more easily than others from the cultural world of the subcontinent to that of the plateau. And, if the Indic original—whatever its language—was a written rendition of an originally oral composition, then the Tibetan translation is at least two versions removed from the original, perhaps more. In addition, even though texts attributed to Saraha extant in the "original" Indic language, usually Apabhraṃśa, are sometimes assigned *rāga*s that are keys to their oral performance—as by the Newārs—they probably are *not* exact transcriptions of an orally performed song. This is so because, as noted earlier, Apabhraṃśa,[320] though it may have begun as a spoken tongue, was by the late medieval period strictly a literary language. It might have been a "demotic" language rather than a "high" literary language like Sanskrit, but it was a literary language, nonetheless. Thus, unless Saraha's songs are older than the evidence suggests, it is likely that any Indic-language version of them we possess is itself a "translation" from whatever language he actually spoke into Apabhraṃśa. In short, although an "original" oral version may lie at the root of some—or, less likely, all—of Saraha's songs, and although enduring song-traditions like those of Indian sants or the Newārs of Nepal are suggestive of what an oral original *might* have been like, strictly speaking, that version remains inaccessible to us.

Saraha's Prosody

Regardless of these textual-historical issues, nearly every extant song we have that is attributed to Saraha is in one of two languages:

Apabhraṃśa or Tibetan. The texts in Tibetan purport to be translations from some Indic language, likely Apabhraṃśa but possibly Sanskrit or some other tongue, as well. Since, effectively, we have Indic songs by Saraha only in some form of Apabhraṃśa, we will try to convey a sense of the poetic forms employed in that language by providing some examples from the Great Brahmin's most famous text, the *Dohā Treasury* (or, to Tibetans, *People Dohā*). According to the pioneering study by Muhammad Shahidullah,[321] there are twelve different metrical schemes found in the Apabhraṃśa of the *Dohā Treasury*, of which three are paramount: the dohā, the *pādākulaka*, and the *aḍillā*. All of these are known in Sanskrit prosody but are adapted in Apabhraṃśa, especially by the employment of end rhymes.

The dohā (*dodhaka* in Sanskrit), the verse form, or meter, from which the text takes its name, is the most common, with nearly forty occurrences out of 112 Apabhraṃśa verses. It is best described simply as a rhyming couplet. Here is a typical instance:

> vāddho dhāvai dhadihahiṃ mukko ṇicala ṭhāi /
> emai karahā pekkhu sahi viharia mahuṃ paḍihāi //

> (Bound, it runs in all directions, freed it stands motionless;
> look at the camel, my friend: the paradox is clear to me!)[322]

Much could be said about the specific metrical patterns—for example, the occurrence of caesuras, stressed and unstressed syllables, and so forth—found in this and other dohās but suffice it to say that the rhythm and syllable count—here and elsewhere in dohā literature—are seldom as precise as is typical in the highly regimented forms of Sanskrit poetry.[323] This, in turn, places a premium on the end rhyme, which is the most consistent and striking feature of any dohā.

In its Apabhraṃśa form, the second most common form in the *Dohā Treasury*, the pādākulaka, also employs end rhyme. It typically consists of four lines, each shorter than a typical dohā line. Usually, as in the following, the first two lines rhyme and the last two rhyme, but the rhyme sound of the first pair differs from the rhyme sound of the second pair:

dekkhahu suṇahu parisahu khāhu /
jighahu bhamahu vaiṭhṭha uṭhṭhāhu /
ālamāla vyāvahareṃ pellaha /
maṇa cchaḍḍu ekākāra ma callaha //

(Look, listen, touch, eat,
smell, move, sit, stand.
Throw off conventional nonsense—
give up cognition, don't move from the singular!)[324]

Here, we might note two things beyond the end rhymes. First, we must pause to admire the wonderful use of alliteration in the first "couplet," where the repeated imperative ending *-ahu* (or *-āhu*) gives great force to the lines. Second, there is no certainty—here or in any other pādākulaka—that the two couplets placed together here were originally intended to be paired; we find in the *Dohā Treasury* not only that some pādākulaka couplets stand on their own (perhaps having lost their other pair) but also that while some pairings of couplets appear quite natural, others seem somewhat artificial, suggesting that pādākulakas may sometimes have been created by juxtaposing two short rhyming couplets composed in different contexts. I would argue that the verse cited above is a case in point, since although one *can* make sense of the two couplets as forming a single semantic unit, their connection is not self-evident.

The third form worth noting, the aḍillā, also consists of four short lines, but at least in the case of Apabhraṃśa, the end rhyme (or at least an end assonance) is consistent throughout. Here is an example:

bhavahi ujjai khaahi ṇivajjai /
bhava-rahia puṇu kahi uvajjai /
viṇṇa vivajjia jou vajjai /
acchaha siriguruṇaha kahijjai //

(In existence it arises, in destruction it disappears;
beyond existence, how can it arise again?
It transcends distinctions and leads on to union—
the resplendent masterful guru declared, "It is thus.")[325]

Here, we will remark only that the verse is given strong semantic and poetic unity through the quadruple end-rhyme, but will draw attention, too, to the alliteration, for instance the *bha-* with which each of the first two lines begins, the repetition of initial *v-* in the third line, and the two *-ha* endings in line 4. As with the other forms, much more could be said, but I hope this gives the reader some sense of the prosody of these Apabhraṃśa verses.

When we turn to Tibetan versions of Saraha's texts, we find ourselves in a far different sonic and rhythmic universe from that of India, especially that of the Apabhraṃśa dohās. Here, end rhyme disappears; verses are generally rendered in four lines, even if the original was a couplet; and metric regularity reigns supreme: the majority of Saraha's poetic corpus in Tibetan (certainly in the case of the *Dohā Treasury*) consists of nine-syllable lines, though other line lengths also occur. Here, we will present in phonetic form the Tibetan versions of the three verses cited above in Apabhraṃśa, followed, as before, by parenthetical translations; the proper Tibetan spelling may be gleaned from the note for each. Syllables that receive emphasis are underlined. (Note that the Tibetan does not always yield the same translation as the equivalent Apabhraṃśa verse.)

The first example, a classic two-line dohā, is split into four lines of nine syllables each, with each pair of lines corresponding to one line of the couplet. Note that the syllabic emphases here are not uniform, with lines 1 and 4 following one pattern, and lines 2 and 3 another.

ching dak ni chok chu ra dro wa chom /
tong par gyur na mi yo ten par ne /
go dok nga mo ta bur dak gi tok /
bu kyö nam kyang rang la char te tö //

(When bound, they begin to run in every direction,
but when released, they stand stock still:
I see this to be like the camel paradox;
look into yourselves intently, my children!)[326]

The second example is a translation of a pādākulaka verse, which in Apabhraṃśa involves two pairs of rhyming couplets combined into a single four-line verse. As with the dohā, the verse is rendered in four lines of Tibetan. Although the lines of the Apabhraṃśa pādākulaka are shorter than those of the dohā, the Tibetan version (again) provides nine syllables for the first three lines and, curiously, eleven for the fourth line:

tong dang tö dang rek dang dren pa dang /
za nom kyam dang dro dang duk pa dang
chel chol tam dang len ma gyur pa la /
sem so she na chik gi nam pa le mi kyö //

(There's seeing and hearing and touching and knowing
and eating, smelling, traveling, and going and staying,
[there's] chitchat, stories, and back talk:
when you know "these are mind," you won't move from the
singular.)[327]

The aḍillā verse, which in Apabhraṃśa often involves four lines with identical or similar end rhymes, is also rendered in four lines in Tibetan and, as with the pādākulaka and dohā, each line is usually nine syllables in length:

ngö por kye wa ka tar rang zhin na /
ngö po nam pang chi ne chi zik kye /
dö ne kye me rang zhin yin pa la /
de ring pel den la ma ten par tok //

(If the nature of arising things is like the sky,
then after things are abandoned, what could arise?
That which from the start has not arisen
is realized today through the glorious guru's teaching.)[328]

Although much more could and should be said about the prosody of both the Apabhraṃśa and Tibetan versions of Saraha's poetry, two points deserve emphasis: (a) The Apabhraṃśa versions are extant in a literary language but a literary language that likely bears the imprint of a lost oral original—and certainly these versions may be, and have been, performed orally. (b) The Tibetan versions, or translations, cannot possibly reproduce the prosody of the original and understandably recast the verses in styles and rhythms familiar from Tibetan poetic traditions. Those styles and rhythms are common not just in translations but also throughout the "native" Tibetan canon, and although the translations are obviously literary creations, they, too, may be—and are, at times—sung, just as many other types of Tibetan verse may be sung. Thus, although we must concede the "literary" nature of the Saraha works extant in either Apabhraṃśa or Tibetan, we also must recall that in both Indic and Tibetan traditional culture the oral may flow into the written and the written become oral, and that they should not be seen as belonging to two utterly separate realms of discourse.

Saraha's Images and Symbols

One of the glories of Saraha's verse is its evocative employment of images, symbols, similes, and metaphors. A whole book could—and should—be dedicated to the topic, but here we must content ourselves with exploring just a few selected aspects of the Great Brahmin's use of literary devices. Saraha's images and symbols are woven into dohās, performance songs, vajra songs, and other poetic expositions of his view of reality and tantric practice, and they are also found in those mysterious utterances known as symbol-songs. In his dohās and other "standard" songs, images and symbols may be analyzed in various ways. Here, we will divide them topically: some refer to atmospheric, aquatic, and earthy aspects of the physical cosmos, some to plants and animals, and some to human types and the things they construct.

In terms of the physical cosmos, one extremely common image is that of the sky, or space, which typically is a symbol of emptiness, the ultimate reality that must be realized by practitioners, as well as the true nature of the mind that blissfully realizes emptiness:

> The sky is naturally pure from the start:
> when you look and look at it, seeing will stop. (PD 36)

———

Mind is to be grasped as like the sky;
as naturally sky-like should mind be grasped. (PD 45)

The sky is without birth, aging, or death,
[so] wherever you look, there's only sky. (AD 8)

Milking and milking the sky, you draw down the [moon]
drops and drink them. (AD 29)

Not identifying variety within the sky realm,
don't torment yourself by strenuous efforts of body, speech,
or mind. (CD 29)

Among celestial bodies, the sun and moon are given special prominence. The sun tends to refer to the luminous nature of mind, although it may also symbolize the red drop that resides at the navel cakra and is moved through the subtle body in tantric practice, as well as the channel to the right of the central channel in the subtle body. The moon sometimes suggests a mere reflection of true reality but more often symbolizes either the white bodhicitta drop, typically found at the crown cakra, that must be drawn down and transformed through tantric practice, or the channel to the left of the central channel in the subtle body:

By the pure light-rays of his sunlike gnosis
that supreme person turns ignorance into awareness.
(QD 54)

Hey! The sun is free from clouds and its rays are all-pervasive,
but to the eyeless they appear as darkness;
the connate is all-pervasive,
but to fools, thatness is very far away. (MM 11)

[When] the drops of sun and moon [combine], there is
deathless sky:
the sun in the mode of great bliss is most beautiful. (AD 26)

The reflection of the moon is partless and devoid of
objectivity;
even if sought, it is not [there], and even if viewed, it is not
seen. (BT 28)

Just as the jewellike moon shines
in the great, black darkness [of night],
so supreme great bliss overcomes
every evil notion in a single instant. (PD 116)

Where sun and moon don't enter in:
repose there, you fools. (PD 28)

Another common image is that of water, either as a part of life or in its more impressive manifestations, in oceans, rivers, ponds, waterfalls, and so forth. Water taken on its own may be a symbol of transience but more often refers to the fundamental purity of the mind, the yogin's experience of it, the process of purification, or all three:

This world, which is like a water bubble,
has the self-nature of connate emptiness. (PS 4:3)

Direct your primordial cognition into oneness, O yogin—
know that it's like water poured into water. (PD 34)

Drink up the cool, pain-removing
nectar waters of the guru's pith instructions. (PD 67)

Just as salty seawater
drunk up by the clouds turns sweet,
the stable mind works for the aims of others
and turns even the poison of sense objects into nectar. (KD 11)

Just as ice that's melted into water is fit for drinking,
so everything that appears is felt as nonarising great bliss.
(BT 101)

Oceans, rivers, and other bodies of water may variously refer to turbulent worldly existence, the ultimate nature of reality and mind, or a mode of practice:

Fools must thoroughly know the limits,
and know how to part the sea of confusion. (PD 33)

The sound of *kṣa kṣa* (destruction) can dry up the oceans.
(AD 33)

The qualities of nonrecollection are [like] an untroubled ocean:
there is no recollection; there are no waves on the water. (BT 43)

[Between] the near and far shore, fierce currents flow;
Saraha says, [perform] sky concentration. (PS 3:5)

Though rivers may vary, in the sea they are one;
though falsehoods are many, they're destroyed by a single truth. (KD 4)

The mind, like a river, submerges dualistic views,
possessing gnosis, spurning nothing, and not covered up. (QD 55)

Meditate on bliss as akin to an aimless river. (QD 24)

The boat goes downstream, and a boatman [guides it] with his pole;
let it go—and by letting it go, you'll know the other [shore] through the connate. (PS 3:3)

[Suchness] is all-pervasive, like a waterfall,
like an uninterrupted waterfall. (BT 40)

A final set of images from the physical world worth noting is connected to precious substances found in the earth and valued by humans, especially gold and jewels. Gold is often used in an alchemical context, to show the possibility of transformation through tantric practice, while jewels serve both as grantors of wishes and as symbols of purity, especially the pure nature of mind:

> All dharmas take on the same taste, as if turned to gold by an
> elixir. (QD 33)

> Always serve the wheel-turning king who's skilled in the
> methods
> of changing all dharmas to bliss, as elixir [1028] turns
> [metals] to gold. (QD 55)

> To the mind, which like a wish-fulfilling gem
> brings about [all] desired results, I prostrate. (PD 43)

> Suppressing the evil of self-view, you suppress all evils,
> so sanctify this jewel that is your mind. (QD 70)

> Hey, friends! The mind, like a jewel in the ocean, is
> thatness—ah!
> Lion's milk poured into the horn of a water buffalo:
> by that blazing jewel, you will obtain [freedom]. (CD 47)

Within the biological realm, Saraha deploys both vegetative and animal imagery. Of plants, unspecified flowers appear often, typically with reference to their fragrant scent and delectable nectar, which may symbolize tantric enjoyment of the senses. Of named flowers, the most common, by far, is the lotus, which may refer to an offering material or a quality of the feet of a guru or buddha, but most commonly is a symbol of the pure nature of mind or, in a more tantric register, either the cakras in the subtle body or the female sex-organ:

> Using the senses, don't be occluded by the senses:
> [be] like lotus petals untouched by water. (PD 78)

———

> The mind, which is like a lotus born from the mud of existence,
> is never covered by any fault. (MM 36)

———

> The amulet box of the heart, the lotus flower at the center:
> someone possessing methods applies them, and it opens. (MT 24)

———

> [When the vajra] resides within the mother's lotus,
> the bodies are bound [together] and nectar drips. (AD 1)

Another vegetative symbol is the tree, which is the focus of a brilliant extended metaphor toward the end of the *People Dohā*, worth quoting in full:

> The sublime tree of nondual mind
> grows over everything in the triple world;
> flowers of compassion bear the fruit of benefiting others,
> and its name is Supreme Benefit to Others.

The sublime tree of emptiness sends forth flowers,
which are the many varieties of sublime compassion;
its eventual fruit is spontaneously accomplished:
this bliss is not just another mind state.

The sublime tree of emptiness lacks compassion:
it has no roots or flowers or leaves,
[but] anyone who turns [emptiness] into a referent
will fall down and break their limbs.

Two trees are within a single seed,
and that's why the fruit is one;
anyone who thinks them indivisible
is free from saṃsāra and nirvāṇa. (PD 129–32)

Many denizens of the animal kingdom appear in Saraha's songs, of which the most common are the lion, which symbolizes the yogin's power and confidence, and the elephant, which suggests spiritual power, grace, and spontaneity, though it can also symbolize the "wild" mind that must be trained:

The yogin is without concepts. . . .
. . . .
like a lion roaming in and out of the forest. (VM 11)

———

Just as the lion's roar in the forest
frightens all the tiny deer
but moves the lion cubs to rejoice,
so when this great bliss, nonarising from the start, is taught,
wrongheaded fools are frightened,
but the hairs of the fortunate bristle with joy. (MM 17)

———

Let the elephant of mind wander free,
let it inquire into its own nature,
let it drink from the mountain lake
[reflecting] the sky and rest on the shore, enjoying itself.
(PD 119)

Like an elephant tamed when prodded by a goad,
when [mind] is left inactive, it's like an elephant that's been
[tamed]. (BT 106)

Three other animals often encountered are the bee, symbolizing yogins' delight in whatever they encounter; the deer, which is prone to delusion or fear; and the snake, which is often suggestive of the poisons that are our defilements:

Just as honey dwells within a flower
and the bees come to know this,
[the wise] do not reject existence or nirvāṇa—
how will fools ever understand? (KD 14)

Reality has an equal taste, like flowers for bees. (BT 22)

Just as deer tormented by error
run toward the water in a mirage,
so [when] fools are tormented by desire for something,
regardless of how they strive for it, it grows ever more distant.
(MM 41)

Improper [gurus], who are like venomous snakes,
are stained by their flaws. (PD 1)

Don't examine primordial nature in every aspect;
if you examine [thus], you're snakebit—enough said. (QD 4)

Other animals mentioned by Saraha include the cow, dog, tiger, camel, rhinoceros, raven, and swan, whose symbolic import we cannot explore here.

In the human realm—which is, after all, Saraha's true concern—various representative "types" and abodes are mentioned. Types include the guru, who is perfection itself; brahmins and ascetics, who symbolize empty ritualism and religious charlatanism; the yoginī, who embodies the mysteries of Transgressive Tantra and transcendent gnosis; and the mad, children, and drunkards, who may be regarded either as pitiable or as exemplifying the nonconceptual freedom of the accomplished practitioner:

If the guru's sayings have entered your heart,
it's like seeing treasure in the palm of your hand. (PD 21)

Brahmins don't know thatness:
pointlessly, they recite the four Vedas. (PD 2)

Seated in lotus posture [194] with eyes closed,
[ascetics] whisper in people's ears and deceive them;
teaching others, such as widows and nuns,
they bestow consecration and collect their guru fees. (PD 6)

> Mind-itself is the yoginī, who has accomplished thatness:
> know her as pledged to the connate. (PD 106)

> Live like a crazy person [acting] freely without calculation,
> like a small child engaged in doing nothing. (MM 35)

> Release the essence of mind to do what it will:
> mind like that of a drunkard who's free from deeds. (QD 25)

Finally, also noteworthy is Saraha's mention of human abodes, including palaces, houses (which may symbolize both the body and interiority), and—in a typically Indian move—the forest:

> The unconventional yogin whose mind [roams] the town
> enters the royal palace and flirts with the women. (QD 39)

> Because the vital winds move in the empty house [of the body],
> [people] contrive in multiple ways. (KD 22)

> Some fools, bound by the categories of thought,
> seek the owner elsewhere, even though he's at home. (MM 14)

> Not going to the forest, not sitting at home,
> when cognition knows [thatness] wherever you are,
> then everything abides forever in eternal awakening. (PD 124)

Two of the works surveyed in the last chapter, the *Vajra Secret Song* (VS) and *Key Instructions* (KI), are themselves classifiable as symbol-songs, consisting as they do of a series of apparently unrelated one-line sayings that implicitly evoke experiences of the connate, the great seal, or some other index of ultimate reality but seldom mention them explicitly, and because these texts were almost completely ignored by Tibetan traditions, most of the "translation" work is left up to the reader.[329] Like those in the dohās, performance songs, and vajra songs, the images in symbol-songs range widely among natural phenomena, denizens of the animal realm, various types of humans, and human edifices and products, such as foods, drinks, and medicines, as well as common human experiences and activities. Religious ideas and practices, both Buddhist and Hindu, are mentioned, but infrequently, and again, the link between any given saying and the ultimate attainment of Buddhism is almost never made explicit. Nevertheless, guided by the symbolic associations we have detected in Saraha's dohās and other song forms, we may hazard guesses as to the symbolism of several sayings in the *Vajra Secret Song*:[330]

- VS 123—"Through *kalpas* of fear and desire, the sky is unmoved"—exploits the common Buddhist association between a clear and empty sky and the pure nature of mind, which may in fact be realized through entering a sky-like or space-like meditative state.
- VS 350—"Don't look at sea foam after it's disappeared"—suggests that when distracted by the superficial, "frothy" emanations of reality, we should return our focus to the groundless depths out of which they arise: the unchanging "oceanic" mind.
- VS 134—"The sun's rays destroy the mass of darkness"—may be read as an allusion to the natural luminosity of mind,

which always shines and, when realization dawns, dispels the dark night of delusion.

- VS 462—"The lotus remains free from the flaws of mud"—evokes a classic Buddhist and Indic image of the process whereby a bodhisattva rises above the muck of saṃsāra without abandoning concern for those mired in it.
- VS 465—"Gold that enters an alloy is still pure"—makes it clear that the dualistic distinction between "pure" realization and "impure" saṃsāra is arbitrary and false, for in the end, there is only a single, indivisible, pure reality.
- VS 174—"The supreme jewel should not be hidden"—can be read as a reference to such supreme virtues as altruistic bodhicitta or such fundamental qualities as the pure nature of mind—both of which should be manifest rather than concealed.
- VS 241—"Don't follow a lion [hoping] to rein it in"—seems to refer to the power and independence of a spiritually advanced adept, who cannot be controlled, or even imitated, by ordinary beings.
- VS 491—"The way of the elephant is without limits"—similarly evokes the ease, grace, and power with which an awakened being moves through the world.
- VS 51—"The solitary rhinoceros is free from suffering"—will connote for a Buddhist the path of the solitary buddha (*pratyekabuddha*) but implies more generally the impermeability and confidence enjoyed by those who are spiritually advanced.
- VS 141—"Observe the bee that fetches nectar"—may be read as referring to the Vajrayāna adept who, broadly speaking, "enjoys" sense pleasures while transmuting them for spiritual purposes or, more specifically, tastes various forbidden sexual fluids in the context of a tantric consecration or ritual feast.

- VS 87—"The words spoken by the king cannot be changed"—may easily be interpreted as referring to the word of the tantric guru, which never can be transgressed.
- VS 160—"Place at the crown of your head the captain who has taken you to the island"—can be interpreted as advising us to value someone—the guru—who leads us across the stormy ocean of saṃsāra to the tranquil island of realization, or nirvāṇa.

Not all the sayings in the *Vajra Secret Song* (or the *Key Instructions*) are so amenable to religious interpretation, however. Some seem to be commonplace observations, on the order of "A person who leaves home and lives in the forest is happy" (VS 52), or "A brahmin drunk on liquor changes for the worse" (VS 207), or "A mother rejoices when her child comes to her lap" (VS 510). Other sayings involve unusual images or ideas, such as "The burden carried on the elephant's back ends up in the stomach of an ant" (VS 42), or "The cemetery guards relax in the treetops" (VS 296), or "A blanket of frog hair is neither new nor old" (VS 522). If the former examples do not immediately yield up a religious or mahāmudrā interpretation because of their ordinariness, the latter are problematic because of their obscurity. However, the interpretive genius of religious scholars never should be underestimated, and no doubt every one of the 540 lines in the *Vajra Secret Song* could be plumbed for deeper meanings—although I have neither the ingenuity nor the space to attempt such analysis here.

One other text in which such one-line sayings occur is the *Twelve Verses of Instruction*,[331] a short exhortation to realize the nondual, nonconceptual, unchanging supreme reality, which in its middle portion gives one-line descriptions of the natural behavior of various animals—but here, the intent is not so much to indicate the ultimate as to convey what it means to live and practice based on habit rather than discernment; in this sense, animal behavior (like that of unreflective humans, like brahmins) is to be avoided by those intent on spiritual freedom.

CHAPTER 4

The Message and the Method

Saraha as Religious Teacher

ALTHOUGH SARAHA is important as a poet, it is the doctrines and practices conveyed in his poems (and other works) that have sealed his reputation, both in India and Tibet, as one of the great masters of tantric Buddhism. Here, I will attempt to sketch the main outlines of his teaching, by examining the terms he uses to designate ultimate reality and the various guises through which he teaches his disciples to understand and attain that ultimate. I identify these personae as Saraha the Critic, Saraha the Radical Gnostic, Saraha the Tantric Yogin, and Saraha the Mainstream Buddhist.

Saraha's Ultimate

Like many a mystic, Saraha repeatedly insists that ultimate reality is ineffable—beyond predication, description, or expression. For instance, he observes that "the primordial nature can't be expressed in words" (PD 40) and that "the essential meaning is without what is expressed or the act of expression" (BT 8). Put another way,

> Bereft of colors, qualities, letters, or examples,
> it cannot be spoken, and it's useless for me to point it out.
> (PD 72)

In short, says Saraha elsewhere, "I have nothing to express" (PD 35). And yet, also like mystics everywhere, Saraha knows that the ultimate reality, and experience of it, are so crucial to true happiness and freedom that it is, quite simply, the most important thing there is. Therefore, he must say something, and say something he does, employing a wide range of terms to denote the ultimate, of which we will survey only the most common, providing examples of each.

One common term, used either as a noun or adjective, is simply the *ultimate* itself (S. *paramārtha*; T. *döndam*) or its synonym, the *supreme* (S. *uttama*; T. *chok*), both of which connote the most true, the most real, the most important—literally, the highest—matters that any person could possibly know:

> All the Archer has to say is this:
> Hey! Come to know everything as the stainless ultimate. (PD 75)

> Since the nonarising ultimate shines on everything,
> all [things] appear as beyond thought. (BT 76)

> The ultimate is unspoken, while the relative is merely logic;
> the path of nirvāṇa is samsaric appearance itself. (MT 21)

> My friends, you must come to know supreme holiness,
> that transformation supreme among the supreme. (KD 29)

> Saraha says, this is supreme;
> what use is the vile ox of self,
> which destroys beings on its own. (PS 4:5)

Of Mahāyāna Buddhist terms for the ultimate nature of things, *emptiness* (S. *śūnyata*; T. *tongpanyi*) is perhaps the most pervasive, and it is employed by Saraha over one hundred times in the texts translated here. It is traceable to the texts of the Pāli canon and other early collections but takes on central importance in the Great Vehicle Perfection of Wisdom literature and the philosophical schools that arose from it, most notably the Madhyamaka, which was initiated by Saraha's purported disciple, Nāgārjuna—although it is an important topic in Yogācāra texts, as well. Emptiness is always a negation, although sometimes it seems to have a more negative cast, sometimes a more positive one, and often it seems simply to point beyond any predication whatsoever:

All dharmas posited by thought are empty on their own;
they're free from conditions, so none exists as we conceive.
(QD 5)

The sense domains themselves are completely pure and
cannot be taught;
you should take them solely as being empty. (PD 84)

Like tongues of flame spreading through a forest,
in an instant turn all appearances that come
before you into the root of mind, emptiness. (PD 90)

With the hands of emptiness tear apart—ah!—
your own cognitive flaws. (PS 4:1)

Emptiness is sealed by appearances,
and appearances are sealed by emptiness. (BT 111)

Emptiness of indivisible mind is the level of vastness. (ST 33)

Those able to apply themselves to perfection
dissolve particulars and abide in emptiness. (CD 92)

The cognate terms *thatness* (S. *tattva*; T. *denyi*), *suchness* (S. *tathatā*; T. *dekonanyi*), and *thusness* (S. *tathatā*; T. *deshinyi*), any of which might also be translated as "reality," or "the real," are even more common in Saraha's works than emptiness, occurring (in one or another variant) almost 140 times in the selections translated here.[332] Although these terms are not as ancient as emptiness—they occur rarely, if at all, in Mainstream sūtras—*thatness*, *suchness*, and *thusness* occur frequently in the Perfection of Wisdom sūtras and all subsequent Mahāyāna literature. There, they serve as an indicator of the ultimate—conveying the sense, "*that*'s the way things are," "*such* are things" or "*thus* is true reality"—without specifying that reality in either positive or negative terms; in this way, the term is left open to multiple interpretations, so that Mādhyamikas might regard it as emptiness, Yogācāras as mind-only, buddha-nature theorists as luminous awareness, and so forth. A somewhat similar term used by Saraha is *that* (S. *tat*; T. *dé*), an impersonal designation for the ultimate most familiar from Upaniṣadic contexts. Here are a few instances, which should convey some sense of the way Saraha uses these terms:

Thatness, the connate nature,
is neither a thing nor a nonthing. (PD 23)

Hey! Infants are ignorant of thatness,
but I realize that they don't move from thatness. (MM 15)

Alas! Look at how thatness points to itself:
you have to look with undistracted mind. If you don't,
. . . .
you'll lose the jewel of thatness amid the thicket of things.
(QD 11)

Although it can't be expressed, it has no suffering;
although it can't be contemplated, it's the bliss of thatness.
(KD 12)

Hey! Let undistracted mind observe itself by itself;
when its own thatness is realized by itself,
then distracted mind dawns as mahāmudrā,
and signs are liberated within great bliss. (MM 18)

Knowing thatness as it is, is taught as natural freedom.
(BT 24)

Whatever there is, is suchness,
[so] whatever is seen is the ultimate. (AD 8)

Since lucid suchness is itself unsullied,
the dancing girls sway with suchness.

In knowledge of suchness,
there is no grasping, and there is no essence. (SI 13)

The unconventional yogin whose mind [roams] the town
. . . .
[is] aware that all sense objects are thusness. (QD 39)

When you're realized, everything is that,
[for] no one knows anything other than that.

Study is that, apprehension and meditation are that,
treatises explaining the essence are also that;
[but] there is no view that indicates that—
it depends solely on the guru's word. (PD 19c–20)

Reality (S. *dharmatā*; T. *chos nyid*), the *reality sphere* (S. *dharmadhātu*; T. *chöying*), and the *reality body* (S. *dharmakāya*; T. *chöku*) are partially overlapping terms—also familiar primarily from Mahāyāna literature—that refer, respectively, to the real, or true, nature of all dharmas; the sphere, or realm (more akin to space than a "place"), in which dharmas exist as they truly are; and the "body" of a buddha that fully realizes, and is identical with, reality as it truly is. None is used with great frequency by Saraha, but a few examples are worth citing:

Seeing luminous reality with certainty,
you'll realize fully the time and means of serving the guru.
(QD 23)

Those of the cut-off lineage . . .
. . . .
are insensitive to the anguish [brought on] by karmic
tendencies
and won't see the meaning of stainless reality. (CD 26)

Not conceiving existence and nirvāṇa as two—
this, it's explained, is the abiding nature, the reality sphere.
(QD 10)

Therefore, all appearances are the reality body,
wandering sentient beings are buddhahood,
every karmic formation is the reality sphere from the start.
(MM 10)

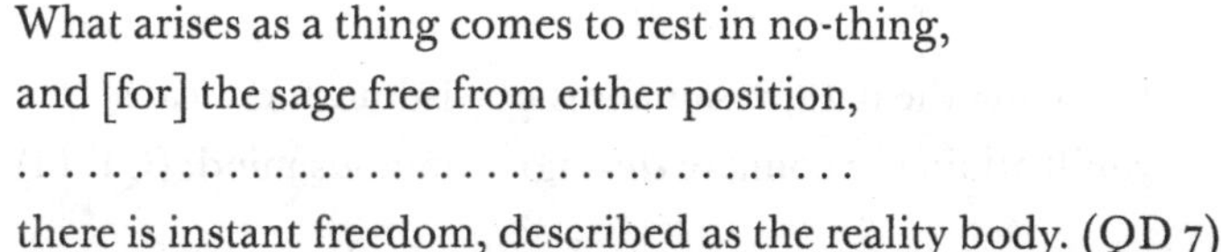

What arises as a thing comes to rest in no-thing,
and [for] the sage free from either position,
. . . .
there is instant freedom, described as the reality body. (QD 7)

Connate (S. *sahaja*; T. *lhenkyé*)—alternative translations include "coemergent," "simultaneously arisen," "innate," "together-born," and "complementarity-in-spontaneity"—is among the terms for ultimacy Saraha mentions most often, around sixty times in the works translated here. It is especially prominent in his most influential text, the *People Dohā*, but is found elsewhere, as well. It may be used as either a noun ("the connate") or an adjective (for example, "the connate nature"). It is a complex term, deeply rooted in tantric discourse,[333] that in Indic traditions carries with it a variety of connotations, including the metaphysical simultaneity of reality and appearance; the epistemological coalescence of subject and object; in a tantric vein, a realization of the nature of things that is inseparable from an experience of bliss or luminosity, or both; and, in the realm of conduct, a spontaneous way of being in the world. In Saraha's context, it seems above all to suggest the nonduality of the ultimate and the conventional, which are separable only conceptually, such that every possible event or experience may serve as a portal to ultimate freedom. Here are several typical instances:

> Cognition purified of stains is the connate:
> at that time, no discordant factors can enter in. (PD 125)

> Earth, water, fire, wind, and space
> don't exist apart from the connate's single taste. (QD 10)

> Realizing the natural sameness of wisdom and means,
> you'll attain the connate through luminous mind. (QD 61)

> Though the connate is all-pervasive
> and near, to fools it's very far away. (KD 3)

> Although the five senses may pass on, the connate remains. (AD 13)

As a flawless lotus expands from a single root,
the connate nature abides in all beings. (BT 15)

All buddhas, sentient beings, and dharmas
are connate with your own pure mind-itself. (BT 49)

Saraha designates the ultimate as *mahāmudrā* (T. *chakya chenpo*), the great seal or great symbol, nearly as often as he calls it "the connate." Like the connate, mahāmudrā has its origins in tantric circles, although unlike the connate, it is not discussed much outside the Buddhist tradition. As noted in the introduction, it may be one of four "seals" of ritual and contemplative accomplishment in the tantras, but taken on its own—as it often was in the mahāyoga and yoginī tantras—it came to refer either to a female consort for sexual-yoga practice or, increasingly, the ultimate nature of mind and reality, the nondual realization of that reality, and the buddhahood that results from that realization. In Tibet, where it became a vital term in nearly all Buddhist traditions, it came further to signify a particular style of formless meditation on the nature of mind, which would lead to full awakening.[334] Here are some examples of Saraha's usage of the term in its "ultimate" sense:

Mind-itself on its own is taught as mahāmudrā. (BT 94)

Mahāmudrā is unchanging great bliss, and
independent of any cause, it is the result beyond thought;
mahāmudrā is the perfected result. (BT 7)

The stainless truth is mahāmudrā,
arising as an experience that's oceanic or sky-like. (BT 21)

In all conduct on the path, abide in mahāmudrā,
and rest within the nonarising, abiding nature of things. (BT 68)

[From] reliance on mahāmudrā free from object and subject,
knowledge arises freshly on its own. (BT 82)

Within nonduality, relax and rest in mahāmudrā. (ST 16)

Another term commonly used by Saraha is *primordial* (S. *nija*; T. *nyukma*), also translated as "innate," "inborn," or "original," which typically is an adjective modifying such terms as *nature*, *mind*, *cognition*, or *gnosis*,[335] and which, as the term implies, is the natural purity, luminosity, and bliss—the awakened mind—with which all of us are born, and which we have possessed from beginningless time, yet typically failed to recognize:

Every being is fooled by the seal of existence,
and no one takes up their primordial nature. (PD 25)

The primordial nature is naturally empty. (AD 5)

The primordial nature can't be expressed in words,
but it may be seen through the eye of the guru's pith
instructions. (PD 40)

When you abide in the primordial state, whatever you do, it's
blissful;
one endowed with the essence of luminous-recollection
apprehension
is free from dualistic fixation and rests in the primordial
nature. (BT 62)

When you train on the path, primordial gnosis is your sole
concern. (QD 34)

When primordial cognition is purified,
then the hermit enters realization of "I." (MM 16)

Another way in which Saraha characterizes the ultimate is as *mind* (S. *citta*; T. *sem*) or *mind-itself* (S. *cittatvā*; T. *semnyi*). The centrality of mind to the cosmos, and especially within the lives of sentient beings, has been vouchsafed throughout the history of Buddhist thought. After all, we suffer and take rebirth in saṃsāra because our deluded mind leads us to act in unwholesome ways, and we awaken to full liberation when our mind turns to the truth and practices of the path, above all through training the mind. Furthermore, there is a sense in which the world is "mind made," since the environments in which we live are themselves products of the intentional actions of sentient beings. This much all Buddhists acknowledge, but some, particularly in the Yogācāra school of Indian Mahāyāna, go so far as to suggest, like a Western idealist (or perhaps a phenomenalist), that the cosmos is in some sense made of mind, is "concept-only" (*vijñaptimātra*) or "mind-only" (*cittamātra*). And most thinkers who posited such an ontology also asserted that the "mind" of which the cosmos was made is primordially pure, luminous, and awakened.

This is mind-itself, which is synonymous with our innate capacity for buddhahood, our buddha-nature (S. *buddhadhātu*; T. *sangyé kyi kham*) or tathāgata matrix (S. *tathāgatagarbha*; T. *deshin shekpei nyingpo*). Saraha definitely upholds the centrality of mind, occasionally seems to uphold a mind-only ontology, and most certainly is concerned with mind-itself:

Mind is itself the single seed of everything,
whence existence and nirvāṇa are projected;
to the mind, which like a wish-fulfilling gem
brings about [all] desired results, I prostrate. (PD 43)

The mind relies on the baseless;
don't view things as different from your own [mind] forms.
(PD 101)

Since mind is essentially pure,
it is itself the stainless supreme stage. (PD 128)

All buddhas, sentient beings, and dharmas
are connate with your own pure mind-itself. (BT 49)

The illusionist, mind-itself, is [like] the sky:
[since it is] without edges or center, who can know it? (MM 21)

The dawning of mind-itself, mahāmudrā,
is the miraculous dawning of whatever there is. (BT 97)

Although pure, empty, and nondual, mind-itself is characterized by several essential qualities, of which the two most important are luminosity, or clarity (S. *prabhāsvara*; T. *ösel*), and great bliss (S. *mahāsukha*; T. *dewa chenpo*). Luminosity is regarded as a characteristic of the mind even in early Buddhist scriptures but takes on special importance in the Mahāyāna, where it is synonymous with buddha-nature: the fact that our mind is essentially pure and luminous assures that we all will someday become buddhas. Luminosity also is highly important in Vajrayāna traditions, such as the Guhyasamāja, where it refers to the realization of the empty nature of mind and reality during the completion stage, which becomes the basis for attainment of a buddha's reality body. Here are a few examples from Saraha:

> Seeing luminous reality with certainty,
> you'll realize fully the time and means of serving the guru.
> (QD 23)

———

> You'll attain the connate through luminous mind;
> It emerges by increasing like a waxing moon. (QD 61)

———

> Apart from mind, not a single external
> object can be said to exist,
> and mind-itself is completely luminous. (SI 8)

———

> The lamp of the connate that is hard to transcend
> . . . .
> [is] nonarising, empty, luminous, and impartial. (MT 6)

———

The mahāmudrā of union, which is beyond thought,
is blissful, luminous, and nonconceptual, like the sky. (VM 3)

The other important characteristic of mind-itself is great bliss, which is an aspect of advanced yogic experience but also has a metaphysical side. Although the term is certainly rooted in the higher tantras, we should remember that even in early Buddhist texts, bliss is commonly said to be an attribute of nirvāṇa, while one of the aspects of a buddha described in Mahāyāna is the enjoyment body (S. *sambhogakāya*). Furthermore, in the Hindu Upaniṣadic tradition, one of the qualities of the ultimate, brahman, is bliss, or joy (*ānanda*), along with reality (*sat*) and awareness (*cit*). In any case, for Saraha, great bliss is another way of indicating the highest reality:

In this supreme great bliss,
no self or other exists. (PD 30)

———

Your own self-awareness is a habit-form of great bliss. (PD 92)

———

Just as the jewellike moon shines
in the great, black darkness [of night],
so supreme great bliss overcomes
every evil notion in a single instant. (PD 116)

———

Since it is nonexistent, nonarising, and unceasing throughout
the three times,
thatness that doesn't change into anything else,
it is the abiding nature of inherent great bliss. (MM 9)

———

Mahāmudrā is unchanging great bliss. (BT 7)

———

Since all [things] are undifferentiated, they are one in great bliss—
it's like ice that has melted into water. (BT 104)

———

The pure nature of unchanging great bliss, as well as the connate,
are the true nature of mind and are qualities
of the utterly pure nature of all the tathāgatas. (CD 60)

Despite his mockery or rejection of them in certain contexts, Saraha also at times unapologetically uses terms that were rejected by most Buddhist philosophers because of their Hindu overtones. In a theological context, these include the *one* (S. *eka*; T. *chik*), or *oneness* (S. *ekatvā*; T. *chiknyi*), which denotes the single reality (for instance, brahman) behind the apparent diversity of phenomena; the *lord* (S. *īśvara*; *hara*; T. *wangchuk*), an epithet of Śiva but also a more general term for a powerful creator god; and the *protector* (S. *tāyin*; T. *kyobpa*), which may in some contexts refer to Viṣṇu:

Residing namelessly between the duality of subject and object:
when the parts collapse, [that's] the essential nature of the one. (CD 9)

———

The aggregates, sense spheres, and sense fields, and all our limbs
dwell in unmanifest subtlety within the realm of oneness. (CD 40)

Can that sacred lord be taught to anyone
any more than bliss to a lustful virgin? (PD 72)

The supreme lord . . . is waveless. (PD 99)

When you bind the supreme colorless lord to the body,
then you'll fully accomplish the unexcelled through play.
(AD 32)

The protector alone is selfhood; others are in contradiction.
(PD 98)

Saraha also employs the—to Buddhists—philosophically suspect terms *self* (S. *ātman*; T. *dak*), also found in compound form in such expressions as *self-nature* (T. *daknyi*) and *self-awareness* (S. *svasaṃvitti*; T. *rangrik*), *essence* (S. *sara*; T. *nyingpo*), and *inherent nature* (S. *svabhāva*; T. *rangshin*), which can be and are used in various ways in Indic philosophical systems but in Hindu contexts often designate an unchanging reality of the sort supposedly rejected by Buddhists:

Abide in the blissful thatness of self, and don't torment
yourself. (PD 26)

This world, which is like a water bubble,
has the self-nature of connate emptiness. (PS 4:3)

Even when it's polluted by the mud of subject and object,
the root is the great self-nature, unchanging throughout the
three times. (BT 16)

The blissful taste of the connate
is the uninterrupted self-nature. (SI 20)

All beings are pervaded by shining self-awareness. (BT 3)

[Mind-itself] is the stainless essence, uncovered by extremes.
(QD 4)

Pointing out essence by way of essence, the pure supreme guru
points others toward realization [1025], and thereby points to
himself. (QD 32)

In this single inherent nature, categories are completely
abandoned. (PD 121)

Abide in mahāmudrā, the nondual inherent nature. (QD 6)

Inherent nature is formless, bereft of distinctive forms.
(KD 32)

In the beginninglessly pure sky-like inherent nature,
there is nothing to abandon or obtain. (MM 39)

Saraha also seems to go against the grain of the axiomatic Buddhist assertion of impermanence, by describing the ultimate as the *unchanging* (S. *akṣara*; T. *gyurmé*), or the *permanent* or *eternal* (S. *nitya*; T. *takpa*)—although to be fair, permanence often is ascribed to nirvāṇa in early Buddhist literature, and to buddha-nature or the reality body in Mahāyāna sūtras, treatises, and commentaries. Here are just three examples of Saraha's employment of the term:

The qualities of the nonarising are unchanging, like a rock,
nor do they follow after, [as] the mere sound of an echo does.
(BT 44)

[Mahāmudrā] is formless and all-pervasive,
unchanging and [present at] all times. (BT 70)

Permanent mind-itself is the changeless eternal realm;
. . . .
and permanent mind-itself, mahāmudrā, reaches the eternal realm. (DT 2)

Lest, however, we think that all of Saraha's designations of the ultimate are off the beaten track of standard Buddhist discourse, it is important to conclude this section by noting that he does, on numerous occasions, employ such familiar terms as *liberation* (S. *vimokṣa*; T. *namtar*), *freedom* (S. *vimukti*; T. *namdrol*), *nirvāṇa* (T. *nyangenlé depa*), and *awakening* (S. *bodhi*; T. *jangchub*):

The self-nature of all the buddhas of the ten directions and the three times:
this very path of the yogins is the door to liberation. (CD 4)

Knowing the path of liberation as suchness,
abide within concept-free self-emergence just as it is. (BT 78)

[Know that] there is no internal or external referent, no self or other;
knowing thatness as it is, is taught as natural freedom. (BT 24)

[In] showing the path to freedom, there is no examination of particulars—
the childish don't know this. (CD 18)

When you free your own mind-stream, . . .
you'll obtain supreme nirvāṇa. (PD 42)

Insects in excrement are attached to the smell
and consider pure sandalwood foul;
likewise, those who reject nirvāṇa
are attached to the miasma at the source of existence. (KD 9)

When cognition knows [thatness] wherever you are,
then everything abides forever in eternal awakening. (PD 124)

You should practice perfect gnosis—
for those [who do], pure sublime awakening
and sublime special attainments will emerge. (TV 12)

Spurn the straight path but don't take up another;
awakening is near, so don't go far away. (PS 2:2)

We see, thus, that Saraha employs a wide range of terms to denote the ultimate, which is at once the highest reality, the highest realization, and the highest attainment: *the connate*, *mahāmudrā*, *the primordial nature*, *emptiness*, *thatness*, *suchness*, *that*, *reality*, *mind*, *mind-itself*, *luminosity*, *great bliss*, *the one*, *the lord*, *the protector*, *self*, *essence*, *inherent nature*, *the unchanging*, *liberation*, *freedom*, *nirvāṇa*, and *awakening*. Each term has its own history and resonances, and certainly no two terms for ultimacy are wholly identical. Furthermore, at least one term, *emptiness*, seems to be in tension with all the others (and perhaps itself) because it apparently undercuts every possible affirmative description of reality. Yet we must recall that for Saraha, emptiness may at times serve as an "affirmative" negation that clears the way for the assertion of various positive qualities, so it may not, in fact, contradict the other terms for ultimacy. In any case, it is quite clear that the terms are sufficiently synonymous that if we substitute one for the other in any given passage, very little of Saraha's meaning is likely to be lost. In this sense, the terms have what Tibetan philosophers call "a single essence but different contextual meanings."[336] Or, as Saraha puts it,

A single thing is seen [by] recollection as many concepts,
while nonrecollection is one, and [yet] is manifold. (BT 23)

Yet, lest we grow complacent with notions of uniformity, he reminds us repeatedly of the nonduality of the one and the many and, more broadly, of the emptiness of all dichotomies, proclaiming:

> When I observe oneness, I don't see a one. (MM 15)

However it may be characterized, the ultimate is not simply a reality that sits "out there" or "in here"—it must be *attained*, and the surest way to attaining it is epistemic and experiential, through knowing and tasting the ultimate for oneself. This, after all, is what the Buddha did on the night of his awakening, and what all Buddhists since him have (at least in theory) striven to do, as well. Epistemically, the songs of Saraha are replete with terms that revolve around the ideal of transcendental knowing, pristine awareness, or gnosis (*jñāna*), which not only in Buddhism but also in many other Indic traditions is regarded as a sure way to attain liberation—more reliable, according to some, than the paths of devotion (*bhakti*) or ritual and ethical works (*karma*). The knowledge-related terms used by Saraha include *realization* (S. *adhigamana*; T. *tok*), *understanding* (S. *avabodha*; T. *gowa*), *wisdom* (S. *prajñā*; T. *sherab*), *awareness* (S. *vidyā*; T. *rikpa*), and, simply, *gnosis* (S. *jñāna*; T. *yeshé*). As with terms for the ultimate, these epistemic terms are distinct yet also, for Saraha's purposes, roughly synonymous. Here are some examples, which should suffice to indicate their range and usage:

> When you're realized, everything is that,
> [for] no one knows anything other than that. (PD 19)

———

> One's own aim is nonarising true realization free from duality. (MT 9)

———

Concepts without realization are like clouds in the sky,
and when there's realization, it's empty thatness and inherent nature. (VM 15)

The supreme precious symbol brings understanding by itself alone. (QD 32)

When unbodied thatness falls into everyone's house,
at the time it's understood, there is nothing at all. (CD 33)

With discerning wisdom, see appearances as they should be seen. (QD 59)

O Protector, the wisdom briefly summarized in the key points of your word
exerts control like a skillful princess. (SS 15)

By the pure light-rays of their sunlike gnosis
[the guru] turns ignorance into awareness. (QD 54)

The essential meaning is without what is expressed or the act of expression;
the sphere of awareness is nonrecollection, in which everything is expressed. (BT 8)

The nondual unification of permanence and annihilation
settles into oneness;
it is known [through] awareness [derived from] scripture and
pith instructions. (ST 37)

Meditate on gnosis uncovered by extremes;
mind without meditation or meditation object is without
inherent nature. (QD 26)

Undifferentiated gnosis is the sole singularity;
the naturally settled mind pervades itself. (QD 35)

The distinctive gnosis, which is suchness,
is independent of duality and is uninterrupted bliss. (MT 7)

It is important to note that the realization, or gnosis, insisted upon by Saraha not only is nonconceptual knowledge but also carries with it a distinct experiential character, which often, though not always, carries affective or aesthetic overtones. This is captured in such common terms as *experience* (S. *anubhāva*; T. *nyongwa*), the *single taste* (S. *ekarasa*; T. *rochik*), *bliss* (S. *sukha*; T. *dewa*), *passion* (S. *rāga*; T. *döpa*), and *joy* (S. *ānanda*; *gawa*) or *enjoyment* (S. *bhoga*; T. *longchö*):

Uninterrupted experience is ineffable:
you should know how to apply it to your mind-stream. (BT 20)

When experience dawns, you'll be free from discordant
grasping. (BT 99)

Gaining the experience intended by yoga, you'll [become] a complete buddha. (MT 22)

Inquire into concepts, which are just this primordial gnosis, where all grounds, paths, and buddhas have a single taste. (QD 8)

Just as the Ganges and other rivers
[take on] a single taste in the salty sea,
all the various mental labels and mental events
[take on] a single taste in the reality sphere: know this! (MM 22)

All dharmas have a single taste in emptiness,
and when you become perfect, there's nothing to obtain. (CD 94)

Nondual knowing is like water and milk:
diverse [things] have the uninterrupted single taste of great bliss. (MM 28)

The experience of the self-dawning nondual yoga is bliss,
and when you give up the entity conceptualized as the self,
you're as vast as the limits of the sky. (ST 11)

Abide in the blissful thatness of self, and don't torment yourself. (PD 26)

Supreme great bliss overcomes
every evil notion in a single instant. (PD 116)

Immeasurable, greatly blissful inherent gnosis
[shines] impartially like the light of the sun and moon.
(CD 4)

The blissful savor of the inherent nature of beings—
that experience alone is a meritorious mind. (SS 15)

Turn everything in this whole triple world
to a single color: great passion. (PD 29)

If you're not freed from bondage by enjoying sense objects,
then say I, the Archer, "you don't know thatness." (PD 22)

Seizing the naked, the yogin is joyous:
he pervades the whole sky, becoming firm. (AD 2)

As long as they appear in the reality sphere,
all things are enjoyed as untainted. (CD 49)

Abiding in your own joy,
you'll have no fear of birth or death. (AD 25)

In short, Saraha in his songs designates ultimate reality in a variety of ways, both epistemological and metaphysical, both "negative" and "positive," and he deploys several key epistemic and experiential terms to describe what it is like to realize that ultimate. In the next sections, we will turn to the actual methods prescribed by the Great Brahmin for attaining freedom, through his personas as Saraha the Critic, Saraha the Radical Gnostic, Saraha the Tantric Yogin, and Saraha the Mainstream Buddhist.[337] The reader will note that the last three designations echo but do not precisely replicate the three types of tantra described in the introduction: Radical Tantra, Transgressive Tantra, and Mainline Tantra.

Saraha the Critic

Saraha has much that is "positive" to teach about how to attain the ultimate, but before turning to the various guises in which he does so, we must recognize that he "clears the field" for such teaching through his fierce criticism of nearly every social, religious, ethical, and philosophical convention of his time. Indeed, Saraha has a reputation for being one of the most outspoken critical voices ever to appear on the Indian scene.[338] His derisory stance may bring to mind for some the refrain sung by the inimitable Groucho Marx, as Professor Quincy Adams Wagstaff, in the 1932 film *Horse Feathers*: "Whatever it is, I'm against it." This impression of Saraha is understandable, given that his most influential work, the *Dohā Treasury*, or *People Dohā*, devotes its first eighteen or so verses—and many others—to a sarcastic demolition of a variety of Indic religious ideas and practices, not only Hindu and Jain but Buddhist, too, and that such critiques are scattered elsewhere in his works, as well. Before commenting on the accuracy of this image of Saraha, we will survey some salient instances of his critical spirit.

We have already seen in the biographical traditions that by living with a low-caste woman, Saraha (like many of the great adepts) courted the opprobrium of people obsessed by notions of caste purity. His rejection of a cornerstone of the Indian social system, as we have seen, is made quite plain in the song attributed to him by the Tibetan historian Tāranātha, where he sings of himself as a brahmin who lives with "a girl who works with bamboo" and who sees "neither caste nor no caste," living as a monk yet "wander[ing] with this wife of mine." [339]

Saraha provides further evidence of his rejection of notions of caste purity in the *Queen Dohā*, where he describes women suitable to serve as a yogin's great seal (*mahāmudrā*), his partner for sexual yoga practice, as including nymphets, laundresses, harlots, or pickers of rags (QD 43). Further on, he speaks of how a yogin who has practiced sexual yoga with his consort "dissolves into nonconceptual sky" (QD 46), so that even when he lives with her in a cremation ground,

> [he] sleeps with a carefree mind in ghost-haunted places;
> he makes friends with outcastes, and draws the corpse cart
> along.
> "This is forbidden conduct"—he's not to be held to that
> standard. (QD 47)

By the same token, he instructs his listeners,

> Enjoy yourself in a cobbler's hut:
> even though [it's filthy], you won't get covered in dirt.
> (PD 69).

And, on the most basic level,

When cognition fully ceases,
bodily bonds are broken;
when [things] taste the same in the connate,
then there is no low-caste or brahmin. (PD 57)

If Saraha seems to mock the very foundations of the traditional Indian social structure, he is even more pointed in his critique of religion. His most famous attack on the practices and practitioners of his day comes at the outset of his *People Dohā*, where he denounces members of his own caste, brahmins, for their ignorance, their vain incantation of the four Vedas, their pointless oblations, and their spiritual charlatanism (PD 2–6). Later in the same collection, he asks,

What use are lamps and food offerings to the gods?
What do they do? What use is imparting secret mantras?

Pilgrimage spots and austerities are useless.
Can you win liberation by immersion in water?
(PD 15c–16b)

Furthermore, he is quite explicit in his rejection of the Hindu gods:

When you take Brahmā and the Pervader [Viṣṇu]
and the three-eyed [Śiva] as the basis of everything in the world
and make offerings to all of them, then countless
[virtuous] karmas you've collected will be completely wasted.
(PD 61)

It is not just "Hindus" that Saraha assails; he decries equally the practices of the Jain community, which, as we know, was founded around the same time as Buddhism and long competed with it for patronage, including in the medieval period. Saraha describes Jain yogins thusly:

> Long nailed, their bodies smeared with filth,
> unclothed, they pluck out their hairs:
> the Digambaras are deceived [in thinking] the self
> will gain liberation on a path consisting of pain. (PD 7)

He continues in an ironic tone:

> If nakedness leads to freedom,
> then why aren't dogs and foxes free?
> If plucking out hairs leads to freedom,
> then women with plucked-out hair must be free. (PD 8)

In short, sings Saraha at the outset of the *Body Treasury*,

> Long-hairs grasping at self and agent,
> brahmins, naked ascetics, experimenters,
> materialists who assert a [physical] basis for reality
> [all] claim to know everything but aren't self-aware—
> they've been deceived and are far from the path to liberation. (BT 1)

But Saraha does not spare his Buddhist coreligionists, either. In the *People Dohā*, he complains,

> Those so-called novices, monks, and elders,
> and, likewise, renunciant clerics—
> some are involved in explaining sūtras,
> while others are seen grasping for mind's single taste.

Some run along with the Great Vehicle,
the authoritative treatises of the textual tradition. (PD 11–12b)

Elsewhere, he observes,

The path of the perfections, with its progressions, entrances, stages, and so forth,
which gives up the quick path, is cause for a long samsaric [sojourn]. (BT 18)

And if a fellow Buddhist replies that the heart of the tradition is to be found in meditation, Saraha has a response to that claim too:

You won't gain liberation through false contemplation,
which is like being held tight by the net of an illusory display. (PD 35)

And he adds,

The whole world is fooled by contemplation,
and no one can point to their primordial nature. (PD 37)

What's more, Saraha's scorn is reserved not only for practitioners of earlier Buddhism and the nontantric Mahāyāna; he directs it as well at proponents of the Vajrayāna. In the *People Dohā*, he declares,

No tantra, no mantra, no contemplative object, no contemplation:
all of them are causes for delusive cognition. (PD 26ab)

Along similar lines, he sings in the *Queen Dohā* of the vajra gnosis, which is "beautiful in its abiding nature":

Devoid of maṇḍalas or fire offerings,
free from mantras, seals, or consecrations,
it can't be accomplished through any tantra or treatise.
(QD 31)

Other well-known tantric concepts and practices are criticized elsewhere. In the *Speech Treasury*, he describes how "the yoga with signs"—visualizing oneself as a tantric deity—"does not touch the signless meaning" (ST 27) and is "the road to the three samsaric spheres" (ST 45). Commenting on subtle-body practices, he remarks in the *Mind Treasury*,

Drawing [energies] up and down and turning the cakras
is a way of drawing out methods, but you won't attain the deepest truth.

Even if you seize, expel, join, and ignite [breath energies],
you're no different from an asthmatic fool—you're the same.
(MT 24c–25b)

Similarly, he notes in the *Queen Dohā*,

Serving the sublime one, listening to them, and applying what you've heard;
obtaining blessings [because] "virtues arise from consecration";
resting conceptuality in concentration, then [engaging in] application and meditation
after gaining certainty about the benefits [of practice]; behaving unconventionally—
all of them are practices based on contrivances and wrong ideas. (QD 76–77a)

Finally, in the *People Dohā* he asks enthusiasts of tantric sexual yoga,

> Those who do not know the nature of everything
> but would accomplish great bliss at the time of copulation
> are like thirsty [deer] who chase a mirage:
> dying of thirst, will they find celestial waters? (PD 112)

Put in more technical terms,

> Since experience based on the action seal
> is contrived, it emerges through conditions,
> and because it depends on other [factors], it is not suchness.
> (BT 65)

On the broadest plane, Saraha's critique of religious practice extends to every form of human behavior, such that his advice sometimes seems to amount to "do nothing":

> The essential is free from virtues and flaws,
> truth requires no deeds at all,
> while the mind that's done with deeds is great bliss itself.
> (QD 77b–d)

In short, so much for religion.

Saraha is a critic not only of social stratification and nearly every imaginable form of religious practice but of philosophy itself. Near the outset of the *Body Treasury*, he shows his contempt for the four major Indian Buddhist philosophical schools, singing:

> Vaibhāṣikas, Sautrāntikas, and Māntrikas,
> Yogācāras, Mādhyamikas, and others
> point to each other's flaws and argue—

not knowing thatness, where appearance and emptiness are
equally sky-like,
they turn their backs on the connate. (BT 2)

More broadly, Saraha consistently mocks the myopic pretensions of scholars and philosophers, who are "tormented by thirst in the sorrowful desert of ambiguous treatises and will perish [there]" (PD 67) Indeed, he says,

The scholars all explain their treatises,
not realizing that buddha is in the body.
. . . .
When you realize this, there's no room for questions,
[but] shameless scholars don't realize it. (PD 82)

In the *Queen Dohā*, he notes the falsity of every "symbol or convention that you label" (QD 75) and the importance of clearing away "the husk of logical complication" (QD 79), so as to comprehend what is true, real, and essential. And, in the *King Dohā*, he uses a striking simile to illustrate the limitations of the intellect:

When [winter] winds lash and roil the waters,
it's as if water, although soft, turns to stone;
when fools are disturbed by concepts, what's formless
becomes very solid and hard. (KD 17)

Indeed, not just intellect but mind itself may be a problem:

When you thoroughly search mind and dharmas,
you won't find even an atom of essence. (MM 23)

At the same time, however, Saraha asserts that "seeking without knowing, the mind chases words" (BT 12) and awakening will be gained only "when cognition changes to noncognition" (PD 45); later, he exults in how "when my mind is undermined, I certainly see the yoginī" (PD 103). At the most basic level,

> the mind that can't be viewed as outside or in
> cannot be conceived by anyone, for there is no mind.
> (QD 24)

And that which is to be realized—true reality, the connate nature, the great seal—is beyond language:

> Every being is [trapped in] syllables,
> and not a one is without syllables,
> but when you're without syllables,
> it's then that you know syllables. (PD 107)

One important consequence of the rejection of language and thought—especially dichotomous thought—is that the dualities through which we understand and operate in the world are effaced. Thus, the distinction between self and other, saṃsāra and nirvāṇa, pure and impure, suffering and pleasure, and even good and bad, simply do not apply. In the *Speech Treasury*, for instance, Saraha describes reality as a state in which "self and other are not two" (ST 2), and in the *People Dohā*, he says that we are "free from saṃsāra and nirvāṇa" (PD 132). Regarding behavior, he sings in the *Queen Dohā*,

> Even the concept of "the good" is a sickness plunging you into saṃsāra,
> and when you label an act as evil, its result still can't be interrupted. (QD 73)

The consequences of this stance for a yogin's conduct seem dramatic indeed:

> Behaving like a crazed elephant and acting like a fool,
> behaving without regard for dos and don'ts, like an elephant
> plunging on impulse into a pond: his mind ever crazed,
> he performs the basest of deeds yet is free, says Saraha.
> (QD 50)

How such injunctions are to be understood is a question we will address later; for now, suffice it to say that Saraha's rejection of philosophical categories appears to have radical implications for a range of fields from ontology to metaphysics to ethics.

At the deepest level, the reason Saraha rejects language and thought is that the ultimate nature of all phenomena, from atoms to the mind, from form to omniscience, is their emptiness (*śūnyatā*), their lack of inherent existence (*svabhāva*). As he sings at the end of the *Mahāmudrā Pith-Instruction*, "In sublime truth, there is no existent" (MM 44). As deluded beings, however, we believe—either instinctively or based on reflection—that somehow, somewhere, there must exist a true self that is the foundation of the cosmos. We are reinforced in this belief by the immediacy and apparent persistence of our body and senses and by the apparent precision and coherence of language and concepts. But all these deceive us: everything is empty and baseless, no such self will ever be found, and all our fine-spun theories are vain exercises in imputing complexity where there is only simplicity, and something where there is nothing.

In short, Saraha makes it very clear that *any* exercise of the intellect—whether day-to-day dichotomous thinking, the study of scriptures and commentaries, logical analysis and argument, contemplative reflection, or perhaps even the use of language itself—

ignores the empty nature of things, and his urgent injunction "Don't divide, unite, / don't separate things into particular classes" (PD 29) implies that language and thought pave the way to spiritual rack and ruin. Thus, if we are to be free, we must simply recognize, with Jack Kerouac, that the Buddha is "philosophy's dreadful murderer."[340]

Saraha the Radical Gnostic

Although Saraha himself acknowledges that "yogins desiring great gnosis / may proceed by stages or instantaneously" (QD 80), many of his most striking claims convey the impression that the corollary of his critique of all social, religious, and philosophical norms is an insistence on a direct, unmediated entry into the nondual and nonconceptual gnosis of the ultimate, a sort of "pathless path." The persona I call Saraha the Radical Gnostic declares in the *Body Treasury* that "mahāmudrā is manifest awakening in an instant" (BT 72), and in a verse from the *People Dohā* that is virtually a charter for meditation on the great seal, he sings:

> When mind is pointed out by mind,
> . . . .
> [then] just as salt dissolves in water,
> so mind dissolves into its inherent nature.
> When self and other are seen to be the same,
> what use is striving in contemplation? (PD 96)

The way in which mind points to mind is as follows:

> Mind is to be grasped as like the sky;
> as naturally sky-like should mind be grasped;
> when cognition changes to noncognition,
> you'll obtain thereby unexcelled awakening. (PD 45)

As he explains further in the *Mahāmudrā Pith-Instruction*,

> Just as the sky is sky without reference points,
> so the empty is empty without meditation;
> nondual knowing is like water and milk:
> diverse [things] have the uninterrupted single taste of great bliss. (MM 28)

And the way in which we "suddenly" enter this space-like meditation is simply to drop concepts and *be* in it:

> If this mind, so tightly bound,
> is relaxed, it will be freed, no doubt. (PD 52)

Or, as he puts it in the *Queen Dohā*,

> The free mind settles into its own nature,
> which requires no labels or analysis: it is just as it is;
> the result is unhindered and exists on its own from the start,
> so you needn't be bound to antidotes for your hopes and fears. (QD 74)

Within a sky-like meditation—which in fact overflows the boundaries between meditation and nonmeditation—we can see all thoughts and things exactly as they are: as manifestations of our original nature, our natural mind. In the *Mahāmudrā Pith-Instruction*, Saraha advises,

> Not holding your breath, not binding it,
> let uncontrived knowing relax like a little child;
> when conceptual recollection arises, observe its own suchness:
> Don't conceive of water and waves as two different things. (MM 30)

Furthermore, just as one must go beyond concept and contemplation, one must also transcend action and inaction:

> Making no effort whatsoever, with no view of [what] to take up or cast aside,
> not distinguishing middle from extreme—the middle is the straight path. (BT 17)

> The jewel of trust is a wish-fulfilling treasure of instruction:
> settle into it without mental action or inaction. (BT 83)

> When concepts occur in the mind, the yogin
> should relax and settle down, like petals of cotton or wool;
> abandoning action, let your own mind observe itself. (VM 9)

In several texts, (most notably the *Body*, *Speech*, and *Mind Treasuries*), Saraha sets his radical approach within the context of the four symbolic realizations mentioned earlier: *recollection* (S. *smṛti*; T. *drenpa*), *nonrecollection* (S. *asmṛti*; T. *drenmé*), *nonarising* (S. *anutpāda*; T. *kyemé*), and *beyond thought* (S. **atibuddhi*; *T. lodé*).[341] The first two are the most common and the most crucial, for they describe, respectively, the way we misconstrue reality and the way we can overcome our error. *Recollection* is, of course, a venerable term in accounts of Buddhist meditation: it is mindfulness, or remembrance, or recognition of the object of meditation, whatever that may be; typically it involves bringing the object to mind when one has lost concentration. Here, it stands in more generally for any deliberate application of the conceptual mind, which, as we have seen, is something akin to the original sin for Saraha. As shown in the following three examples, the way in which we eliminate it is by "nonrecollection," by simply dropping thought and allowing our original nature to shine unimpeded:

> Within nonrecollection, equipoise is great bliss;
> within great bliss, you abide in continuous nonconceptuality.
> (BT 14)

———

> In the domain of nonrecollection, there is nothing to see,
> and since it lacks a basis, there is nothing to study. (BT 79)

———

> The yoga of signs is the road to the three samsaric spheres:
> entities with signs contain the seeds of carelessness,
> while the yoga of nonrecollection is equivalent to the center of the sky. (ST 45)

The third and fourth symbolic realizations, then, are simply elaborations on the characteristics of the reality we must see: *nonarising* indicates the fact that our original nature is beyond either origination or cessation, because it has always been what we truly are, while *beyond thought* indicates that this nonarising reality transcends all understanding or predication:

> The qualities of the nonarising are unchanging, like a rock,
> nor do they follow after, [as] the mere sound of an echo does.
> Beyond thought and unobjectified,
> the qualities of mahāmudrā are like the sky. (BT 44)

Another term employed by Saraha to express his gnostic radicalism is *cognitive disengagement* (S. *amanasikāra*; T. *yila mijepa*), which is most closely associated with the great Indian tantric master Maitrīpa, and also may be translated by such phrases as "nonmentation," "unthinking," "mental inactivity," or "nonconceptual realization."[342] The notion of cognitive disengagement negates the classical Buddhist mental factor of "cognitive engagement," or mentation (S. *manansikāra*; T. *yilajepa*), whereby we deliberately bring some object within the purview of cognition. As with nonrecollection, cognitive disengagement points to the need for an immediate and total abandonment of our conceptual mind and our direct entrance into a state in which we see reality as it is, as shown in the following examples:

> Abide continuously in thatness and practice only that
> contemplation—
> this cognitive disengagement and stainless contemplation are
> no-mind. (KD 32)

———

> In the mahāmudrā of cognitive disengagement,
> there is not even an atom to prompt meditation;
> nonseparation from true nonmeditation is supreme
> meditation. (MM 31)

———

> Nongrasping cognition is the yogic contemplation of
> nonaction;
> don't meditate on anything, don't seek anywhere:
> when there are no concepts, that's the equal taste of cognitive
> disengagement—ah! (CD 36)

In all the passages cited above, Saraha's spiritual radicalism is quite uncompromising, and his advice seems to be, don't think anything or do anything, and don't even meditate in the usual sense—just see your own mind, and everything else, as the pure, empty, blissful reality from which they have never parted. Here, however, an important qualification must be introduced, for it is quite clear that the sudden gnostic awakening Saraha promotes is *not* completely unmoored or independent; quite to the contrary, it depends almost entirely upon the one indispensable element of religious life for those intent on freedom: the guru.

The importance of the guru for Saraha and for those following a guru[343] in India and Tibet, whether as bestower of tantric consecration, as teacher, or as object of devotion, cannot be overstated. The theme is especially prominent in the *People Dohā*:

> [Realization] depends solely on the guru's word.
> If the guru's sayings have entered your heart,
> it's like seeing treasure in the palm of your hand.
> (PD 20d–21b)

———

> For someone who thinks on unrooted thatness,
> seeing by way of the guru's pith instructions will suffice.
> (PD 39)

———

> That which from the start has not arisen
> is realized today through the glorious guru's teaching.
> (PD 65)

———

> If the guru doesn't express the teaching,
> then the student won't understand. (PD 68)

———

If you hold tight the guru's precept, and strive in it,
the connate will emerge—there is no doubt. (PD 71)

The centrality of the guru is affirmed in other texts, as well. In the *Alphabetical Dohās*, Saraha affirms that "when you comprehend the sky through a proper guru, that's awakening" (AD 11). In the *Queen Dohā*, he describes the guru through a series of metaphors that make clear his indispensability: he is "the kingly physician," "the supreme ship that delivers us / from saṃsāra's deep, vast sea," "the powerful friend who's attained great bliss / . . . [possessed of] sunlike gnosis," "the wheel-turning king who's wise in the ways / of changing all dharmas to bliss, as elixir turns metals to gold," the one whose "mind, like a river, submerges dualistic views" (QD 53–55). In short,

The root of every special attainment is the vajra master,
the perfectly purified cause who himself embodies all results.
(QD 62)

According to the *Body Treasury*, "The disciplinary vows of the secret [vehicle] are fulfilled by respect for the guru" (BT 35). And, according to the *Speech Treasury*,

The guru teaches the doctrines, scriptures, commentaries,
and special instructions;
those desiring to realize the specific characteristics [of things]
through scriptures and reasoning
will attain it from those holding the special instructions
taught by the guru:
when you make reverence [to the guru], you obtain great bliss
in an instant. (ST 5)

Or, more simply,

> The word of the self-aware guru is stainless mahāmudrā.
> (ST 31)

In a couple of instances, Saraha goes even further, stating that "encountering [everything] as the intention of the sublime guru, / you will be free from the samsaric path" (MT 21) and, even more strongly:

> Pointing out essence by way of essence, the pure supreme guru
> points others toward realization, and thereby points to himself. (QD 32)

Most radically, perhaps,

> There is no dharma that's not the guru. (QD 38)

Though these last three statements seem extreme, they make sense when we consider that (a) there is only a single reality, (b) the guru has thoroughly identified with that reality, and therefore (c) the guru *is* that reality. In another sense, because all reality is "it" or "that," all reality can teach us about itself, so in that sense, too, reality and the guru are inseparable. In any case, devotion and supplication to the guru are essential to Saraha's gnostic subitism and are inseparable from any attainment we hope to gain:

> Understand the root through service to the glorious guru;
> when you can unify the basic mind with thought,
> the mind will be cut off and die and be of a single nature. (AD 24)

> To the sublime speech of the sole guru, I bow down. (SS 7)

My eyes full of joyous tears as my hair
stands on end, my eyelashes moist,
bowing beneath the burden of greatly firm devotion—
to the sublime, wish-fulfilling guru, I prostrate. (SS 13)

Saraha the Tantric Yogin

As noted in passing, one of the primary functions of the guru is to grant tantric consecration, and it is evident that Saraha's understanding of the path to freedom is undergirded by such consecrations and the complex practices they entail. Indeed, it is impossible to understand Saraha's social and religious critique or his radical gnosticism without appreciating their location within a larger Vajrayāna context, particularly that of the late and highly esoteric yoginī tantras, which seem to have been the Great Brahmin's touchstone. Proof of Saraha's reliance upon the tantras should not be required, but if it is, we might simply observe that (a) every text attributed to him in the Tibetan Tengyur is found in the Tantra (*gyu*) section; (b) the vast majority of his corpus—including texts from which radically gnostic statements may be extracted—contains explicit or implicit references to tantric ideas and practices; and (c) many, if not all, of his texts are suffused with tantric terminology, including such seminal works as the *People* and *Queen Dohās*, the *Body*, *Speech*, and *Mind Treasuries*, the *Performance Songs*, and the *Alphabetical Dohās*—not to mention his lengthy commentary on the *Buddhakapāla Tantra* and his sādhanas and other ritual texts. His scattered references to such tantric deities as Vajrapāṇi, Heruka, and Hayagrīva, not to mention his frequent evocation and celebration of yoginīs (on which more shortly), are further proof of his immersion in the world of Vajrayāna in general and the yoginī tantras in particular.

Although receiving consecrations from a qualified guru is the sine qua non for tantric practice, Saraha seems at times to dismiss their importance, singing, for instance:

> The disciplinary vows of the secret [vehicle] are fulfilled...
> not by defining the individual outer, inner, and secret
> consecrations
> and their categorization into vase, secret,
> wisdom-gnosis, and essential definitive-word [consecrations];
> what arises from common powers cannot affect mahāmudrā.
> (BT 35)

The key point here is that *common*, or mundane, powers arising from these consecrations and the practices they entail are unworthy of a yogin's attention; implicitly, however, there are uncommon, or transmundane, powers—realization of the nature of reality and attainment of full awakening—that may also result from consecration, and *they* are certainly worth pursuing. In the late, highly esoteric, and sometimes transgressive yoginī tantras, the consecrations usually are fourfold, involving a vase, secret, wisdom-gnosis, and fourth, or word, consecration. In the Indic context, the secret and wisdom-gnosis consecrations involved ritual sexual union and ingestion of the resultant sexual fluids. In later Vajrayāna systematizations, the vase consecration became the basis for practice of the contemplative and ritual "transformation of seeing" known as the generation stage, while the secret, wisdom-gnosis, and fourth consecrations empowered the initiate to practice the subtle-body yogas of the completion stage, which lead directly to buddhahood. Although in his songs Saraha rarely emphasizes the importance of consecration, when he does so, he is emphatic, as in two instances from the *Queen Dohā*:

Alas! People deprived of the precious consecrations
are like lowly śūdras aspiring to be king;
deceived about the tantras of awareness bearers,
they're condemned by *ḍāka*s and fall to vajra hell.
(QD 16)

Suffused with the taste of consecration and seeing with the eye of instruction,
when you touch the dust of the [guru's] feet, knowledge becomes awareness. (QD 58)

And, when we turn to Saraha's sādhanas, the references are plentiful. Here are some examples from his Buddhakapāla sādhana:

Just as a fully assembled vina
can't sound forth without strings,
so, if I am unconsecrated,
I will not perfect mantra and contemplation. (SB p. 1450)

I, who am stuck in the mire of saṃsāra,
[request] consecration [by] the yoginīs,
who are greatly renowned for their mercy—
please free me through consecration. (SB p. 1450)

Thus, I again request the yoginīs,
who are treasuries of knowledge, "Please consecrate me."
May I, when I [receive] the consecration
of nonarising, become Heruka. (SB p. 1450)

The role of yoginīs (also variously referred to as ḍākinīs, goddesses, or mothers) in such later Vajrayāna systems as the mahāyoga and yoginī tantras cannot be overstated. They are crucial characters in virtually all the tantric traditions discussed by Saraha, including those of the male deities Buddhakapāla and Lokeśvara, on whom he composed sādhanas. Coming in both mundane and transmundane varieties, they serve multiple functions in the higher tantras: bestowing blessings, making offerings, energizing the practitioner's meditation, granting consecrations, or appearing as flesh-and-blood consorts for sexual yoga practices.[344] Often, they simply serve as symbols for tantric bliss and freedom—almost like a female equivalent of the guru, who is typically conceived as male. Here are just a few of the many verses in which Saraha celebrates the yoginī:

> [When] the lord of the house has eaten, the lady of the house
> enjoys [her meal]:
>
> . . . .
>
> the yoginī's conduct is beyond compare.
> She's consumed her lord and beautified inherent nature;
>
> . . . .
>
> Mind-itself is the yoginī, who has accomplished suchness:
> know her as pledged to the connate. (PD 103–5)

> Through the voice of the yoginī, the connate is realized. (AD 25)

> When there's enjoyment of the supreme connate,
> then one's own and others' karmic tendencies are destroyed;
> yoginīs [both] serene and wrathful accomplish this—there is
> no doubt. (AD 30)

The empty is naturally mixed with compassion;
emptiness is indivisible and uninterrupted.
I see the empty yoginī,
riding through the sky, milking it, drinking it, being in it.
(US 2:1)

The ḍākinī's blessing is a symbol of realization. (KI 1:1)

All of the preceding should suffice to prove that tantric consecration is indeed a part of Saraha's religious universe.

Once consecration has been obtained, the disciple typically engages in the procedures of the generation stage – a complex set of practices, described in sādhanas, in which we change the way we see ourselves and the world, visualizing ourselves as a divine buddha-deity, our environment as a pure land or maṇḍala, and other beings as deities, while regarding all words and sounds as mantras. In generation-stage practice, we typically enact a "psychodrama" in which we deconstruct our ordinary way of seeing and conceiving ourselves, then reconstruct ourselves in divine form at the center of a magnificent palace, or maṇḍala, then send purifying blessings, in the form of mantras and rays of light, to all sentient beings, who themselves are divinized and absorbed into us. We ourselves then dissolve into emptiness and arise again instantaneously as the deity—with whose body, speech, and mind we are supposed to continually identify, both in meditation and in our everyday interactions. As we have seen, Saraha the Critic dismisses the importance of "tantras and mantras." He also asserts that "all [the aspects of] the generation stage—outer, inner, and profound— / are to the seal of [the] completion [stage] as tiny stars to the sun and moon" (ST 32) and occasionally dismisses the "yoga with signs" involved in the generation stage (ST 14, 27). Nonetheless, in his songs, he sometimes refers positively to such generation-stage topics as mystic syllables and maṇḍala circles:

> The ruler of the stars . . .
> emanates its emanations—
> that is the sublime maṇḍala circle. (PD 117)

———

> The pledge seal is a yoga with signs,
> and the result, the maṇḍala of deities, is for the sake of beings. (BT 93)

———

> The sound of *ṭha* expresses mantras,
> and taking up the syllable *ṭha*, you obtain the abiding [reality]. (AD 11)

And, when we turn to Saraha's commentary on the *Buddhakapāla Tantra* and the various sādhanas attributed to him in the Tibetan Tengyur, we encounter ample references to deity visualizations, maṇḍalas, mantras, and other aspects of generation-stage practice. Thus, although he sometimes seems to dismiss it, we may be certain that Saraha was familiar with generation-stage practices, even if they were not his primary concern.

Certainly, he was most concerned with the practices involved in what came to be known as the completion stage, in which the practitioner manipulates various physical and mental forces within the subtle body so as to gain full awakening. The reader will recall that, as part of his critique of religion, Saraha mocked many of these techniques too—including various breathing exercises, manipulation of the cakras, behaving eccentrically, and practicing sexual yoga. Despite his own critique, however, Saraha frequently describes and extols completion-stage techniques, and we must assume that his apparent dismissal of these and other tantric practices is based on his fear that they will become a source of attachment and pride for the unwary practitioner, while for someone sufficiently mature, they are a key to realization.

Thus, because completion-stage practices are carried out within the body—more specifically the subtle body that interpenetrates our coarse physical body—it is reasonable to read many of his verses in celebration of the body as implicitly referring to advanced yogic techniques involving seventy-two thousand channels (S. *nāḍī*; T. *tsa*), the biotic drops (S. *bindu*; T. *thiklé*) and vital winds or energies (S. *prāṇa*; T. *lung*) that move within the channels, and the energy centers (S. *cakras*; T. *korlo*) that mark places where the outer channels intersect with (and, typically, constrict) the all-important central channel (S. *avadhūti*; T. *uma*). Thus, he sings in the *People Dohā*,

> Accomplish supreme great bliss [through] that very [body]
> you've taken on, which arise, abides, and dies. (PD 24)

Later, he adds,

> Some, who've gone to all the major and minor [pilgrimage]
> sites
> and elsewhere, claim realization [based on] what they've seen,
> but I, who am virtuous, rightly see for certain that there is
> no [pilgrimage] site outside the body's bounds. (PD 59)

And,

> The bodiless is hidden within the body:
> knowing this, you'll be free. (PD 109)

Elsewhere, he exclaims,

> Hey! If you want to meditate on your inherent nature
> through taking to heart the yogic view,
> [know that] the mountain of your own body is the supreme
> abode,
> and mind-itself is the accomplisher of timely yoga. (VM 7)

The body is closely related with the senses, and these, too, Saraha celebrates, writing, for instance:

> Hey, sirs, you must look to your senses:
> I'm certain of nothing but this. (PD 54)

And,

> Rely on form, sound, smell, taste, touch, and dharmas:
> all dharmas are unconditioned and nonarising. (QD 34)

And finally,

> There's seeing and hearing and touching and knowing
> and eating, smelling, traveling, and going and staying,
> [there's] chitchat, stories, and back talk:
> when you know "these are mind," you won't move from the
> singular. (PD 66)

In the yoginī tantras and other advanced esoteric systems, the way in which one is freed within the body—meaning the subtle body—is through a series of practices that involve moving wind-related energies from the outer channels—usually represented by two "side" channels—into the central channel, and then gaining proficiency in moving energies and drops up and down in the central channel, inducing various states of gnosis, or bliss, or both. Often, the sequence culminates with the absorption of the vital winds, the drops, and awareness into a drop at the heart cakra, where we purify the subtlest mental and physical aspects of ourselves and create the buddha bodies that are the fruition of the Mahāyāna path. There are many ways to describe these culminating practices. Saraha does not lay out a particular system or sequence but does allude to certain operations and concepts. For instance, he declares,

> When you make [mind] like the sky, the vital winds are bound,
> and when you thoroughly know sameness, they entirely dissolve;
> . . . .
> When wind and fire and the lord [of earth] have ceased
> and the nectar flows, the vital winds enter the mind;
> when [all] four conjoined [vital winds] enter a single abode,
> then supreme bliss can't be contained within the sky.
> (PD 46–47)

This partly metaphorical and partly technical instruction refers to the necessity to "stop" the breath by bringing the vital energies related to it into the central channel and experiencing great bliss there—a bliss that is both bodily and gnostic. That bliss, or joy, is induced when "the nectar flows," that is, when the fluids, or drops, residing within the various cakras of the central channel of the subtle body are moved up and down by the yogin. As we have seen, a common yoginī-tantra way of articulating that process divides the resultant experiences into four joys: joy, supreme joy, cessative joy, and connate joy, the last of which is usually regarded as the culminating event and sometimes equated to awakening itself. Saraha occasionally refers to these four,[345] but he rarely expounds them in detail. More often, he simply describes the "dripping" of "nectar" or "liquid" or "camphor" from the "sky"—which is usually understood as the descent of the white, "male" drop residing throughout one's life at the crown cakra, and also referred to as the bodhicitta.[346] In systematic accounts, the arrival of the drop at the throat cakra induces bliss, its arrival at the heart cakra induces supreme bliss, its arrival at the navel cakra induces cessative bliss, and its arrival at the "secret" or "root" or genital cakra induces the connate bliss, tantamount to full realization.

The joys may be induced through a process described as "inner fire" (S. *caṇḍalī*; T. *tumo*), which is stoked by the inrush of vital winds to the red, "female" drop at the navel cakra, which, like a bellows, generate great heat there. That heat then rises like a thin flame up through the central channel to the crown, where it melts the white drop and sets off its dripping, or descent. Saraha refers to this practice—famous as one of the "six dharmas of Nāropa"—only in passing.[347] More often, he mentions what sometimes are called "consort practices": techniques of sexual yoga, practiced with a flesh-and-blood yoginī that help to induce the movement of vital winds into and within the central channel, so as to produce gnostic bliss or joy. In the *Queen Dohā*, he describes how

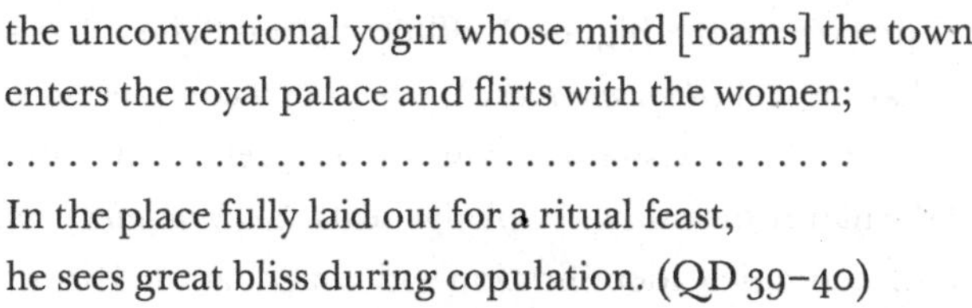

> the unconventional yogin whose mind [roams] the town
> enters the royal palace and flirts with the women;
> . . . .
> In the place fully laid out for a ritual feast,
> he sees great bliss during copulation. (QD 39–40)

He goes on to describe the various characteristics possessed by a proper consort, which include her being low caste, sixteen years old, "redolent of blue lotus," "little given to concepts," and "lustrous with passion," hence "with her left-handed ways, [able to apply] herself eagerly to her secret abilities" (QD 41–45). Practice with a consort is often described using the common terms for penis and vagina, namely, vajra and lotus, as in these two passages from the *Alphabetical Dohās*

> When the vajra resides within the mother's lotus,
> the bodies are bound [together] and nectar drips;
> [when] the ḍombī maiden embraces you around the neck,
> camphor drips down and springtime branches [bloom].
> (AD 1)

> Join the lotus and vajra, join them, and accomplish sameness.
> (AD 20)

Two other terms for a female consort are the great seal (*mahāmudrā*) and the action seal (*karmamudrā*). Although, as we have seen, Saraha typically uses *mahāmudrā* to connote the ultimate, its realization, or the fruit of the tantric path, he does occasionally use it to refer to a flesh-and-blood woman (for example, QD 46), and he refers to the action seal frequently in his *Body*, *Speech*, and *Mind Treasuries*. The action seal, as noted in the introduction, is one of four seals to spiritual practice in the higher Buddhist tantras. The other seals are the dharma seal (*dharmamudrā*), which in a completion-stage context may involve a visualized consort or a preliminary appreciation of the nature of reality; the pledge seal (*samayamudrā*), which entails either complete identification with a meditation deity or the compassionate expression of one's realization; and the great seal, which, as we have seen, is complete and final realization of the nature of mind and reality.

Consort practices, in turn, are part of a larger set of transgressive tantric "performances" or conduct (S. *caryā*; T. *chöpa*), undertaken by a yogin (or yoginī) at a particular point in their spiritual career when it is necessary to realize nonduality not just intellectually or in abstract meditation but socially, viscerally, and directly. This is where the yogin turns to such practices as inhabiting cremation grounds, dressing and acting as if mad, and attending ritual feasts or "clan circles" (*gaṇacakra*) where participants engage in song, dance, consumption of forbidden drinks and foods, and sexual yoga. Such behavior certainly is noted—and for the most part endorsed—by Saraha, as the following excerpts show:

> Live like a crazy person [acting] freely without calculation. (MM 35)

> Sometimes he enters the cremation ground, and practices the [five] lamps,
> and sleeps with a carefree mind in ghost-haunted places;
> he makes friends with outcastes and draws the corpse cart along.
> "This is forbidden conduct"—he's not to be held to that standard.
> He joins in musical gatherings, amusing himself with song, dance, and flute;
> he should never tire in the least of uplifting his mind
> through the dance of Heruka and songs sung by the six [yoginīs] and others. (QD 47–48)

I delight in vajra songs and interrupt idle talk;
may all beings purify knowing and engage in blissful dance.
(CD 30)

The empty one, [whose] forehead [cakra] abides in the sky,
is naked, unclothed by virtue or nonvirtue;
even when eating and drinking, he abides in nirvāṇa. (AD 2)

Although such behavior was regarded by many—Buddhist and non-Buddhist alike—as an antinomian rejection of all social and cultural norms, it is clear that within the context of the higher Vajrayāna systems in general and the yoginī tantras in particular it was a necessary part of the practitioner's path, which helped clear the way for the culminating practices conducted within the central channel of the subtle body, in which one attains complete buddhahood—a state identical to the blissful, luminous, nondual realization of the ultimate celebrated by Saraha the Radical Gnostic but, in this case, achieved not instantaneously but through a progression of esoteric and sometimes transgressive practices described in the later Vajrayāna systems.

Saraha the Mainstream Buddhist

Just as Saraha's more radical claims cannot really be comprehended outside their tantric context, so the great tantric systems, even at their most antinomian, cannot be understood apart from the basic Buddhist religious project of which they are a part. As was the case with Vajrayāna, we must concede that Saraha the Critic—especially at the outset of the *People Dohā* and the *Body Treasury*—dismisses many of the ideas and practices associated with Mainstream and Mahāyāna Buddhism. It is also true that he completely, or largely, ignores many important Buddhist concepts and categories, including, to name just a few, refuge, merit, the six realms of saṃsāra, the twelve links of dependent arising, serenity and insight meditation, the six perfections, and buddha-nature. Nevertheless, there is good evidence from his corpus that he adheres to many basic Buddhist values and techniques—including renunciation of saṃsāra, cultivation of love and compassion, attainment of wisdom realizing the ultimate, and the pursuit of nirvāṇa. Indeed, these are foundational to his entire project, for the radical, esoteric, and sometimes transgressive practices he espouses require previous mastery of basic Buddhist virtues: without renunciation, altruism, and deep insight, such practices almost certainly would lead to physical, psychological, and spiritual ruin.

In the previous section, we noted that Saraha celebrates the body, the senses, and even desire as necessities on the path to awakening. However, his verses also contain "standard" Buddhist warnings about ensnarement by any of these. Of the body, he writes,

> While the body's machinery is reckoned to be momentary,
> permanent mind-itself is the changeless eternal realm;
> bodily manifestations are naturally destroyed on their own,
> while permanent mind-itself, mahāmudrā, reaches the eternal
> realm. (DT 2)

———

> Unknowing fools think, "The body [is real],"
> [but] the corpse[-like] body is like a poisonous snake with a
> severed neck:
> I don't see any owner residing within it,
> and some say, "It's a corpse within a corpse." (DT 6)

Of the senses, he observes,

> Using the senses, don't be occluded by the senses:
> [be] like lotus petals untouched by water. (PD 78)

> Don't be bound by fixation on sense objects!
> . . . .
> The fish, the moth, the elephant, the bee,
> and the deer: observe what they're like. (PD 86)

> Beasts don't comprehend what suffering is;
> by contrast, the wise here comprehend
> suffering and drink the nectar of sky,
> while others are attached to sensuous things. (KD 8)

> To the one who [regards] appearances equably and [makes] the senses
> and their objects disappear—I bow down. (SS 2)

> Transcend the senses through the pure inherent nature. (AD 7)

> Omniscience is nondual and free from fixation on sense objects. (MT 20)

More specifically, he warns against attachment to the pleasure entailed by tantric sexual practices:

> Someone [conjoins] vajra
> and lotus and revels in bliss.

Why? [Real bliss] cannot be taught, so
how can they fulfill the hopes of [beings in] the triple world?
(PD 112)

Experiencing the action seal produces pride,
while cultivating the practice of suchness is the path to
freedom. (ST 34)

By desiring to see the lotus joined with the vajra
and by a path of desire, you will not be freed [into] thatness.
(ST 35)

Since experience based on the action seal
is contrived, it emerges through conditions,
and because it depends on other [factors], it is not suchness.
(BT 65)

Broadly speaking, Saraha rejects desire, attachment, grasping, fixation, and other "acquisitive" emotions and attitudes, often associated with the senses:

Alas! Don't be attached to things you desire:
when cognition's attached to an object of desire,
it's an illness afflicting the supreme mind of great bliss,
a blow to the stainless mind by the sword of desire. (QD 12)

Just as deer tormented by error
run toward the water in a mirage,

so [when] fools are tormented by desire for something,
regardless of how they strive for it, it grows ever more distant.
(MM 41)

Just as someone who acts like a worm will be bound,
[so] those attached to tastes will be bound,
but someone who can eat away this thicket
will continually turn all the wheels [of Dharma]. (CD 95)

Childish ignorance is the cause for entering into samsaric conditionality,
[so] those with weakened wisdom grasp at things and do not accomplish the aims of self or others.
Even [as] a blazing lamp cannot appear to the blind,
[so] those intent on the aims of self and others grasp at things, grasping at self by themselves. (ST 3)

Samsaric beings are entwined like trees by vines,
and thirst in the miserable desert of grasping at self. (QD 2)

Whatever you're fixated on: let it go! (PD 19)

The corollary of Saraha's dismissal of desire and its associated emotions is that he values their opposite, nongrasping, nonfixation, detachment, and renunciation—which, of course, have been primary Buddhist values from the tradition's very inception, reflecting a spiritual aspirant's proper reaction to the delusions and suffering that constitute saṃsāra.

The opposite of saṃsāra is nirvāṇa, the most common term in Mainstream Buddhism for the ultimate attainment. Saraha often insists, like Nāgārjuna,[348] that there is no difference at all between saṃsāra and nirvāṇa, or "existence" (S. *bhava*; T. *sipa*) and peace (S. *śānti*; T. *shiwa*),[349] and occasionally derides those who are obsessed with attaining nirvāṇa (PD 14; CD 16), but he also sometimes makes positive references to the ideal:

When you free your own mind-stream, there's certainly no other [way]:
you'll obtain supreme nirvāṇa. (PD 42)

———

Nirvāṇa is taught by way of the three vehicles;
not knowing this, you don't see suchness. (CD 18)

———

"Nirvāṇa" means emergence from conceptuality, which is synonymous with the nature of the reality body. (CB 1149)

———

The empty one, [whose] forehead [cakra] abides in the sky,
is naked, unclothed by virtue or nonvirtue;
even when eating and drinking, he abides in nirvāṇa. (AD 2)

———

When conditionality and the path to nirvāṇa are taught
and realized as nonarising, that is mahāmudrā. (BT 81)

———

If you want to enter the city of nirvāṇa,
then by cultivation of the great yoga [applied] like continuous rain to what is encountered
. . . .
you will quickly [attain] the union [at the end of] the path, and not turn back. (ST 12)

In Mainstream Buddhism, two key methods for reaching nirvāṇa are morality, or ethics, and meditation, or contemplation. While Saraha denies that there is any ultimate difference between virtue and vice, occasionally suggests that nonaction is preferable to action, and in his tantric guise sometimes espouses practices that appear to contravene conventional morality, elsewhere, he upholds basic Buddhist ethics, singing, for instance:

Not working to benefit others,
not bestowing gifts on the needy:
this, alas, is the fruit of saṃsāra—
better you should toss out selfhood. (PD 134)

Mind is devoid of all harmful actions;
it's not covered up by deeds like getting or taking. (QD 37)

The stages of the basic instruction taught by the guru are long,
and through those stages compassion and other pure virtues
themselves arise in the heart dwellings of the faithful. (SS 11)

[When you] don't abandon the supreme rarity that is the guru, all good qualities emerge. (ST 48)

> [Those] who [bring about] the desired goals of beings
> through perfect generosity, reveal those goals through the
> attribute of love. (CD 1)

While Saraha often mocks meditators and meditation and asserts that he sees no difference between meditation and nonmeditation (PD 95, 122) or meditator and object of meditation (QD 14, 26), he does employ and recommend various contemplative techniques. Many of those, as we saw in the previous section, are tantric, but others can be traced back to Mainstream Buddhism, in spirit, if not in terminology:

> Meditate clearly with the mind that enters everything.
> (QD 23)

> Meditate on bliss as akin to an aimless river. (QD 24)

> Meditate on gnosis uncovered by extremes. (QD 26)

> Meditate on the nature of ultimate mind. (QD 30)

> Knowing [your own basic] clarity, meditate stably upon it—
> the unmoving mind is held there as your very nature. (KD 36)

> When you obtain uninterrupted contemplation,
> you're free and won't see anything apart from this. (CD 62)

You should meditate first on love. Then, after compassion, meditate on joy and, last of all, equanimity. (SB p. 1444)

The mention of the four immeasurables leads naturally to a consideration of distinctly Mahāyāna aspects of Saraha's teaching, including the bodhisattva ideal and an emphasis on the bodhicitta or "great compassion" that seeks the benefit of others:

Someone who strives in the manner of a bodhisattva is a bodhisattva. (CB 1150)

For those who have become bodhisattvas,
it won't be difficult to become a perfect buddha. (CD 52)

Luminosity, mahāmudrā, and the primordial essential nature,
which do not change at all, are one in bodhicitta. (BT 87)

The realized conduct themselves without calculation,
so when destitute, foolish beings come before them,
tears well up by force of their unbearable compassion. (MM 37)

Unattached conduct upheld by compassionate means is as vast as the sky. (ST 15)

Emanations that emerge on their own through unthinking
compassion
are like a precious jewel that emerges without increase or
decrease. (CD 35)

We have already seen, in our discussion of Saraha's notion of the ultimate, that Mahāyāna concepts like emptiness and mind-only are a key to his approach. He is also distinctly Mahāyānist in his insistence that emptiness and compassion, or wisdom and method, must be balanced in practicing the path:

Bereft of compassion and abiding in emptiness,
you won't attain the supreme path,
but if you meditate only on compassion,
you'll remain in saṃsāra and won't win liberation.
Someone who's able to join the two
doesn't abide in saṃsāra and won't abide in nirvāṇa. (PD 17–18)

The sublime tree of emptiness sends forth flowers,
which are the many varieties of sublime compassion. (PD 130)

Emptiness and compassion are indivisible and nonarising.
(BT 26)

Finally, Saraha's notion of the outcome of the Mahāyāna path, buddhahood, is deeply informed by pretantric Great Vehicle categories, which typically divide the awakened state into two, three, four, or more "bodies" (S. *kāya*; T. *ku*). The twofold scheme posits a reality body (S. *dharmakāya*; T. *chöku*), which was discussed earlier, and form body (S. *rūpakāya*; T. *zugku*). The threefold scheme includes the reality body and two form bodies: the sublime enjoyment-body (S. *sambhogakāya*; T. *longku*) and various magical emanation bodies (S. *nirmāṇakāya*; T. *trulku*). The fourfold scheme adds an essence body (S. *svabhāvikakāya*; T. *ngowonyiku*) to those three. This is expounded in some detail in the *Queen Dohā*:

> The reality body, complete enjoyment-body, and emanation body,
> as well as the essence body, are clearly known through cause and result;
> nonduality empty of exaggeration and deprecation is the reality [body],
> its essential bliss is the great enjoyment[-body].
>
> Its various [appearances] to beings are the emanation [body],
> and nondual gnosis is the [essential] self of them all.
> . . . .
> The results are two: fulfilling the aims of oneself and of others.
> Though labeled as cause or result, [the bodies] are essentially indivisible:
> the twofold form-body emerges by virtue of prayer and compassion,
> like a fine vase, a wish-granting tree, or a precious jewel.
> (QD 63–65)

Elsewhere, it is expressed more concisely:

> The reality body, enjoyment body, and emanation body are indivisible,
> and the essential nature is beyond the domain of thought.
> (BT 71)

In the passages excerpted in this section, then, Saraha shows that despite his critical, radical, and sometimes transgressive rhetoric, he remains in many respects a Mainstream Buddhist, adhering (at least conventionally) to the saṃsāra-nirvāṇa dichotomy and affirming the importance of such basic Mainstream and Mahāyāna values as renunciation, virtue, meditation, and the necessity to balance wisdom and compassion on the path to awakening. Put another way, just as the nay-saying Saraha the Critic cannot be appreciated except by reference to the positive assertions about reality made by Saraha the Radical Gnostic, and the gnostic Saraha must be seen within the context of the esoteric ideas and practice of Saraha the Tantric Yogin, so the Vajrayāna Saraha cannot be comprehended except against the background of the Mainstream and Mahāyāna Buddhism of which Vajrayāna was a part, socially, practically, and conceptually. Thus, Saraha's various guises—and his multiple and sometimes conflicting teachings—may in fact be reconciled, and his outlook shown to be unitary, such that, to return to the comment from the *King Dohā*, "The king sees Saraha appearing in various guises, although he is one" (KD 1). But is this really so? That is the question we will consider briefly in the final section of the chapter.

One Saraha, or Many?

There is much to be said for regarding Saraha as a unitary figure in the manner sketched above. For one thing, it aligns us with Tibetan tradition, which—with occasional exceptions—regards Saraha as a single individual who lived in India and composed all the texts attributed to him, whether found in the Tengyur or extracanonical sources. Furthermore, by articulating a relationship among the various "guises" of Saraha we have identified, we smooth over apparent contradictions in the corpus, whereby, for instance, Saraha the Critic may seem at odds with Saraha the Radical Gnostic, and

Saraha the Radical Gnostic in tension with Saraha the Tantric Yogin or Saraha the Mainstream Buddhist. Through such a hermeneutics, we can imagine a Saraha who—in the style of many a Mahāyāna Buddhist thinker—is simultaneously a critic *and* an affirmative mystic, a transgressive tāntrika *and* a "standard" Buddhist. Imagining Saraha thus can make him more comprehensible and perhaps more palatable, in that his radical critiques and gnostic affirmations may be located within his Vajrayāna context and his tantric persona shown to be part of a larger project that aligns with Mainstream and Mahāyāna Buddhism in terms of both theory and practice. In this way, Saraha—much like the Buddha himself—would be seen as utilizing the discerning teacher's skillful means to espouse different attitudes, ideas, and techniques for different audiences of different capacities in different contexts.

There are, however, several problems with the notion of a unitary Saraha. First, as we saw in chapter 2, the assumption that a single individual composed all the texts attributed to Saraha—whether Apabhraṃśa "originals" or Tibetan translations—is by no means a safe one, for even in Tibet, the authorship of the *Queen* and *King Dohās* was up for debate, and a number of other texts credited to the Great Brahmin might plausibly be assigned to the likes of Śavaripa, Balpo Asu, Vairocanavajra, or Padampa Sangyé. Indeed, the widely varying rhetorical, topical, and terminological emphases from one text (or set of texts) to another could be taken as evidence that they were in fact composed by a social critic, a radical gnostic, a tantric yogin, and a conventional Buddhist who lived at different times and perhaps in different cultures. Furthermore, the attempt to harmonize the disparate Sarahas into a single figure runs up against the inescapable fact that there exists an overall imbalance in voices, or personas, found in the texts, such that Saraha the Radical Gnostic is probably most common, followed by Saraha the Tantric Yogin, Saraha the Critic, and Saraha the Mainstream Buddhist. If the preponderance of the first and the relative scarcity of the last is taken as a measure of importance, then it may be that Saraha is not a standard Buddhist occasionally prone to radically gnostic or transgressive tantric rhetoric but a true social and religious radical who invokes ordinary Buddhist ideas and practices only as an occasional sop to convention.

Which of these two is the "real" Saraha? Perhaps neither. The notion of a unitary Saraha not only flies in the face of much textual and historical evidence but threatens to "normalize" a figure who defies domestication as surely as he defies conceptual constructs. At the same time, the assertion of multiple Sarahas threatens to split into incoherence a body of texts that, for all the problems they pose, do seem to be held together, at least loosely, by a set of partially overlapping images, concerns, and instructions—those represented by Saraha the Poet, Saraha the Critic, Saraha the Radical Gnostic, Saraha the Tantric Yogin, and Saraha the Mainline Buddhist. In the end, I think we must affirm that the Saraha found in texts ascribed to him is a genuinely radical figure but that his social and religious critique and gnostic radicalism must be understood in the context of the Vajrayāna in general and the yoginī tantras in particular, and that Vajrayāna must be recognized not as a complete departure from the concepts, values, and practices of pretantric Mainstream and Mahāyāna Buddhism but as a particular late Indic instantiation of them. We might conclude with an admonition from the *King Dohā*:

> If you examine whether mind is one or many,
> you give up clarity and tumble into existence;
> seeing in this way, you tumble into a hole—
> what could be more pitiful than that? (20)

As with mind, so with the mind's great poet, Saraha, who is neither one nor many.

CHAPTER 5

Saraha's Legacy

All that remains in this part of the book is to briefly note Saraha's aesthetic, religious, and philosophical legacy in precolonial South Asia, the pre-1959 Tibetan cultural sphere, and the modern world, both in Asia and the West.

Saraha's Legacy in Premodern South Asia

Although the Tibetan Tengyur is replete with translations of various Buddhist tantric songs composed in Indic languages in the late first and early second millennium CE, precious few have been preserved in their Indic form, whether in Apabhraṃśa or some other linguistic register. Of those that do survive, the most notable are the short, personalized songs found in Munidatta's *Treasury of Performance Songs* (including four by Saraha) and the aphoristic couplets collected in the *Dohā Treasuries* attributed to Saraha, Tilopa, and Kāṅha/Kṛṣṇācārya. That this is all we have in the "original" from a once-thriving Buddhist tantric culture can be attributed to the almost complete disappearance of Buddhist institutions and culture from the subcontinent, starting around 1200 CE. With the destruction, around that time, of the great Buddhist monasteries of the Gangetic plain, along with their libraries, nearly every literary record of late north Indian Buddhism that had not by then been transmitted to Nepal or Tibet was irretrievably lost, including most of the Indic-language works of Saraha. (Recall that nearly every surviving specimen we have of his Apabhraṃśa work was discovered in Nepal or Tibet.) Yet although the works of Saraha and other Buddhist siddhas were effectively obliterated from Indian cultural memory for the better part of a millennium, they were known and sung among the Buddhist Newārs of Nepal and continued to exercise an aesthetic and even a religious influence on the non-Buddhist traditions that remained and developed on the subcontinent.

Aesthetically, the dohā form mastered (if not originated) by Saraha and his ilk proved very durable and useful, especially for those north Indian poets and religious figures who eschewed Sanskrit versification in favor of more vernacular expressions. These figures, who are typically styled as sants ("saints," more or less), represented a range of different religious movements, including esoterically inclined Nāth siddhas like Gorakhnāth (twelfth century); worshippers of a formless God (sometimes styled the Name, or Rām) like Kabīr (d. 1519), Nānak (1469–1539), and Dādū (1544–1603); various poets—such as Sūrdās (1478–1583), Mīrabaī (1498–1546), and Tukārām (1608–50)—who were devoted to more tangible forms of the divine, like Kṛṣṇa or Viṭhobhā; and ecstatic minstrels like the Bauls of Bengal.[350] In general, they were critical of caste distinctions and pedantic scholarship while embracing direct, ecstatic experience of the divine and affirming the centrality of the guru to the attainment of that experience. Much of the sant poetry of the second millennium is composed in dohās (the term *sākhī*—or "witness"—is often used as well), which echo not only the main verse style used by Saraha but also his critical spirit, his symbolic terminology, and his love of wordplay and paradox. Thus, for instance, the eleventh-century Jaina poet Rāmasiṃha sings of pandits:

> You've read a lot, your mouth is dry, you're still a fool;
> Read only that one letter which takes you to the auspicious abode.[351]

Gorakhnāth, a figure revered in both Nepal and India, expresses the bliss of realization of the connate:

> The spring has burst forth, I have drunk the nectar of
> immortality, I have pierced the thousand-petaled lotus;
> Where there is moonlight without the moon, there I saw Lord
> Gorakhnāth.[352]

Along similar lines, the great nonsectarian master Dādū sings,

> Come, says Dādū, let's go to that land where neither moon
> nor sun can go,
> where neither night nor day can enter and all is merged in the
> connate.[353]

Dādū's disciple, Rajjab (seventeenth century), laments humans' inability to take advantage of the spiritual opportunities presented to them:

> Dogs and crows throw themselves on dead carcasses, ignoring
> vessels full of cooked food.
> Says Rajjab: Such is the tendency of the mind, which gives up
> nectar and eats poison.[354]

Finally, some of the strongest echoes from Saraha are found in Kabīr, whose *Bījak* is among the richest collections of dohās/sākhī in all of Indic literature. Here is just a small sampling:

> The guru's word is one, ideas about it are endless;
> Sages and pandits exhaust themselves, the Vedas can't touch
> its limit.[355]

———

Moving within limits: humans; moving without limits: the saint;
Dropping both limits and no limits—unfathomable thought.[356]

Do one thing completely, all is done; try to do all, you lose the one.
To get your fill of flowers and fruit, water the root.[357]

Make the guru your burnisher: polish, polish your mind;
scour, scour with the word: make consciousness a mirror.[358]

On the peak of emptiness: shimmer of cymbals, rain of nectar, drops of love;
Kabīr says: Listen, friend, seeker: each taste gives bliss.[359]

Examples from Kabīr and other sants could be multiplied almost ad infinitum. Clearly, each of the poets cited here functioned within his own linguistic, cultural, and religious setting—one quite different from that of Saraha and other Buddhist mahāsiddhas. Nevertheless, these excerpts should suffice to show that many premodern South Asian religious movements of the second millennium CE bore the unmistakable imprint of both the aesthetic style and the thematic concerns of their tantric Buddhist predecessors, including Saraha.

Saraha's Legacy in the Pre-1959 Tibetan Cultural Sphere

While Saraha's works—along with the rest of Buddhist culture—largely disappeared from South Asia (Nepal and other Himalayan regions excepted) between the thirteenth and nineteenth centuries, working there only in subterranean ways, they were at the same time gaining a powerful foothold in Tibet, along with Indic Buddhism in general and the traditions of the great tantric adepts in particular. Indeed, as we saw in chapters 1 and 2, Saraha became for Tibetan tradition something like a mahāsiddha for all seasons, whose legends were transmitted, whose works were translated, whose songs were sung, cited, and discussed, and whose name and image implanted itself in the lineages, dreams, visions, and artworks of the masters of the nascent Buddhist orders of the early second millennium CE.

Aesthetically, the introduction of Saraha's works to Tibet in the eleventh and twelfth centuries through the efforts of translators and transmitters such as Marpa, Balpo Asu, Kor Nirupa, and Padampa Sangyé helped to hasten the development of a Tibetan equivalent of the dohā, which like the translations of Saraha's songs lost their distinctive Indic end-rhyme and followed established Tibetan metrical conventions. Although few Tibetans could read or understand the Great Brahmin's songs in the Indic original (where such existed), they could read (or hear) the Tibetan versions, and the tone and style they detected in Saraha's songs—especially the *People*, *Queen*, and *King Dohās*—echoed the critical spirit and confident tone they heard in their own secular "songs of myself," known as *gur*. Wedded to Buddhist themes and images, *gur* became the main term for songs of spiritual experience composed by countless Tibetan masters of the second millennium, from early figures like Marpa, Milarepa (eleventh–twelfth century), Lingrepa Pema Dorjé (sometimes called "the Saraha of Tibet," 1128–88), Godrakpa Sönam Gyaltsen (1170–1249), and the third Karmapa, Rangjung Dorjé (1284–1339), down to later poet-yogins like Pema Karpo (1527–92), Panchen Losang Chögyen (1570–1662), Shar Kalden Gyatso (1607–77), and Shabkar Tsokdruk Rangdrol (1781–1851).[360] All of these, directly or indirectly, owed a debt of gratitude to Saraha—and to the scholars who brought his work to the plateau at the dawn of the Tibetan renaissance.

Saraha's aesthetic influence in Tibet would not have been as pronounced as it was had he not been identified early on as the human source of the mahāmudrā, or great seal, teachings on the nature of mind that loomed so large for the religious orders that arose beginning in the eleventh century, such as the Kadam, Sakya, and Kagyu. We have already detailed some of the ways Saraha was integrated into the mahāmudrā lineages of various Tibetan schools. As the seminal figure in such lineages, he was quoted constantly in texts on mahāmudrā theory and practice composed within the various orders, especially the Kagyu, and his main poetic works, particularly the *People Dohā*, were given more or less detailed commentarial treatment by several important Tibetan scholars, including Pharpuwa Lodrö Sengé (twelfth century), Chomden Raldri (1227–1305), the third and seventh Karmapas, Karma Trinlepa, the First Jamyang Shepa (1648–1721), and Mipham Gyatso (1846–1912). Only those by Chomden Raldri, Karma Trinlepa, and Jamyang Shepa have been explored by modern scholars,[361] and delving into the others would be a worthy project. Here, however, we will content ourselves with examining briefly how Saraha might be positioned in three debates concerning the interpretation of the great seal that played out over the centuries in Tibet, both between and within various Buddhist orders. Specifically, we will see how his works might be utilized by those favoring (a) instantaneous or gradual approaches to achieving the great seal of buddhahood, (b) Sūtra, Mantra, or "third-way" interpretations of mahāmudrā, and (c) explanations of the emptiness synonymous with mahāmudrā as an affirming or a nonaffirming negation.

(a) Debates over instantaneous and gradual approaches to awakening seem to have arisen quite early in the history of Buddhism, but they became especially intensive in the eighth and ninth centuries

CE, when the question was addressed among Mahāyāna Buddhist philosophers in India, members of the nascent Chan tradition in China, and by Indian, Chinese, and Tibetan scholars at the court of King Tri Songdetsen in Tibet.[362] The issues in the latter-day debates were complex but may be summarized as follows: Those favoring a gradual approach to awakening asserted that, given the deluded state in which we start the path, it is necessary first to establish a solid foundation in Buddhist moral teachings and engage in serenity meditation only when our morality is unimpeachable and our desires few. By the same token, realizing the nature of mind and reality through Buddhist wisdom teachings will be possible only when we have attained a degree of meditative stability and have sufficient intellectual comprehension of those teachings. When we gain insight into the nature of reality (for example, as emptiness) with a settled, serene mind, we are transformed from ordinary beings into holy beings (*ārya*), destined for eventual awakening through whatever sūtra- or tantra-based techniques we may apply. Those advocating an instantaneous, or immediate, approach to awakening—the subitists—insisted that no amount of ethical preparation, meditative training, or philosophical analysis could possibly issue in true realization, which, by definition, lies beyond all calculation, conceptuality, or causal analysis or manipulation. Thus, our only alternative is to drop these and enter immediately into our own true nature, which is, and always has been, empty, luminous, and pure. Once we realize our true nature, all other aspects of the path—morality, meditation, the various perfections—will arise as spontaneous expressions of our profound comprehension of the ways things are.

At the debate conducted before King Tri Songdetsen, the subitists were represented by the Chinese Chan master Heshang Mohoyan and some Indian and Tibetan tantric masters, while the gradualists were led by the Indian philosopher Kamalaśīla. The actual outcome of the debate is uncertain, but there is no doubt that in the wake of the event, Indian styles of Buddhism came to predominate in Tibet over those originating in China. Since, however, Indian Buddhism already contained within it both subitist and gradualist tendencies, the debate before the king did little to resolve the tension between the two positions, which in fact continued to play off against one another throughout the history of Buddhism in Tibet. Some traditions, such as the Sakya and Geluk, tended to emphasize the gradual approach, while others, such as the Nyingma and Kagyu, showed more subitist inclinations. Nevertheless, each school contained elements of both approaches, and there was general agreement that subitism was appropriate only to those karmically fortunate few who could draw on significant previous training, either in this life or a previous one, while for most of us, some version of the gradual path was necessary. It also was agreed that, regardless of how rapidly or slowly we have proceeded, the transition from sentient being to buddha at the end of the path is, indeed, instantaneous. As for Saraha, while he might at first glance seem most easily enlisted for the subitist side, we must recall that Saraha the Radical Gnostic, who instructed his disciples to abandon thought and see reality directly, was only one of the Great Brahmin's guises, and that Saraha the Tantric Yogin and Saraha the Mainstream Buddhist might just as easily be quoted to support the idea that our progress toward awakening must necessarily proceed by stages, until we are ready for the final leap into full awakening. Indeed, Tibetan masters inclined toward subitism (for example, many Kagyupas) will tend to quote the radical-gnostic Saraha in support of their stance, while those upholding gradualism (for example, most Gelukpas) will either quote the tantric-yogin or mainstream-Buddhist Saraha—or, just as commonly, explain how his apparently subitist statements must be understood as part of a broader, gradual progression toward awakening.[363]

(b) Although, as we know, the term *mahāmudrā* originated in the Buddhist tantras, at first denoting a ritual hand-gesture or the clear visualization of oneself as a buddha-deity, and somewhat later a female consort for sexual yoga practice, by the beginning of the second millennium CE, it had increasingly become an index of ultimacy, referring, inter alia, to the ultimate nature of mind and reality, a type of meditative practice that aimed to realize that nature, and the final outcome of that realization, full buddhahood. And as the great seal became both wider and deeper in its connotations, it moved beyond its tantric roots and came to be associated with the standard terminology and practices of Mahāyāna, and even Mainstream Buddhist traditions, such that, for instance, Maitrīpa and his circle of disciples at least suggested that there was a sūtra-based mahāmudrā that corresponded to the better-known tantric usages of the term. Thus, when great-seal texts and traditions were transmitted to Tibet in the eleventh and twelfth centuries, the term had a broad range of meanings, and Tibetan scholars and yogins could select from a large menu of options the sense of the term they deemed most appropriate. Among the most significant figures in this regard was Gampopa Sönam Rinchen (1079–1153), the great organizer of the Kagyu traditions started by Marpa and Milarepa. Not only did Gampopa institute monasticism among the Kagyu but he also placed mahāmudrā at the center of the Kagyu worldview, describing it in various ways. Among his most enduring—and controversial—claims was that there was a mode of teaching and receiving the great seal that did not require prior tantric consecration; all that was needed was for the master to point out the true nature of mind to the disciple, then bless them—and realization would ensue. In this sense, Gampopa, and other Kagyupas in his wake, upheld the idea of a sūtra-based mahāmudrā that was just as valid and effective as that of the tantras. Their contention was strongly rejected by the great Sakyapa scholar Sakya Pandita Kunga Gyaltsen (1182–1251), who insisted that the great seal could be practiced only after receiving tantric consecration and that Kagyu claims to the contrary were the result of wishful thinking and mistaken historical analysis.[364]

Over the following centuries, nearly every Tibetan scholar concerned with mahāmudrā—a great many—would take a position on the dispute, with most Sakyapas defending Sakya Pandita's tantra-only stance, Kagyupas defending some version of Gampopa's analysis, and Gelukpas, who came late to the discussion, usually supporting the Kagyu view. Over the years, the discussions were nuanced enough that it was not simply a binary choice between the tantra-only mahāmudrā described by Sakya Pandita and the tantra-plus-sūtra mahāmudrā model suggested by Gampopa. Especially among the Kagyu, important variations were suggested, as in Dakpo Tashi Namgyal's delineation of a Sūtra mahāmudrā (essentially the Perfection of Wisdom), a Mantra mahāmudrā (completion-stage practices of the unexcelled yoga-tantras, such as the six dharmas of Nāropa), and an Essence mahāmudrā, a sort of third way that both combines and transcends elements of the Sūtra and Mantra approaches and is implicit in the songs and teachings of the Indian mahāsiddhas, including Saraha.[365] Thus, Saraha comes to be identified in many Kagyu circles with a special understanding of the great seal that is neither Sūtra nor Mantra alone but somehow combines and supersedes the two. Where such a threefold division of mahāmudrā is not recognized, as among the Geluk, Saraha is cited primarily as an exponent of the Mantra system, whose verses must be read in light of the completion stage of the unexcelled yoga-tantras.[366] Among traditional Sakyapas, the view of Sakya Pandita—that mahāmudrā is solely a tantric idea and practice—has continued to hold sway, and so Saraha has been regarded as solely a tantric figure. It should be noted, however, that the overarching Sakya path-and-result system (*lamdré*) includes many contemplations of the nature of mind that resemble what elsewhere is called "mahāmudrā."[367] As for Saraha himself, it should be evident by now that, just as with the sudden-gradual debate, he can be enlisted here for any side one chooses: Saraha the Radical Gnostic appears to be espousing a way that goes beyond Sūtra or Mantra and directly engages the essence of reality, while Saraha the Tantric Yogin clearly alludes to Vajrayāna processes such as consecration and the generation and completion stages, and Saraha the Mainline Buddhist might almost be read as espousing a version of Sūtra mahāmudrā. The interpretation we support will depend on how we weigh the evidence in Saraha's texts, and that, as we have seen, is no easy matter.

(c) As noted in the previous chapter, "emptiness" is always a negation in Buddhist discourse, but just what *sort* of negation it is has been much debated. Although there was occasional controversy on the matter in India, it was in Tibet that the question was contested most vigorously. The question became especially acute with the appearance, in the fourteenth century, of the works of the Jonang master Dölpopa Sherab Gyaltsen (1292–1361), who drew on his own distinctive reading of Madhyamaka, Yogācāra, buddha-nature, and Kālacakra-tantra literature to formulate an interpretation of emptiness that came to be referred to as Shentong (extrinsic, or other, emptiness). According to this view—adopted in various forms by many thinkers in the Nyingma and Kagyu traditions—emptiness is an "implicative" negation, in which the existence of a permanent, partless, and independent self in anything worldly is denied but the reality of what is extrinsic to saṃsāra—namely, such unchanging buddha-qualities as purity, luminosity, bliss, and so forth is implicitly (or explicitly) affirmed.[368] To most Sakyapas and all Gelukpas, such a stance smacked of absolutism, or the "extreme of eternalism" (*yöta*), and they insisted repeatedly that emptiness is a simple, universal negation, which refers to the absence of inherent existence, or self, in *any* concept or entity, whether worldly or "transcendental," and does not imply any "leftover" reality, not even nirvāṇa.

According to this Rangtong (intrinsic, or self-emptiness) view, all concepts and entities are empty in exactly the same manner, such that a buddha is empty in just the same way as a sentient being is empty. At the same time, say Rangtongpas, it is precisely the absence of any inherent existence anywhere in anything that allows for the operation of dependent arising, the axiomatic Buddhist causal law that subsumes all persons and phenomena, whether conventional or ultimate.[369] The Rangtong position was criticized by Shentongpas for debasing the ultimate, bringing it down to the level of mere worldly convention; for their part, Rangtongpas replied that spiritual transcendence was, indeed, possible, but through the operations of dependent arising—and certainly not through the mistaken view of emptiness asserted by the Shentongpas.

The Rangtong-Shentong debate sometimes turned on the sort of philosophical questions just mentioned, but it also was contested in scriptural terms. Thus, the same passage in Nāgārjuna's corpus might be given either a Rangtong or a Shentong reading, or different works might be given primacy, so that, for instance, Rangtongpas tended to favor Nāgārjuna's "texts on reasoning" and their interpretation by Candrakīrti, while Shentongpas focused on Nāgārjuna's "songs of praise," the Yogācāra texts of Asaṅga, and buddha-nature literature. The philosophical stance of the tantras remained a much-contested question, and to the degree that Saraha's corpus emerged from a tantric milieu, his position in the Rangtong-Shentong debate is hard to pin down with certainty. Given his focus on gnostic realization and positive characterizations of the ultimate, amply illustrated in the previous chapter, he may seem to have a more natural affinity with the Shentong position.[370] However, as we saw earlier, his actual employment of the noun *emptiness* or the adjective *empty* leaves the matter unsettled, with his use of the negation sometimes appearing to short-circuit all predication whatsoever. Thus, depending on how we read his verses, Saraha might with equal justification be identified as a Shentongpa, a Rangtongpa, or simply a mystic who seeks to undermine the duality framing the dispute and directly point to the ineffably blissful *experience* of empty, luminous reality, the great seal for which all sentient beings thirst, even though they already possess it.

Saraha in the Modern World

The very fact that a book such as this is being written testifies to the fact that Saraha has emerged as a figure in his own right in the modern world, both in Asia and the West. Without entering into the intricate debate as to when "modernity" begins in South Asia, Tibet, or elsewhere, I would suggest that where Saraha is concerned, modernity begins with the publication, by Indian and Western scholars, of verses and verse collections attributed to him, in the first three decades of the twentieth century, for that is the source of the "modern" study and appreciation of the Great Brahmin. The way Saraha is imagined by modern people—so often shaped by Western ideologies and practices—is, of course, not precisely the way he was imagined by Indians in 1000 CE, Nepalis in 1200, or Tibetans in 1600, but some continuities are evident, as well—and we must recall that in "premodernity" he was imagined in many different ways, both within and between various Buddhist cultures. Here, we will touch briefly on some modern linguistic, aesthetic, religious, and philosophical takes on Saraha in South Asia, the Tibetan cultural sphere, and the West.

In South Asia, the discovery and publication of texts by Saraha and other "medieval" siddhas helped to fill in the historical picture of the pre-Muslim era in the subcontinent. Since most of the texts were esoteric and tantric in nature, this led to a certain ambivalence among scholars. The overt or covert sexual references in the songs, in particular, accentuated the tendency among early-twentieth-century Indian historians—no doubt encouraged by the British for their own political and cultural reasons—to see "medieval" (for example, Pāla-dynasty) tantric culture as reflecting a sad decline from the "classicism" of the Gupta and other earlier eras—and as a major factor in north India's susceptibility to Muslim invasion early in the second millennium and the contemporaneous decline and eventual disappearance of Buddhism from much of the subcontinent.[371] For such scholars, Saraha and his ilk certainly would be of interest but would not stand out as beacons of Indic civilization in the way that Aśoka, Pāṇini, Patañjali, Kālidāsa, or the emperor Harśa might. Not all early Indian scholars took such an approach, however. For instance, Mahendra Prasād Yādava, in his foreword to Rāhula Sāṃkṛtyāyana's edition and translation of Saraha's songs, describes him as promoting "a formless path in which yoga is combined with devotion and meditation"[372]—thereby evoking the perspectives and practices of sants like Kabīr, which were known and widely respected throughout India.

Also, whatever cultural judgments Indian scholars might (or might not) pass on Saraha and the mahāsiddhas, they agreed that the songs that had been discovered and published were valuable testimony to a phase in the development of Indic languages that more or less directly preceded the rise of the modern vernaculars, hence was an important transition point between Sanskrit and Prakrit culture on one side and "modern" languages on the other. As suggested earlier, scholars are not unanimous on the actual form of Apabhraṃśa reflected in Saraha's dohās or the performance songs collected by Munidatta. Nor, in fact, do they always agree on the "proto" language reflected in such texts. Bengalis have described it as proto-Bengali, but scholars from Odisha have argued that they most clearly prefigure Oriya.[373] This is not a dispute that can concern us here; it is worth noting, however, that in this context, Saraha and the mahāsiddhas are being invoked as important bearers of language, whatever one's view of the tantric culture that gave rise to them.

In the Tibetan cultural sphere, traditional ways of imagining and interpreting Saraha effectively held sway until the mid-twentieth century, when the onset of Chinese rule on the plateau led to the dismantling of some, and state oversight of other, traditional institutions within Tibet and a significant diaspora of Tibetans to India (and later to the West), where efforts were made to preserve various aspects of traditional culture, including Buddhist monasteries, lineages, and texts. It is difficult to assess the state of discourse about Saraha in Tibet itself over the past seven decades, though it should be noted that the Chinese have sponsored major publishing projects, which make the works of Saraha and countless other Indian and Tibetan masters available to a wider reading public in accessible formats, including bound books and web-based libraries. Among Tibetans who settled outside the plateau after the mid-twentieth century, traditional ways of reading Saraha seem largely to have held sway. His works are known, cited, and interpreted by scholars in all the major Buddhist orders, but in a traditional style that could just as easily have been utilized in 1724 as in 2024.[374] In that sense, the Saraha gradually constructed by Tibetan tradition throughout much of the second millennium continues to be transmitted today, whether to Tibetans or to non-Tibetans who study with Tibetan teachers.[375]

Some interesting exceptions, however, are found in the realm of poetry. Typically, modern Tibetan verse hews to the formal and thematic dictates established in the previous millennium, when religious concerns predominated, and when poets break with traditional forms (experimenting, for instance, with free verse) they usually eschew or minimize religious content. At least two modern figures go against this grain, however.

Gendun Chöpel (1903–51), a "renegade" Gelukpa monk who

helped Rāhula Sāṃkṛtyāyana find caches of Indian Buddhist texts (including the Long Apabhraṃśa *Treasury* by Saraha discussed earlier) and later spent twelve years living in India and Sri Lanka, acquainted himself with modern languages, ideas, and mores to a greater degree than any Tibetan before him. He wrote a considerable amount of poetry (occasionally even in English), and although he generally worked within classical Tibetan poetic forms, his references and ideas were anything but traditional. For instance, he utilizes an uncommon but perfectly acceptable twelve-syllable line to express the following striking geopolitical sentiments:

> Oh, the English government possesses a power that is not just talk;
> We need not fear the troops of any enemy.
> Because many nations with different tongues have united
> Fish need not despair that they use water to extract tea from tea leaves.[376]

And, in a more personal vein that seems to echo the authors of dohās and performance songs, he confesses in the prologue to his treatise on erotics,

> With little shame in myself and great faith in women,
> I am the kind who chooses the bad and discards the good.
> Although I have not had the vows in my head for some time,
> The guts of pretense were destroyed only recently.
> . . . .
> The author is Gendun Chöpel,
> The place it was written is the city of Mathurā,
> The difficult texts were written by an old Brahmin,
> The practical lessons were given by a Muslim girl.[377]

Chögyam Trungpa Rinpoche (1939–87) was born in Tibet and received his early education there and in India but pursued his higher education in England and eventually settled in North America, where he established the Vajradhatu organization, Shambhala Training, and Naropa University. He wrote verse, in both Tibetan and English, that ranged widely in prosody and theme but often attempted to combine the Tibetan dohā style and "crazy wisdom" he attributed to Saraha and other mahāsiddhas with modern concerns and references. Thus, in a poem called "Cynical Letter" written originally in Tibetan and translated by him into English, he concludes:

The laughing poet
Has run out of breath and died.
The religious spin circles, in accordance with religion;
If they had not practiced their religion, they could not spin.
The sinner cannot spin according to religion;
He spins according to not knowing how to spin.
The yogis spin by practicing yoga;
If they don't have chakras to spin, they are not yogis.
Chögyam is spinning, watching the spinning/samsara;
If there is no samsara/spinning, there is no Chögyam.[378]

Although modern in certain respects, these brilliant lines could well have been composed by Saraha, Milarepa, or some other great Buddhist poet of the past. In his English-only verse, however, Trungpa Rinpoche often moves beyond Tibetan tradition in both style and references, as when he writes, in "Missing the Point":

Brain hemorrhage
Sick pigeon
Trust in the heart

Good soldier
Neat girl in the cosmic whorehouse—
Our minds becoming bigger and smaller
As if they were Lynn's mustache
Which gets bigger and smaller as he talks.
. . . .
Who is instigating all this?
Maybe the uranium that makes atom bombs
Shooting star
Allegorical presentation of the dharma
Historical confirmation of the antidisestablishmentarian
sophistication of the seemingly sane society of the
past.
July Fourth
Flash of fireworks—
At the same time,
Lingering thought tells me
My private secretary is really drunk.[379]

Unmoored from any Tibetan original, this passage, like much of Trungpa Rinpoche's poetry, seems as indebted to the American Beats (with whom he was quite familiar) as to any traditional sources, yet behind even this we can at least faintly detect the contrarian, creative spirit of a figure like Saraha, now transposed into a different, very modern key.

Trungpa Rinpoche is in many ways a culturally transitional figure, who carries Saraha and the tradition he represents over to Western culture in a new and interesting way. Allen Ginsberg, who studied under Trungpa for almost two decades and helped him establish the Jack Kerouac School of Disembodied Poetics at Naropa University, saw his teacher providing

> millennial practical information on attitudes and practices of mind speech & body that Western Poets over the same millennia have explored, individually, fitfully, as far as they were able—searching thru cities, scenes, seasons, manuscripts, libraries, backalleys, whorehouses, churches, drawing rooms, revolutionary cells, opium dens, merchant's rooms in Harrar, salons in Lissadell.[380]

Not only that, Ginsberg saw Trungpa as a sort of white knight who could save Western verse from "beat bleakness," exclaiming, "At last! To the rescue! Carrying the panoply of 25 centuries of wakened mind-consciousness. . . . The poet of absolute Sanity and resolution, 'having drunk the hot blood of the ego.'"[381] If Ginsberg is right, then a direct poetic and spiritual line exists between Saraha and the Beats (and beyond), making Saraha an ancestor of certain modern Western cultural attitudes as surely as he is the forefather of the Indian sants or the mahāmudrā poets of Tibet. And, to the degree that Buddhism has in fact affected American and other Western poetries in the past seventy or more years, Ginsberg is probably right.[382]

There are ways other than the poetic whereby Saraha has entered the modern Western imagination. For many scholars and practitioners, he has become an emblematic figure, who is variously, or all at once, a rebel, a mystic, and a philosopher. One of the main scholars to promulgate such a view was Herbert Guenther, who, in two major studies and translations of works by Saraha, saw him as rejecting the complacent philistinism of the society around him and teaching Buddhism through song and metaphor as "a practical discipline rather than an intellectual pastime," which aims

> to bring about a change in outlook and to introduce a person to certain experiences which, though not very frequent in

> a high degree of intensity, have occurred in a high degree among a few men at all times and places. . . . The decisive factor in teaching is to bring about certain experiences that are felt to be valuable in their own right rather than to discuss the contents in propositions.[383]

These experiences, for Guenther, are what might be described as mystical, and they may be understood within an existentialist framework, in which existence supersedes essence, or through a gnostic framework, in which the key focus is on awareness, described by Guenther as "basic to man," and divisible into "objective referential" awareness of external objects, "objective nonreferential" awareness of internal objects, and "nonobjective nonreferential" awareness, which involves dwelling in the open dimension of being. The last, which Saraha teaches, is also "presential awareness,"

> out of which by creative imagination (*gom*), we may build a world of aesthetic appreciation (which may lend itself to fulfilling man's metaphysical need), and by acting out of this awareness (*chöpa*) may order a world of values. . . . The presential awareness is not so much the awareness of man's possibilities as it is the possibilities themselves as a functional unit pervading and sustaining all human traits, values, and experiences. The transition from the closed world of ordinary thought and action with their frustrating limits to the open dimension of potentiality and unlimited possibilities is made through disciplined contemplation and insight, which reinforce each other and culminate in an indissoluble unity.[384]

In short, as Guenther says of Saraha elsewhere,

> His insistence on the immediacy of experience—its spontaneity, its wholeness, its ecstasy—marked a quest for the authentic Self that resolutely refuses to lose itself in abstract speculations about the self. In so doing, Saraha set himself squarely within the ancient Indian tradition of "inwardly directed" thought, a tradition whose offshoots include Buddhism and whose stress on the transformation of the self continues in our times in ideas like the [Jungian] "process of individuation."[385]

Thus, somewhat in the same way as Ginsberg indirectly turns Saraha into a poet for our times, Guenther turns him into a thinker for our times: a rebel against conventional ways of thinking and living, a mystic who values ecstatic experience and gnostic awareness above dry analysis, and a philosopher who understands that "love of wisdom" has more to do with living authentically in the world than with parsing propositions.[386]

Perhaps, though, Ginsberg and Guenther place too much of a burden on Saraha, romanticizing him to a degree that the Great Brahmin's texts and contexts simply can't support. It is tempting to say, Don't try to make Saraha a paradigm for thought, life, and song in our time, or for all times; rather, be content to see him as the colorful late-first-millennium Buddhist figure that he was, and his works as expressions of a South Asian tantric milieu that was interesting and important in its own right and produced significant echoes in subsequent Indic and Tibetan culture. In other words, let Saraha be Saraha.

However, the reader who has followed this far will understand that, properly speaking, there is no single Saraha we can identify amid the panoply of myths and texts associated with him, and that, in fact, *Buddhists* in both India and Tibet were themselves making up Saraha stories, Saraha lineages, and perhaps even Saraha texts almost from the very start, telling tales of his life and reading his works so as to add meaning to their own lives in their own times. If we accept that this is what premodern Buddhists did, we begin to see that this is what all humans do in their search for meaning in their own worlds, bodies, emotions, and minds. With that understanding, we see that reading ancient works like those of Saraha through modern eyes is an inevitable part of the process of cultural transmission and appropriation wherever and whenever it occurs. That does not mean that we can say just anything about Saraha—we still must be moored to stories about him and writings attributed to him—but it does mean that, like any classic figure, he cannot be (for he never has been) confined to some tiny corral of cultural specificity, and it means that although our research may lead us, like the myopic ruler addressed in the *King Dohā* (KD 1), to fragment Saraha into "various guises," we are not amiss if we seek to see him as he asked to be seen: as one—and that one, a tenth-century Indian, may have something to teach to twenty-first century people about how to unseal our innate but long-hidden sense of how to think, feel, speak, and live as embodied beings in the world, living joyously and generously in light of a deeply felt insight into the way things are.

Selected Texts

CHAPTER 6

Dohā Treasury Song (People Dohā)

Note: *Italics* indicate verses found in Tibetan whose equivalents are missing from the Bagchi edition of the Apabhraṃśa; lines or verses enclosed in curly brackets are present in the Bagchi edition of the Apabhraṃśa, but their equivalents are missing from the Tibetan. The bracketed "text divisions" interspersed throughout the translation are based on those found in the commentary by Karma Trinlepa (KT)

---

[193] In the Indian language: *Dohakoṣagīti*; in the Tibetan language: *Do ha mdzod kyi glu* (*Dmangs do ha*).[387]

I bow down to the youthful Mañjuśrī.

[Critique]

Improper [*gurus*], *who are like venomous snakes,*
are stained by their flaws
and will certainly sully good people:
just to see them should make you afraid. (1)

Brahmins don't know thatness:[388]
pointlessly, they recite the four Vedas. (2)

They purify earth, water, and *kuśa* grass,[389]
and sit at home, burning sacrificial fires;
their burnt offerings are meaningless,
and the smoke just damages their eyes. (3)

With staff or trident, in the guise of a god,
they expound on difference or "I am that";[390]
they're equally ignorant of good and bad,
and divert beings into falsehood.[391] (4)

Smearing their bodies with ash,
they pile their hair atop their heads;
staying at home lighting their fires,
they sit in a corner ringing their bells. (5)

Seated in lotus posture [194] with eyes closed,
they whisper in people's ears and deceive them;
teaching others, such as widows and nuns,
they bestow consecration and collect their guru fees. (6)

Long nailed, their bodies smeared with filth,
unclothed, they pluck out their hairs:
the Digambaras are deceived [in thinking] the self
will gain liberation on a path consisting of pain.[392] (7)

If nakedness leads to freedom,
then why aren't dogs and foxes free?
If plucking out hairs leads to freedom,
then women with plucked-out hair must be free.[393] (8)

If raising one's tail leads to freedom,
then the peacock and yak must be free;

if eating food off the ground leads to freedom,
then why aren't horses and elephants [free]? (9)

The Archer says, It's never the case
that Digambaras are liberated;
bereft of blissful thatness,
they have only their bodily hardships. (10)

Those so-called novices, monks, and elders,
and, likewise, renunciant clerics—
some are involved in explaining sūtras,
while others are seen grasping for mind's single taste.[394] (11)

Some run along with the Great Vehicle,
the authoritative treatises of the textual tradition,[395]
or meditate on nothing but maṇḍalas and cakras;
and some wallow in explaining the meaning of the fourth
[consecration]. (12)

Still others conceive [thatness as] the element of space
or [see] everything in terms of emptiness—
for the most part, they [all] live in disagreement. (13)

Others, bereft of the connate,
apply themselves to meditation on nirvāṇa—
not even a few of them will accomplish
the ultimate; on the contrary, they will not. (14)

Can someone who aspires to [the ultimate]
win liberation by sitting in contemplation?
What use are lamps and food offerings to the gods?
What do they do? What [195] use is imparting secret mantras? (15)

Pilgrimage spots and austerities are useless.
Can you win liberation by immersion in water? (16)

{Bereft of compassion and abiding in emptiness,
you won't attain the supreme path,
but if you meditate only on compassion,
you'll remain in saṃsāra and won't win liberation.} (17)

{Someone who's able to join the two
doesn't abide in saṃsāra and won't abide in nirvāṇa.} (18)[396]

[The connate in general]

Hey you! Whatever is said is wrong, and a lie: cast it off!
Whatever you're fixated on: let it go!
When you're realized, everything is that,
[for] no one knows anything other than that. (19)

Study is that, apprehension and meditation are that,
treatises explaining the essence are also that;
[but] there is no view that indicates that—
it depends solely on the guru's word. (20)[397]

If the guru's sayings have entered your heart,
it's like seeing treasure in the palm of your hand;[398]
the primordial nature is unseen by fools—
"fools," says the Archer, "are deceived by error." (21)

Without contemplation, without renunciation,
staying at home with your wives;
if you're not freed from bondage by enjoying sense objects,
then say I, the Archer, "you don't know thatness."[399] (22)

If it's manifest, what's contemplation [do]?
If it's hidden, you only encounter darkness;
thatness, the connate nature,
is neither a thing nor a nonthing—
thus does the Archer ever loudly lament. (23)

"Accomplish supreme great bliss [through] that very [body]
you've taken on, which arises, abides, and dies"—
although the Archer proclaims secret words,
worldly beasts of burden don't understand. What's to be done? (24)

It lacks contemplation, so what is there to think on?[400]
It's inexpressible, [196] so how can it be explained?
Every being is fooled by the seal of existence,
and no one takes up their primordial nature. (25)

No tantra, no mantra, no contemplative object, no
contemplation:
all of them are causes for delusive cognition;
don't pollute mind's pure nature with contemplation:
abide in the blissful thatness of self, and don't torment yourself. (26)

Eating and drinking and enjoying copulation,
fill up the cakras again and again;
by such a dharma you'll accomplish the transworldly:
step on the head of foolish worldlings and move on. (27)[401]

Where wind and mind do not move,
where sun and moon don't enter in:
repose there, you fools, your breathing [relaxed]—
the Archer has taught all these pith instructions and gone
away.[402] (28)

Don't divide, unite,
don't separate things into particular classes:
turn everything in this whole triple world
to a single color: great passion. (29)

In that, there is no beginning, middle, or end,
no existence and no nirvāṇa;
in this supreme great bliss,
no self or other exists. (30)[403]

In front, in back, and in [all] ten directions,
whatever you see is thatness;
[I,] the protector, have excised error this very day,
so don't ask anyone else. (31)

Where senses have subsided
and your own essence has been experienced,
that, my friends, is where the connate is:
ask the guru to make it clear. (32)[404]

Where cognition's bound, where vital winds have dispersed:
on this place repose your limbs;
fools must thoroughly know the limits,[405]
and know how to part the sea of confusion.
This is supreme great bliss—Saraha has taught and gone away.
(33)[406] [197]

Hey! This is self-awareness:
don't turn it into error;
thing and nonthing are bondage for sugatas;[407]
without distinguishing existence from sameness,

direct your primordial cognition into oneness, O yogin[408]—
know that it's like water poured into water. (34)

You won't gain liberation through false contemplation,
which is like being held tight by the net of an illusory display;[409]
trusting the truth in the words of the sublime guru,
the Archer says, "I have nothing to express."[410] (35)

The sky is naturally pure from the start:
when you look and look at it, seeing will stop,
just as at the time of cessation. (36)[411]

Because of their flaws, the childish are fooled about the
primordial [nature]:[412]
intensely critical of everyone,
flawed by pride, they cannot point to thatness;
the whole world is fooled by contemplation,
and no one can point to their primordial nature. (37)

No one can point to root of the mind;
in terms of the triple connate,[413]
they don't know how to make clear where it arises,
where it subsides, and where it abides. (38)

For someone who thinks on unrooted thatness,
seeing by way of the guru's pith instructions will suffice;
"the nature of saṃsāra is the [nature] of mind"—
fools should know precisely what the Archer has said. (39)

The primordial nature can't be expressed in words,[414]
but it may be seen through the eye of the guru's pith instructions;

delighting in good and bad [alike], eat them up—[415]
there's not an iota of fault in this. (40)

When primordial cognition has been purified,
then the guru's virtues will enter your heart;
realizing this, seeing not a single mantra
or tantra, the Archer takes up this song. (41)

[The connate in detail]

Beings are bound by their individual actions,
and when [198] they're freed from action, cognition is freed;
when you free your own mind-stream, there's certainly no other
[way]:
you'll obtain supreme nirvāṇa.[416] (42)

Mind is itself the single seed of everything,
whence existence and nirvāṇa are projected;
to the mind, which like a wish-fulfilling gem
brings about [all] desired results, I prostrate. (43)

When mind is bound, you're bound;
when it's released, you have no doubts;
what will bind the fool
quickly frees the wise.[417] (44)

Mind is to be grasped as like the sky;
as naturally sky-like should mind be grasped;
when cognition changes to noncognition,
you'll obtain thereby unexcelled awakening.[418] (45)

When you make [mind] like the sky, the vital winds are bound,
and when you thoroughly know sameness, they entirely dissolve;
when you're able [to act] as described by the Archer,
you'll quickly abandon what changes and moves. (46)

When wind and fire and the lord [of earth] have ceased
and the nectar flows, the vital winds enter the mind;
when [all] four conjoined [vital winds] enter a single abode,
then supreme bliss can't be contained within the sky.[419] (47)

In house after house, they tell news of this, but
abiding great bliss is completely unknown;
all beings, says the Archer, are betrayed by concepts,
and no one accomplishes the inconceivable. (48)

Thatness exists in each and every
living being, yet it goes unrealized;
since everything by nature has a single taste,
gnosis can't be surpassed by concepts. (49)

Yesterday, today, tomorrow, and other times, too,
beings assert the fulfillment of their aims;
alas, it's like a cupped [hand] filled with water:
when it trickles out, they don't feel the loss. (50)

To perform a deed or not to perform a deed:
when your realization [199] *is sure, there is no bondage or freedom;*
it's beyond syllables, but which of a hundred yogins
who claim to explain it can point it out? (51)

If this mind, so tightly bound,
is relaxed, it will be freed, no doubt;

the things by which fools are bound
completely free the wise. (52)[420]

When bound, they begin to run in every direction,
but when released, they stand stock still:
I see this to be like the camel paradox;
look into yourselves intently, my children! (53)

Hey, sirs, you must look to your senses:
I'm certain of nothing but this;
in the presence of a person who's done
with action, you must cut the cord of mind. (54)

Don't think you'll [be freed] when binding the vital winds,
wooden yogin, and don't focus on the tip of your nose;
hey, that's not it—attach yourself to the supreme connate,
and rightly spurn the nose tip of existence.[421] (55)

Now, when the waves of vital wind [crash] within collected cognition,
[mind] trembles and quivers, and becomes quite unruly;[422]
when you realize the connate nature,
then your self-nature is stabilized. (56)

When cognition fully ceases,
bodily bonds are broken;
when [things] taste the same in the connate,
then there is no low-caste or brahmin. (57)

This is the Lunar River,[423]
this is the Ganges River,
this is Vārāṇasī and Prayag,
this is the moon and the illumining [sun]. (58)

Some, who've gone to all the major and minor [pilgrimage] sites
and elsewhere, claim realization [based on] what they've seen,
but I, who am virtuous, rightly see for certain that there is
no [pilgrimage] site outside the body's bounds.[424] (59)

In the center of the pistil of the petaled lotus
there are natural scents and colors;
get into distinctions, fools, and you induce sorrow; [200]
don't bring fruitless torment upon yourself.[425] (60)

When you take Brahmā and the Pervader [Viṣṇu]
and the three-eyed [Śiva] as the basis of everything in the world
and make offerings to all of them, then countless
[virtuous] karmas you've collected will be completely wasted.[426] (61)

Hey! Listen, children: those who [claim to] know that the taste of disputation abides in perfect purity
may explain the world, recite [texts], and so forth, but they cannot [really] know.[427] (62)

Hey! Listen, children: the taste of thatness
cannot be taught through multiplicity;
[entering] the supreme abode of bliss [requires] abandoning concepts:
it's like giving birth to a being.[428] (63)

Thought is stopped, cognition is overcome:
where overt pride is severed,
you realize that [mind] is the supreme nature of the illusory,
so why bind it with contemplation? (64)

If the nature of arising things is like the sky,
then after things are abandoned, what could arise?
That which from the start has not arisen
is realized today through the glorious guru's teaching.[429] (65)

There's seeing and hearing and touching and knowing
and eating, smelling, traveling, and going and staying,
[there's] chitchat, stories, and back talk:
when you know "these are mind," you won't move from the
singular.[430] (66)

One who does not drink up the cool, pain-removing
nectar waters of the guru's pith instructions
will be tormented by thirst in the sorrowful desert
of ambiguous treatises and will perish [there]. (67)[431]

If the guru doesn't express the teaching,
then the student won't understand;
how, and by whom, can the nectar[-like]
taste of the connate be taught?[432] (68)

Swayed by grasping at valid cognition,
the fool gets only the details;
enjoy yourself in a cobbler's hut:
even though [it's filthy], you won't get covered in dirt. (69)

When begging, you use a clay bowl from the gutter,
but if I were a king, [201] *what use would it be?*
Give up categories completely and abide in thatness,
and you'll spontaneously accomplish naturally unmoving equipoise.
Abiding in nirvāṇa, you beautify existence;
don't treat one disease with the medicine for another. (70)

Thoroughly abandoning concepts and what is conceived,
you should live in the way that a small child does;
if you hold tight the guru's precept, and strive in it,
the connate will emerge—there is no doubt. (71)

Bereft of colors, qualities, letters, or examples,
it cannot be spoken, and it's useless for me to point it out;
can that sacred lord be taught to anyone
any more than bliss to a lustful virgin?[433] (72)

Thoroughly sever [ideas of] thing and no-thing [in your mind],
and every being will completely dissolve there;
when cognition is immobile and stable in its own abode,
then it's freed from samsaric things on its own. (73)

When there's no knowledge of self or other at all,
then you'll obtain the unsurpassed body;
thus, through that very teaching, you'll come to proper
knowledge
by yourself and within yourself with unerring certainty. (74)

Things are neither atomic nor nonatomic,
nor even mind; they are without fixation from the start;
all the Archer has to say is this:
Hey! Come to know everything as the stainless ultimate.[434] (75)

He lives in the house but she searches outside;
she's seen the lord of the house but she asks the neighbors;
the Archer says, You must know your very own nature,
but neither contemplation nor its objects can be expressed by
fools. (76)

When the guru teaches and I [think I] know it all,
will I obtain liberation through thorough analysis?[435]
Though you wander in sense domains and suffer affliction,
in the grip of vice, you will not attain the connate. (77)

Using the senses, don't be occluded by the senses: [202]
[be] like lotus petals untouched by water;
anyway, yogin, resort to the root:
if you possess a poison spell, how can poison harm you?[436] (78)

You may make ten thousand offerings to the gods,
but you bind yourself thereby, so why do it?
[Practicing] in such a way, you won't be able to sever
saṃsāra, realize the primordial nature, or transcend [sorrow].[437]
(79)

Eyes unblinking, mind undistracted,
vital winds stopped, you think you understand, thanks to the
glorious guru;
[but] when at death time[438] the flowing vital winds
no longer move, what's a yogin[439] to do? (80)

As long as you descend to the city of sensory objects,
you never extend beyond yourself.[440]
You must think about what you're doing right now, and hey!—
entertain that most difficult idea.
Who it is and where it abides:
you won't see that there. (81)

The scholars all explain their treatises,
not realizing that buddha is in the body.
A trained elephant has a stable mind:

no longer coming or going, it's at ease.
When you realize this, there's no room for questions,
[but] shameless scholars don't realize it.[441] (82)

Living beings who do not change at all:
how can they age or die?
The stainless intelligence taught by the guru
is a treasure of thatness—what other could there be? (83)

The sense domains themselves are completely pure and cannot be taught;
you should take them solely as being empty,[442]
like a raven that flies from a ship,
circles and circles, and lands there again. (84)

Just by seeing a black rope
that [looks] like a snake, [beings] are afraid.
Friends! Even a person who's sublime
can be bound by the flaw of [seeing] double. (85)

Don't be bound by fixation on sense objects!
Hey, you fools! The Archer says,
The fish, the moth, the elephant, the bee, [203]
and the deer: observe what they're like. (86)

Whatever is projected from the mind
is just the nature of the protector.
Do water and waves differ?
Existence and [nirvāṇa] have the same nature as sky.[443] (87)

If you carry out in a sublime [manner] what's been taught,
what you've heard, and what's intended [by the guru],

then stupidity will subside in the heart
like dust motes effaced by sunlight.[444] (88)

Just as when water is poured into water
the [mixture] you get tastes the same as water,
the mind in which flaws and virtues are the same,
will not be seen by anyone, O Protector.
There is no antidote for fools.[445] (89)

Like tongues of flame spreading through a forest,
in an instant turn all appearances that come
before you into the root of mind, emptiness. (90)

If cognition thinks of something pleasant
[and] cherishes it, then it sinks into the heart;[446]
even the pain of [stepping on] a single
sesame husk will never produce such suffering.[447] (91)

It is like that and it is not like that:
my friends, look at the pig and the elephant.[448]
That the wise dissolve error is like the need
for a wish-granting jewel: it's a great wonder!
Your own self-awareness is a habit-form of great bliss.[449] (92)

At that time [everything] is the same as sky.
Is it right to speak of kālakūṭa *poison?*[450]
When cognition apprehends the sky-like inherent nature
and that cognition turns into noncognition,
then the connate nature is utterly beautiful. (93)

In house after house they discuss it,
but abiding great bliss is not really known;[451]

all beings are burdened by anxiety, says the Archer,
and there's no one who realizes the unthinkable. (94)

Since I've given up [discerning such] qualities [as] bliss and secrecy,
I see no difference between meditation and nonmeditation;
others think [to attain it] [204] *through pointing to sense domains,*
[but] thinking of thatness, they have no realization, and their nature[452]
is blocked. (95)

When mind is pointed out by mind,
then conceptuality abides in motionless stability;
just as salt dissolves in water,
so mind dissolves into its inherent nature.
When self and other are seen to be the same,
what use is striving in contemplation? (96)

Within the connate, every scripture is seen,
and the many things you wish for clearly appear.[453] (97)

The protector alone is selfhood; others are in contradiction:
this philosophy is proven in house after house.
When the one is consumed, everything [else] is burned,
yet she goes outside to search for the lord of the house. (98)

She doesn't see him when he comes or goes,
and even if he sits there, she doesn't recognize him;
the supreme lord, which is waveless,
turns into unsullied contemplation.
Let the water and lamp illumine themselves alone.[454] (99)

I don't accept or reject coming or going,
and I meet a sensuous girl I've never [seen] before.[455] (100)

The mind relies on the baseless;[456]
don't view things as different from your own [mind] forms—
that way, you place buddha in your palm,
and when body, speech, and cognition are indivisible,
then your connate nature is beautiful.[457] (101)

[When] the lord of the house has eaten, the lady of the house
enjoys [her meal]:
she should delight in any sense objects she sees.
The children have become quite weary
of the game I have played,
[but] except from that mother, no offspring are born;
the yoginī's[458] conduct is beyond compare.[459] (102)

She's consumed her lord and beautified inherent nature;
that very mind replete with objects of attachment
should let go of attachment and detachment and dwell in the
middle—
when my mind is undermined, I certainly see the yoginī.[460] (103)

When eating and drinking, there's nothing to think. [205]
My lady friend, whatever appears as external
to the mind cannot, I take it, be indicated;
the yoginī of illusion is beyond compare.[461] (104)

And in the triple world, the stainless doesn't emerge or abide:
fire blazes because of its tinder,
a moonstone emits water through no power of its own—
[the yoginī's] methods hold sway in every realm. (105)

Mind-itself is the yoginī, who has accomplished thatness:
know her as pledged to the connate.[462] (106)

Every being is [trapped in] syllables,
and not a one is without syllables,
but when you're without syllables,
it's then that you know syllables.[463] (107)

A calligrapher may not know how to read,
and [brahmins] are undermined by reciting meaningless Vedas;
if you don't know the sublime mind and its opposite,
well, it's that from which [things] rise and where they set. (108)

As it is outside, so it is within:
abiding continuously on the fourteenth level;[464]
the bodiless is hidden within the body:
knowing this, you'll be free. (109)

I recited[465] the first four syllables,[466]
but when I drank elixir, I forgot them;
someone who knows the single syllable[467]
doesn't know its name.[468] (110)

Amid the three forests is a single syllable;
at the center of the three letters is a deity;[469]
someone who has fallen from these three
is like an untouchable [posing as] a Vedic [teacher]. (111)

Those who do not know the nature of everything
but would accomplish great bliss at the time of copulation
are like thirsty [deer] who chase a mirage:
dying of thirst, will they find celestial waters? (112)

{Reflection on aggregates, elements, fields, senses, and objects:
they're just water;
in these new, new dohā verses I speak, there are no secrets.} (112a)

{You scholarly types: be patient with me: here there are no
concepts;
what I've heard the guru say, why should I declare it in secret?}[470]
(112b)

Someone [conjoins] vajra
and lotus and revels in bliss.
Why? [Real bliss] cannot be taught,[471] so
how can they fulfill the hopes of [beings in] the triple world?[472]
(113)

Either the bliss [produced] by [tantric] methods is momentary
or that very [experience] becomes both [method and wisdom];[473]
anyway, [it's attained] through the guru's kindness,
but out of a hundred, only a few know it. (114)

Friends! [206] The profound and the vast
are not separate, nor do they [have] their own nature;[474]
at the time of the fourth joy, the connate,
you know the primordial experience. (115)

Just as the jewellike moon shines
in the great, black darkness [of night],
so supreme great bliss overcomes
every evil notion in a single instant. (116)

When the sun of suffering has set,
the ruler of the stars [the moon] rises along with the planets;

abiding thus, it emanates its emanations—
that is the sublime maṇḍala circle. (117)

Hey, you fools! Examine mind with mind,
and you'll free yourself from every lowly view;
by virtue of your abiding in supreme
great bliss, sublime special attainments [will be yours]. (118)

Let the elephant of mind wander free,
let it inquire into its own nature,
let it drink from the mountain lake
[reflecting] the sky and rest on the shore, enjoying itself. (119)

When picked up by the elephant trunk of sense objects,
he seems on the verge of being overpowered and killed,
but the yogin, like the elephant keeper,
will reverse that very situation.[475] (120)

Someone who's certain that saṃsāra is nirvāṇa
does not think they belong to separate categories;
in this single inherent nature, categories are completely
abandoned—
I've clearly realized the stainless. (121)

The very cognition of a referent
is empty of referents;
since duality is faulty,
no yogin meditates upon it. (122)

There is no difference between meditation with a referent
and without a referent, or between meditation and nonmeditation—
by nature, they're aspects of bliss;

the utterly unsurpassed arises on its own—
it's known through reliance on the guru's timely methods. (123)

Not going to the forest, not sitting at home,
when cognition knows [thatness] wherever you are,[476]
then everything abides forever in eternal [207] awakening,
so what is saṃsāra, what is nirvāṇa? (124)

Cognition purified of stains is the connate:
at that time, no discordant factors can enter in;
it's like on a limpid lake:
the foam is itself water and into [water] dissolves. (125)

Awakening's not in the forest and not at home:
thus, thoroughly knowing distinctions,
you should stabilize everything in nonconceptuality,
through the inherent nature of stainless mind. (126)

That is self, and this, therefore, is other:
those who distinguish deep meditation from some
[object of] meditation must free [themselves] from bondage to that;
indeed, their own nature is completely free.[477] (127)

Don't be in error about self and other:
everyone is always buddha;
since mind is essentially pure,[478]
it is itself the stainless supreme stage. (128)

[Fruition]

The sublime tree of nondual mind
grows over everything in the triple world;

flowers of compassion bear the fruit of benefiting others,
and its name is Supreme Benefit to Others.[479] (129)

The sublime tree of emptiness sends forth flowers,
which are the many varieties of sublime compassion;
its eventual fruit is spontaneously accomplished:
this bliss is not just another mind state.[480] (130)

The sublime tree of emptiness lacks compassion:
it has no roots or flowers or leaves,
[but] anyone who turns [emptiness] into a referent
will fall down and break[481] their limbs.[482] (131)

Two trees are within a single seed,
and that's why the fruit is one;
anyone who thinks them indivisible
is free from saṃsāra and nirvāṇa. (132)

When a needy person comes around
and leaves with their hopes unfulfilled,
they'll pick up a clay cup tossed out the door—
better they should toss out the householder and take up residence.[483]
(133)

Not working to benefit [208] others,
not bestowing gifts on the needy:
this, alas, is the fruit of saṃsāra—
better you should toss out selfhood. (134)

This completes the Dohā Treasury, *the syllables of ultimacy that genuinely point to suchness; it was composed orally by the lord of yogins, the glorious Saraha.*

CHAPTER 7

The Inexhaustible Treasury

A Song of Instruction (Queen Dohā)

[1020] In the Indian language: *Dohakoṣopadeśagīti-nāma*; in the Tibetan language: *Mi zad pa'i gter mdzod man ngag gi glu zhes bya ba* (*Btsun mo do ha*).[484]

I prostrate to the ever-youthful Mañjuśrī.

[1. The Natural State]

Amazing, the secret language of ḍākinīs!

Bowing with folded hands before the bodhisattva,
the blissful protector whose nature is Buddha,
Dharma, and Saṅgha, I will explain
the state of naturally nondual mahāmudrā. (1)

Samsaric beings are entwined like trees by vines,
and thirst in the miserable desert of grasping at self;
like a young prince, stateless and apart from [his father],
they have no occasion for bliss, their minds in agony. (2)

"The gnosis of thusness won't come through examination;
it's free from deeds and accumulates no karma."

When Saraha, who knows for himself, declares this,
then all the scholars' hearts [1021] are full of poison. (3)

The meaning of genuine mind-itself is hard for all to
    comprehend;
it's the stainless essence, uncovered by extremes.
Don't examine primordial nature from every angle;
if you examine [thus], you're snakebit—enough said. (4)

All dharmas posited by thought are empty on their own;
they're free from conditions, so none exists as we conceive.
When you know their thusness, their natural state of release,
there is no seeing or hearing, so there is no discord. (5)

All who conceive of "things" are said to be like cattle;
those who conceive of "no-things" are more foolish still—
while those who exemplify these as the lighting and dousing of a
    lamp
abide in mahāmudrā, the nondual inherent nature. (6)

What arises as a thing comes to rest in no-thing,
and [for] the sage free from either position,
[even] when examining the notions of fools,
there is instant freedom, described as the reality body. (7)

The childish say, "There's a level of great bliss apart
from that freedom"—but that's the same as water in a mirage;
inquire into concepts, which are just this primordial gnosis,
where all grounds, paths, and buddhas have a single taste. (8)

A person who realizes this is unbound;
without shaking off dust, they're not dusty in the least.

Where's the line between defilement and its cure?
The individual who tries [to find it] is bound to saṃsāra. (9)

Earth, water, fire, wind, and space
don't exist apart from the connate's single taste.
Not conceiving existence and nirvāṇa as two—
this, it's explained, is the abiding nature, the reality sphere. (10)

[2. Pitfalls]

Amazing, the secret language of ḍākinīs!

Alas! Look at how thatness points to itself: [1022]
you have to look with undistracted mind. If you don't,
your distracted mind won't realize thatness,
and you'll lose the jewel of thatness amid the thicket of things. (11)

Alas! Don't be attached to things you desire:
when cognition's attached to an object of desire,
it's an illness afflicting the supreme mind of great bliss,
a blow to the stainless mind by the sword of desire. (12)

Alas! Don't look at cause and result as two:
there is no cause for a thing to arise, nor any result;
if the yogin's mind is deranged by the poison of hope and fear,
then the abiding connate gnosis will be bound. (13)

Alas! Don't say that thatness lacking inherent nature exists in
meditation:
if meditated and meditator are conceived of as two,
then conceptuality apprehending duality abandons bodhicitta—
such people have sinned against themselves. (14)

Alas! Those preparing for certain knowledge should partake
as much as they can of nectar drops from the guru's mouth;
when those who know the time and means serve in an untimely way,
they're like the blind [trying to] rob the royal coffers. (15)

Alas! People deprived of the precious consecrations
are like lowly śūdras aspiring to be king;
deceived about the tantras of awareness bearers,
they're condemned by ḍākas and fall to vajra hell. (16)

Alas! Having learned the supreme meaning from virtuous friends
but not holding it sublime, utterly rejecting it with debased mind,
you're like a person suffering from cataracts who gets haughty:
throughout a great eon you'll bring yourself nothing but pain. (17)

Alas! If you come to the level of stability but don't keep your vows,
you're like a person condemned by the king and held: [1023]
your life breath held by the iron hooks of ripening [acts],
molten metal poured into your mouth—it's unbearable! (18)

Alas! If you realize the abiding nature but your conduct's debased,
you're like a king who's deposed from the throne and made a sweeper;
spurning inexhaustible great bliss itself,
you're bound by the very touch of samsaric pleasures. (19)

Alas! Yogins who've seen their own mind
without complication but strive to complicate

are like [people] who obtain a jewel but search for trinkets:
try though they might, they never [reach] the essential place. (20)

[3. Contemplation]

Amazing, the secret language of ḍākinīs!

Holding bodhicitta and realizing bodhicitta—
gnosis with effort and effortless [gnosis]—
arise from the nectar-like word of the sublime one
and shine in between the sun and moon. (21)

From the nose tip[485] of a trustworthy male and from
a qualified mudrā emerges a unified mind:
through that, form and other qualities of things change color;
this is to be known through a pacifying[486] pith-instruction. (22)

Seeing luminous reality with certainty,
you'll realize fully the time and means of serving the guru;
it's attained through the Perfection of Wisdom and other sūtras—
meditate clearly with the mind that enters everything. (23)

The mind that can't be viewed as outside or in
cannot be conceived by anyone, for there is no mind.
I lift this song to the vajra peak of eternal abiding nature:
meditate on bliss as akin to an aimless river. (24)

The mind swayed by complication amid gathered crowds:
its inherent nature is stable, it doesn't project or engage;
release the essence of mind [1024] to do what it will:
mind like that of a drunkard who's free from deeds. (25)

Meditate on gnosis uncovered by extremes;
mind without meditation or meditation object is without inherent nature.
The utmost, beyond hope and fear, is the vajra mind:
even if it goes to hell, it does not suffer. (26)

Even if it abides in the supreme result, there's nothing more to gain.
So, spurning the help and harm brought on by pleasure and pain,
through good conduct or bad it does not wax or wane:
this gnostic realization without duality is all there is. (27)

If you claim that Buddha is great, know you're a fool;
when actionless conceptuality seeks nothing at all,
there's no need to seek for virtue, for in [mind] there's no disharmony:
there's no attaining thatness through any tantra or treatise. (28)

Mind without attachment or aversion is free from the stain of causes;
experiencing great gnosis itself, which looks at nothing,
the yogin who pacifies samsaric poisons—
whether [straight] like a monk or [bent] like a bow—holds sway in every realm. (29)

The yogin who does not close their eyes or meditate
should [go] to distant places and unpeopled spots,
and, with unstained notions free from attachment or anger,
meditate on the nature of ultimate mind. (30)

[4. Encounter]

Amazing, the secret language of ḍākinīs!

Devoid of maṇḍalas or fire offerings,
free from mantras, seals, or consecrations,
it can't be accomplished through any tantra or treatise:
this vajra gnosis is beautiful in its abiding nature. (31)

The supreme precious symbol brings understanding by itself alone:
it's like a snake in a basket, beautiful to none but [its owner].
Pointing out essence by way of essence, the pure supreme guru
points others toward realization [1025], and thereby points to
himself. (32)

It's fine to be able to engage with sounds and such that link
the three drops—powerful like sky, a jewel,
and the sun—with concepts, recollection, and nonrecollection;
all dharmas take on the same taste, as if turned to gold by an
elixir. (33)

When you train on the path, primordial gnosis is your sole
concern;
the one who shows that path by symbols is the pure supreme
guru.
Rely on form, sound, smell, taste, touch, and dharmas:
all dharmas are unconditioned and nonarising. (34)

The fortunate are wise to nonarising
and so perforce are wise to everything born.
Undifferentiated gnosis is the sole singularity;
the naturally settled mind pervades itself. (35)

Knowing the single nature of the appearing self and other,
hold tightly without distraction to thatness alone;
[since grasping] itself is a sickness of mind, relinquish it,
and when you fixate on nothing, you'll take up bliss. (36)

Mind is devoid of all harmful actions;
it's not covered up by deeds like getting or taking.
Free from effort, without the conditions for temporary events,
this seal of manifold appearances is a grand spectacle. (37)

When you see everything up close at the sublime one's timely
[prompt],
there is no dharma that's not the guru;
a finger pointing to the sky doesn't see sky;
so it is with the guru pointed out by the guru. (38)

The unconventional yogin whose mind [roams] the town
enters the royal palace and flirts with the women;
as one who's eaten leftovers recognizes leftovers,
he's aware that all sense objects are thusness. (39)

In the place fully laid out for a ritual feast,
he sees great bliss [1026] during copulation;
the yogin possessing symbols and vows
[understands] well that existence and peace are the same:
mahāmudrā. (40)

[5. Connection]

Amazing, the secret language of ḍākinīs!

The yogin in whom gnosis has arisen is fearless,
so with potent methods, he should enter a low-caste town
and search for an outcaste [woman]; the one he selects
will little by little beguile him and grant him great [bliss]. (41)

As much as he can, he should give her things that betoken
reverence, with a mind lacking [notions of] "mine."
Wandering everywhere, he should examine [women's] qualities
and gradually come to know them by caste, by color—by their
collection of qualities. (42)

His very own daughter, sister, or niece,
a nymphet, a laundress, a harlot, or picker of rags,
women black, white, red, yellow, or dark maroon;
and women with moles: these are mudrās for easy connection. (43)

Sixteen years old, very beautiful, golden haired,
redolent of blue lotus, breasts firm and strong, slim waisted,
wide hipped, vulva folded in and lustrous with passion:
with her left-handed ways, she applies herself eagerly to her
secret abilities. (44)

Trusting, steadfast, little given to concepts:
the mudrā with these three signs should be ripened by consecration;
apprehending her qualities, [the yogin] should grant her gnostic
awareness,
and right then take hold of the primordial-gnosis seal where all
tastes the same. (45)

The mahāmudrā who concentrates queenly fluids:
when [the yogin's] collected them [from her] at the proper time,
he dissolves into nonconceptual sky.
Sometimes he frequents the bazaar and observes the true
as it truly is, letting truth play out on its own. (46)

Sometimes he enters the cremation ground, and practices the [five] lamps,[487]
and sleeps with a carefree mind in ghost-haunted places;
he makes friends with outcastes, [1027] and draws the corpse cart along.
"This is forbidden conduct"—he's not to be held to that standard. (47)

He joins in musical gatherings, amusing himself with song, dance, and flute;
he should never tire in the least of uplifting his mind
through the dance of Heruka and songs sung by the six [yoginīs][488] and others.
He should cover his back and adorn his limbs with copper. (48)

He should bind his [hair] atop his head in a circular topknot,
and ornament all his limbs with pieces of bone,
then wrap [his torso] with elephant hide on top and tiger skin below,
and wield in his hands a khaṭvāṅga and bell. (49)

Behaving like a crazed elephant and acting like a fool,
behaving without regard for dos and don'ts, like an elephant
plunging on impulse into a pond: his mind ever crazed,
he performs the basest of deeds yet is free, says Saraha. (50)

[6. Commitment]

Amazing, the secret language of ḍākinīs!

The one who shows all the manifold dharmas
to be of a single taste is just the sublime guru;
that supreme sublime lord, who [extracts essence] like a swan
with its bill,
should with reverent mind be raised to the pure place at your
crown. (51)

Unified mind: it's the guru who points it out,
and the place where it's shown is the student's very heart;
through realization of that, the kindly hero
destroys all sufferings in a single instant. (52)

Observe this fact, and acknowledge [the guru's] kindness
by constantly revering that kingly physician;
he, and he alone, is the supreme ship
that frees us from saṃsāra's deep, vast sea. (53)

So, trust that sublime vessel, and honor unflinchingly in every
way
that most powerful friend who's attained great bliss;
by the pure light-rays of his sunlike gnosis
that supreme person turns ignorance into awareness. (54)

Always serve the wheel-turning king who's skilled in the methods
of changing all dharmas to bliss, as elixir [1028] turns [metals] to
gold;
the mind, like a river, submerges dualistic views,
possessing gnosis, spurning nothing, and not covered up. (55)

Uncontrived thought and transformed thought
emerge from the sublime guru's nectar-like word;
"mind" and "mental events": these conventionally
labeled [distinctions] are transformed. (56)

They [become] the yogin's friends through the guru's lotus word:
through it, all [things] are transformed into spiritual friends;
hidden in every tantra, apart from convention,
the secrets of the buddhas are known to none. (57)

Suffused with the taste of consecration and seeing with the eye of
instruction,
when you touch the dust of the [guru's] feet, knowledge[489]
becomes awareness.
Shoot the arrow of the empty at manifold relative things,
and induce [the ultimate] experience by means of empty
appearance. (58)

And, with discerning wisdom, see appearances as they should be
seen.
The source of that wisdom is the master, unsurpassed and pure,
through whom all defilements become supreme,
and no concept[-born] pain can change them back. (59)

[Gnosis] surely emerges from essential pith-instructions,
and surely is attained through that sublime lord's power;
therefore, any [guru] who is blessed to possess the transmission
should always be served with respect by those wise to time,
means, and service. (60)

[7. Fruition]

Amazing, the secret language of ḍākinīs!

Realizing the natural sameness of wisdom and means,
you'll attain the connate through luminous mind;
it emerges by increasing like a waxing moon,
and it's enjoyed like rice irradiated by the sun and moon. (61)

The root of every special attainment is the [1029] vajra master,
the perfectly purified cause who himself embodies all results;
in order that [we] act in accord with the Sugata's words,
the bodhisattva, the blissful protector, has spoken well. (62)

The reality body, complete enjoyment-body, and emanation body,
as well as the essence body, are clearly known through cause and
result;
nonduality empty of exaggeration and deprecation is the reality
[body],
its essential bliss is the great enjoyment [body]. (63)

Its various [appearances] to beings are the emanation [body],
and nondual gnosis is the [essential] self of them all.
The nature of the creature and creator is inconceivable,
but the power of developing [mind] suppresses all fear. (64)

The results are two: fulfilling the aims of oneself and of others.
Though labeled as cause or result, [the bodies] are essentially
indivisible:
the twofold form-body emerges by virtue of prayer and
compassion,
like a fine vase, a wish-granting tree, or a precious jewel. (65)

The inapprehensible body is utterly beautiful;
it appears for disciples in various forms,
all of them unthinkable emanations.
Whoever contemplates the nonconceptual, self-emergent gnosis
will contemplate each and every result.
[As for] this path that's the essence of the unsurpassed Great Vehicle:
carrying the result onto the path, abide in the result from the start.
The completion of others' aims is the supreme result. (66–67)

It emerges mainly through purification and other [practices].
The great release, where action has been purified, surely is gained
through the power of an uninterrupted mind that's without hope.
When in some precious person this divine substance arises,
each and every evil is instantly quelled and dissolved,
and lions, crazed elephants, [1030] tigers, and she-bears,
wild beasts, venomous snakes, fire, and ravines,
royal punishment, poison, and thunder and lightning—
all are [seen to be] the essential [body], hence do no harm.
When you destroy the great enemy—conceptuality—you destroy all enemies.
Suppressing the evil of self-view, you suppress all evils,
so sanctify this jewel that is your mind. (67–70)

[8. Instruction]

Amazing, the secret language of ḍākinīs!

A person who knows the secret of body, speech,
and mind is someone without the toxin of stupidity,

while [for] someone who dualistically thinks of actions in terms
of virtue and vice,
whatever they try to do, it's explained, is conjoined with evil. (71)

People behaving that way only bind themselves,
and sick from incessant longing, plunge into saṃsāra.
With logic [you get] what you do not need and deplete what
sufficed before;
[when you] imagine something, the images block you from
liberation. (72)

Even the concept of "the good" is a sickness plunging you into
saṃsāra,
and when you label an act as evil, its result still can't be
interrupted.
The mind that does not label abides like sky,
and nonabiding sky itself is free from conventions. (73)

The free mind settles into its own nature,
which requires no labels or analysis: it is just as it is;
the result is unhindered and exists on its own from the start,
so you needn't be bound to antidotes for your hopes and fears. (74)

And so not a single symbol or convention that you label
is correct, for what is [correct] is [only] in the domain of the wise.
Indivisible cause and result—this is essential mind:
when trying to experience it, you need not search all around. (75)

Serving the sublime one, listening to them, and applying what
you've heard;
obtaining blessings [because] "virtues arise from consecration";
[1031]

resting conceptuality in concentration, then [engaging in]
application and meditation
after gaining certainty about the benefits [of practice]; behaving
unconventionally—
all of them are practices based on contrivances and wrong ideas.
The essential is free from virtues and flaws,
truth requires no deeds at all,
while the mind that's done with deeds is great bliss itself. (76–77)

Those obsessed with the five sciences[490] and such are in a demon's
grasp,
their minds suffused with the poison of grasping at things;
[the yogin] whose mind spurns externals and settles within
and hews to the essential should reflect on this very point. (78)

[Tired of] the husk of logical complication and clearing it away,
realizing this unsurpassable true essence that arises
from [focusing one's] faculties on the primordial
truth, you'll abide on the fourteenth ground.[491] (79)

Yogins desiring great gnosis
may proceed by stages or instantaneously;
set on the essential stage, that of gnosis,
they must win mahāmudrā for beings. (80)

This completes the Dohā Treasury That Establishes the Unsurpassed Essence, *which was composed by the lord of yogins, the glorious Saraha.*

CHAPTER 8

Dohā Treasury

A Performance Song (King Dohā)

[1013] In the Indian language: *Dohakoṣa-nāma-caryāgīti*; in the Tibetan language: *Do ha mdzod ces bya ba spyod pa'i glu.*[492]

I bow down to Ārya Mañjuśrī.
I bow down to one who has utterly destroyed the power of Māra.

Just as motionless water turns
to waves when moved by surging winds,
so the king sees Saraha appearing
in various guises, although he is one. (1)

Just as fools, viewing things topsy-turvy,
see a single lamp as two,
so—alas!—they see thought, where viewer
and viewed are not-two, to be two things. (2)

Though multiple lamps may blaze throughout a house,
the sightless dwell in darkness; just so,
though the connate is all-pervasive
and near, to fools it's very far away. (3)

Though rivers may vary, in the sea they are one;
though falsehoods are many, they're destroyed by a single truth;
though shades of darkness are many, they're destroyed
when the [1014] single sun appears. (4)

It's just as clouds absorb water
from the sea and then fill the earth with rain,
yet the sea, as limitless as sky, does not diminish:
it doesn't increase or decrease. (5)

The inherent nature itself, spontaneous accomplishment
replete with the conquerors' fulfillment:
through it, beings arise and cease,
although within it there is no thing nor nonthing. (6)

Rejecting sublime bliss, they wander elsewhere,
pinning their hopes on conditioned bliss;
the honey within their mouths, so near,
will be far away if they do not drink it up. (7)

Beasts don't comprehend what suffering is;
by contrast, the wise here comprehend
suffering and drink the nectar of sky,
while others are attached to sensuous things. (8)

Insects in excrement are attached to the smell
and consider pure sandalwood foul;
likewise, those who reject nirvāṇa
are attached to the miasma at the source of existence. (9)

Just as an ox's footprint filled
with water will in time dry up, so

in a stable mind whose fulfillment is unfulfilled,
fulfillment eventually will dry up. (10)

Just as salty seawater
drunk up by the clouds turns sweet,
the stable mind works for the aims of others
and turns even the poison of sense objects into nectar. (11)

Although it can't be expressed, it has no suffering;
although it can't be contemplated, it's the bliss of thatness—
just as when, although thunder terrifies us,
the rainfall will ripen our crops. (12)

It is not first or last or otherwise,
it does not abide in beginning, middle, or end;
for one whose cognition [1015] is thoroughly fooled by concepts,
emptiness and compassion are expressed in words. (13)

Just as honey dwells within a flower
and the bees come to know this,
[the wise] do not reject existence or nirvāṇa—
how will fools ever understand? (14)

Just as a form on a mirror's surface
is foolishly seen [as real] by fools,
just so, the mind that denies the truth
mostly relies on what is not true. (15)

Although the scent of a flower is formless,
it's perceptible and all-pervasive;
likewise, through the formless inherent nature
you will come to know the maṇḍala circle. (16)

When [winter] winds lash and roil the waters,
it's as if water, although soft, turns to stone;
when fools are disturbed by concepts, what's formless
becomes very solid and hard. (17)

When confusion is manifest, gnosis can't manifest;
when confusion is manifest, suffering manifests.
Just so, a shoot emerges from a seed,
and leaves emerge from their cause, the shoot. (19)

If you examine whether mind is one or many,
you give up clarity and tumble into existence;
seeing in this way, you tumble into a hole—
what could be more pitiful than that? (20)

Wholly attached to the pleasure of kissing,
fools say, "This is the ultimate";
emerging from the house, outside the door,
they ask for news of sensuous forms.[493] (21)

Because the vital winds move in the empty house [of the body],
[people] contrive in multiple ways;
through torment that comes with having faults,
the yogin falls from the sky [1016] and into a swoon. (22)

As brahmins pour offerings
of ghee and rice into the blazing fire,
they fixate on [the bliss] produced by distilling
the substance of sky, and say, "This is thatness." (23)

Some, who have raised the light to their crown,
enjoy stroking the uvula with their tongues;

this binds them and churns them up,
yet they arrogantly assert, "We are yogins." (24)

Their own awareness they teach to others as awareness of thatness;
saying, "Whatever binds you is itself freedom;"
fools, who don't know how to appraise a jewel,
discern the color [green] and call a trinket an emerald. (25)

They assume that brass is actually gold:
carried away by experiences, they think they've achieved the ultimate;
attached to the bliss found in dreams,
they say of the impermanent aggregates, "They're permanent bliss." (26)

They [think] they've understood the syllables *e* and *vaṃ*, and
distinguishing the [four] moments, they set forth the four seals;[494]
they claim that spontaneous accomplishment arises from experiences,
but this is like fixating on a mirror's reflection. (27)

Just as deer under the power of error will run
uncomprehending toward the water of a mirage,
so fools cannot slake their thirst and are bound,
saying that whatever is, is the ultimate—and taking it for bliss. (28)

There is relative truth [and also] the mind
that does not cognize and turns into nonmind;
My friends, you must come to know supreme holiness,
that transformation supreme among the supreme. (29)

The nonrecollecting mind enters concentration—
it is utterly purified of defilement.
Just as a mud-born [lotus] is not covered by mud, likewise
the conqueror's qualities are uncovered by worldly faults. (30)

Also, all things must certainly be viewed as deceptions;
transcending the world, seize the moment and practice
equanimity;
[while] those with dogmatic thoughts are bound, [1017]
the self-originated, unthinkable nature abides. (31)

Appearances, clear from the very first, are nonarising, while
inherent nature is formless, bereft of distinctive forms:
abide continuously in thatness and practice only that
contemplation—
this cognitive disengagement and stainless contemplation are
no-mind. (32)

Thought, mind, and mental appearances have that very nature,
the world and what seems other[worldly] have that very nature,
all the various visible things and acts of seeing have that very
nature,
attachment, anger, confusion, and even bodhicitta have that very
nature. (33)

A lamp blazes in the darkness of confusion;
as long as someone categorizes
through thought, they will not give up the mental
stains—they should think on the nature of nonfixation. (34)

It cannot be refuted, it cannot be proved,
it cannot be grasped, it cannot be conceived;

fools are bound by the categories of thought,
while the indivisible connate is utterly pure. (35)

Examination in terms of the one or the many [yields] no oneness:
just by knowing [this], beings are completely freed;
knowing [your own basic] clarity, meditate stably upon it—
the unmoving mind is held there as your very nature. (36)

Reaching the land of expansive joy,
the seeing mind expands,
and is thereby useful for this and that:[495]
even when pursuing sensuous things, it doesn't differ. (37)

Joy gives rise to the shoots
of bliss and the leaves of supreme [emanation];
when it doesn't diffuse in the ten directions,
uncomplicated bliss is the fruit itself. (38)

The why, where, and what do not exist,
so they are useful for this or for that;
the very forms to which we are deeply attached—
or are unattached—are emptiness. (39)

[If I am] like a pig obsessed with worldly muck,
what fault can there be in a mind become stainless?
How can someone who's not covered
by something be bound by it? (40)

This completes the Dohā Treasury: A Performance Song, [1018] *composed orally by the glorious Saraha, lord of yogins.*

CHAPTER 9

Stages of Self-Blessing

[1276] In the Indian language: *Svādhiṣṭhānakrama*; in the Tibetan language: *Rang byin gyis brlab pa'i rim pa*.[496]

I bow down to the glorious Vajrasattva.

Lord of illusory emanations who specially teaches about self-blessing
and fully savors, to the utmost, his play with the glorious Vajralāsyā:
since anyone's praise even of one such as Vajrāmṛta Śrī is
naturally in error,
how can I express it? Who else is there? I bow down fully to the
Blessed One. (1)

To the one who alone [possesses] the beautified body of the
conqueror [residing] in Abhirati [Akṣobhya],
to the one, unchanging, who rouses from sleep the hearts of the
wise,
to the one who [regards] appearances equably and [makes] the
senses
and their objects disappear—I bow down. (2)

To the one wielding the complex vajra weapon of the glorious
blissful inherent nature,
to the one who, bedecked with the uncomplicated stainless
natural wisdom, is all- [1277] pervasive,

to the one who, like a wish-fulfilling willow cane, cuts the net of defilements in the three abodes,
to the glorious queen marked [by] vajra words—I bow down in every way. (3)

Completely mindful of the Goddess of Vajra Limbs (Vajrāṅginī),
who blissfully goes to the sole place where bliss is free from defilement,
with my neck bent down under the heavy load of unbreakable devotion,
to the dust of her lotus feet I bow the crown of my head. (4)

To the very one who himself is embellished by rays of kindness,
who destroys the mass of darkness through encircling, jeweled light,
who sees himself at play [from] afar with his unsullied eye—
to Guru Vairocana, I perfectly prostrate. (5)

To the one who, the concordant causes having befallen, dwells joyously on the riverbank between becoming and peace,
to the glorious triple guru whose mind expands through the sky-river of gnosis,
to the glorious Vajralāsyā and the assembly of consorts, whose nature is Prajñāpāramitā,
to the sublime mind of the sublime lord who alone is the teacher of the three abodes—I go for refuge. (6)

To the one whose mind is settled in the domain of sameness and who, like a naturally powerful
mantra, makes a show of extracting the poisonous juice of saṃsāra,

to the one whose ground is not the ground of senses or thoughts,
and who has cleansed the stench
from the hut of the three kinds of beings—to the sublime speech
of the sole guru, I bow down. (7)

To the one who dwells perfectly in recollection, and who,
applying the guru's
oral teaching to freeing the breath and [undoing] the knots at the
heart-lotus,
destroys the darkness in the hut of the three abodes like the light
of the noon sun
and counteracts foolishness—I, intent on discipline, bow down.
(8)

By[497] even the slightest recollection of the dust of the guru's
feet,
the glorious one, completely accomplished in projecting [1278]
good qualities,
will, if [spiritually] accomplished, turn what is by nature
unpleasant
into supreme bliss—there is nothing to be accomplished apart
from that. (9)

I, who worship the dust of the guru's feet, [if I] have not wearied
of the mass of arrow-like pains of aging, sickness, death, and
various [other] sufferings,
will be unable to apportion to embodied beings the nectar of
gnosis
and will be greatly sorrowful, regardless of what I do. (10)

What's not in the domain of thought is not in the domain of
anyone;
the stages of the basic instruction taught by the guru are long,
and through those stages compassion and other pure virtues
themselves arise in the heart dwellings of the faithful. (11)

All these entities are one,
and the nature of the many is partless;
by freedom from indulging in fixation,
the yoga of effort will be manifest. (12)

My eyes full of joyous tears as my hair
stands on end, my eyelashes moist,
bowing beneath the burden of greatly firm devotion—
to the sublime, wish-fulfilling guru, I prostrate. (13)

First lightly placing my hands at my crown,
joyously joining hands together [as if] holding a jewel,
then threading mind-made flowers with perfect devotion,
I say, "Please put on this garland that I have knotted and strung
together." (14)

O Protector, the wisdom briefly summarized in the key points of
your word
exerts control like a skillful princess;
the blissful savor of the inherent nature of beings—
that experience alone is a meritorious mind. (15)

Moist with youthful compassion, you teach the path without
precedent,
[saying,] "There are no beings to be led nor any beings." O great
wonder!

Just stepping onto [the path], we'll [experience] continuous,
matchless bliss
and see then that there is not the slightest difference between
existence [1279] and peace. (16)

This completes the Stages of Self-Blessing, *composed by the lord of yoga, glorious Saraha the Great.*

CHAPTER 10

Excerpts from *The Gnostic: A Commentary on the "Buddhakapāla Tantra"*

[1145] In the Indian language: *Śrībuddhakapālatantrasya pañjikājñānavatī-nāma*; in the Tibetan language: *Dpal sangs rgyas thod pa'i rgyud kyi dka' 'grel ye shes ldan pa zhes bya ba.*[498]

I bow down to glorious Heruka.

To her [whose state] is to be accomplished, whose subtle form,
emerging from supreme bliss, bestows the sixteen joys,[499]
[who] knows completely the sounds on the drops in front and
within, [who is] the true nature of the mind,
[who is] the basis of one's own joy, and [who possesses] the
essential requisites for awakening, the collection of good
qualities of the form [body],
[who knows] the nature of entities and nonentities, [and imparts]
the various classes [of teachings] that clear away fear of
existence—to her I bow down.

[Here,] I will explain a little
how the gurus explain
and how other tantras see

the *Buddhakapāla Tantra*,
which is explained by various classes [of teachings].

With regard to that, for now I will teach (1) the expresser, (2) the expressed, (3) the purpose, and (4) the special purpose. (1) The expresser is the tantra; (2) the expressed is the meaning of the tantra; [1146] (3) the purpose is manifesting deity yoga; and (4) the special purpose is performing deeds on behalf of sentient beings.

[Buddha] enters into the form of the Blessed One himself and other teachers, and [here] teaches in the form of the Blessed Lady, [who symbolizes] self-nature. [The teaching] was heard from the Blessed Lady by Vajrapāṇi. [1146: 5]

[5b7] *This speech was heard by me thusly at one time.*

[1146: 5] Saying the phrase "this speech" with reference to the tantra collection that [the Buddha] has explained [refers to] effecting the collection [of the tantra]. "Heard" means whatever has been heard from the Blessed One, in every detail. As to "by me thusly" [S. *evaṃ mayā*]: *e* refers to earth, which is of the nature of Locanā; *vaṃ* refers to water, which is of the nature of Māmakī; *ma* refers to fire, which is of the nature of Pāṇḍaravāsinī; and *yā* refers to wind, which is of the nature of Tārā. These four syllables are properly explained to be the four seals: when beings are sealed by the nature of emptiness, those are the seals. The phrase "was heard by me" does not refer to hearing by way of ear consciousness. What, then? [It refers to hearing] at a single time. As to "at one time": Time has three aspects: the time of bliss, the time of suffering, and pervasive inconceivable time itself. [When] the winds enter [the central channel] is the time of bliss; [when] the winds emerge [into the world] is the time of suffering, and the nature pervading the nonduality of these is pervasive inconceivable time. [1146: 16]

[5b7] *The Blessed One dwelled at the center of the ornate great maṇḍala of the vajra body, speech, and mind of all the tathāgatas, together with all the tathāgatas and [many] yoginīs. He also dwelled together with the chief [arhats] who were free from passion, [such as] Ārya Ānanda and others; and tens of thousands of billions of bodhisattvas, [such as] Ārya Avalokiteśvara and others.*

[1146: 16] As to "the Blessed One" (S. *Bhagavan*; T. *Chomdendé*): he is "blessed" on account of his fulfillment of good fortune (S. *bhaga*); he also blessed on account of his conquest (T. *chom*) of the four māras. It is in this sense that he is said to be "the Blessed One."

As to "the vajra body, speech, and mind of all the tathāgatas": [1147] since it refers to "all" and refers to "tathāgatas," it is "all the tathāgatas." Their vajra body, speech, and mind is *vajra* because its cuts down the mountain of unknowing. Unknowing is lack of knowledge about the aggregates, sense fields, and sense spheres, which is synonymous with "knowledge obscurations." "Vajra" is nondual gnosis, which is synonymous with "form of wisdom."

As to "at the center of the ornate great maṇḍala": it is "an ornate great maṇḍala" because it is great and it is also ornate, and [because] it is a maṇḍala (T. *kyilkor*: "center-circle"). "Center" means essence; "circle" means taking that up, so it's said to be "taking up the essence." This should be applied to the explanation to the effect that the Blessed One first attained final nirvāṇa at the center of that [maṇḍala]. Why specifically should this be so? "All tathāgatas" refers to Vairocana and the other [four] of the five buddhas, who are the [purified] nature of the five aggregates. "Yoginīs" refers to Yamadaṃṣṭrī and the other [goddesses of the maṇḍala]. "Dwelled" is synonymous with "adorned by those" [tathāgatas and yoginīs].

That abode is said to be circular, because the Blessed One is said to be surrounded [there] by Ārya Ānanda and other members of the saṅgha who are free from passion. And not solely "those free from passion"; saying "Ārya Avalokiteśvara and others" is synonymous with saying "completely surrounded by Ārya Avalokiteśvara and other great bodhisattvas." The expression "he dwelled together with tens of thousands of billions of bodhisattvas" is synonymous with "enumerating eighty [1148] thousand billion." Those persons who strive [in the manner] of bodhisattvas are bodhisattvas. "Dwelled together with" is synonymous with "dwelled together with bodhisattvas at the center of that maṇḍala." [1148: 4]

[6a3] *Then, having properly explained all the tantras and mantras with vajra words at that great vajra site, the Blessed One, the lord of all the tathāgatas, perfectly joined his vajra with his [consort's] lotus and attained final nirvāṇa within the queen's vagina. Having witnessed this final nirvāṇa, all the bodhisattvas and all the yoginīs were astonished, and looking at one another, [thought,] "Oh, my, how is it that the Blessed One, the lord of all the tathāgatas, has attained final nirvāṇa at the center of this ornate great maṇḍala?"* [6a7]

[1148: 4] How did the Blessed One attain final nirvāṇa? "Then" [S. *atha*] means "right afterward." *A* is the form of a drop; *tha* is the tathāgata at whose heart the drop resides. It is with the distinctive true nature of [the Blessed One] in mind that it says "with vajra words." "Vajra" is the essence of the nondual wisdom gnosis that abides in the emanated circle; "words" refers to the natural methods for residing in the Dharma wheel. The natural nonduality of these is the Blessed One.

"At that great vajra site" refers to the site at the level of great Vajradhara: the dharma [or heart] cakra and the emanation [or navel] cakra taken together. Why, specifically, is that so? It's [because] it is said that [the Buddha] "properly explained all the tantras and mantras." The phrase "all the tantras" includes the *Guhyasamāja* and others; "mantras" refers to *a*, *hūṃ*, and others. "Properly explained [those]... at that site" is synonymous with "great bliss." It is specifically with the Blessed One's dissolution in mind that it says, "the lord of all the tathāgatas"—that is, Vajradhara. Thus, it is said that the level of great Vajradhara, glorious lord of all the buddhas, emerges from the method of all the buddhas, which is the real nature of all dharmas—and that is synonymous with "producing all the buddhas." [1149]

"Perfectly joined his vajra with his [consort's] lotus" refers to the perfect bliss [experienced] through the joining that is the vajra's penetration of the lotus. "Within the queen's vagina" refers to the vaginas of Yamadaṃṣṭrī and the other [maṇḍala goddesses].

"Final nirvāṇa" is synonymous with the bodhicitta's dissolution into form. "Final" means in all ways; "nirvāṇa" means emergence from conceptuality, which is synonymous with the nature of the reality body. "Having witnessed this final nirvāṇa" means having seen the reality body. As to "all the bodhisattvas": there are the bodhisattvas, and all of them are [present], so all the bodhisattvas are the eyes and the other senses. "All the yoginīs" refers to conjoining the self-natures of method and wisdom; it is synonymous with the defining characteristics of the wisdom [realizing] the absence of inherent nature and [the defining characteristics] of skillful means. Who are they? The yoginīs are of the nature of all the channels.

"Were astonished" is synonymous with "were amazed." "Looking at one another" means the bodhisattvas and the yoginīs looked at each other. What do they say? "Oh my [*e ma'o*]!" *E* is said to be wisdom, *ma* to be method, and *'o* to be the why—that's the meaning.

"The Blessed One" is synonymous with "the concentration that conjoins the self-nature of wisdom and method." "The lord of all tathāgatas" is Vajradhara, who is the self-nature of all the tathāgatas. As to "at the center of this ornate great maṇḍala": [1150] any maṇḍala that is ornamented by the passion-free saṅgha, many bodhisattvas, all the tathāgatas, and an assembly of yoginīs is the maṇḍala that is the ornate great maṇḍala; and [the Blessed One] abides at the center of that.

"'How is it that [he] has attained final nirvāṇa?'" is synonymous with "'How is it that [he] has attained the reality body?'" [1150: 5]

[6a7] *Then the bodhisattva Vajrapāṇi appealed to the yoginī Citrasenā, saying, "Oh goddess, is there some simple method by which sentient beings of little merit may gain greater ability?* [6b1]

[1150: 5] In consternation, [Vajrapāṇi] questioned Citrasenā. "Then" is synonymous with "immediately." "The yoginī Citrasenā" is the root of abiding in the secret. The variety [*citra*] of that [secret] is wondrous; the grouping [*sena*] is the gnosis of great bliss, and that itself is the Mahāyāna. Conjoining both, she is said to be the yoginī, hence the goddess.

As to "the bodhisattva Vajrapāṇi appealed [to the yoginī Citrasenā], saying": "Vajra" is nondual gnosis, and [*pāṇi*] is someone who holds that in their hand, so he is Vajrapāṇi. Someone who strives in the manner of a bodhisattva is a bodhisattva; further, because he is a being, he is a great being [*mahāsattva*]. Beings [S. *sattva*; T. *sempa*] are said to have two aspects: those of good fortune and those of bad fortune. "Appealed [to the yoginī Citrasenā], saying" is synonymous with "asked this." [Asking] what she would think or say, [Vajrapāṇi] calls out, "oh, goddess."

"Of meager merit" means those whose cognition is untrained; hence they are of meager merit and are sentient beings of meager merit. As to "may gain greater ability": there are many [types of] ability; "may gain greater [ability]" is explained as being what is established by mind. "Is there some simple method" is the assertion of the question asked of the goddess, as to whether there is some [1151] simple method [for gaining greater ability]. [1151: 1]

[Translator's note: There follows, in both the tantra and the commentary, a detailed version of Vajrapāṇi's question, omitted here, which specifies the number of mantras taught in the sūtras and tantras and lists the number of mantra recitations required of various sorts of beings, based on their level of spiritual development.]

[7a2] *Having heard thusly, the yoginī Citrasenā looked at the face of the Blessed One, leering at him with desirous sidelong glances. Then, her mind moved by compassion but displaying extreme ferocity, she destroyed Māra's army completely. Then, [once more,] the powerful lady who is mistress of all the tantras, the great goddess residing [in the maṇḍala], leered [at the Blessed One].* [7a4]

[1153: 12] As to "having heard thusly [*evaṃ*]":

> The excellent [syllable] *e*
> is adorned in the middle by *vaṃ*;
> it is the basis of all bliss,
> the casket of buddha jewels.[500]

[What] drips down "in the middle" of [*e*] refers to the dripping [of the bodhicitta]. What is meant by that? The meaning is [that] when the bodhicitta descends, omniscience will come about. "The yoginī Citrasenā" is the root of abiding in the secret. *Citra* [T. *natsok*] evokes wonder and is synonymous with "the collection of all roots." She is said to be a yoginī because of her inner experience of great bliss. She is not a yoginī bereft of methods; thus, it is said:

> Homage to the ḍākinī,
> [who] in [1154] human form has ways of moving [through the sky],

the yoginī possessing methods,
[who] ever emanates from the maṇḍala.[501]

Because of that, Citrasenā dwelled in sexual embrace with the Blessed One. "At the face of the Blessed One" refers to the nature of great bliss [expressed] on the central face [of the Buddha]. "Looked" is synonymous with "inner experience." "With . . . sidelong glances" and so forth are easy to understand.

As to "destroyed Māra's army completely": Māra is the senses and so forth, which are synonymous with "destroyed the mass of conceptions related to [the senses]." Who, then, is the special [being] who [accomplishes] that? "It is the goddess who is thus." As to [that]: The one who, abiding thus in the great secret, plays in the emanation cakra and the dharma cakra is the goddess. What does that imply? Perfectly collecting [both] method and wisdom, she experiences great bliss.

As to "[powerful] lady who is mistress of all the tantras": since there are tantras, and all of them, all of the tantras, refer to the *Guhyasamāja* and so forth, the powerful lady who is mistress of them all is Citrasenā. Alternatively, the phrase "all of the tantras" is to be taken as [connoting] *a* and other of the sixteen syllables of the enjoyment [or throat] cakra; thus the phrase "all of the tantras" is rightly explained as referring to the enjoyment cakra. "Mistress of all the tantras" refers to the great-bliss [or crown] cakra. "Powerful" is rightly explained as inner fire—this clearly explains the very nature of mantra. [1154: 18]

[7a4] *Merely because of this [leering], a mantra emerged from the head of the Blessed One:* oṃ buddhe siddhe susiddhe amṛta arje buddha kapāla spoṭanipātaya trāsaya hūṃ ho phaṭ. *Going forth with supreme [force], the mantra destroyed the* nāgas *living below the seventh level,*

turning them to dust, then returned and entered the mouth of Citrasenā; emerging from her lotus, it went back into the [Buddha's] skull. [7a5]

[1154: 19] It is taught that "merely by this leering" refers to "the accomplishment of mantra through inner fire." "A mantra emerged from the head of the Blessed One" refers to the bodhicitta seed. Since it maintains the body, it is the skull. Since *kaṃ* maintains the senses, [1155] it is the skull. *Kaṃ* maintains bliss, and *haṃ* is the indestructible bodhicitta seed. Thus, it is asserted that from that abode "a mantra emerged."

> Actions are posited to be fourfold,
> indestructible forms are four;
> through the four colors of this body,
> the four actions are accomplished.[502]

Again,

> Through the conjoining of vowels and consonants,
> the seeds of that are properly collected;
> the gnostic meditates on the seed
> of the fruitional drop that abides in the head.[503]

Therefore, the abode of all mantras is the indestructible mother. It is said that when mentally labeled mantras are projected in that abode, then special attainments are obtained.

What is the mantra? The mantra *oṃ buddha* and so forth has eight [poetic] feet. "Emerged" means it went forth. Where did it go? "[To those] living below the seventh level" means it dissolved into those seven [levels of nāgas] that are depicted; it is of the nature of *ka* and the other [syllables]. The mantra emanates from that and dissolves back into that. As to "destroyed the nāgas": "nāgas" and so forth is literal; [destroying] them is synonymous with destroying and demolishing the sense domains and the senses.

"Returned" is synonymous with "came back to that image and remained there." "Citrasenā" refers to entering inside the avadhūti. "[Into] the mouth" should be thought of as meaning that when one categorizes the vital winds abiding naturally in a subtle way, the mantra abides in them. "Emerged from her lotus" is synonymous with "emerged and departed from the drop that had entered her lotus." As to "went back into the [Buddha's] skull": the skull is to be thought of as the subtle entity that abides in the indestructible root. Alternatively, Citrasenā and [1156] the other [yoginīs] should be taken literally. "Dust" refers to the bodhicitta [drops] that emanate from the seventy-two thousand channels. [1156: 2]

[7a5] *The nāgas who were being destroyed by the power of the mantra were terrified of being turned to dust. All the nāgas possessing great magical powers—Vasuki and so forth—came forth, and all the others of their poisonous ilk came forth: Karkoṭaka, Śaṅkapāla, Takṣaka, Ananta, Padma, Mahāpadma, and so forth.* [7b1]

[1156: 2] "The nāgas . . . Vasuki and so forth" is easy to understand. Thus, it is said,

> From the great-bliss cakra there are eight [channels],
> and also [eight] from the enjoyment cakra,
> four from the dharma cakra,
> and also twelve from the emanation cakra.[504]

Thus, all the bodhicitta [drops] emerge from the thirty-two channels. It is also said,

When the bodhicitta [drops]
fill up these channels,
you will obtain buddhahood
and the state of Vajradhara.[505] [1156: 9]

[7b1] *Turning toward the yoginī Citrasenā, all the nāgas asked, "Oh, goddess, tell us what we should do." [She replied,] "Do whatever [accords with] the Buddha's inner experience." As soon as this was heard, the Blessed One, at the center of the ornate great maṇḍala, opened up his skull, and from it emerged a text. These words came out of the sky:*

"Oh, Citrasenā! Take this [text];
this great king of tantras
will benefit sentient beings—
there is no higher yoginī [tantra].
It is called the Buddha Skull,
and will benefit sentient beings."

Hearing this, the yoginī Citrasenā took hold of the text and delivered it directly to Vajrapāṇi. [7b4]

[1156: 9] "Turning toward the yoginī Citrasenā" means turning toward the face of the great yoginī. "All the nāgas" means Vasuki and the others. "Asked" means they properly requested. The eight channels abiding in the heart [cakra] are the real nature of the eight nāgas. The form of the drop in the middle is synonymous with "the Blessed One [in union] with Citrasenā. "'Oh, goddess, tell us what we should do'" [asks] the goddess Citrasenā what to do. As to [the answer,] "do whatever [accords with] the Buddha's inner experience": Buddha is the five aggregates. "As soon as" means what happens next—which is that one should do whatever [accords] with inner experience.

"This was heard" means the perfect conjoining of *e* and *vaṃ*, merely through the emanation of the bodhicitta. Where is that? "At the center of the ornate great maṇḍala," which is the central [channel] with its four cakras. Where does [the maṇḍala] come from? From the Blessed One, meaning the Blessed One's appearing in the form of the drop. "Opened up his skull" simply refers to the skull, [1157] which is synonymous with "opening and concealing the skull, which is the nature of vowels and consonants."

"Text" means all the dharmas collected into one; alternatively, the text is bodhicitta—referring to the land of Malaya[506]—which is the head. *Kaṃ* is bliss; *ta* is the spreading of that. Through that, the indestructible mind that is in the form of the drop is the text. "Emerged" is synonymous with "emanated." As to "emerged from the sky": the sky is the place where dharmas emerge. "Words" are just the words from "the proper conjoining of vajra and lotus" to "the vajra emerged."

At the time of the text's emergence, the gods in the sky sounded forth various musical sounds. As to "Oh, Citrasenā, take this [text]": the goddess is called, by saying "Ah, goddess, take this text." "Will benefit sentient beings" means "will effect the benefit of all sentient beings." "This great king of tantras" is synonymous with "the king, or chief, of the inner tantras, the *Guhyasamāja* and so forth." Which particular tantras? Saying "there is no higher yoginī tantra" [points] to a [tantra whose] nature is beyond the speech of Locanā and others. What is the name of the tantra? The *Buddha Skull*. Buddha is taught to be the vajra; the skull is explained as the lotus, which is the place of origin of all dharmas; this is synonymous with "because of that, it is a tantra of wisdom and method."

"Hearing this" means the emanation of the bodhicitta that is of the nature of wisdom and method. As to "Citrasenā": *citra* (various) means "wondrous"; *senā* is synonymous with "great bliss." What came of this? "She properly took hold of the text." As to that, there is [1158] Malaya; and there is *kaṃ*, which is bliss [*sukha*] and is indestructible; and there is *ta*, which effects spreading. Properly taking up the text that is bodhicitta is synonymous with "any sentient beings there are, [that is,] Citrasenā."

As to "delivered it to Vajrapāṇi": *vajra* means "unbreakable," and whoever has that in their hand [*pāṇi*] is Vajrapāṇi. "[Delivered it] directly" is synonymous with "gave it right up." Why did she do that? It was for the purpose of granting Vajrapāṇi the secret consecration. [1158: 6]

CHAPTER 11

Sādhana of the Glorious Buddhakapāla

[1443] In the Indian language: *Śrībuddhakapālasādhana-nāma*; in the Tibetan language: *Dpal sangs rgyas thod pa'i sgrub thabs zhes bya ba*.[507]

I bow down to the glorious Buddhakapāla.

To the blood drinkers possessing profound qualities,
the supreme inherent nature of all entities,
the ones who delight in benefiting sentient beings,
to those in the various classes [of deities], I prostrate.

Just as [this practice] that was taught by [my] guru
came in stages through the guru transmission,
so, in order that sentient beings may understand it,
I will explain this sādhana.

First, [you,] the yogin, should sit comfortably. At your heart is a moon disk arising from the original vowel [*a*]. On top of that is the syllable *hūṃ*, [emanating] five light-rays; these should be considered as the self-natures of the five tathāgatas. Then, emerging from the light-rays of that *hūṃ*, Yamadaṃṣṭrī and the other offering goddesses emanate. You should make offerings of the five nectars to Heruka [1444] who is in sexual union with Citrasenā and surrounded by the twenty-four yoginīs, Sumālinī and so forth. Having made all offerings properly, invite before you the three jewels and so forth and confess your transgressions and so forth. In the yoga tantras, you meditate first on compassion, [but] in this yoginī tantra, you should meditate first on love. Then, after compassion, meditate on joy and, last of all, equanimity.

Then, imagine a *hūṃ* standing on a sun [disk] at your heart. Then, ignited by a wind maṇḍala below, light-rays are emitted from the *hūṃ* and perfectly consume countless bodies. Think of everything as emptiness. Then, through the transformation of a *raṃ*, a sun disk appears. On top of the sun disk there is a *hūṃ*, which transforms into a double vajra. In the center of the double vajra, imagine a simple *hūṃ*. From the *hūṃ* comes a black vajra; through the emission of its light-rays, the perimeter of lattice fences should be secured. Contemplate how, through the transformation of that [black] vajra, the ground is a double vajra. Contemplate how, in the middle of the vajra ground, there is a triangular dharma source. Then, imagine the four great elements in the center of that.

Imagine that *yaṃ* transforms into a wind maṇḍala marked by two bow-shaped banners. As all the physical cakras that move within the [central] channel dissolve into it, the yogin should dwell in the center. This is said to be the purity of wind. Observe *raṃ* transform into a red triangular fire maṇḍala marked by seven blazes; imagine you effect that as [drops] drip down from [the openings of] the eighteen channels. Imagine that *vaṃ* transforms into a white circular water maṇḍala, [1445] marked by vases; imagine that all the cakras in the channel dissolve into the water maṇḍala. Imagine that *laṃ* transforms into a yellow square earth maṇḍala, [1445] marked by vajras. Thus, you should meditate on being blessed by the four letters of the four great elements.

Then, imagine that the four great elements transform into a cubical, tiered mansion, adorned by four doors and four archways, adorned by lattice and half-lattice, beautified by netting [set with] bells, and embellished with eight pillars. Imagine that the center of this [mansion] is embellished with an eight-petaled lotus. Imagine that in the center of [the lotus] is a corpse, whose true nature is that of the reality sphere. On it, the thirty-two basic syllables—*a* and so forth—in two circles of sixteen sound-syllables transform into a moon disk, which is the very pure mirrorlike gnosis. On that, the thirty-four pillars and other [adornments], with the addition of the six [syllables] *ya*, *ra*, *wa*, *la*, *ḍa*, and *ḍha* become forty. Then, the two circles of [forty] syllables transform into eighty and become a sun disk, which has the nature of the gnosis of equality. At the center of the [sun disk], imagine the syllable *hūṃ*, [symbolizing] wisdom and method, which has the nature of the gnosis of discernment. Imagine that the *hūṃ* transforms into Heruka Buddhakapāla, in sexual union with Citrasenā.

He has one face and four arms, glittering like white moonlight on jasmine flowers and emitting light like a jewel. It is understood from the pith instructions that in his right [hands he holds, respectively,] a chopper and skull-cup, and in his left a khaṭvāṅga and vajra. His wisdom consort, [1446] Citrasenā [usually depicted as red], with one face and two arms, is in sexual union with Heruka. She is naked, lacking a garland of heads or offering substances. Completely blissful, she [possesses] the beauty of [both] awareness and form [incarnate]. In her right [hand] she holds a hand drum and a chopper, in her left she wields a khaṭvāṅga and holds aloft a skull-cup.[508] Meditate upon her as the Blessed Lady Rūpinī.

On the eastern [lotus-]petal is a white-colored Sumālinī; on the northern petal is a yellow-colored Kāminī;[509] on the western petal is a blue-colored Bhīmā; and on the southern petal is a black-colored Durjayā. These [goddesses] stand in half-dance pose[510] on sun disks; imagine them holding a chopper and skull-cup in their [right and left] hands [respectively]. On the four intermediate petals are four skull-cups brimming with nectar. The central petal is adorned by a garland of vajras.

The eight segments of the second level are adorned by lotus garlands: on the eastern segment is Subhamekhalā, on the northern segment is Rūpiṇī, on the western segment is Vijayā, on the southern segment is Kāmiṇī, on the northeast segment is Kāpalānī, on the southeast segment is Mahāśastrā,[511] on the northwest segment is Grathantī,[512] on the southwest segment is Māradadū.[513] Each of these yoginīs is red in color and stands on a sun seat; they are in half-dance pose and hold a chopper and skull-cup in their [right and left] hands [respectively].

The eight segments of the third level are adorned by vajra garlands: on the eastern segment is Tārinī, on the northern segment is Bhīmadarśanā, on the western segment is Lāmā, on the southern segment is Ajayā, on the northeast segment is Śubhā, on the southeast segment [1447] is Tāḍakā, on the northwest segment is Kālarātri, on the southwest segment is Mahāyaśā.[514] Each of these yoginīs is red in color and stands on a sun seat, holding a chopper and skull-cup in the [right and left] hand [respectively].

At the eastern door is a white-colored Sundarī, at the northern door is a yellow-colored Vasudhā,[515] at the western door is a red-colored Subhagā, and at the southern door is a black-colored Priyadarśanā. Each of these yoginīs, who possess the nature of Maitreya and other [bodhisattvas], stands on a corpse and sun disk, in a dancing pose with the left leg extended [and right one bent]. Each has one face and two arms and holds a chopper [in the right hand] and a skull-cup [in the left hand]. View them as completely [one with] Heruka.

Except for the door guardians, the yoginīs are in half-dance posture. They are wrapped at the waist in a tiger skin, wear bone ornaments, and gather red light-rays [within]. Their yellow hair blazes upward. Contemplate how from all their orifices blood and semen come forth, and that at the time of the Blessed One's perfect [awakening], the yoginīs instantaneously reach perfection through *hūṃ*. Contemplate yourself, along with the twenty-four yoginīs, thusly.

Then, having made offerings, the twenty-four goddesses drink the five nectars from the skull-cup. Then, imagine *a* in the lotus of Citrasenā and *hūṃ* on the vajra of Heruka. The vajra of the Blessed One and the lotus of Citrasenā are conjoined. Greatly impassioned with desire and attachment, the twenty-four goddesses make requests, and the sexual substances [appear] in the middle of the sun disk. Seeing the sexual substances, [the goddesses] are aroused by the songs of the door guardians, who are of the nature of Maitreya and so forth:

Well, if you ignore [1448] worldly fame,
How can you not have pleasure?
If you hear the commitments,
you'll give up all displeasure—
be aroused by Sundarī.

Without emptying the mind,
make known the notion of thatness;
bewildering people who fear existence,
associate with the yoginīs—
be aroused by Vasundharā.

If you hear the words of the blue principal [deity],
don't forsake activity;
if he doesn't appear, all beings
will fall into rebirth and be joyless—
be aroused by Subhagā.

Renowned but not indulging in perverse
pride, see natural emptiness;
forsaking all things,
join the company of the yoginīs—
aroused by Kīrtidarśanā.

As soon as these songs of arousal [have been sung], from the sexual substances [emerge] *a* and *hūṃ*, and from those two, a chopper and vajra. From the chopper and vajra [emerges] a blue-colored Heruka with one face and four arms. This principal deity—possessing the signs described before and proclaiming *hūṃ*—is in half-dance pose. The epitome of terror and wrath, he is attired in tiger-skin garments and holds a garland of forty-nine [blood-]soaked heads, which is proffered for the purpose of offering. He laughs loudly and is seen as the main embodiment of greatly fierce compassion.

He [wears] shoulder ornaments, neck rings, and bracelets,
and is bound by a [bone] girdle at his naked waist;
His anklets make a tinkling sound,
completely destroying all the māras.
At his topknot he wears a perfect crown
ornamented by the heads of the five buddhas.
He's the deity with a half-moon
and a double vajra [atop] his head.
[With his head ornaments], nose rings, throat ornaments,
bangles, and girdle,
he's a protector bearing the five mudrās.
Smeared with ashes, fearsome,
and adorned [1449] by pearly skulls,
he's the hero bringing freedom from saṃsāra,
possessing the nature of the seed of awakening.
Your breath unmoving, contemplate him thus.

The principal wisdom-consort, Citrasenā, is naked: she wears neither a garland of heads nor any ornaments, and, [though] completely lacking in offering substances, she is blissful. She has one face and two arms. Her hair hangs freely, and she is white colored. Her transformed face terrifies with her partially bared fangs. In her right [hand] she holds a hand drum and a chopper, in her left she wields a khaṭvāṅga and holds aloft a skull-cup.[516] Contemplate her as the goddess of the perfection [of wisdom].

Now, ritual [offerings] should be made to your own seven places—heart, throat, crown, two shoulders, two eyes, secret place, and body as a whole—through these mantras: *oṃ, haṃ, hraiṃ, hreṃ, ho, hēṃ*, and *hāṃ*.[517] At the heart, from *hūṃ* comes vajra mind; at the throat, from *āḥ* comes vajra speech; at the crown, from *oṃ* comes vajra body. With body, speech, and mind thus blessed, you should invite the gnosis being: contemplate that from *hūṃ* on a moon disk at your heart, hooklike light-rays [go forth] and, when you proudly recite the mantra *oṃ buddha ka pā li ni āh khaṃ graṃ drūṃ śrū aḥ aḥ aḥ hūṃ hūṃ hūṃ phaṭ*,[518] the gnosis being is drawn down and enters into the pledge being—imagine they are fused like milk and water.

Thus, the hero, having witnessed this perfection, drips at the root cakra. With those drippings, all the tathāgatas compassionately bless the various yoginīs. Eight [more] yoginīs—wearing various costumes, endowed with youthful forms, twelve years of age—are generated and take up positions in the sky. They hold eight vases filled to the brim [1450] with bodhicitta and ornamented at the rim by mango leaves. All of them are quite pure and exclaim, "May Heruka be victorious!" Having been seen by the protector, you should request the higher consecrations:

> I, who am stuck in the mire of saṃsāra,
> [request] consecration [by] the yoginīs,

who are greatly renowned for their mercy—
please free me through consecration.

Just as a house without offspring
is empty when [the owner] dies,
just so, if I am unconsecrated,
I will be devoid of all gnosis.

Through those verses, the secret consecration is taught.

Just as a fully assembled vina
can't sound forth without strings,
so, if I am unconsecrated,
I will not perfect mantra and contemplation.

Through those verses, the wisdom-gnosis consecration is taught. It is also said that if you are unconsecrated, your faults will multiply. [Say,]

As a foolish person who is unconsecrated,
I say, "Please consecrate me!"
Until I dwell in buddhahood,
make me your student, lest I go to hell.

Through those verses, the faults of being unconsecrated are shown.

Thus, I again request the yoginīs,
who are treasuries of knowledge, "Please consecrate me."
May I, when I [receive] the consecration
of nonarising, become Heruka.

Then, the yoginīs, saying "May [Heruka] be victorious," bathe and consecrate the Blessed One. Merely by [the granting of] the outer and secret consecrations, drums resound in the sky, and a rain of sandalwood and flowers falls. The consecrations complete, the yoginīs dissolve into the root cakra. Each of the circles of the maṇḍala is sealed by its own lineage. Then, you should offer [1451] the Blessed One songs of praise, offerings, and the five nectars.

Then, imagine that *yaṃ* transforms into a wind maṇḍala. On top of that is *raṃ*, which transforms into a fire maṇḍala. On top of that is *aṃ*, which transforms into a skull-cup. In the center of the skull-cup, *vi*, *mu*, *ra*, *śu*, and *ma* transform into the five nectars, and *go*, *ku*, *da*, *ha*, and *na* transform into the five meats. Then, the wind ignites the fire, and when the fire heats the skull-cup, vapors emerge that are like a vajra in aspect. In order to cool down [the contents], [there appears in] the center [of the skull-cup] a finger-high *oṃ*, which transforms into a moon disk in the nature of nectar. Through the blessings of *oṃ*, the nectar descends like snow, cooling [the contents of the skull-cup].

The gods should be satisfied by the three suchnesses.[519] Then, contemplate how the maṇḍala circles are eternally like a dream or an illusion. At your navel is *āḥ*, at the heart is *hūṃ*, at the throat is *oṃ*, and between the eyebrows is the indestructible *haṃ*, which possesses [the nature] of sound and drop. [Then,]

The earth and the other of the four great elements
are divided among the four cakras.
Blessings occur during the four [daily] retreat sessions.
Perfection emerges from the four lotuses.
By the nature of the four joys,
you are completely stabilized in the four applications.[520]

By the form of supreme joy,
the doer of deeds, naturally

possessing the glorious form of Vajrasattva,
plays blissfully, whatever the occasion.
When you meditate on the coming and going of vital winds,
they dissolve and great bliss arises.

The [main] directional petals of the eight [at the heart cakra
in the central] channel
are in the nature of the four great elements,
while the four intermediate petals,
which have the nature of the five nectars,
exist in the form of offerings.

The divisions of body, speech, and mind
are rightly said to be twenty-four,
and the outer maṇḍala
is also twenty-fourfold:
Citrasenā dwells at the center [1452]
together with the Blessed One.

At the center of the sixty-four-[branched] emanation (navel) cakra is *oṃ* within a physical drop. At the center of the eight-[branched] heart cakra is *hūṃ* within a physical drop. The light-rays of the *oṃ* go upward, while the light-rays of the *hūṃ* go downward; when both are collected back, they dissolve into their [respective] drops and bliss is obtained. Thus should you contemplate the emergence and entrance [of breath].

When you have applied yourself to this practice for six months, you will accomplish [your aim]—there is no doubt. If you grow weary while meditating, then recite the [following] mantra: *oṃ hrīḥ buddha hūṃ ka pā li ni āḥ*. *Oṃ* is [recited] for entering, *hrīḥ* for emerging, *buddha* for abiding, *hūṃ* for enjoying, *ka pā li ni* for retiring, *a* for rising. Thus, recite the mantras as a six-part practice. When you apply yourself to this, you will become a buddha—there is no other [way]. That is the root mantra. The essence mantra is *oṃ buddha ka pā li ni / oṃ hrīḥ hai hūṃ phaṭ*. The near-essence mantra is *oṃ ka pā la vajrī ni hūṃ haṃ dura kṣe hūṃ phaṭ*.

[The food-offering mantra is] *oṃ ma hā ka pā la vajra ce tri pru ca tre a lamba ne pri nay a sarva bhū ta mā rāna mā yay a sarva mā rāna kī la ya sarva duṣṭana / uccha ta ya sarva vighnana vi tray a dra ma ya*[521] *bhagavati yakṣa rakṣa / sa pi śa ca na śo ṣa ya tra ya sapta pā tā la ga ta na sa ra sa ra pra sa ra hūṃ hūṃ hūṃ phaṭ phaṭ phaṭ*. The maṇḍala should be emanated in each of the four daily sessions and the food offering made, [employing] the mantra of food offering to all the elemental spirits.

This completes the Sādhana of the Glorious Buddhakapāla, *which was orally composed by the great master Saraha.*

CHAPTER 12

Sādhana of Lokeśvara Who Subdues the Three Worlds

[535] In the Indian language: *Trailokyavaśaṃkaralokeśvarasādhana-nāma*; in the Tibetan language: *'Jig rten dbang phyug 'jig rten gsum dbang du mdzad pa'i sgrub thabs zhes bya ba.*[522]

First, you should set up a scroll painting [of the deity] in a pleasant location, and before it, in the middle of an earth maṇḍala, you should make a moon disk out of saffron, while reciting the mantra *vajra picture hūṃ.*[523] After that, when you have invited his eminence Lokeśvara Who Subdues the Three Worlds through the mantra *jaḥ hūṃ baṃ please enter the lotus hoḥ*, you should make offerings to him in the center of the maṇḍala. Ask him to come, by using the mantras *oṃ Subduer of the Three Worlds vajra flower hūṃ please take up residence svāhā* and then *oṃ vajra sage muḥ*.

[Then,] you should imagine at your own heart a red *oṃ* syllable, which transforms into a [536] sun disk. On top of that is a red *hrīḥ* syllable. Through the light-rays from that [*hrīḥ*], the tathāgata Amitābha is summoned, offerings are properly made, evil is confessed, and so forth. [Then,] through the skillful means of the Subduer of Three Worlds, light is made to enter the seed syllable at one's own [heart].

When those [procedures] are complete, instantly imagine yourself as Lokeśvara, whose body is entirely red with a great redness, who has one face, two hands, and three eyes, and whose long hair is [tied up] in a crown ornament. He holds in his [right] hand [183a] an elephant goad marked by a vajra and [in his left] a triple noose with which two sheep are tied. Seated in vajra posture upon a red lotus, he is adorned with silk scarves and fine vestments.

Imagine that buddhas, bodhisattvas, vajra yoginīs, and deities possessing various magical emanations grant consecration. You should contemplate the tathāgata Amitābha atop your head. Then, on a sun disk at your heart, contemplate a trio of syllables, which you recite: *hrīḥ hūṃ yaṃ*. After that, recite the two mantras of vajra self-nature: *Oṃ I am of the inherent* [537] *self-nature of the gnosis of emptiness* and [*Oṃ*] *I am of the vajra self-nature of the vajra self-nature of all dharmas*.

After that, you should give dough offerings [to the hungry ghosts] while reciting *oṃ hrīḥ āḥ hūṃ Hāritī with power over demons svāhā*. [Then,] send forth the torma mantra: *aṃ āṃ traṃ hrī the assembly of the powerful heroes and heroines together with their entire retinues a a a va ta ra a va ta ra please come from the ten directions and please, guardians of the world, [accept] this torma gṛḥṇa gṛḥṇa hūṃ svāhā*. This should be animated by deity yoga.

This completes the Sādhana of the Subduer of Three Worlds, *which emerged in stages from Oḍiyāna and was orally composed by Saraha.*

CHAPTER 13

Alphabetical Dohās

[1091] In the Indian language: *Kakhasya dohā-nāma*; in the Tibetan language: *Ka kha'i do ha zhes bya ba.*[524]

I bow down to the Blessed One, Śrī Heruka.

(Ka) [EA 1098–99]
[When the vajra (*kakuliṣa*)] resides within the mother's lotus
(*kamala*),
the bodies (*kāya*) are bound [together] and nectar drips;
[when] the ḍombī maiden (*kumārī*) embraces you around the neck,
camphor (*kapūra*) drips down and springtime branches [bloom]. (1)

(Kha) [EA 1099]
The empty one, [whose] forehead [cakra] abides in the sky
(*khasama*),
is naked (*khama*), unclothed by virtue or nonvirtue;
even when eating (*khā*) and drinking, he abides in nirvāṇa;
seizing the naked (*khama*), the yogin is joyous:
he pervades the whole sky (*khasama*), becoming firm. (2)

(Ga) [EA 1099–1100]
[When] you milk and milk the sky (*gamana*), and then drink it up,
the Ganges (*gaṅgā*) and Yamuna are dammed up;
stable amid existence, you'll cut off going (*gama*) and coming. (3)

(Gha) [EA 1100–1101]
Glorious Heruka delights in the sound of the bell (*ghaṇṭana*):
embraced by Nairātmyā, he copulates [1092] [with her] again and again (*ghanahana*);
the yoginī transfers the winds again and again (*ghanahana*):
the housemistress (*gharanī*) changes into primordial cognition. (4)

(Ṅa)[525] [EA 1101]
The primordial (*ṇinaya*) nature is naturally empty,
the primordial (*ṇaya*) housemistress does not project virtue or nonvirtue;
when the yogin is able continually (*ṇirantara*) to produce bliss,
the darkness of night (*ṇasi*) is cut away and empty luminosity comes to be. (5)

(Ca) [EA 1101–2]
One in proper possession of the four (*cautha*) joys
—hey!—must hold the mind apart from the four (*cautha*) extremes;[526]
the four (*cau*) moments are understood though the speech of a proper guru,
while the four (*cau*) drops[527] are not known by those with foolish tendencies. (6)

(Cha) [EA 1102]
Transcend (*chaḍa*) the senses through the pure inherent nature,
transcend (*chaḍa*) desirable things and entities and nonentities,
cast aside (*chaḍahūṃ*) chattering and storytelling—in this way,
giving up (*chaḍa*) these tastes, enjoy the sky! (7)

(Ja) [EA 1102–3]
The sky is without birth, aging (*jari*), or death,
[so] wherever (*jājhā*) you look, there's only sky;

whatever (*jiseng*) there is, is suchness,
[so] whatever (*jo*) is seen is the ultimate. (8)

(Jha)[528] [EA 1103]
Just as multiple flowers (*ṇavahuli*) depend upon their [particular] seeds,
so in various [ways] the aggregates come to be (*jhana*);
since the bee can drink nectar both thin and thick through its nose (*ṇase*),
it is sustained for a very long time—there is no (*ṇihina*) doubt. (9)

[EA 1103: Ña is the same as Ṅa.]

(Ṭa) [EA 1103–4]
Hey! The speech drop of the proper guru descends (*ṭala*):
through movement (*ṭalīna*) in the basic ground, the drop drips from the sky;
hey, yogin: don't chatter (*ṭalamalana*) about the wrong path:
when you chatter (*ṭalamala*), you don't realize the connate. (10)

(Ṭha) [EA 1104]
The sound of *ṭha* expresses mantras,
and taking up the syllable *ṭha*, [1093] you obtain the abiding [reality];
when you take it up properly (*ṭhaṇa*), you project concentration,
and when you comprehend the sky (*ṭha*) through a proper guru, that's awakening. (11)

(Ḍa) [EA 1104–5]
[Through] uttering mantras and taking up the *ḍombī*,
the inner fire ([*caṅ*]*ḍālī*) burns and the liquids drip down;
the *ḍamaru* sounds forth the indestructible sound:
playing the *ḍamaru* [evinces] the voice of the yoginī. (12)

(Ḍha) [EA 1105]
When something passes on (*ḍhaliya*), it resolves into a single aspect,
and when mind passes on (*ḍhaliya*), the supreme connate comes to be:
although the five senses may pass on (*ḍhaliya*), the connate remains;
why would the hidden (*ḍhaḍha*) housemistress not see any entities? (13)

(Ṇa)[529] [EA 1105–6]
The primordial (*ṇija*) nature is naturally empty,
and when you understand primordial cognition (*ṇiyamana*), you're not covered by virtue or nonvirtue;
the primordial housemistress (*ṇayagharī*) is driven on by the connate:
continually (*ṇibara*) reliant upon it, she isn't bound by birth or death. (14)

(Ta) [EA 1106]
Gain knowledge in reliance upon the three dimensions (*tatraya*) and the three textual [collections],
and as for the three syllables (*tri*[*-akṣara*]), rely on the words of Saraha and meditate;
through the contemplation of sameness (*tulla*), the mind
observes thatness (*tattva*): what's to be done by explanation? (15)

(Tha) [EA 1106–7]
Rely (*thira*) upon the moon in the sky;
if you forsake what abides (*thana*) [at the crown], how will you [obtain] a fortunate body?

When you rely (*thira*) upon what abides [at the crown], the vital winds will dry up,
and when you rely (*thira*) upon what's stable, your life span will increase. (16)

(Da) [EA 1107–8]
Through the words of Saraha, everything is burned up (*daha*) and you become immortal;
destroy the [tortoise (*duli*)] milk of duality by bathing in supreme bliss,
When you know the two (*duyi*) drops, that is the pure inherent nature,
and the suffering (*duḥkha*) of evil folk [who conceptualize] entities and nonentities doesn't exist. (17)

(Dha) [EA 1108]
The nature of the *dha-*(*ḍombī*) is to sit washing and rinsing;
even though she washes (*dhabanta*) and rinses, she does not see sitting or going.
The washerwoman (*dhaḍombī*) should take up Saraha's words; [1094]
[averting] trickery (*dhuta*), assume the nature of sky. (18)

(Na) [EA 1108–9]
In various (*nana*) ways, [mind-itself] passes on into the one;
worldlings who don't understand (*nabuche*) speak in various ways.
[In order] to nullify (*nase*) fear [of kings and robbers], you pay a toll:
there is no (*namu*) existence, no nirvāṇa, nor anything else. (19)

(Pa) [EA 1109–10]
The five (*pañca*) nectars are to be put into the nose;[530]
join the lotus (*pauma*) and vajra, join them, and accomplish sameness.
Make offerings with lotus (*pauma*) flowers to the one seated in vajra posture [Vajrasattva];
if you don't know the thatness of the lotus (*pauma*), it's not royal great bliss. (20)

(Pha) [EA 1110]
The mind that projects and collects (*phira*) [maṇḍalas] is like the sky;
Even if you don't see projections (*pharanata*), desire to be like the sky.
The syllable *phaṭ* (*phaṭkara*) and the syllable *hūṃ*—how they project [is within emptiness]:
they project (*phari*) like [beneficence from] a wish-fulfilling tree. (21)

(Ba) [EA 1111]
[By] the ponds where the closed Brahmā flowers of the forest (*bana*) open
and lovely and uplifting desirable fruits [appear on] spring branches [when the vajra (*bajra*) mind is seized],
earnestly subjugating (*basa*) [demons] and beautifully dancing,
the yoginī who goes or stays (*biharànahi*) rouses her own body. (22)

(Bha) [EA 1111–12]
As for the *bhaga* (female organ) itself: the nature of the *bhaga* is empty:
it's without virtue or nonvirtue—so say (*bhana*) I, Saraha;
through the speech of the guru, the five desirable things may be enjoyed (*bhañjana*):
mind-itself does not indulge in error (*bhati*)—it is sky. (23)

(Ma) [EA 1112]
Forcing the liquor (*maya*) to drip down again and again,
understand the root (*mūla*) through service to the glorious guru;
when you can unify the basic (*mūla*) mind with thought,
the mind will be cut off and die (*mari*) and be of a single nature. (24)

(Ya) [EA 1112–13]
When (*yabing*) we speak of the *naḍa* and the drops,
then, through the voice of the *yoginī*, the connate is realized;
just so (*yeseng*), based on abiding in your own joy,
you'll have no fear of birth or death (*yama*). (25)

(Ra) [EA 1113–14]
[When] the drops of sun (*ravi*) and moon [combine], [1095] there is deathless sky:
the sun (*ravi*) in the mode of great bliss is most beautiful,
the alchemist's way (*rasanā*) brings down drop after drop,
and day and night (*rātrin*) they are slain within primordial cognition. (26)

(La) [EA 1114]
Hey (*le hūṃ*)! The housemistress of the vital winds arises inside the house;
Take in (*le hūṃ*) the nāḍa and drops: that's the uncontaminated dharma.
There are *lalanā*, *rasa*[*nā*], and avadhūti:
[when] the drops drip down (*lambhi*), that is most wondrous, so you drink them. (27)

(Wa)[531] [EA 1114–15]
Playfully drink the supreme (*wara*) liquid—ah!
Vajrayoginī (*wajra*[*yogi*]*nī*) playfully emanates;

when the glorious heroine (*birā*) delights in the connate,
then the hand drum sends forth (*wabaji*) the indestructible
sound. (28)

Śa [EA 1115]
The sound of the natural, spontaneous, indestructible (*śaya*) sound,
the [moon] drops (*śaśadharana*) dripping down are the yoginī's
protection;
the cooling (*śitatakāra*) words of Saraha are a destructive sound:
milking and milking the sky, you draw down the [moon] drops
and drink them. (29)

(Ṣa)[532] [EA 1116]
When there's enjoyment of the supreme connate (*sahaja*),
then one's own and others' (*ṣabara-abara*) karmic tendencies are
destroyed;
yoginīs [both] serene and wrathful (*sama-asama*) accomplish
this—there is no doubt.
Hey! I, Saraha (*saraha*), say, "Don't you doubt it!" (30)

(Sa) [EA 1116]
All (*saya*) these entities are alike in being nonentities;
don't abandon them because of error about emptiness (*sunyu*)
and compassion.
Enjoy the connate (*sahaja*) joy continually:
whoever possesses the supreme connate (*sahaja*) cannot be
bound. (31)

(Ha) [EA 1116–17]
Hey! Be satisfied by laughter (*hāsa*) or the arising of various [joys].
Hey! Whether deprived (*hariya*) [of things] or filled [with them],
fools have no joy;

when you bind the supreme colorless lord (*harahara*) to the body,
then you'll fully accomplish the unexcelled through play (*hele*). (32)

(Kṣa) [EA 1117–18]
When it falls into the object (*kṣale*),[533] bodhicitta is spoiled;
the sound of *kṣa kṣa* (destruction) can dry up the oceans.
As [when] something rough (*kṣarasana*) is made smooth, the sharpness of concentration turns [sorrow] into joy.
Hey! The naked (*kṣamana*) gives lie to all [distinctions]—there's no doubt at all! (33)

This completes the Alphabetical Dohās, *which was taught orally by the lord of yoga, the glorious great brahmin, Saraha.*[534]

CHAPTER 14

Ornament of Springtime

A Dohā-Treasury Song

[26] In the Indian language: *Vasantatilakadohakoṣagītikā-nāma*; in the Tibetan language: *Dpyid kyi thig le do ha mdzod kyi glu zhes bya ba.*[535]

I prostrate to the glorious Heruka.

I, a youth[536] who sees the flowers
of spring, the pomegranate,[537] the three bodies,
and other [delights], am intoxicated. (1)

Desiring Heruka, [I say,]
here, at the very beginning of spring,
please be my protector,
and don't let me die of passion. (2)

May [I] enjoy sweet-smelling
ambhakāruna flowers.
The *śaripa*,[538] it is said, beats his drum,
the caṇḍalī carries the lamp,
and the master painter descends.[539] (3)

I hope the young man will come;
now, at the beginning of spring,

may you be my protector,
and don't let me die of passion. (4)

Looking in the ten directions,
I don't see anything but you,
And in the fire[540] of my passion, [27]
I don't even think of my own body. (5)

Through our prayers
to the four transmission-yoginīs,
may the Blessed One be roused. (6)

This completes the Ornament of Springtime: A Dohā-Treasury Song, *composed by master Saraha and transmitted by Kṛṣṇācārya.*

CHAPTER 15

Four Songs from the *Treasury of Performance Songs*

[Excerpted from Munidatta, *Caryāgītikoṣavṛtti*; Tibetan: *Spyod pa'i glu'i mdzod kyi 'grel pa*.][541]

(1)

Through their own active construction of saṃsāra and nirvāṇa,
worldly beings bind themselves by wrong views. (1)

I, the inconceivable yogin, do not know
how birth and death could exist. (2)

Just like birth and death,
the living and the dead can't be distinguished. (3)

Those who are unconcerned[542] here with birth or death
[seek to] perfect alchemical elixirs. (4)

How can those who roam around in the moving
and immobile [worlds] escape aging and death? (5)

Is birth due to karma or karma due to birth?
Saraha says, this matter is unthinkable. (6)

(2)

No sound, no drop, no orb of the sun or moon:
the mind-king is essentially free. (1)

Spurn the straight path but don't take up another;
awakening is near, so don't go far away.[543] (2)

Don't pick up the mirror to look at your bracelet;
selfhood is known for certain by oneself. (3)

Those who go along this or the farther shore
will perish in the company of evil people. (4)

Saraha says,[544] the trench on the left
and the abyss on the right are the straight path—ah! (5)

(3)

The body is a boat, cognition is the oar;
the speech of the sublime guru gives you the oar. (1)

[Except] by holding mind-itself steady, the people in the boat
have no other means of going to the farther shore. (2)

The boat goes downstream, and a boatman [guides it] with his
pole;[545]
let it go—and by letting it go, you'll know the other [shore]
through the connate. (3)

[On] the path, fearsome obstacles turn up;
the waves of existence agitate everyone. (4)

[Between] the near and far shore, fierce currents flow;
Saraha says, [perform] sky concentration. (5)

(4)

With the hands of emptiness tear apart—ah!—
your own cognitive flaws;
the path of practice according to the guru's word—ah!—
how could you turn back on that? (1)

Marvelous! In the sky born from *hūṃ*
take up what moves erratically;[546]
you'll go to the far shore by conquering
your manifold flickering illusions. (2)

Wondrous! In the confusion of worldly existence
—amazing!—self and other are seen;
but this world, which is like a water bubble,
has the self-nature of connate emptiness. (3)

Where there is nectar, there is no poison—ah![547]
The self-nature of mind is under others' sway. At home,
I understand what I have drunk—ah!—
and I shall consume my vile relatives. (4)

Saraha says, this is supreme;[548]
what use is the vile ox of self,
which destroys beings on its own.
Amazing! I behave as I like. (5)

CHAPTER 16

The Mahāmudrā Pith-Instruction Called "Dohā Treasury"

[1266] In the Indian language: *Dohakoṣa-nāma-mahāmudropadeśa*; in the Tibetan language: *Do ha mdzod ces bya ba phyag rgya chen po'i man ngag.*[549]

I bow down to the glorious Vajrayoginī.
I bow down to the connate gnosis, the greatly blissful reality body.

Just as things and no-things, appearance and emptiness,
the wandering and the not-wandering, the moving and the
unmoving—
all things, none excepted, do not ever move
at any time from the nature of sky. (1)

Although the sky is described as "sky,"
an essence of sky is not at all established;
moreover, is, isn't, both is and isn't,
and neither is nor isn't transcend objective characterization. (2)

Thus, among sky, mind, and reality,
there exists not the slightest difference;
the different names are only temporary labels,
nothing but false and meaningless words. (3)

All dharmas are your own mind, [1267]
and there's not an atom of any dharma not included in mind;
whoever realizes nonmind from the start
attains the sublime purport of the conquerors of the three times. (4)

[Mind] is designated as the "casket of dharma,"
so there are no wrong dharmas within it;
it is the connate nature from the beginning. (5)

Its thatness is not an existent that can be taught,
and since it's inexpressible, who could understand it? No one. (6)

If an owner exists, then [their] wealth exists,
[but] how could that which is unowned from the start exist?
If mind exists, it's reasonable that all dharmas exist,
[but] how can anyone realize dharmas in nonmind? (7)

When you seek out everything appearing as mind
and dharmas, you can't find them, nor is there any seeker. (8)

Since it is nonexistent, nonarising, and unceasing throughout the three times,
thatness that doesn't change into anything else;
it is the abiding nature of inherent great bliss. (9)

Therefore, all appearances are the reality body,
wandering sentient beings are buddhahood,
every karmic formation is the reality sphere from the start,
and labeled dharmas are like a rabbit's horn. (10)

Hey! The sun is free from clouds and its rays are all-pervasive,
but to the eyeless they appear as darkness;

the connate is all-pervasive,
but to fools, thatness is very far away. (11)

Since beings don't realize nonmind,
mind-itself is tightly bound by mental labeling. (12)

Just as the mad, overtaken by demons,
powerlessly and pointlessly suffer, so
beings seized by the great demon of conceptual grasping
at self only suffer pointlessly. (13)

Some fools, bound by the categories of thought,
seek the owner elsewhere, even though he's at home;
some take mirror images to be true;
some, forsaking the root, [only] prune the foliage—
whatever they do, [1268] they don't notice they're deceived. (14)

Hey! Infants are ignorant of thatness,
but I realize that they don't move from thatness;
since I know the beginning and end as mine,
when I see "I," one selfhood remains—
[but] when I observe oneness, I don't see a one. (15)

Since it is free from seen and seer, it is inexpressible,
and who will understand this inexpressibility?
When primordial cognition is purified,
then the hermit enters realization of "I."[550] (16)

Lion's milk is not [placed] in inferior vessels,
and just as the lion's roar in the forest
frightens all the tiny deer
but moves the lion cubs to rejoice,

so when this great bliss, nonarising from the start, is taught,
wrongheaded fools are frightened,
but the hairs of the fortunate bristle with joy. (17)

Hey! Let undistracted mind observe itself by itself;
when its own thatness is realized by itself,
then distracted mind dawns as mahāmudrā,
and signs are liberated within great bliss. (18)

Because all pleasures and pains [encountered]
in dreams lack inherent nature when you wake up,
who, greatly aroused by notions of hope
and fear, will think of accomplishment or cessation? (19)

Because all dharmas of saṃsāra and nirvāṇa
lack inherent nature when their thatness is seen,
when ideas of hope and fear come to an end,
why make efforts to accept or reject? (20)

All sights and sounds are equivalent to illusions, mirages,
and reflections: they are insubstantial;
the illusionist, mind-itself, is [like] the sky:
[since it is] without edges or center, who can know it? (21)

Just as the Ganges and other rivers
[take on] a single taste in the salty sea,
all the various mental [1269] labels and mental events
[take on] a single taste in the reality sphere: know this! (22)

Even someone who thoroughly searches the sky realm
sees that it's without edges or center: it's complete cessation;
likewise, when you thoroughly search mind and dharmas,

you won't find even an atom of essence.
Even the mind that thoroughly searches is nonreferential,
so that very not-seeing of anything is seeing. (23)

Just as a raven that flies from a ship
circles in [all] directions and lands there again,[551]
even the desirous mind that's lost track of the teaching
lands back in primary mind-itself, in the primordial [nature]. (24)

Untroubled by conditions, with the anxiety of hope
and the gambling hall of fear destroyed, vajra mind,
mind-itself, which cuts the root, is like the sky. (25)

When you're in nonmeditation, there's nothing for cognition to do;
the primordial self-nature of ordinary mind
is unpolluted by contrived imaginings:
in the naturally pure mind, contrivance is unnecessary. (26)

Don't hold it, don't release it: let it rest on its own;
if you don't realize this, there is no point to meditation,
[while if] you realize it, there is no meditative object or meditator. (27)

Just as the sky is sky without reference points,
so the empty is empty without meditation;
nondual knowing is like water and milk:
diverse [things] have the uninterrupted single taste of great bliss. (28)

Thus, throughout all three times,
there's no cognitive engagement, and within primordial nonseparation,
maintaining thatness is what we conventionally label "meditation." (29)

Not holding your breath, not binding it,
let uncontrived knowing relax like a little child;
when conceptual recollection arises, observe its own thatness:
Don't conceive of water and waves as two different things. (30)

In the mahāmudrā of cognitive disengagement,
There's not even an atom to prompt meditation;
nonseparation from true nonmeditation is supreme [1270]
meditation. (31)

The taste of nondual connate great bliss:
just as water poured into water has a single taste,
so, when [mind] abides within [reality] as it is,
cognition fixated on grasping at referents is completely pacified.
(32)

Hey!
In the yoga of the nondual primordial [nature],
what things are there to accept or reject?
Since, my son, I [myself] don't give up
any dharma, I don't say, "Do this." (33)

Just as a jewel is a nonentity,
so the practitioner of yoga is a nonentity:
even when [people] chatter about various [mental] formations,
the yogin's thought doesn't go beyond oneness—
and when there's oneness, even the one does not exist. (34)

The various aspects [of things] are unrooted:
live like a crazy person [acting] freely without calculation,
like a small child engaged in doing nothing. (35)

Oh!
The mind, which is like a lotus born from the mud of existence,
is never covered by any fault:
[through] the pleasures of eating, drinking, and copulation[552]
and even utter torment of body and mind—
the various ways in which someone behaves—
[mind remains] uncovered, neither bound nor freed by anything. (36)

The realized conduct themselves without calculation,
so when destitute, foolish beings come before them,
tears of unbearable compassion well up;
[the realized,] having reversed self and other, become beneficence itself. (37)

When objects are analyzed, they are [seen to be] free of the three reference points;[553]
they are incorrect, like dreams and illusions;
without the hindrance of attachment, there is neither joy nor sadness:[554]
they're the same as the unreal illusions [created by] an illusionist. (38)

In the beginninglessly pure sky-like inherent nature,
there's nothing to abandon or obtain;
[in] the mahāmudrā of cognitive disengagement,
don't hope for any result. (39)

Since the hopeful mind is nonarising from the start,
what could there be to abandon or obtain?
If there were something to be obtained by someone, [1271] what would it be?

If there were something to be obtained by someone,
what could teaching the four seals[555] do? (40)

Just as deer tormented by error
run toward the water in a mirage,
so [when] fools are tormented by desire for something,
regardless of how they strive for it, it grows ever more distant. (41)

The completely pure inherent nature, nonarising from the
outset,[556]
has within it not the slightest distinction,
so cognition that labels is purified within the [reality] sphere:
it is merely labeled as "Vajradhara." (42)

Just as, in a desert mirage
the apparent water and [real] water seem to be nondual,
so cognition that labels, pure from the beginning, is awake:
it can't be expressed through the duality of permanence and
annihilation. (43)

Like a wishing jewel or a wish-granting tree,
it completely fulfills your hopes through the power of prayer:
and although the world is a relative convention,
in sublime truth, there is no existent. (44)

This completes the Mahāmudrā Pith-Instruction Called "Dohā Treasury," *orally composed by the ascetic, the glorious Saraha.*

CHAPTER 17

Body Treasury

An Immortal Vajra Song

[1221] In the Indian language: *Kāyakoṣāmṛtavajragītā*; in the Tibetan language: *Sku'i mdzod 'chi med rdo rje'i glu.*[557]

I bow down to the youthful Mañjuśrī.

Hey! Long-hairs who grasp at self and agent,
brahmins, naked ascetics, experimenters,
and materialists who assert a [physical] basis for suchness
[all] claim to know everything but aren't self-aware—
they've been deceived and are far from the path to liberation. (1)

Vaibhāṣikas, Sautrāntikas, and Māntrikas,
Yogācāras, Mādhyamikas, and others
point to each other's flaws and argue—
not knowing thatness, where appearance and emptiness are
    equally sky-like,
they turn their backs on the connate. (2)

Body, speech, and mind shine like cotton and oil [ablaze] in a lamp:
together in just that way, they shine like a self-illumining lamp;
all beings are pervaded by shining self-awareness:
because of its inseparability, it is the nonarising nature. (3)

The mind that apprehends [1222] a self wanders amid various recollections;
within inherent nature, anything at all may appear.
Although all [beings] abide in a state akin to darkness,
the lamp of yoga blazes when it encounters just that [darkness]. (4)

The essential meaning transcends the domain of logic;
obscured by the power of recollection, it's clearly evident.
A nonconceptual ascertaining cognition is the path to nonrecollective bliss;
without progression, the result appears, beyond thought. (5)

From the treasury of connate mind,
pure and impure appear in the form of saṃsāra and nirvāṇa;
although they appear, they are one in being nonarising—
without inherent nature, thatness is conventionally [described] as immovable. (6)

Mahāmudrā is unchanging great bliss, and
independent of any cause, it is the result beyond thought;
mahāmudrā is the perfected result—
conventionally, it is indicated as the goal of the path. (7)

The essential meaning is without what is expressed or the act of expression;
the sphere of awareness is nonrecollection, in which everything is expressed. (8)

Differential understanding [arises] through aspirational knowledge,
but there can be no falsehood in nonrecollection;

distinct results [occur] through effort on the path,
but there can be no truth in recollection. (9)

You may rest for a while in different [states] through the power of equanimity,
but there can be no duality in nonarising;
you may apply such terms as *cognitive engagement* and *disengagement*,
but there can be no effort in what's beyond thought. (10)

Although recollection arises conditioned by appearances,
it does not transcend the condition that is empty nonrecollection;
that nonconceptual object is actionless and unobserved—
what an error, to seek one's self from others. (11)

Hey! It's difficult to realize suchness as vajra-like;
seeking without knowing, the mind chases words.
It's difficult to encounter the meaning of nondoing;
when the nature of doing is known as nondoing,
that's the unique intention of the conquerors, beyond the sense domain. (12)

The body is the unchanging reality, hollow inside;
[suchness] does not abide [1223] in the body and is beyond deed and doer.
The result will not be seen through a path that's a polluted path;
within nonarising, the mind of the conqueror makes no distinctions. (13)

Within nonrecollection, equipoise is great bliss;
within great bliss, you abide in continuous nonconceptuality.

[In] cognitive engagement, appearances are purified on their own
ground;
the condition is the luminous gnosis of unceasing recollection. (14)

As a flawless lotus expands from a single root,
the connate nature abides in all beings.
[The mind] may be polluted by virtue of wrongly seeing an
existent other,
but just like a lotus flower that is pure from the outset,
by virtue of seeing rightly, [the mind] is unmoving mahāmudrā. (15)

Even when it's polluted by the mud of subject and object,
the root is the great self-nature, unchanging throughout the three
times.
Consciousness, the vital winds, the lower door, mantras, and so
forth
are from the start free from activity, from self and other, from
giving up and letting be. (16)

Don't think of saṃsāra, don't look to nirvāṇa:
the three times and the three worlds are collected within body,
speech, and mind.
Making no effort whatsoever, with no view of [what] to take up
or cast aside,
not distinguishing middle from extreme—the middle is the
straight path. (17)

When it's free from contrivance, it's the supreme path of the
mind,
while the path of the perfections, with its progressions, entrances,
stages, and so forth,

which gives up the quick path, is cause for a long samsaric
[sojourn];
the connate is[558] the unrivaled and matchless antidote. (18)

In suchness are collected the four bodies,
the five gnoses, and the defilements. On a samsaric path,
you should not engage with any arising object, you should see no
object—
[for] in the essential nature, there is no joy nor nonjoy. (19)

Apprehension, concepts, and duality are the uncontrived reality
body;
the senses do not apprehend freely, they are empty.
Uninterrupted experience is ineffable:
you should know how to apply it to your mind-stream. (20)

The stainless truth is mahāmudrā,
arising as an experience that's oceanic or sky-like.
For senses free from objects, there is no abyss into which to fall;
by apprehending [objects of] recollection, [1224] you become
attached. (21)

By leaving things as they are, you avoid complication;
when there is no rising or setting, concepts go dark.
Reality has an equal taste, like flowers for bees;
flaws and virtues are equally indivisible:
it's a great wonder, but the experience can't be described. (22)

Bliss is indivisible, just like water added [to water];
the connate and the yoga [of bliss] are indivisible.
A single thing is seen [by] recollection as many concepts,

while nonrecollection is one, and [yet] is manifold.
Those who practice the yoga of connate great bliss
and emptiness engage [in the practice] beyond thought. (23)

If you wish to apply the path of attachment to the primordial
meaning,
[know that] there is no internal or external referent, no self or
other;
knowing thatness as it is, is taught as natural freedom.
Although three bodies cannot be distinguished within the reality
body,
when you practice, distinct results arise. (24)

Hey! When you realize inseparability, debased views are quickly
destroyed;
if you know that indivisible nonarising emptiness is the meaning
of whatever you encounter, then there are no grounds for living
in the forest. (25)

[When] you don't know [the meaning of] what is encountered,
compassion with signs
is the cause of tainted conduct [conducive to] remaining in
saṃsāra.
Emptiness and compassion are indivisible and nonarising.
Someone free from fear of saṃsāra and hope for nirvāṇa,
attaining neither body nor mind, settles freely into
nonrecollection;
thatness is not attained by thought [but] is self-arising. (26)

What's characterized as equipoise, postmeditation, or calm
abiding
is not ultimate and cannot be meditated upon by thought.

Body, speech, and mind illuminate form and so forth without effort;
not engaging in [meditations] such as those [focusing on] the nose tip,
shapes, sky, and channels, [just] abide in the primordial [nature]. (27)

All appearances are blissful noncognition:[559]
recollection is mere appearance: merely knowing it as illusion is illuminating.
The reflection of the moon is partless and devoid of objectivity;
even if sought, it is not [there], and even if viewed, it is not seen. (28) [1225]

Recollect that illusory-seeming recollection;
in nonrecollection, nothing [of it] is seen.
Even if it appears as recollection, it is not apprehended;
even if it is affected by recollection, there is no notion of being affected. (29)

Since it is free because it cannot be conceived, it is nonarising;
although recollection arises, there is no engagement with the object.
Leave it on its own in its empty [state], where nothing is established;
however you do it, the seal is uninterrupted. (30)

The four-branched mahāmudrā is fourfold:
(1) the branch of realization of the nonarising meaning;
(2) the branch of the nondifference between the two truths;
(3) the branch of nonapprehended recollection, [based on]
realization that appearances you encounter are nonarising;

and (4) the branch where things are neither refuted nor
established, [based on]
emptiness free from conditions or recollection, and beyond
thought. (31)

With just that as the basis, separation from desire,
[states] involving investigation and analysis,
joy and bliss, and dwelling in isolation, and so forth
are said to be the objects indicated by just that [fourfold]
designation.[560] (32)

Basically, [beings] are said to be high, middling, or inferior.
For the sake of the lowly, the wise have clearly explained
that mahāmudrā does not make its abode anywhere;
it is explained thus for the sake of freeing [us] from accepting
[virtue] and rejecting [nonvirtue].
Not distinguishing pure from debased, effect the special
attainments. (33)

The connate, igniting the inner objective fire, and so forth,
pledges, the suchness of the self, and yogic meditation:
in mahāmudrā, the sameness of all things,
how can you abandon concepts or cultivate the nonconceptual?
(34)

The disciplinary vows of the secret [vehicle] are fulfilled by
respect for the guru,
not by defining the individual outer, inner, and secret
consecrations
and their categorization into vase, secret,
wisdom-gnosis, and essential definitive-word [consecrations];
what arises from common powers cannot affect mahāmudrā. (35)

Since the self-nature of the result [of actions of] body, [1226]
speech, and mind is present in mahāmudrā,
that result is feasible with respect to the essential meaning, but
not with respect to the provisional or definitive meaning:
it is the collected distillate of all the essentials of the path and
result,
the truth of the unsurpassed Great Vehicle, that most distinctive
of vehicles,
and the secret [vehicle], which is the essence of all [vehicles]. (36)

The marks for ascertaining mahāmudrā are
recollection, nonrecollection, nondual nonarising,
and [being] beyond thought—why would it not abide like the
sky? (37)

The exemplary action seal, the path of the dharma seal,
the resultant great seal, and the pledge seal [for] the benefit of
others:
relying on the dharma seal or anything lower, falling to extremes
of hope and fear,
and assuming the flaws [entailed by] frivolous doings, you don't
[reach] the utmost. (38)

Within suchness, antidotes are indivisible, you must leave
[things] alone;
to the extent that concepts appear, they appear in relaxation.
When recollection is freed into its own place, then
nonrecollection is relaxation;
know all enjoyments as appearance, and nonrecollection is
restored. (39)

It is the very experience of inherent nature and possessed of
nonarising purity.
It is all-pervasive, like a waterfall,
like an uninterrupted waterfall,
and like a lamp, it is luminous, it is self-aware bodhicitta:
while unceasing, recollective awareness is empty on its own. (40)

You may ask: What is perfect suchness?
If it exists elsewhere, it should be seen by all,
and although it exists within you, it's hidden, like the guru's face.
Mind-itself is suchness buddha,
but polluted by recollection, it is analyzed as existing elsewhere.
(41)

You may ask: What are the qualities because of which it is
buddha?
Its qualities are like cotton and its whiteness;
mahāmudrā has the quality of suchness,
[where] essential qualities cannot be individually differentiated.
(42)

Mahāmudrā, the fourth [consecration], and all the others
are without individual qualities, without difference;
the qualities of nonrecollection are [like] an untroubled ocean:
there is no recollection; there are no waves on the water. (43)
[1227]

The qualities of the nonarising are unchanging, like a rock,
nor do they follow after, [as] the mere sound of an echo does.
Beyond thought and unobjectified,
the qualities of mahāmudrā are like the sky. (44)

Recollection arises from the mind of sentient beings,
so the empty need not be sought elsewhere;
although it appears as fourfold, it has the quality of oneness,
so why point out four seals? (45)

The [seals] specified above arose as fourfold,
so don't conceive mahāmudrā as threefold;
don't dwell anywhere, and conduct yourself without attachment,
like a bee drinking nectar from a flower. (46)

The gnosis of discernment is the method;
when you encounter a taste, don't fixate on the taste—
[but] this will not be known by all.
Although the essential meaning pervades the six [types] of beings,
beings are bound by recollection, like an insect in a lotus bud.[561] (47)

Because recollection emerges from the mind, it is the cause of error,
[while] when you know without mental engagement, that is buddhahood.
In error, there is no method or wisdom.
Hey! When you know their inseparability, just that is the supreme method. (48)

All buddhas, sentient beings, and dharmas
are connate with your own pure mind-itself.
When [something] merely arises within mental disengagement,
the cognized appearance disappears, and there is no true or false;
therefore, [appearances] are not in the domain of suchness. (49)

For example, [just as] sound does not appear in the visual
domain,
nonconceptuality is not in the domain of concepts;
when, conditioned by emptiness, recollection merely shines forth,
the recollected appearance disappears, and there is no seeing. (50)

Gnosis can never be deaf, blind, or mute;
there is no cause for deafness, blindness, or muteness in
nonrecollection.
It is free from all conventionalities, such as physical matter and
so forth,
and the conventionality "appearances disappear"
[connotes] sweeping away recollection and taking
nonrecollection as nourishment. (51)

Thatness, nonarising, and beyond thought:
by burning and purifying subject and object [1228] in the fire
of nonrecollection and nonarising gnosis and offering up what is
beyond thought,
by virtue of [our] prayers, future rebirths will not occur. (52)

Therefore, mahāmudrā is primary:
it does not rely on anyone, it is not dependent on anything;
it's the same as entering water, [joining] an assembly, sharing
food,
and shaking the city of the Vedas. (53)

Because mahāmudrā is nothing apart from yourself,
when the offering substances, guests, and offering sites you
cognize are known as yourself,
then offerings are offered to your own nonrecollection,
and you revel in the nonarising assembly beyond thought. (54)

Because mahāmudrā relies on nothing else,
your own mind is the meditator and its own meditative object;
your own [mind], beyond thought, is without reference point,
and because thatness is the result, it does not depend on other
[factors]. (55)

Practicing meditation and reciting mantras are your own mind,
and meditational deities are also your own mind;
therefore, ḍākinīs, prophets, and so forth are your own mind:
everywhere recollection appears, mind shows [itself]. (56)

In nonrecollection, everything is nonreferential;
since mahāmudrā is nothing apart from your own [mind],
making offerings and praises to Buddha,
Dharma, and Saṅgha, and so forth, as well as to parents,
the three jewels, inherent nature, and bodhicitta are [all] causes
for recollection. (57)

When there are no differences, the nonarising is freed on its own
ground;
when you are beyond thought, there is no doing or not-doing.
Although there are ways of defining buddhas and sentient beings
individually,
they arise simultaneously as awareness and ignorance. (58)

Although something appears, if it is not conceptualized through
recollection,
then sentient beings themselves are the nonarising result;
if something does not appear but is conceptualized through
recollection,
then buddhahood itself [may be] a cause for the three samsaric
spheres. (59)

What can be upheld in unrecollected cognition?
Although sentient beings appear, they are the same as buddhas;
if you wish to realize buddha [through] recollection,
[know that] although buddhas appear, they are not distinct from sentient beings. (60) [1229]

Thus, the duality of appearance and analysis is unanalyzable, so discard it;
although discarded, it is not other than yourself—[see this,] and the continuum of [samsaric] wandering is cut.
The notion that it is other than yourself is polluted by logic and recollection,
[while] in luminous appearance, mind is nonconceptual nonfixation. (61)

Therefore, freed from dualistic conceptions of existence and nonexistence,
when you abide in the primordial state, whatever you do, it's blissful;
one endowed with the essence of luminous-recollection apprehension
is free from dualistic fixation and rests in the primordial nature. (62)

Thus, mahāmudrā is the highest union,
where recollection, nonrecollection, and nonarising are united.
Nonrecollection, which has the nature of nonconceptuality,
and recollection, which arises [through] temporary conditionality:
these two have a single taste within nonarising,
so that arisen and arising are beyond thought. (63)

Luminosity, emptiness, [their] union, and so forth
are uncontrived, unmade, nonarising, and freed on their own
ground;
that is explained as the three bodies: reality body,
enjoyment body, and the various appearances of the emanation
body,
[while] the primordial [nature] is the essence body,
compassion and emptiness, indivisible and nonarising. (64)

Since experience based on the action seal
is contrived, it emerges through conditions,
and because it depends on other [factors], it is not suchness. (65)

Although the dharma seal is uncontrived,
when it's experienced, its nonestablishment is not seen.
When mahāmudrā is experienced,
[our] various recollections are known to be nonarising. (66)

What appears as a thing is empty of essential nature;
the meaning, the inseparability of sentient beings and nonarising,
is shown by illustrative examples through compassionate
methods. (67)

Although appearances are various, do not move from [the state]
beyond thought,
and always observe the yoga of self-nature itself;
in all conduct on the path, abide in mahāmudrā,
and rest within the nonarising, abiding nature of things. (68)

Because of the wind, rippling waves
arise temporarily in a limpid sea; [1230]
those very [waves] are indivisible from the sea.

Conditioned by recollection, concepts temporarily arise,
while thatness is nonrecollection of those very [things]:
they are nonarising and beyond thought, hence equally
wondrous. (69)

Thus, just as in mahāmudrā there is no previous arising,
so, too, although [things] may arise later through conditions,
they are indivisible from nonarising.
[Mahāmudrā] is formless and all-pervasive,
unchanging and [present at] all times. (70)

Like sky, it does not arise or cease,
and like a rope apprehended as a snake, it is empty of snake;
the reality body, enjoyment body, and emanation body are
indivisible,
and the essential nature is beyond the domain of thought. (71)

Mahāmudrā is manifest awakening in an instant;
it arises as the form body for the sake of sentient beings.
Results correspond to their causes, and the results ripen:
the pure result is acting for the sake of others.
That level is said to be quite beyond expression. (72)

Hey! Uncontrived mahāmudrā is great bliss;
it appears on its own in the vast expanse of nonrecollection.
Its nonarising is pervasive like sky,
abiding within what's beyond thought. (73)

Appearances free from complication are great bliss,
nonrecollection does not conceptualize anything;
various recollections shine forth as mind,
but when they're sought and analyzed, no referent [is found]. (74)

The nonarising is free from grasping,
and because it is free from grasping, it does not move;
recollection is illusory, mere self-awareness,
[which] shines forth without illusion, without liberation, without recollection. (75)

Since the nonarising ultimate shines on everything,
all [things] appear as beyond thought;
that very gnosis that's beyond thought [in] the three spheres
is connate suchness—
determine [that it is] the root of all recollection. (76)

Place nonrecollection in the nonarising realm;
uncontrived thatness is beyond the domain of thought.
It shines with the self-effulgence of mind that recollects and is aware,
and by shining [thus], it associates with samsaric concepts. (77)

Knowing [1231] the path of liberation as suchness,
abide within concept-free self-emergence just as it is;
self-illumining recollection is not established as a thing. (78)

This uncontrived intention, [this] nonarising great bliss,
appears to the senses, so there is nothing to identify;
in the domain of nonrecollection, there is nothing to see,
and since it lacks a basis, there is nothing to study. (79)

Where there is no cognitive engagement, there is mahāmudrā;
the varied and diverse awareness of recollected signs
is just mahāmudrā, in which there are no categories
and [where] realization and nonrealization are not distinguished. (80)

Not abiding in the extremes of permanence or nonexistence, it is free from flaws;
when you realize thatness, [it's] your own, not someone else's.
When conditionality and the path to nirvāṇa are taught
and realized as nonarising, that is mahāmudrā. (81)

Those who don't know thatness desire and strive toward
the action seal, the pledge seal, and so forth,
[which are] mere examples pointing to thatness, not its true meaning,
[while from] reliance on mahāmudrā free from object and subject,
knowledge arises freshly on its own. (82)

Without desire, it abides in the essence of the primordial nature;
knowledge of ordinary appearances is itself thought,
resting on its own in the mind recollecting is and isn't.
The jewel of trust is a wish-fulfilling treasure of instruction:
settle into it without cognitive action or inaction. (83)

Since self-awareness is mahāmudrā itself,
it is taught within, and by, mahāmudrā itself;
don't engage the mind with the objects of various recollections. (84)

Free from outer and inner, the seal is free from dispute,
and one who is alive to mahāmudrā is without desire,
[for] when desire arises, that also is the cause of recollection. (85)

In your own mind, mahāmudrā,
the distinction between recollection and nonrecollection does not arise;

errancy and inerrancy are beyond thought,
[while] expanding conceptually fixated recollection is the cause
of saṃsāra. (86)

Luminosity, mahāmudrā, and the primordial essential nature,
which does not change at all, are one in bodhicitta;
suchness [1232] is free from essential subject or object,
and the meaning of appearance is seen in gnosis itself. (87)

Through mental analysis, you wander amid the sense collections
[known through] recollection,
and arising appearances are seen through wrong [ideas];
engaging consciousness within recollection and nonrecollection
is not a cause for recollection, even with exertion of body, speech,
and mind. (88)

Since there is no duality, saṃsāra has no nature—
this is the nature of varied and shifting recollection;
from the start, it does not exist in the seals at the nose tip,
and thus, [in] the concept-free great seal, you should let go of
acceptance and rejection. (89)

Hey! The inner and outer, profound and nonprofound
generation stage,
the thoroughly established essential nature, breathing in and out,
confirming the action and dharma seals:
these are the stages of thoroughly perfect yoga.[562] (90)

Mahāmudrā is the stage of essential nature;
the pledge seal is the stage of the thoroughly established
[nature],
the seal of the thoroughly established imputed nature;

the action seal is the essence of [the third] consecration
and naturally possesses the methods of the four joys;
the dharma seal is various appearances:
among the four joys, it is the connate [joy]. (91)

As for nonarising mahāmudrā,
it is free from recollection of subject or object, its essence beyond thought;
it is the stainless result, manifest buddhahood. (92)

The pledge seal is a yoga with signs,
and the result, the maṇḍala of deities, is for the sake of beings;
it indicates the holy father and mother, method and wisdom. (93)

Endowed with the four joys, the pledge seal is great;
thus, even if you train yourself in all applications of method,
the profound [wisdom] is established by the dharma seal,
while mind-itself on its own is taught as mahāmudrā. (94)

Isolating recollection of objects through joy,
giving up subjective examination through supreme joy,
isolating recollection through connate joy,
the appearance of cessative joy illumines nonarising recollection—
thus is the profound dharma seal taught. (95) [1233]

Where the gnoses of the four joys arise,
and there is no differentiation, you abide in complete absorption,
and [when] you abide in experiences of realization,[563]
there is in cognition no difference between nonrecollection and concepts—
examples and the path are taught in order to subdue conventionality. (96)

The dawning of mind-itself, mahāmudrā,
is the miraculous dawning of whatever there is, nonarising or arisen;
since it is beyond thought, it is taught as essentially nonarising:
both nonarising things and those that arise
don't differ when left to their essential nature. (97)

Wherever varied recollection may wander,
when you engage in nonrecollection, concepts will not stop;
when knowing is left to its own devices, it will abide.
The cause of birth is apprehending appearances and emptiness as two,
when you understand that they are not different, that is great bliss. (98)

When experience dawns, you'll be free from discordant grasping:
there is no recollection, and there is no such object;
nonrecollection and empty appearances are not different. (99)

In the yoga of signless nonarising,
there is neither equipoise nor postmeditation;
also, whatever recollection of appearance or arising arises,
because you abide in nonrecollection, which is empty thatness,
recollective cognition is inactive, [as] appearance and emptiness cannot be separated. (100)

In the encounter with thatness, the experience of nonarising,
the empty essence of appearances dawns as great bliss;
just as ice that's melted into water is fit for drinking,
so everything that appears is felt as nonarising great bliss. (101)

Equanimity is nonrecollection, but concepts do not cease;
since it is beyond thought, it is freed from foolish meditation:

when you abide in this, the experience of great bliss will occur.
First, the experience of empty appearances occurs,
like recognizing water even when it appears as ice. (102)

Second, without stopping appearances within recollection,
the empty and the blissful emerge as undifferentiated;
just as when ice melts into water,
recollection and nonrecollection dissolve into the [1234] nonarising. (103)

Since all [things] are undifferentiated, they are one in great bliss—
it's like ice that has melted into water;
when [through] knowledge you encounter the nature of everything,
you won't be held by bondage or freedom and won't chase after recollection. (104)

The mind will not be obstructed as it is when bound by worldly concerns;
when worldly concerns are loosened, you are free, and mind-itself is left on its own,
like a flying raven that returns to a ship.
When you know thatness, appearances are enjoyed. (105)

Like an elephant tamed when prodded by a goad,
when [mind] is left inactive, it's like an elephant that's been [tamed].
Recognition of recollection and nonrecollection is harmless;
by knowing appearance and emptiness, you're free from conceptualization. (106)

When you abide within arising, it's inseparable [from
nonarising,] and recollection does not stir;
[realizing] thatness is like the pervasive lord [Viṣṇu] recognizing
all enemies.
Dissolving appearances into emptiness is like salt dissolving into
water:
dissolving recollection and nonrecollection [evokes] suchness.
(107)

In the two aspects of arising, there is no cause for arising,
since when the nonarising gnosis dawns in [mystical] encounter,
recollection appears as gnosis without objects of thought,
without bias:
it blazes on its own, like fire spreading through tinder,
or like[564] the bliss of a youth [who has had] an ineffable
experience. (108)

Although various [things] appear, they will not turn into
recollection,
[as] gently flowing water will not turn into waves;
since it illumines its own essence, recollection is a lamp. (109)

Thus, since mahāmudrā is not taught anywhere,
it's like a *sarkone* bird[565] living in the sky;
since the practice of realization is not brought about through
acceptance or rejection,
it's [like] the *patari* beast,[566] which [lives] without passion.
When you desire the result beyond thought, you accomplish
nothing;
among the supreme medicines, thusness is the *beta* [tree].[567] (110)

Hey! Thus, the wise, who are established in methods,
seal nonrecollection with nonarising;
because it lacks recollection, it is sealed by nonrecollection:
emptiness is sealed by appearances,
and appearances [1235] are sealed by emptiness. (111)

When recollection and appearance arise with the taste of bliss,
they are sealed by emptiness and nonrecollection;
when appearance and recollection, [and] the seal of emptiness
are sealed by those who abide in nonrecollection,
then appearance and recollection arise with the taste of bliss
and are not examined by meditation involving signs—they are
beyond thought involving signs. (112)

Recollection and appearance are sealed by nonarising,
and nonarising is sealed by [going] beyond thought;
since recollection is sealed by nonrecollective bliss,
it does not become nothing, [so you] do not fall to the extreme of
annihilation. (113)

Since abiding and arising are sealed [by emptiness],
they do not become things, [so you] do not fall to the extreme of
permanence;
everything is beyond thought and nonarising,
everything possesses the causes[568] of great bliss—
knowing this, you do not fall to the extreme of indifference. (114)

Recollection is the substance of saṃsāra.
In the realization of nonrecollection,
equanimity should be carried onto the path. (115)

Sought by awareness, emptiness is equanimity,
and since self-awareness free from subject and object is
equanimity,
you should meditate on nondual equanimity that is free from the
two truths.
Contemplation without recognition of anything is supreme
equanimity,
while indeterminate equanimity is not meditation. (116)

Knowing left on its own projects the experience of
nonrecollection,
while the signs involved in recollection are carried onto the path
as nonrecollection.
Bliss carried onto the path is beyond thought and is
nonreferential;
without notions of duality, it is bliss uninterrupted. (117)

Hey! Free of experience, you're free of subject and object
and will see the meaning of thatness, mahāmudrā;
in the great treasure jewel of the utmost result,
may those who desire to abide in mahāmudrā
realize the stainless result. (118)

This completes the Body Treasury: An Immortal Vajra Song, *which was spoken directly by Saraha.*

CHAPTER 18

Speech Treasury

A Gentle Vajra Song

[1238] In the Indian language: *Vākkoṣa-rucirasvaravajragītā*; in the Tibetan language: *Gsung gi mdzod 'jam dbyangs rdo rje'i glu.*[569]

I bow down to the youthful Mañjuśrī.

Hey! Single-pointed concentration is distinguished by the practice of equal taste;
since conceptualizing things and nonthings is the cause of saṃsāra, let it go.
The union of appearance and emptiness is indivisible suchness;
everything arises in the nature of the reality sphere and abides in dissolution [there]. (1)

Within the illumination of nonrecollection, where the aims of self and other are not two,
enumerations of mahāmudrā are infinite and beyond expression;
when "thing" and "nonthing" are completely released, there is no saṃsāra or nirvāṇa:
if a pond has no cover, the circle of the four directions is abandoned.[570] (2)

Childish ignorance is the cause for entering into samsaric conditionality,
[so] those with weakened wisdom grasp at things and do not accomplish the aims of self or others.
Even [as] a blazing lamp cannot appear to the blind,
[so] those intent [1239] on the aims of self and others grasp at things, grasping at self by themselves. (3)

Because there is conceptuality, release and nonrelease require analysis,
while self-awareness, which involves no appearance, is free from all conceptual conventions;
because they lack method, [the ignorant] will not accomplish their own aims and will be [caught up] in signs. (4)

Abiding in the indivisible true meaning, the teacher
teaches the characteristics of entrance into the reality sphere.
The guru teaches the doctrines, scriptures, commentaries, and special instructions;
those desiring to realize the specific characteristics [of things] through scriptures and reasoning
will attain it from those holding the special instructions taught[571] by the guru:
when you make reverence [to the guru], you obtain great bliss in an instant. (5)

Because the guru's deeds are stainless, you should bow to his feet;
the Conqueror explained that when you offer [to the guru], great blessings arise. (6)

Hey! You may fly magically through the sky, but it's just the city [of saṃsāra];
if the liberated exert themselves, they'll no doubt [reach] the level of a conqueror. (7)

Expressed and expression, consecrations and blessings occurring and increasing;
what the student must do beforehand and the sequence of what the master must do;
what the student must do afterward and the consecration into the profound;
[the master,] requested by mudrās, offerings, and praise,
and requested with sweet words, granting the awareness-expressing
consecration and [also] the secret consecration that is based on the consort, [with its] vows,
granting permission [to practice] and afterward spreading the teaching;
[accepting] the substances offered by the student and teaching the promises [required by] the consecration into the profound;
teaching the generation stage and so forth;
teaching the stages of essential nature;
[teaching] what can be said about meditative experience and so forth, all that—
don't dwell on any of it; like a *sarkone* [bird], don't build a nest anywhere;
in the bliss of desirelessness, there is no dwelling.
Because it is without diversity, it is free from basis or basing:
the experience of the self-dawning nondual yoga is bliss,
and when you give up the entity conceptualized as the self, you're as vast as the limits [1240] of the sky. (8–11)

If you want to enter the city of nirvāṇa,
then by cultivation of the great yoga [applied] like continuous rain to what is encountered
by the six sense collections
and [by practice] of nonduality independent of conditions, which encounters
empty, nonarising appearances, you will quickly [attain] the union [at the end of] the path and not turn back. (12)

When you know the inherent nature of sentient beings and buddhas, there is no more effort;
relying on those who practice the equal taste, you'll obtain the result.
When they make that their practice, beings will no doubt be liberated from saṃsāra,
and demons and discord will be overcome. (13)

The yoga with signs is not to be performed, and equanimity isn't yoga;
quickly obtain the gnosis of the wise and extinguish the obscurations.
By practicing with signs, fools may be wise to provisional meaning, but they are bound,
[while] those who rely on the mahāmudrā of equal taste traverse the sky. (14)

If you rely continually on the path of practicing nonduality, you'll win [freedom] in this life;
don't abide in the sphere of illusory appearances, for the objects you conceive do not exist.

For those bound by the eight mundane concerns,[572] supreme
austerity is impotent,
while unattached conduct upheld by compassionate means is as
vast as the sky. (15)

The methods of the four-branched great seal[573] are supreme:
within the singular magical display of the single great seal as
four,
within nonduality, relax and rest in mahāmudrā. (16)

When you possess bodhicitta without taking up or letting go,
you're like an elephant;
through essential realization,[574] a cow, if you so desire, may
appear as a horse.
Striving for the goal of nonconceptuality and nonappearance,
perform yoga. (17)

Within the great bliss of the four bodies, the utmost result,
path bodies, appearing to arise,
possess the power of the three bodies, and are quite free of
concepts;
knowing and what's to be known are [in] the pure domain of
your own mind-stream. (18)

Although the nature of things appears through the conditions for
arising,
they are not experienced as transcending the nonarising domain;
entities, nonentities, equanimity, and so forth—all of these
are indistinguishable, their domain that of nonrecollection and
nonarising. (19)

Mahāmudrā is eternally free from characteristics; [1241]
since the aggregates are pure, it transcends the secret domain.[575]
The characteristics of the four joys are [in] the domain of the [great] seal,
which is not your own mind-stream and is free from wisdom and method. (20)

Since thatness is not grasped by nose-tip [meditation] or other [practices],
even applying yourself to pure thatness is not the ultimate;
abiding in adamantine self-awareness, the hero's yoga,
is not essentially like omniscience. (21)

The ocean's waves are essentially the same as echoes:
you don't get anywhere just by counting them.
Connecting the fulfillment of pledges with the [final] result
is the path of conventional words that define or are defined. (22)

When you think of pledges, where are notions of methods and so forth?
In the domain beyond thought, there is no training.
Through the performance of [tantric] austerities, outer and inner are transformed;
if you possess suchness, you have distinction,
while if you don't possess that, you're the same as the animals. (23)

Since thatness is hidden, meditate on the connate;
although pledges bereft of methods are a contradiction in terms, there is no fault:
without regard for enumerating this [world] or the [world] beyond,

mahāmudrā manifests right this instant,
but if you abandon thatness, you'll never encounter it. (24)

Even hearing of mahāmudrā for an instant—
regardless of whether or not you know scripture—
just by that teaching, by this single root, it is obtained;
someone who, undistracted by recollection,
meditates on the connate meaning will obtain it. (25)

It is your own thatness, so don't seek the Dharma of others;
when you scrounge like a fox or other [beast] in a cremation
ground, your pursuit ends in ruin. (26)

Hey! Just as [when] a brahmin seeks to mingle by going begging
at a low-caste household,
the mingling of good and bad [leads] each to harm the other,
[so] the yoga with signs does not touch the signless meaning.
The signless can never be observed;
signs come to be when time and number are observed. (27)

The stages of generation and completion cannot be conceived as
distinct;
those who combine them in nonduality possess the supreme yoga,
while the ignorant [see] nonrecollection as a domain of
distraction:
leave [1242] the stream of recollection and cultivate that [yoga]. (28)

From the very outset, those on the uncommon,
distinctive secret-mantra [path] abide in essence of truth;
when special attainments are combined, you touch the connate:
distinctive self-aware thatness is beyond the [sensory] domain. (29)

Thatness is the abode of bliss and empty of entities;
since dharmas are pure, the point of natural bliss
is to abide nowhere: transcending the domain of thought,
[thatness] is nonobjective, nonabiding, without a basis: it is
empty. (30)

Evaṃ is the cause for the essential special attainment.
The combination, in the mind-stream, of Vajradhara
and the word of the self-aware guru is stainless mahāmudrā;
while the relative[-level] action seal and the others
are equivalent to the retinue of servants of a wheel-turning king.
(31)

All [the aspects of] the generation stage—outer, inner, and
profound—
are to the seal of completion as tiny stars to the sun and moon.
Cessative joy, joy, supreme joy, and so forth,
and connate joy, which are at the very root of the cakras,
are illumined in the intention to purify them into stainlessness.
(32)

When you possess thatness, you perpetually experience gnosis;
emptiness of indivisible mind is the level of vastness.
Possessing the methods of body and speech, meditate in reliance
upon those methods;
the causes and conditions producing recollection ripen the fruit.
(33)

To draw out the karmically [ripe], apply yourself to methods
[leading to] freedom;
experiencing the action seal produces pride,
while cultivating the practice of thatness is the path to freedom. (34)

By desiring to see the lotus joined with the vajra
and by a path of desire, you will not be freed [into] thatness;
on the other hand, when you rely on experiencing the action seal,
mahāmudrā will ignite [within] your own ordinary body.
Mahāmudrā is all-pervasive; it's equivalent,
for example, to a precious gem or the sky. (35)

The five aggregates and so forth become the supreme secret:
the mundane and the transmundane abide connately,
and suchness, which is pointed out through the kindness [1243]
of the guru, is attained on its own, without need of proof. (36)

The supreme great seal itself is free of stain;
because it is the level to be obtained, it should be engaged.
The nondual unification of permanence and annihilation settles into oneness;
it is known [through] awareness [derived from] scripture and pith instructions. (37)

When you accomplish suchness, there is no problem;
when mahāmudrā shines and you cultivate knowledge,
there is no doubt: you realize suchness—
and when you know just that, practice with the power you've cultivated. (38)

[When] you don't realize thatness and rely on the upper door,
the lower door,[576] and the consort, you're triply scattered
and are just the same as ducks, fish, and beasts. (39)

Having comprehended conventions in the self-aware mind-stream
and scrutinized outer and inner, if you're intent on what lacks inherent nature,
then there may be worldly chatter, but it makes no difference—it's all the same. (40)

Desiring liberation through the doors of truth and conditionality,
desiring to be led on the path to liberation by control of the sense faculties,
beguiled by empty pleasures [like] a childish drunkard:
[for those] intent on doing such deeds, deceived by falsehood, there is no liberation;
one who asserts the reasoning of the Sāṃkhyas and so forth, or of the Jainas or Vaiśeṣikas,
promulgating their views on action, causation, and so forth, will roam around [in saṃsāra]. (41)

Hey! How, then, do we give up saṃsāra?
Since it lacks causes or conditions, abide in mahāmudrā,
the thatness of mind that is not [in] the domain of analysis;
through thatness, you'll be free from signs,
and obtain mahāmudrā in a single life. (42)

Hey! How wondrous! This [is the] experiential domain of secret conduct,
the dawning of nonarising through the Medicine King's realization;
themselves possessing the characteristics of the five gnoses and so forth,
[those in] the highest, most fortunate lineage[577] will see suchness. (43)

Recollection reliant on signs is a cause of distraction;
since the external world has no reference point in suchness,
you should dissolve it into nonrecollection of the experiential
domain of signs. (44)

The yoga of signs is the road to the three samsaric spheres:
entities with signs contain [1244] the seeds of carelessness,
while the yoga of nonrecollection is equivalent to the center of
the sky. (45)

If there are no distinctions, essences do not arise,
so there is no experience of the thought of other people;
those wise to the view of thatness will give rise to what is to be
practiced. (46)

[Through] nonrecollection, give up dwelling in recollection,
concepts, and forms, and dwelling as well in the three spheres;
nonarising thatness is the abode of all special attainments;
nonreference to outer and inner accomplishes everything. (47)

Hey! Whoever possesses mahāmudrā, with its supreme qualities,
pleases the guru and so has the basis for all special attainments;
[when you] don't abandon the supreme rarity that is the guru, all
good qualities emerge.
May those yogins with a mind of faith—
one in a hundred—realize [the meaning of] this text. (48)

This completes the Speech Treasury: A Gentle Vajra Song, *spoken by Saraha.*

CHAPTER 19

Mind Treasury

A Vajra Song on Nonarising

[1246] In the Indian language: *Cittakoṣa-ajavajragītā*; in the Tibetan language: *Thugs kyi mdzod skye med rdo rje'i glu*.[578]

I bow down to the youthful Mañjuśrī.

Hey! The connate gnosis
is suchness experienced on its own,
suchness illuminating awareness, unawareness, and
self-awareness;
[as] a lamp illuminates the dark and [also] illuminates itself by
itself, [gnosis] awakens to itself. (1)

The beautifully colored mud[-born] lotus does not fixate on
mud;
not spurning the stains of subject and object, illuminate the
essential. (2)

Deer that live deep in the forest wander alone;
not fixating on the cause is the result itself.
It shines without appearance, nonappearance, or object, without
fixation;

not mindful of entities or emptiness, it is unforgetting[579]
nonrecollection;
bliss is experience in the three aspects of the connate.[580] (3)

Because of nonfixation, you are beyond the domain of logic;
do not pursue [logic] for the sake of cognizing variety.
Luminous and unequaled gnosis is the very essence:
just as the [brilliance] of the lamp of the sun dispels [1247] the dark,
when self-awareness blazes within itself, grasping and
conceptuality are ended. (4)

Because the obscurations have ended [in it], nonrecollection is
undistracted;
don't give rise to dualistic conventions, such as is or isn't:
mahāmudrā is inconceivable and beyond thought. (5)

The self-aware vajra-bearing yogin [possessing]
the lamp of the connate that's hard to transcend[581]
aims to unify method and wisdom;
[the connate is] nonarising, empty, luminous, and impartial. (6)

The distinctive gnosis, which is suchness,
is independent of duality and is uninterrupted bliss;
it is self-arisen, nonconceptual, and has cut karmic tendencies
from the root. (7)

Although the distinction between sentient beings and buddhas is
unthinkable,
when conduct on the path is pure, that is continuous great yoga;
although recollection is inconceivable,
since it is pure from the start, it dissolves into the realm of
nonrecollection. (8)

One's own aim is nonarising true realization free from duality;
since the result is pure, it is beyond thought, free from objects [or] their nonexistence.
The continuous method for realization is the all-pervasive inherent nature. (9)

While compassion [that fulfills] the aims of beings through[582] [skillful] methods is unthinkable,
gnosis is the realization of the inherent nature, without arising or ceasing;[583]
although bliss may arise [through yogic] methods, if you don't grasp its nonexistence, it is bondage;
the gnosis of freedom arises within oneself in an instant. (10)

Meditator and meditative object are beyond referential thought;
buddhas and sentient beings are inconceivable;
when an object of realization is nonarising, it does not arise in thought;
when thatness is activated, it's indicated by blissful emptiness. (11)

The entities[584] that are objects of meditation emerge through apparent conditions;
relative conventions are accomplished when nonconceptuality is realized;
the appearance of nonduality is without conditions;
natural purity dawns as the arising of magical manifestations. (12)

Not conceptualized [as] separate or not separate, beyond thought,
in the nondual that's to be realized, nonarising becomes the object.
You won't realize thatness by saying it's empty,
and since it's beyond thought, there is no object of which to think. (13)

Those who assert [1248] the permanence of the three extremes[585]
have trouble attaining [thatness];
even if they visualize the four joys, thatness is difficult [to attain];
since the six sense collections possess supreme gnosis on their own,
the appearance of the nondual distillate will dawn on its own. (14)

Hey! Mahāmudrā, free from conceptuality, is the basis of everything,
and because special attainments emerge [from it], it is wondrous, it is greatly marvelous;
having activated the tendency for nonduality, you are freed [into] self-awareness. (15)

Mahāmudrā is free from subject and object;
śrāvakas and other [lesser practitioners] are frightened by the teaching on the characteristics [of things].
When you observe [mahāmudrā] single-pointedly, you'll possess the utmost qualities,
[but] even if you gain single-pointedness, there is nothing at all on which to meditate. (16)

Concepts immolate themselves, and nonrecollection is a healing calm;
nonrecollection and nonappearance are like reflections in a mirror;
being free from conventions, the path is nonarising and beyond thought.
Stainless recollection of signs is taught as a tendency [to acquire]:
free of beginning and end, it cannot be referred to as earlier or later.
Hey! Therefore, the gnosis [that knows] there are no entities is the path to realization. (17)

If you ask how to be free of karmic tendencies,
[well,] they are pacified by not grasping at duality and by
freedom from origin and ending;
when you're free of karmic tendencies, you're without direction,
[yet] devoid of wandering. (18)

Union is the very essence of the Buddha,
[who] spoke of the objects of the threefold wisdom and of method;[586]
beyond exemplification, he transcends the domain of signs. (19)

In [what] arises, the heart of the sublime is not [found],
[but] through application of methods, the six sense collections
are pacified on their own ground
and the five aggregates and so forth [become] a field of pure
qualities;
omniscience is nondual and free from fixation on sense objects. (20)

The ultimate is unspoken, while the relative is merely logic;
the path of nirvāṇa is samsaric appearance itself:
encountering [everything] as the intention of the sublime guru,
you will be free from the samsaric path. (21)

Gaining the experience intended by yoga, you'll [become] a
complete buddha;
on the unmistaken path, there is just the connate. (22)

Hey! In true nonduality, you're freed by secret-mantra symbols,
and your qualities [1249] are akin to an inexhaustible ocean of
jewels;
if you hold to the supreme methods, you'll dwell on the
fourteenth stage,
and wherever you dwell, gnosis is attained on its own. (23)

Those who would gain treasure are fools when it comes to the
aims of self and others;
the amulet box of the heart, the lotus flower at the center:
someone possessing methods applies them, and it opens.
Wherever the channels [intersect] the cakras,
when you're free from desire, even in the sky of nonattachment,
drawing [energies] up and down and turning the cakras
is a way of drawing out methods, but you won't attain the deepest
truth.[587] (24)

Even if you seize, expel, join, and ignite [breath energies],
you're no different from an asthmatic fool—you're the same. (25)

Those desiring realization always look to thatness;
those with sincere respect rely on the supremely rare guru,
and from the supreme guru secret qualities will arise;
possessing worthwhile characteristics, you'll defeat defilement in
battle. (26)

Through the guru, the master who possesses the meaning
of truth itself and possesses the oral transmission,
may beings be freed through the nondual door. (27)

This completes the Mind Treasury: A Vajra Song on Nonarising *[on] the essential secret meaning, which was spoken directly by the glorious Saraha.*

CHAPTER 20

Cognitive Disengagement from Body, Speech, and Mind

[1251] In the Indian language: *Kāyavākcittāmanasikāra-nāma*; in the Tibetan language: *Sku gsung thugs yid la mi byed pa zhes bya ba*.[588]

I bow down to the one who does not dwell at all upon signs.
I bow down to Vajradhara.

Those with distinctive bodily attributes, who utterly defeat the four māras
and who bring about complete yogic freedom,
and who [bring about] the desired goals of beings
through perfect generosity, reveal those goals through the attribute of love. (1)

The mind of the conqueror is the ultimate notion of utter nonabiding:
whoever doesn't think all this in their mind—ah!
You teach the many limbs of enlightened activity
and delight and satiate all the worlds [to the ends] of the sky. (2)

You utter various sounds through the sixty branches of supreme speech,
and although the distinctive concepts in your mind never shake loose from the reality sphere,

all are satisfied and praise [1252] you with gladness;
with love and compassion, you show clearly the maṇḍala of [Sita]
patra,
and you utterly vanquish Mahādeva and Umādevī. (3)

The self-nature of all the buddhas of the ten directions and the
three times:
this very path of the yogins is the door to liberation.
Any who apply themselves to the supreme, principal [reality]
without categorizing—
[they're practicing] the undifferentiated great yoga. (4)

There are those who due to the stain
of unknowing see nothing at all,
and those who, completely binding [ignorance]
through their own luster and splendor, teach through their every
deed. (5)

Those whose forms are pervaded [by] the single taste of no-self
do not abide here at all, yet act [on behalf of] beings. (6)

Through the royal consecrations of the mantra and sūtra
classes—
with the root of all of these being cognitive disengagement—
you shouldn't think in terms of one or two—ah! (7)

Showing the various magic displays of relative recollection,
[experiencing] the single taste in the sphere of the nonreferential
ultimate,
clearing away the darkness of those afflicted by the five poisons
and other diseases,

without seeing the extreme of a beginning or an actual basis for
an ending:
in the uncompounded, cognition has no reference point—ah! (8)

Residing namelessly between the duality of subject and object:
when the parts collapse, [that's] the essential nature of the one.
To know and to do: all [such] conventions
are defilements [induced] by signs [based on] viewing things as
other than they are. (9)

Just as Rāhu consumes the moon,
the childish, who are unseeing and lost betwixt and between,
say, "The essential nature is [found] between distraction and
stability," though it's not;
when uncaused, unconditioned nonarising is [seen] as dual,
then, because of the buildup of wrong views, you can't be
absorbed in [thatness]. (10)

As if colored with drops of gallstone, saffron, or sandalwood,
the beautiful moon may be obscured by the light [1253] of
constellations.
The light of the heart outshines that of the limbs:
"from here to there—that's all": it's difficult to analyze [how] this
occurs.[589] (11)

For those with the quality of desire for enjoyment
in the pure sky, no waxing or waning occurs;
from them emerges a treasury of mental qualities,
which are [like] possession of a stainless jewel. (12)

The view of permanence [brought on] by way of not seeing
[leads the ignorant] to say, "This is reality, the essence indicated
[by buddhas]." This must be transcended,
for even those of supreme thought can't penetrate it,
and tathāgatas, by way of [knowing] nonduality,
know that there is nothing that proceeds from here:
[thatness] is unabiding: it doesn't dwell anywhere. (13)

In this nonobjective [reality], there is freedom from the view of
permanence,
and in any and every direction you might go from here,
you should, without paying heed to fearful sounds,
immediately do what [leads to] happiness. (14)

Hey, friends! Here, all analysis of mind in terms of is or isn't
is the quaking of vital-wind[-borne] concepts and issues in crazy
words;
having gone crazy, you fall into an ocean
and won't be free from the darkness of Brahmā, atoms, or signs. (15)

Desiring to realize thatness that's free from duality
is [like] seeing broken shards turn to jewels [on] the ocean floor;
any austerities performed for the sake of nirvāṇa
[simply] show what unknowing is like. (16)

The primordial [nature], which is free from the two truths and
without exaggeration or underestimation
is not seen anywhere,
[but] it's definitive accomplishment and has in it no inherent
nature:
through not seeing it, you become a conqueror. (17)

Nirvāṇa is taught by way of the three vehicles;[590]
not knowing this, you don't see thatness.
[In] showing the path to freedom, there is no examination of particulars— [1254]
the childish don't know this. (18)

Someone who desires to realize freedom from passion
and abandons sufferings—the three, the eight,[591] and so forth—
is not beyond the two truths, effects the aims of beings
by various ways and means, [and] sends forth light-rays right and left. (19)

An impure, downward-facing full skull is taught to be pure,[592]
the six sense domains and so forth, which are an intertwined thicket, are destroyed;
those possessing omniscience are not seen by anyone:
although praised for their renown and so forth, they [remain] unperturbed. (20)

Hey! If you abide like this, you'll know everything,
but the ocean of existence is turbulent without beginning or end,
and [unknowing] is the root of suffering itself. (21)

As a mud-[born] lotus is not covered by the stains
of defilement- and knowledge-[obscurations],
unmixed colors appear in objects as if distinct,
but they're realized as illusions, like a performer's magical creation. (22)

The power cultivated through various accumulated
formations and temporary dependent arisings:

cultivating it will never result in knowledge,
while by not cultivating it, you'll know everything. (23)

Mixed dharmas: don't establish them at all.
Body, speech, and mind, the seals and so forth—all the stages:
don't cognize them even for an instant.
Worldly treatises and volumes
can't express the self-nature of speech. (24)

The sun and moon [seem to] exist as two,
[but] someone who mixes them together into one
is beautifully adorned, whatever their practice;
by expressing the middle that expresses certainty
as to nonarising, you completely abandon extremes. (25)

Those of the cut-off lineage, who roam in worldly realms
unable to understand the teaching,
are insensitive to the anguish [1255] [brought on] by karmic tendencies
and won't see the meaning of stainless reality,
while whoever is never apart from [thatness],
will quickly and instantly be free from the body apprehended by recollection. (26)

Vajra mind is hard to analyze:
thinking "don't see mind in mind,"
the peak of contemplation is devoid of analysis of outside or inside,
and the yoga that abides in true genuineness
is perfected in the secret sphere of wisdom and gnosis. (27)

Saying "not seeing, you possess all [proper] characteristics"
[means you should] practice without aspiration the clarification
of the body in the equal sphere of nonrecollection
that is expressed by mantra practitioners. (28)

With compassion, you are not covered by physical, verbal, or
mental unseeing;
not seeing duality, you are free from the stains of the triple
[world].
Not identifying variety within the sky realm,
don't torment yourself by strenuous efforts of body, speech, or
mind. (29)

I delight in vajra songs and interrupt idle talk;
may all beings purify knowing and engage in blissful dance.
Don't experience separation from nonobscuration, nonviewing,
and nonpractice,
and [reach] the stage where everything enters and emerges as
uncontrived from the start. (30)

Hey! Since whatever there is, is free from the thinking mind,
the various conceptual cognitions are the recollecting mind;
anything that has form arises purely from rootlessness:
ordinary knowing is their majesty, unapprehended great bliss.
(31)

No characteristics at all are seen; they are without direction or
part.
The expression of analytical concepts by those in error is temporary;
since [meditation] arises from thought, how could thought
meditate? (32)

When unbodied thatness falls into everyone's house,
at the time it's understood, there is nothing at all;
no entity at all is illumined [or] seen. (33)

Whenever nirvāṇa and existence embrace,
dualistic appearances [1256] will dependently arise for you;
the conquerors and others show their emanations completely,
[so] you should practice in all the lineages of the pure. (34)

Emanations that emerge on their own through unthinking
compassion
are like a precious jewel that emerges without increase or
decrease;
since there are no entities, there never is realization:
without releasing or letting be, free your inherent nature
completely. (35)

Nongrasping cognition is the yogic contemplation of
nonaction;
don't meditate on anything, don't seek anywhere:
when there are no concepts, that's the equal taste of cognitive
disengagement—ah! (36)

The sky-like gnosis, the essential meaning that's uncontrived and
free of concepts:
thought may think it, but it's inexpressible—ah! (37)

[As for] this practice of relaxing the six sense collections freely
and naturally,
those skilled in applying the six sense collections do not release
them or let them be;

since the yoga of suchness is free from the notion of [anything] higher,
in thusness you are free: there is no abiding, no inherent nature anywhere. (39)

Whoever perfects luminosity and stops and dissolves [the vital winds],
however much they meditate, they are [indulging in] signs that lead to attachment;
the aggregates, sense spheres, sense fields, and all our limbs
dwell in unmanifest subtlety within the realm of oneness. (40)

Precious jewels may be obtained from the oceanic realm,
[but] they won't be seen by crocodiles and evil beings;
[you must] see that there is nothing to identify in the realm of signs
[involving] envy or other worldly defilements. (41)

Entering by way of the three doors and so forth,
you search by way of conscious awareness and the two truths;
the path of worldly conventions [based on] how things appear,
liberation [through] the three doors and the three trainings,
is the yoga of mental activity involving signs,
while the great yoga does not dwell on that. (42)

Someone who is [1257] like pure crystal
is free from the two stains and is free from existence and nirvāṇa;
as [by a wishing] gem, [for them] everything needed and desired occurs:
because they have completely exhausted the taints, [for them] there are no characteristics. (43)

Because from the outset there are no entities, there are no two truths,
entities are empty of oneness, there are no signs,
and there are no concepts of seeing, hearing, or other extremes;
the conventional apprehension of that "no" as nothingness—
this cannot make sense. (44)

Don't conceptualize all the roots of this!
Whenever you conceptualize this,
even if you calculate for a kalpa, you won't attain thatness. (45)

Like tinder for a torch, like the blaze of a spreading fire,
from the spread of all this, everything is made to burn. (46)

Hey, friends! The mind, like a jewel in the ocean, is thatness—ah!
Lion's milk poured into the horn of a water buffalo:
by that blazing jewel, you will obtain [freedom]. (47)

These solar light-rays that utterly dry up the defilements
take away fear of the lower realms and so forth [induced] by
wrong views:
those who attain [that] cannot be fathomed. (48)

As long as they appear in the reality sphere,
all things are enjoyed as untainted;
just like what is eaten by poisonous snakes, wild pigs, elephants,
and lions,
existence and nirvāṇa are swallowed whole. (49)

Through many hundreds of thousands of inexpressible kalpas,
the seeds for accumulating defilements and so forth
seem single to the mind and so are wrongly [seen] to have a single
fruit. (50)

A lamp will be outshone in all ways
by the light of a jewel that's in [the same] hut. (51)

The minds of those of lower views and conduct, such as śrāvakas
and others, take up the branches[593] and indulge in them,
while for those who have become [1258] bodhisattvas,
it won't be difficult to become a perfect buddha. (52)

In this mind moment there are no limits,
and in this moment all [sense of] multiplicity is reversed;
within the suchness of all dharmas, how can something come
from what is not other than perfection? It cannot. (53)

The essence of the moon is to defeat darkness on the battlefield;
someone who rightly [sees] that the world is like a dream
and rightly sees whatever is false in it:
where will they see form within that unobservability? (54)

Since ultimately there is no existent whatsoever,
a person who has seen the other side and wants to go there
is like a fragrant rhinoceros[594] that goes from here to there.
By breaking through to the [other] side without casting anything aside,
without having gone even once, you break through. (55)

Hey! Someone who doesn't seek by way of the conventional path
is forever liberated and descends into the forest, leaping like a cat;
if you misunderstand power like that of the tiger or vixen,
what good will that do you? None. (56)

When you know thatness, then without thinking and without
concepts,
any object that appears, any form you see, is empty right there;
when you're distracted there, it makes no sense to remain there. (57)

Mindfulness and alertness: don't see any [difference] between the
two;
since all dharmas are empty,[595] they abide within this.
Here, there are no things and nothing to think,
[so] don't take [things or concepts] to be the supreme root. (58)

Hey! All four bodies of all the buddhas are taught to be three:
you should think of this repeatedly, but not see anything at
all—ah! (59)

When there's recollection of [1259] saṃsāra, things [are seen to]
arise dependently;
appearing variously, they don't arise [from] their own essence.
Because of this, the pure nature of unchanging great bliss, as well
as the connate,
are the true nature of mind and are qualities
of the utterly pure nature of all the tathāgatas. (60)

From the start, all dharmas do not emerge as dual;
through recollection of duality and singularity, [it's seen that]
they're free from multiplicity.
Any entity expressed at all is empty of its own [nature];
because they are beyond thought, signs are overcome,
and that which is nonexistent does not abide anywhere. (61)

When you obtain uninterrupted contemplation,
you're free and won't see anything apart from this.

Since all these secret mantras are produced from that root,
there are no existents that emerge from nonexistence—ah! (62)

Those fools who conceptualize it
will not see the supreme meaning even in a hundred kalpas;
all those who swoon before the signs [involved in] mental engagement
are separated from settling in [to the supreme meaning], which is like a kingdom that can't be won. (63)

Bodhisattvas who obtain [just] the lesser [stage of] heat[596]
don't move anywhere and don't feel [ordinary sensations]. (64)

Someone who has entered the path of conceptuality
and mounts the bodhicitta drop on the vital winds
will have that seed drip down into saṃsāra:
they won't obtain proper thatness,
and will be entwined in a netlike thicket. (65)

When the eye of wisdom annihilates the wrong [view of self],
you are liberated right there from the wrong view of other. (66)

[When] you don't strive in austerities and so forth,
the variety of aspects [of things] emerge on their own without self:
empty out causes, conditions, and other connections right here,
and in [1260] this yoga, you'll see that there's no abiding self. (67)

Someone who prattles about [bodhisattva] grounds and arriving at the other shore
is burdened by the net of existence and jumps into the ocean [of saṃsāra],
where, without a boat, they drop into the ocean depths. (68)

This mahāmudrā without beginning or end
is free from existence and nirvāṇa and dries up the ocean of defilements;
in it, the continuum of mind is cut, so don't engage in cognition related to concepts or emptiness. (69)

Someone who [engages in] great austerities [intent] on a goal won't obtain thatness;
engaging in those austerities, they won't touch it—ah! (70)

Since there is no blessing or one who's blessed, it's the great wonder itself:
someone who abides in nonduality free from exaggeration and underestimation
will abide without a basis. (71)

All beings who know thusly
know the meaning of all existence and nirvāṇa;
[since] the dharmas of existence and nirvāṇa are your own mind,
deciding not to look elsewhere is nonconceptuality and itself beyond thought. (72)

There, it's unnecessary to stop concepts of meditation and nonmeditation,
or of signs, or of what's to be abandoned.
What's to be done there? There's nothing to do, [so] when thatness becomes clear,
without thus stopping or abandoning concepts,
when you don't see anything else, and thatness becomes clear,
abide there, and don't see anything else. (73)

Don't act for the sake of nonmeditation: the unconnected
inherent nature
at no time should be conceived as a sign of true knowledge. (74)

The entirety of existence, which is illumined within yourself at
once, is nonconceptual,
and thought that conceptualizes [something] other than that will
not attain the jewel [deep] within the ocean.
Since the apprehension of [things] arising from somewhere and
abiding somewhere [1261] is nonarising,
when you don't stop the stream, subject and object are
nonarising—that's gnosis itself. (75)

In that essential nature, don't abandon stains, and without
meditating on thatness,
roam the jungles freely, [like] an elephant. (76)

Since distracted thinking about the domain of signs is
inconceivable,
[if] you're not distracted by [signs] and the harm [they do],
you won't be cut [or] killed by those unarmed bandits.
Signs themselves are essenceless;
as in the eight examples of illusion,[597] take them as without
inherent nature. (77)

Whatever you see is mind, and since [mind] is not an entity,
all dharmas, which don't abide in nonrecollective thought,
[nevertheless] emerge from it, and having appeared there, are
themselves transcended,
so just not moving anywhere else,
knowing mere thatness, that's cognitive disengagement—ah! (78)

Hey, friends! The concepts arising in thought
are at no time clear,
they lack the causes for clarity;
free from all disputes,
they abide on their own, and so are freed. (79)

All these pretend buddhas
who are not monks fall into the ocean [of existence],
while those who do not observe even a single thing
apart from thatness
are monks who see everything. (80)

An elder monk who cultivates falsehood
cannot emerge from the destitution of existence;
someone who knows as false this stream
of existence will obtain supreme elderhood. (81)

[In] the experiential domain of that yoga,
even if you know all the particulars of deities, mantras,
and seals, you should not strive for them. (82)

Those who know thatness do not see all [particulars],
so no conceptions will arise [for them]
through any other objects
except for [thatness]. (83)

The [1262] subject that does not see
duality in any direction
frees multiple appearances [into] thatness. (84)

Someone whose view is partial
cultivates coarse and subtle recollective awareness of signs;

[for] someone thus habituated,
no activity, however conducted,
will lead to getting the real meaning:
they are quickly bound by destitute signs. (85)

Someone who doesn't cultivate
a focus on this or that position
is without concepts and won't cultivate cognition. (86)

Hey, friends! Nondual gnostic awareness
[comes through] the great unexcelled-gnosis consecration;[598]
the glorious perfect gurus
bestow its obtainment by way of nonbestowal
and consecrate you by way of the supreme yogas—
by way of nonobtainment, everything is completed. (87)

The senses[599] of those who don't know thatness and indulge in evil
are triply tainted through conceptual signs;
they all amass defilement- and knowledge-obscurations. (88)

[Yogins] will be freed without need of wisdom or concentration;
destroying all sorrow through wrathful glances,
[recognizing] nonarising, they don't produce grasping. (89)

Those who think to stop appearances should disengage from
cognition,
[otherwise] all inverted views and concepts
will flow down into the abode of the five defilements;
others, [who] know thatness, empty out the nets of saṃsāra. (90)

The essential secret meaning that clears out the darkness of fools,
rare as an *udumbura* flower,

is known by no one, but makes everything clear;
it's the stainless truth abiding at the heart,
but those engaged in austerities [1263] don't see it. (91)

Those able to apply themselves to perfection
dissolve particulars and abide in emptiness. (92)

Hey, friends! Like [people] in rich and powerful families,
those quick to boast
will never train themselves in gradual [practices]. (93)

All dharmas have a single taste in emptiness,
and when you become perfect, there's nothing to obtain;
when you realize that there is no root,
you'll ascertain nonduality right in the present. (94)

Just as someone who acts like a worm will be bound,
[so] those attached to tastes will be bound,
but someone who can eat away this thicket
will continually turn all the wheels [of Dharma]. (95)

I bow down to Guru Vajradhara, who teaches
without cognitive engagement, [using] whatever ways [he can]
to illuminate the body, speech, and mind of the buddhas. (96)

This completes the Mahāmudrā of Cognitive Disengagement from Body, Speech, and Mind, *spoken directly by the great lord of yogis, glorious Saraha, who is renowned as a second Buddha.*

CHAPTER 21

Two Untitled Songs

[Tibetan: *Sa ra ha'i glu.*][600]

(1)

[59] *I bow down to the Buddha.*

The whole world talks about the deep, the deep,
but only a few rejoice in nonarising.
Ah! Since the depths of the mind are difficult to know,
when you connect with the connate, [mind] is nonexistent. (1)

The nonabiding mind settles without reference point,
and all things are consumed by yogic fire.
Ah! Since the depths of the mind are difficult to know,
when you connect with the connate, [mind] is nonexistent. (2)

The desire for yoga is not taught by the guru,
[but] you must take in the guru's unsurpassed blessing.
Ah! Since the depths of the mind are difficult to know,
when you connect with the connate, [mind] is nonexistent. (3)

If you desire to seek glorious great bliss
and desire to seek the middle, you'll fall blindly into a well.

Deep, deep! You may say everything about the world,
but [real] joy resides in nonarising. (4)

This completes the song of Saraha.

(2)

I bow down to the Buddha.

The empty is naturally mixed with compassion;
emptiness is indivisible and uninterrupted.
I [60] see the empty yoginī,
riding through the sky, milking it, drinking it, being in it. (1)

See where sky joins with sky,
and don't dwell on the ground where you're bound to saṃsāra.
I see the empty yoginī,
riding through the sky, milking it, drinking it, dwelling in it. (2)

[In] such a yoga, you leave the house of the root [of mind]
and [experience] the stainless great taste of compassion.
I see the empty yoginī,
riding through the sky, milking it, drinking it, dwelling in it. (3)

Why do anything different from what Saraha says?
Go and milk the sky day and night.
I see the empty yoginī,
riding through the sky, milking it, drinking it, dwelling in it. (4)

This completes the song of Saraha.

CHAPTER 22

Special Mahāmudrā Instruction for Death Time

[149] [In the Indian language: *Mahāmudrāmārajāla-upadeśa*; in the Tibetan language: *Phyag rgya chen po 'chi kha ma'i man ngag*].[601]

I bow down to the One Who Destroys Māra [*Mārapramardin*].

The formations of birth, abiding, and death come about
through the composite elements, humors, and [karmic] projections;
since these are reckoned to emerge and dissolve [like] a single water bubble,
the idea that they will long endure gives rise to arrogance, attachment, and anger. (1)

There are both [things] that long endure and [things] that do not long endure:
While the body's machinery is reckoned to be momentary,
permanent mind-itself is the changeless eternal realm;
bodily manifestations are naturally destroyed on their own,
while permanent mind-itself, mahāmudrā, reaches the eternal realm. (2)

Just as in an empty house where the owner has died,
outer emptiness, inner emptiness, and in-between emptiness are in essence the same;
when an empty house is destroyed, emptiness can't be divided or categorized,
just like the empty house of bodily manifestations. (3)

[In] nonrecollection, the owner is destroyed on its own and purified on its own,
so outer emptiness, inner emptiness, and in-between emptiness are in essence the same;
thought and cognition have the nature of sky,
[from which] emerge hundreds of thousands of tens of millions of emanations. (4)

Don't think it's proper to forsake this body:
just as—though the noxious breath [150] of a poisonous snake is fleeting—
you curse when you think you see a snake,
[so] recollection is a manifestation of the body's noxious breath. (5)

Unknowing fools think, "The body [is real],"
[but] the corpse[-like] body is like a poisonous snake with a severed neck:
I don't see any owner residing within it,
and some say, "It's a corpse within a corpse." (6)

This completes the instruction of Saraha, in twenty-five lines.

CHAPTER 23

The Summit of Instruction on Suchness: A Dohā Song

[1280] In the Indian language: *Tattvopadeśaśikharadohagīti-nāma*; in the Tibetan language: *De kho na nyid kyi man ngag rtse mo do ha'i glu zhes bya ba*.[602]

I bow down to Ārya Mañjuśrī.

In the unwavering nature of body, speech, and mind,
it's meaningful to take up at once this song of the vajra summit;[603]
when the pure connate
is understood, it must be realized by all. (1)

There are no reasons or cognitive objects,
the suchness of things
has no refutation or proof,
and there are no categories and so forth—so it is explained. (2)

There are no remedies for discord,
and there is no immorality or avarice,
or laziness, anger, or distraction,
ignorance or other [defilements] to be abandoned. (3)

And there is [no] abandonment,
[for] it's explained that there are no entities [to abandon];
nonconceptual [mind] free from all thinking
is mahāmudrā, apart from saṃsāra. (4)

Even if it's one, no explanation hits the mark:
thatness is the path of perfect buddhas; [1281]
without demeaning desirable qualities,
there's no hope [of attaining] the result. (5)

If you ask, "What's the essence of the path
[to] the three [buddha] bodies?" It's nonconceptuality,
which is how suchness is realized;
no one should hope for anything beyond that. (6)

Like a treasury of jewels and the king's
wealth in an ordinary storehouse,
you yourself should abide in what's supremely valuable. (7)

Apart from mind, not a single external
object can be said to exist,
and mind-itself is completely luminous.
Thus, with proper analysis, [you see that] dharmas
do not exist apart from mind. (8)

In the naturally unified nature of all entities,
nothing arises with an inherent nature;
what's essentially nonarising is empty—
it does not exist otherwise. (9)

When, free from the duality and the conventions of existence and
nonexistence, you analyze by way of the one

and the many[604] and other [modes],
they're neither existent nor nonexistent. (10)

Nothing is proved by reasoning.
All dharmas that appear as entities
don't go beyond their essential nature:
they're [all] like an ocean reflected in a mirror. (11)

When everything emerges from the sphere of nonrecollection,
you should then be aware of inherent nature itself;
since neither duality nor nonduality exists,
you shouldn't even settle single-pointedly
into the unsurpassed, indivisible single taste. (12)

Since lucid suchness is itself unsullied,
the dancing girls sway with suchness.
In knowledge of suchness,
there is no grasping, and there is no essence;
the reality body doesn't grasp at anything,
and the essential nature has no categories. (13)

If you analyze in terms of the subject, [you see that]
since [all things] are naturally unified
in the nonarising sphere, there are no differences,
and when there's no exaggeration or underestimation, that's said
to be the primordial [nature]. (14)

The divine mansion and the major and minor marks [of a buddha],
what's taught by the various emanation bodies,
the power of introducing disciples to the path,
and whatever I, the Archer, say—
there isn't even an atom [1281] [of reality] in this. (15)

People with inverted views
are poisoned by [contact with] defiled objects,
but by gradually [understanding] appearances as they are,
they'll dwell in a separate [reality],
which is explained to be luminosity itself. (16)

Essencelessness without inherent nature
admits no distinctions and no duality;
the gnosis that transcends thought in the three spheres
is a name or sign to be described as "this."
I,[605] the Archer, don't apprehend [a thing]. (17)

If you don't realize the indivisible single taste,
dharmas will appear dualistically,
so you won't gain good fortune
and won't reach the supreme level. (18)

The nature of thatness
is free on its own from refutation and proof;
when you don't move from within nonduality,
whatever gnostic cognition there is
is one and not separate. (19)

The blissful taste of the connate
is the uninterrupted self-nature,
like a flowing river or the sky,
abiding forever without change. (20)

Thinking of signs [and] pursuing concepts
never [produces] knowledge;
the unconceived cannot be analyzed,
so where does objectless meditation get you? (21)

Even nonmeditation does not exist,
and if you ask the meaning of the example, [it's this:]
the minds of all the buddhas are the same. (22)

Dance songs and musical offerings
sound forth in every direction,
as yoginīs circle to the left. (23)

The inherent nature without reference point
effortlessly enters everywhere;
overcoming all notions of apparent duality,
[you'll] obtain the inexpressible, aspectless result. (24)

This completes the Summit of Instruction on Reality: A Dohā Song, *which was taught orally by the great lord of yoga, the glorious Saraha.*

CHAPTER 24

Dohā Song of View, Meditation, Conduct, and Result

[11] In the Indian language: *Bhāvanādṛṣṭicaryāphaladohagītikā-nāma*; in the Tibetan language: *Lta bsgom spyod pa 'bras bu'i do ha'i glu zhes bya ba.*[606]

I bow down to Ārya Mañjuśrī.

The various things [that appear] are just your mind-itself,
saṃsāra and nirvāṇa are indivisible [in] yoga,
and buddhas and sentient beings are nondual,
as in the example of water and waves. (1)

In a single instant of yogic realization,
mind-itself, which has given up things and no-things,
clears away the eye defects of the five poisons inherent in
saṃsāra,
as a small lamp [clears away] darkness. (2)

The mahāmudrā of union, which is beyond thought,
is blissful, luminous, and nonconceptual, like the sky;
pervasive and widespread, it's the essence of great compassion:
although it appears, it's without inherent nature, like a moon in
water. (3)

Although luminous, it's free from all conventions of middle or extremes,
and uncovered by anything, stainless, free from hope and fear;
like a mute person dreaming [12], you don't know what to say:
this immeasurable, greatly blissful inherent gnosis
[shines] impartially like the light of the sun and moon. (4)

Hey! The greatly wondrous self-emergent yoga,
the uncontrived primordial mind, is the reality body,
while the contriving mind won't obtain yogic union;
see, therefore, how unbounded are the regions of bliss. (5)

The yogin who gains the path of natural accomplishment is blissful
and free from concepts, so it's impossible for hatred or desire to emerge—
so say I, Saraha, an adept of Hayagrīva. (6)

Hey! If you want to meditate on your inherent nature
through taking to heart the yogic view,
[know that] the mountain of your own body is the supreme abode,
and mind-itself is the accomplisher of timely yoga. (7)

Binding the senses and setting boundaries[607] will turn into bliss,
and even distractions are not to be spurned on that account;
when you know the things you encounter as mind, they become meditational deities.
Not suppressing knowledge, you gradually give up concepts. (8)

When concepts occur in the mind, the yogin
should relax and settle down, like petals of cotton or wool;

abandoning action, let your own mind observe itself,
and if anger or desire occurs, know them as demons! (9)

The root of concepts is the mind,
and because [mind] does not exist, concepts do not exist.
[For] the yogin who meditates on recollection or nonrecollection,
this mind, forever unestablished, dissolves into itself. (10)

When you don't desire to meditate, you obtain the result,
buddhahood;
the yogin is without concepts, like a small child,
like a bee tasting flowers in a garden,
like a lion roaming in and out of the forest,
like various breezes blowing everywhere. (11)

Mind-itself that's conscientious is supreme conduct;
without blocking your inherent nature, act like a lunatic,
unattached to those behind you, not fixated on those in front.[608]
In brief, in practicing view, meditation, and conduct,
yogins conduct themselves with whatever conduct is beneficial. (12)

Various appearances are essentially [13] mind:
whatever you encounter is unestablished, it's mahāmudrā.
The nonappearing result, buddhahood, emerges within appearance,
and when you think on that, it's the sublime special attainment.
Outer and inner—everything—is connate,
as in a flowing-river yoga of nonconceptuality.[609] (13)

Also, don't search anywhere other than mind;
cognitive disengagement[610] is the path of mahāmudrā:
when there's realization without hope for the result, it's
mahāmudrā. (14)

Concepts without realization are like clouds in the sky,
and when there's realization, it's empty thatness and inherent
nature;
view, conduct, and result are indivisibly connate,
and when you realize their indivisible nature, that's the supreme
result. (15)

This completes the Dohā Song of View, Meditation, Conduct, and Result, *composed by the master Saraha.*

CHAPTER 25

Twelve Verses of Instruction

[1273] In the Indian language: *Dvādaśopadeśagāthā*; in the Tibetan language: *Man ngag gi tshigs su bcad pa bcu gnyis pa*.[611]

I bow down to glorious Vajrasattva.

Bodhicitta is peace;
whoever abides in it
will be peaceful like the sky.
What emerges from body, speech, and mind
does not change [it] in the least (1)

Transcended by perfect gnosis,
[concepts] become nonconceptual peace.
Pacified concepts are buddha itself,
and thatness is omniscience itself;
whatever concepts emerge
[from] seeing entities and [more] entities
are nonconceptual gnosis. (2)

Beings grasp at difference in things,
[but] they have the [same] inherent nature as all things;
[that nature] abides individually in all [things],
so each [exists] distinctively. (3)

[In inherent nature,] there is no arrogance or foolishness;
how could you one-sidedly grasp at
a self in [multi]dimensional entities?
It is nonconceptual gnosis.[612] (4)

As for[613] the nature of animals and so forth:
I will explain the essence [1274]
of what emerges from just one topic;
apprehend it with a perfect mind. (5)

A tiger lives in a cave.
A frog [lives] in a great hollow.
A cat's hair stands on end.
Bulls and so forth shake their bodies.
A snake does not eat.
Birds go through the sky.
A firefly emits light.
A camel attracts snakes.

A peacock conquers thirst.
A bee consumes poisons.
Waterfowl control their senses.
The lion has no fear.
An owl sees at night.
A vulture recognizes gems.
A snake[614] produces venom.
A peacock eats poison.
A duck knows the future.
A parrot is skilled with words.
A bumblebee collects nectar.[615]
[These] and other animals go about in self-awareness.

A swan distinguishes milk from water.
A bee's buzzing is quite melodious.
A heron's tears capture beings.
A snake's eyes can hear.
From a deer emerges musk.
A weevil smells with its eyes.
Fish that live in the water
stop inhaling and exhaling.[616] (6–9)

It should follow, then, that brahmins
who recite malicious [mantras will attain] supreme gnosis.
[For] the tiger and all other living beings,
qualities naturally come about
through the emergence of previous tendencies,
[and while] they may possess worldly knowledge,
that's not austerity and they are not free. (10)

They dwell in individual [forms]
[according to] what emerges from previous tendencies;
if just that were gnosis,
then animals would be free. (11)

Knowing this and abandoning fixation,
you should practice perfect gnosis—
for those [who do], pure sublime awakening
and sublime special attainments [1275] will come to be. (12)

This completes the Twelve Verses of Instruction, *which was taught orally by the Great Brahmin Saraha.*

CHAPTER 26

Key Instructions

[81a] [In the Indian language: **Marmopadeśa*; in the Tibetan language: *Gnad kyi gdams pa*].[617]

[1. View]

I bow down to glorious Heruka.

The ḍākinī's blessing is a symbol of realization.

1. The sesame illuminates the lamp.
2. Be like medicine effected by mantras.
3. The peacock's food is not for others.
4. Sandal is the scent of the deer's musk gland.
5. Waves of water are the sea itself.
6. The nature of clarity is like white cotton.
7. Though a mountain cannot be shaken, it is no different from glacier water.
8. Garlic and its odor are not different.
9. The quality of the sun and moon is clarity.
10. Don't look for the tracks of a bird.
11. The sky is not a topic for logical analysis.
12. The dimensions of a maṇḍala are symmetrical.
13. A zombie is like a jewel in the world of activity.
14. The wondrous crystal jewel is incomparable.

The symbols of the view were taught to Kamalaśīla by the Great Hunter Saraha.

[2. Meditation]

I bow down to glorious Heruka.

The ḍākinī's blessing is a symbol of meditation.

1. In a cemetery in an opening in the jungle, you'll make the acquaintance of Nairātmyā.
2. You should think of sunrise.
3. Be like a person from the karma clan.
4. Even if you offer a jewel at your crown, you're like a dog in an empty house.
5. Medicine is ruined [when] carried into the sky.
6. Be like a great river flowing downstream.
7. A sage should sit on a kuśa-grass seat.
8. Be like a lamp free of wind.
9. Wipe off the silvery white mirror.
10. Don't be like an unpleasant person.[618]
11. A turtle is a metal bowl in the sun.
12. An expert archery student makes effort.
13. An arrow maker has a singularly focused mind.
14. The main instruction will surely free you.
15. Be like an ornament made of gold.

The symbols of meditation were taught to Kamalaśīla by the Great Hunter.

[3. Conduct]

[81b] *I bow down to glorious Heruka.*

The ḍākinī's blessing is a symbol of conduct.

1. Is the bride seized by a madman?
2. A trained elephant can kill a wild boar.
3. Fish are very widespread in the sea.
4. Forests may be deeply scorched by fire.

5. Sometimes, you must ride a fast horse.
6. Display the sharp chopper.
7. The jackal plays in the cremation ground.
8. You should always add white saxifrage to food.
9. The hawk's dexterity is certainly fearsome.
10. The fox plays in the cremation ground.
11. Be like an alcoholic who sees things.
12. Illusory flowers spring forth.
13. [See yourself] mirrored as a lion, my son.
14. The tiger has no reason to fear.
15. Always hold the lamp aloft.
16. A mounted elephant always goes fast.

The symbols of conduct were taught to Kamalaśīla by the Great Hunter.

[4. Fruition]

I bow down to glorious Heruka.

The ḍākinī's blessing is a symbol of fruition.

1. Anthers originate from the center of a lotus.
2. The light of a crystal appears from within.
3. Who drew the designs on the peacock?
4. A rainbow is a magical emanation of the sky.
5. Nonconceptuality is brimming with hoped-for jewels.
6. You can't fly without wings.
7. A fire on a drilling seat can be extinguished with effort.
8. Wood consumes itself by itself.
9. Gold coloring is extracted from an earthy base.
10. A person without enemies may be careless.
11. What cognition is there in a person stirred from sleep?
12. See how the cat toys with the mouse.

13. The clouds in the sky, the sky, the sky are formed in the realm of the sea.
14. The sky's magical emanations are a great marvel.
15. A moon reflected in water has no multiplicity.

The symbols of fruition were taught to Kamalaśīla by the Great Hunter.

[5. The Path]
I bow down to glorious Heruka.
The ḍākinī's blessing is a symbol of the path.

1. Restraint is not beyond measure.
2. Observe the way the rabbit moves along.
3. There is little scope in a hawk's heart.
4. Always ride on the top of a wheel.
5. The child of a potter does not have much scope.
6. A sword with a sharp edge should be cherished.
7. A fire whipped up by the wind turns the jungle into a cremation ground.
8. Observe the brahmin spinning thread.
9. The person who is done with deeds is supreme.
10. A timid [person] is a human corpse.
11. A lamp [82a] mustn't be disturbed by wind.
12. Cut the churn rope of saṃsāra.
13. Be like the sun shining in a cloudless sky.
14. Take the breeze[-blown] southern clouds as a symbol.
15. A child is deceived by this rainbow.
16. Observe the master of a castle that's at a crossroads.
17. Give life to the fire in a jewel cache.
18. The sky! The sky! Liberation is certain.

The symbols of the path were taught to Kamalaśīla by the Great Hunter.

[6. Experience]

I bow down to glorious Heruka.

The ḍākinī's blessing is a symbol of experience.

1. The full moon [arrives] in stages.
2. A rainbow beautifies the sky.
3. What can a young person say or understand?
4. [Your mouth] full of water, you cannot speak.
5. Be like a clear shape in the morning mist.
6. A poor woman with a treasure is a great wonder.
7. Sea salt dissolves into the water itself.
8. A bird cannot go beyond the sky.
9. Don't let your mind be deceived by an enemy, or even a friend.
10. A sharp sword is a great marvel.
11. A king's consort does not fear.
12. The fox does not frighten the lion.
13. A bird does not exert itself in the sky.
14. The sky and a magical emanation do not differ.
15. Some [people] can eat the sky.
16. If dirty water is left alone, it will clear.
17. "This very thing is and is not"—who says this? Who understands? Who?

The symbols of experience were taught to Kamalaśīla by the Great Hunter.

[7. The Key Point]

I bow down to glorious Heruka.

The ḍākinī's blessing is a symbol of the key point.

1. Kill the lion, the elephant, and the wild boar.
2. Be like a rootless tree trunk.

3. The deer in the forest enters the snare.
4. Send the raven [into] the sky, where it is happy.
5. Be like a reflection in clear water.
6. The sky can't be partitioned[619] by pigments.
7. A picture is not disturbed by wind.
8. The great ocean is unmoved in its depths.
9. Fortunate are the timid.
10. A stuffed lion terrifies the child.
11. Observe in your mind the behavior of the bee.
12. Let your sorrow over a dead child settle in your mind.
13. The person who holds a lamp in their hand gets to the point of everything, then mixes outer and inner within the sky.

The symbols of the key point were taught to Kamalaśīla by the Great Hunter.

Notes

1. Henceforth, I will refer to them as "mahāsiddhas" in a Buddhist context and "siddhas" in Hindu contexts. The term favored by mid-twentieth-century Indian scholars was "Sahajiyā," meaning those dedicated to the connate (*sahaja*), which in later tantric Buddhist literature (and also in certain Hindu traditions) refers to the "natural mind" or "innate primordial mind" (*nijacitta*) that is coemergent with great bliss. See, for example, Kvaerne 1975; Davidson 2002b.
2. On Guenther's translations, see R. Jackson 1994; on ethics, see R. Jackson 1996; on Saraha in the Geluk tradition, see R. Jackson 2009; 2019, 363–79; on Saraha as philosopher, see R. Jackson 2022. My translation of the *Dohā Treasury Song* is found in R. Jackson 2004, 53–115, and my translation of the *Inexhaustible Treasury: A Song of Instruction* (*Dohākoṣa-upadeśagīti,* which Tibetans call the *Queen Dohā* [*Rgyal mo do ha*], the title by which I will refer to it) is found in R. Jackson 2012.
3. But see, for instance, Guenther 1993; Schaeffer 2005; and Brunnhölzl 2023.
4. Das (1902) 1979, 1262a.
5. Bendall 1905, 32, 36, 29, 39, 56, 75, 77, 79–81, 84–85.
6. Grünwedel 1916.
7. Śāstrī 1916.
8. Shahidullah 1928.
9. Bagchi 1935, 1938.
10. Tucci 1930, 140.
11. Sāṃkṛtyāyana 1957, 2–35.
12. There is also a second edition (Dasgupta [1946] 1976). His later *Introduction to Tantric Buddhism* (Dasgupta 1958) also draws to some degree on Saraha.
13. Snellgrove 1954.

14. Guenther 1952. This was later revised, retitled, and reissued (Guenther 1976).
15. Guenther 1969. The work also includes a full translation of an important biography of Saraha by the sixteenth-century Tibetan commentator Karma Trinlepa (Karma 'phrin las pa), pp. 4–7.
16. Kvaerne 1977. These works were also translated by Cleary (1998), where they are given a distinctively Zen interpretation.
17. Abhayadatta 1979, 41–43; Dowman (1985) provides an alternative translation of the same text.
18. Jo Nang Tāranātha 1983, 2–3.
19. Guenther 1993; for a detailed critical review, see R. Jackson 1994.
20. Bhayani 1997.
21. R. Jackson 2004, 53–115.
22. Schaeffer 2005.
23. Thrangu Rinpoche 2006.
24. Passavanti 2008, 438–39, 451–56.
25. Stenzel 2008.
26. Braitstein 2014.
27. Mathes 2019.
28. See Dowman 2020, 15–30; Brunnhölzl 2020, 44–45, 61–63, 79–80, 283, 349; 2021, 25–154, 237–40, 348–50, 373–75, 387–92; 2023, 171–236, 245–71, 317–23, 509–22; 2024.
29. Mathes and Szántó 2024.
30. Braitstein et al. forthcoming.
31. Nandy 2000, 1.
32. See, for example, Shahidullah 1928; Bagchi 1938, Sāṃkṛtyāyana 1957; Kvaerne 1977; Bhayani 1997; Mathes and Szántó 2024.
33. See, for example, Abhayadatta 1979, 41–43; Schaeffer 2005, 17–18.
34. Tucci 1930, 143, 149.
35. Schaeffer 2005, 10 (altered slightly).
36. For a survey of scholarly views through the first two-thirds of the twentieth century, see, for example, Joshi (1967) 1977, 270–71.
37. For the Atiśa citation, from the autocommentary to the *Lamp on the Path to Awakening* (*Bodhipathapradipa*), see Atiśa 1983, 118; for the Nāropa citation, from the *Commentary on Consecration* (*Śekoddeśaṭīkā*), see CC 262a5, 262b2, 278b6; and the translation in Gnoli and Orofino 1994, 257, 261, 262, 330. For the Bhavabhaṭṭa citation, from his commentary on the *Catuḥpīṭha*

Tantra, see Szántó 2012, vol. 1, 99, 102, 411–12. There also is a fragmentary quotation, which may well be from the *Dohā Treasury* (A. verse 106b; cf. R. Jackson 2004, 113 = PD 128c), in the *Buddhakapāla Tantra* (9:10); see, for example, Luo 2010, 5, 59. For a recent overview, see Mathes and Szántó 2024, 11–13.

38. There are references to practices associated with "ḍākinī" or "*bhāginī*" tantras that appear in the work of the seventh-century logician Dharmakīrti and an apparent quotation from the *Dohā Treasury* in a text attributed to the sixth-century philosopher Bhāviveka. For Dharmakīrti, see, for example, Hatley (2016, 40–41), who notes that the tantras referred to are almost certainly Hindu rather than Buddhist; for Bhāviveka, see Seyfort Ruegg 2010, 149–51. Although Seyfort Ruegg is not persuaded that Saraha lived as early as the sixth century, since the text in question may *not* be by the philosopher Bhāviveka, he does believe it possible that, given the antiquity of Apabhraṃśa and the tentative dating of other tantric sources cited in the text, Saraha may have lived considerably earlier than the scholarly consensus assumes.
39. This is Apabhraṃśa verse 27 (cf. R Jackson 2004, 67 = PD 30;), which echoes HT 2.5.68; cf. Snellgrove (1959) 2010, 1:114, 2:84–85.
40. Schaeffer 2005, 52. Drakpa Dorjé further argues that the usual reading of "Saraha" as "arrow shooter" or archer is more appropriate to Saraha's disciple, or granddisciple, Śavaripa, who, as his name indicates, is connected to a tribal group, the Śabaras, who are well known for their proficiency in bow hunting, hence archery.
41. As Schaeffer (2005, 52) notes, the fifteenth-century Sakyapa scholar Drakpa Dorjé argued that the true Tibetan term ought to be *mda' 'dzin*, which means something like "arrow holder"—with *sara* indicating "arrow" and *ha* being a contraction of the Indic *graha*, indicating "holding" or "handling."
42. See, for example, Strong 2002, 140–42.
43. The claim that Saraha was the disciple of Nāgārjuna is found in Tucci (1930). In Tibetan tradition, the order is almost always reversed. For a good discussion of the "Rāhulabhadra problem," see Schaeffer 2005, 50–55.
44. For discussion of this ambiguity, see Brunnhölzl 2023, 812n1117.
45. Granted, *medieval* is a term most appropriate in the context of European history, but it is a commonplace among scholars of India (no doubt

influenced by European models of periodization) to refer to the period between the collapse of Harsha's Vardhana dynasty shortly after 650 CE and the permanent arrival of Muslim rulers late in the twelfth century as "medieval" (although cf. Davidson [2002a, 26–27], who refers to this time span as "early medieval"), and I will follow that convention.

46. See, for example, Guenther 1969, 7; Schaeffer 2005, 13.
47. Bhayani (1997, xii), citing with approval the view of S. K. Chatterji, affirms that the language was western Apabhraṃśa; this view contradicts that of Shahidullah (1928, 55), who concluded that the language was eastern Apabhraṃśa. More recently, Péter-Dániel Szántó (personal correspondence, July 7, 2021) has observed that there seem to be both western and eastern elements in Saraha's Apabhraṃśa verses. And in any case, despite its "colloquial" appearance relative to Sanskrit, Apabhraṃśa is a literary language, hence it may not be the native tongue of the "historical" Saraha, if there was such a person.
48. "Southern" Apabhraṃśa is associated with the area now in the northern part of Maharashtra, which, in the context of the whole subcontinent, is better described as west-central. Western Apabhraṃśa, which may have been the earliest form of the language, is associated with Punjab and other parts of the northwest, as well as the Saurashtra region of present-day Gujarat. Eastern Apabhraṃśa flourished mostly in Bengal and nearby regions. See, for example, Tagare (1948) 1987, 15–22; Merendale 1964.
49. To be clear, inscriptional and literary evidence shows that Buddhism also maintained a presence in the south but to lesser degree than in the northwest or northeast. See, for example, Majumdar 1966, 414–25.
50. See, for example, Majumdar 1964, 1966; Thapar 2002, 405–89; Davidson 2002a, 25–74.
51. For concise accounts, see, for example, Thapar 2002, 405–12; Davidson 2002a, 48–62.
52. See, for example, Majumdar 1964, 44–82; 1966, 24–32; Huntington and Huntington 1989, 1990.
53. There is considerable debate over the application of the feudalism model to India. For discussion, see, for example, Thapar 2002, 440–52; Davidson 2002a, 137.
54. Davidson 2002a, 113–68.
55. See, for example, Majumdar 1964, 366–411; 1966, 474–529; Thapar 2002, 456–81.

56. Doniger and Smith 1991, 115.
57. See, for example, Huntington and Huntington 1989, 1990.
58. See, for example, Majumdar 1964, 178–231; 1966, 297–361; Thapar 2002, 466–74.
59. See, for example, Majumdar 1964, 257–365; 1966, 398–466.
60. This was, of course, more often a matter of principle than practice, as the work of Gregory Schopen and others has amply demonstrated. See, for example, Schopen 2004; van Schaik 2020.
61. See, for example, Basham 1959, 232–345; Davis 1997; Samuel 2008.
62. Lorenzen 2002, 25.
63. Tsong-ka-pa 1977.
64. White 2000, 9.
65. The term is that of Benoytosh Bhattacharyya, cited in Urban 2003, 1 (epigraph).
66. See, for example, White 2000, 15–18; Urban 2003, 1–43; Samuel 2008, 229–70.
67. Tsongkhapa was criticized by contemporaneous Tibetans for overlooking the fact that many early Buddhist tantric texts do *not* describe the practitioner's self-identification with a buddha-deity. White's definition is multivalent but seems unduly influenced by Hindu ideas. The definition of Tantra as the religion of sex and violence is open to the obvious objections that it (a) exaggerates the place of a particular feature of *some* tantric traditions and (b) fails to appreciate the complex context in which such rhetoric (and practices) were embedded. While this particular understanding of Tantra has largely receded in the scholarly world, it still runs rampant in popular culture.
68. See, for example, Padoux 2002.
69. For other such lists, see, for example, Goudriaan (1979, 7–9), who notes eighteen characteristics of Hindu Tantrism, Davidson (2002a, 117), who provides a set of characteristics of Buddhist Tantra, and Harper and Brown (2002, 2–5), who describe tantric traditions more broadly "in terms of process rather than as a static structure of characteristics": the *processes* are visualization, verbalization, identification, internalization, concretization, and transformation, which are *accomplished by* ritual yoga, the body, maṇḍala, cakra, mantra, yantra, pūjā, or icons, and *guided by* a guru or deities or both, *with the goal of* enlightenment, liberation (*mukti*), worldly power, or pleasure (*bhukti*).

70. For good summaries of various views, see, for example, White 2000, 18–24; Davidson 2002a, 171–73; Samuel 2008, 232–35. See also Bharati 1970; Snellgrove 1987, vol. 1; the essays in Harper and Brown 2002; and Wedemeyer 2013.
71. See, for example, Samuel 2008, 291–323.
72. Qvarnström 2000, 597.
73. See, for example, Cort 1987, 2000; Dundas 2000; Qvarnström 2000.
74. Dundas 2000, 233.
75. See, for example, Gupta, Hoen, and Goudriaan 1979; Goudriaan and Gupta 1981; White 2000; Harper and Brown 2002; Samuel 2008, 229–309.
76. See, for example, Dimock 1989; Flood 2000; Hayes 2000.
77. On the first, see, for example, Davidson 2002a, 183–86; on the last two, see, for example, Lorenzen 1972.
78. See, for example, White 2003.
79. Davidson 2002a, 183.
80. See, for example, Lorenzen 1972, 1–95; 2000; Samuel 2008, 243–46.
81. See, for example, Muller-Ortega 1997; White 2009.
82. See, for example, Avalon (1913) 1972; Beane 1977; Brooks 2000; Goudriaan 2000; Samuel 2008, 252–58.
83. See, for example, Abhinavagupta 1989; Padoux 1990, 30–85; Mishra 1993; Muller-Ortega 2000.
84. See, for example, White 1996; Samuel 2008, 276–78.
85. See, for example, Davidson 2002a, 202–33; Sferra 2003; Samuel 2008, 258–68; Gray 2023, 5–47.
86. See, for example, van Schaik 2020.
87. See, for example, Williams 2009. For a detailed treatment of skillful means, see Pye 2003.
88. See, for example, the discussions in Joshi (1967) 1977, 235–327; Snellgrove 1987, vol. 1; Williams, Tribe, and Wynne 2000, 192–244; Davidson 2002a; Gray 2023.
89. See, for example, Joshi (1967) 1977, 255–60.
90. See, for example, Williams, Tribe, and Wynne 2000, 202–17; Gray 2023, 148–58. The Nyingma tradition of Tibetan Buddhism divides the tantras into six classes: action, performance, yoga (or "method," *upāya*, or "both," *ubaya*), mahāyoga, anuyoga, and atiyoga. The New Translation traditions of Tibet typically accept four classes: action, performance, yoga, and

unexcelled yoga (*yoganiruttara*)—with the fourth divisible into "father" tantras, which roughly correspond to mahāyoga, and "mother" tantras which roughly correspond to yoginī tantras (or the Nyingma anuyoga).

91. See, for example, Wayman 1973, 237–39; Lessing and Wayman 1978, 141–203; Tsong-ka-pa 1981, 67–179; Snellgrove 1987, 1:232–35; Williams, Tribe, and Wynne 2000, 205–7. As Williams, Tribe, and Wynne note, many of the texts classified as action tantras are not designated as tantras, often being identified instead as sūtras, kalpas, or dhāranīs.
92. For details, see Tsong-ka-pa 1981, 70–76.
93. See, for example, Wayman 1973, 237; Lessing and Wayman 1978, 205–13; Tsong-ka-pa 1981, 181–203; Snellgrove 1987, 1:232–35; Williams, Tribe, and Wynne 2000, 207–8.
94. See, for example, Wayman 1973, 236–37; Lessing and Wayman 1978, 214–49; Snellgrove 1987, 1:209–43, 267–70; Williams, Tribe, and Wynne 2000, 209–10; Tsongkhapa 2017.
95. See, for example, Snellgrove 1987, 1:209–13; Williams, Tribe, and Wynne 2000, 210–11.
96. This is usually shortened to *Compendium of Principles* (*Tattvasaṃgraha*), which is not to be confused with a philosophical treatise of the same name by the eighth-century master Śāntarakṣita.
97. The *Litany* is also sometimes categorized among the higher tantras; see, for example, Wayman 1973, 234.
98. See Williams, Tribe, and Wynne 2000, 231–33.
99. See, for example, Snellgrove 1987, 1:266–70.
100. See, for example, Wayman 1973, 235–36; Lessing and Wayman 1978, 251–337; Snellgrove 1987, 1:132–33, 177–78, 206–8, 243–303; Cozort 1986; Dudjom Rinpoche 1991, 241–372; Samuel 2008, 259–67.
101. See Davidson 1991; Gray 2023, 40–47.
102. See, for example, Fremantle 1971, 24–25; Campbell and Thurman 2020, 463–66.
103. See, for example, Cozort 1986, 39–61; Tsong Khapa Losang Drakpa 2013.
104. See, for example, Cozort 1986, 63–128.
105. See, for example, Williams, Tribe, and Wynne 2000, 210–13.
106. See Fremantle 1971; Campbell and Thurman 2020.
107. See Kittay and Lozang Jamspel 2020.
108. For Nāgārjuna, see, for example, Thurman 1995, 250–60; for Āryadeva, see, for example, Wedemeyer 2007.

109. See, for example, Williams, Tribe, and Wynne 2000, 213–17.
110. Tsuda 1974; Gray 2007; Gray 2023.
111. Snellgrove (1959) 2010; Gray 2023.
112. Newman 1987, 2000; Wallace 2004, 2010.
113. For Nāropa, see Gnoli and Orofino 1994.
114. English 2002.
115. See, for example, Kvaerne 1975; Davidson 2002b; Loseries 2015. Other translations for the term have included "the innate," "the simultaneously arisen," and "the together-born." For an analysis of Saraha's usage of the term through the lens of his commentator Advayavajra, see Mathes 2015b. For discussion of usages of the term in Hindu Tantra, see Hayes 2015.
116. See, for example, R. Jackson 2019, 35–40.
117. See, for example, Sāṃkṛtyāyana 1934, 209–30; Dasgupta (1946) 1976; Abhayadatta 1979; Dowman 1985; Kapstein 2000; Davidson 2002a, 169–335; Linrothe 2006; Lopez 2019.
118. Kapstein (2000, 52) dates the translation to about 1100.
119. For alternate accounts and accountings of mahāsiddhas, see, for example, Schmid (1958), who lists eighty-five, and Jo Nang Tāranātha (1983), who discusses around sixty.
120. See, for example, Dudjom Rinpoche 1991, 445–504.
121. Based on Abhayadatta 1979, 285–88; Dowman 1985.
122. See, for example, Chimpa and Chattopadhyaya 1970; Jo Nang Tāranātha 1983.
123. See Abhayadatta (1979, 289–307), whose translator lists works contained in the Peking edition of the Tibetan Tengyur. Searches of the Narthang or Dergé editions would yield results that are largely, if not precisely, similar.
124. See, for example, Shahidullah 1928, 57–66; Templeman 1994; Loseries 2015; Brunnhölzl 2019, 4–8.
125. See, for example, Schomer 1987; Templeman 1994, 16–26; Brunnhölzl 2019, 4–7. As Schomer (1987, 64) notes, the earliest known specimen of an Apabhraṃśa dohā is found in Kālidāsa's drama *Vikramorvaśīya* (*Ūrvaśī Won by Valor*), datable to the fourth or fifth century CE.
126. See, for example, Kvaerne 1977; Templeman 1994, 30–34; Brunnhölzl 2019, 8.
127. See, for example, Templeman 1994, 26–30; Brunnhölzl 2019, 7. See also Snellgrove (1959) 2010, 1:101, 2:62 (HT 2.4.6–10).

128. See, for example, Shahidullah 1928, 9–24; Dasgupta (1946) 1976, 3–109; Dowman 1985, 1–32; R. Jackson 2004, 16–42; Lopez 2019, 1–15.
129. HT 2.4.6–10, in Farrow and Menon (1992, 207); cf. Snellgrove (1959) 2010, 1:101. The original is in Apabhraṃśa; I have modified the translation slightly.
130. See, respectively, Farrow and Menon 1992, 208–9; Kvaerne 1977.
131. See, for example, Guenther 1976; Snellgrove 1987, 278–303; R. Jackson 1992; Williams, Tribe, and Wynne 2000, 235–38.
132. Beyer 1974, 258.
133. Davidson 2002a; I express somewhat similar views in R. Jackson 2004.
134. Wedemeyer 2013.
135. See, for example, Jo Nang Tāranātha 1983; Gray 2023.
136. See, for example, PD 22. Although Tibetan translations will sometimes use "Saraha"(*sa ra ha*) and sometimes "the Archer" (*mda' bsnun*), the Apabhraṃśa versions known to me uniformly use "Saraha"—so presumably when we encounter "the Archer" in a Tibetan translation, it is simply because the translator opted to translate the name rather than transliterate it.
137. See, for example, PD 59, 113; PS 1.2, 4.4–5; KD 40; MM 15, 33.
138. See, for example, PD 78, 105.
139. See, for example, VM 6; SB.
140. See, for example, PD 103, 106.
141. OS 1–6.
142. Respectively, PD 33, 41; QD 3.
143. Schaeffer 2005, 19. Cf. KD 1.
144. Schaeffer 2005, 20.
145. Tucci 1930.
146. Schaeffer 2005, 13–14.
147. It is found in the Peking and Narthang editions (P 5091 and N 3873, respectively) but not the Dergé.
148. Schaeffer 2005, 20. Pharpuwa likely was familiar with the comment, noted above, by Balpo Asu.
149. Schaeffer 2005, 129. In this case, the sometimes ambiguous name Śabareśvara clearly refers to a siddha who is not Saraha.
150. Passavanti 2008, 451–56.
151. Based on the version in the Peking edition of the Tengyur, in Abhayadatta (1979, 318–20; folios 29–33); for alternative translations, see Abhayadatta 1979, 41–43; Dowman 1985, 66–69; Schaeffer 2005, 17–18.

152. Passavanti 2008, 451–56.
153. A "gnostic" (*jñāna*) form of the bodhisattva Avalokiteśvara.
154. The Tibetan for "without husbands" is *bdag med*, which also means "no self"—a notion that females are said, in Buddhism, to embody or symbolize.
155. Reading *dga'* for *gda'*.
156. Reading *dga'* for *gda'*.
157. Reading *brdar* for *gdar*.
158. There are numerous lists of these "ornaments" (*chas*), which include various adornments and accessories common to yogins, each symbolizing a particular spiritual attainment. See Steinert n.d., s.v. "*dpal gyi chas*."
159. Schaeffer 2005, 26–27.
160. Roerich and Gendun Chöpel (1949) 1976, 1039.
161. Schaeffer 2005, 24–25.
162. Schaeffer 2005, 22–24.
163. See Guenther 1969, 4–7; Schaeffer 2005, 20–22.
164. Dakpo Tashi Namgyal 2019, 143–44.
165. Schaeffer 2005, 28–30; cf. Norbu 2022, 155–57.
166. Schaeffer 2005, 30–32.
167. As Schaeffer (2005, 53–56) notes, the Sakya scholar Drakpa Dorjé (b. 1444) changes the order so that Saraha is a tantric yogin *before* he is a monk, so that his tantric activities do not compromise his ordination status.
168. As Schaeffer (2005, 56) also notes, Drakpa Dorjé omits mention of Saraha's singing of the three dohā collections, likely because, like a number of Tibetan scholars, he doubted the legitimacy of the *King* and *Queen Dohās*—a point to which we will return in the next chapter.
169. It may be recalled that in some sources, Saraha himself is said to have been named Rāhulabhadra during the monastic phase of his career; see Schaeffer 2005, 50–56.
170. This Kāṅha (S. Kṛṣṇa) is presumably not to be confused with the mahāsiddha Kāṅha/Kṛṣṇācārya who is credited with several famous performance songs and a commentary on the *Hevajra Tantra*.
171. Roerich and Gendun Chöpel (1949) 1976, 841.
172. See, for example, TR 251 (folio 10a), 253 (folio 11a), and 256 (folio 12b), where Saraha heads up one or another major Cakrasaṃvara lineage, and TR 285 (folio 27a), where he is named as the human source of the lineage

of the *Guhyagarbha Tantra*, a text of special importance to the Nyingma tradition.

173. But see Schaeffer 2005, 49–119.
174. Dakpo Tashi Namgyal 2019, 143–45. Note that the dates for Marpa, Milarepa, and many other early Tibetan masters are contested even among Tibetans, with no clear consensus evident among the earliest sources. On Marpa, see Ducher 2017, 301–6; on Milarepa, see Quintman 2015.
175. Jo Nang Tāranātha 1983, xi–xii, 214.
176. R. Jackson 2019, 442–44.
177. Personal communication from Charles Manson, August 31, 2020; see also Karmapa n.d.
178. The four syllables are *a-ma-na-si*, Sanskrit for "cognitive disengagement," a central teaching of the mahāsiddha Maitrīpa, and one that occurs in works attributed to Saraha, as well.
179. Abboud, Kane, and Price 2017, 14. Slightly edited for consistency.
180. Abboud, Kane, and Price 2017, 15.
181. Abboud, Kane, and Price 2017, 16. For a brief recounting of the dream by Marpa's later hagiographer Tsangnyön Heruka (1452–1507), see Nālandā Translation Committee 1982, 42.
182. Choephel and Martin 2012, 217.
183. Recall that Saraha and Śabareśvara are both names for the Great Brahmin—but that Śabareśvara may also refer to his disciple or granddisciple Śavaripa. For discussion of this song, which because it is self-contained within the frame of Karma Pakshi's song, I classify among Saraha's Tibetan paracanonical songs, see chapter 2, text 31.
184. Gamble 2020, 154.
185. Gamble 2020, 155.
186. Gamble 2020, 156. Cf. Schaeffer 2005, 41–42.
187. On Padampa, see, for example, Edou 1996, 32; Schaeffer 2005, 88–96; Sorensen 2011. On Tsongkhapa, see, for example, Thurman 1982, 50.
188. Schaeffer 2005, 175–77.
189. Mathes and Szántó 2024, 11.
190. For a brief survey along similar lines, see Stenzel 2008, 34–72.
191. For editions and translations from Indic languages, see Śāstrī 1916; Shahidullah 1928; Bagchi 1935, 1938; Snellgrove 1954; Sāṃkṛtyāyana 1957; Bhayani 1997; R. Jackson 2004; Mathes and Szántó 2024. See also the discussions in Schaeffer 2005, 79–99; Brunnhölzl 2024, 3–6.

192. According to Tibetan tradition, he also addressed dohās to the queens and king; these texts, which will be summarized below, are found only in Tibetan.
193. See, for example, Sāṃkṛtyāyana 1957, 459–67.
194. See Schaeffer 2005; Mathes and Szántó 2024, 11–16, 27–28.
195. The first verse is fragmentary.
196. Śāstrī 1916; cf. the discussion in Brunnhölzl 2023, 40–41; Mathes and Szántó 2024, 13–14. Although Advayavajra is a name often associated with Maitrīpa, many scholars, both in premodern Tibet and the modern academy, consider the Advayavajra credited with the commentary to be a separate individual from the great eleventh-century scholar and master; see, for example, Brunnhölzl 2023, 41; Mathes and Szántó 2024, 22–23.
197. Bagchi (1938, 72–148) includes the text of the Advayavajra commentary in which he found the Apabhraṃśa verses. There is a Tibetan translation of this commentary, as well, though it differs in important ways from the extant Sanskrit version; for an English translation of the Sanskrit version, see Mathes and Szántó 2024.
198. Mathes and Szántó 2024, 16–20, 313–74.
199. See Bagchi 1938, 12–13; verses 3–10, and 12 are translated in Schaeffer (2005, 103–4). See also the discussion in Mathes and Szántó (2024, 12–13), which suggests that 1101 is simply the date of "publication," with the text itself showing signs of having been edited as much as a half-century earlier.
200. This verse (no. 9 here) is also found in the *Dohā Treasury* attributed to Tilopa; see, for example, R. Jackson 2004, 131.
201. For editions, see Śāstrī 1916; Shahidullah 1928; Bagchi 1938; Mathes and Szántó 2024, 55–192 (where it is embedded in a new edition of Advayavajra's commentary); for translations, see Shahidullah 1928; Snellgrove 1954; R. Jackson 2004; Mathes and Szántó 2024, 195–312 (where it is embedded in a translation of Advayavajra's commentary). Here, I will follow R. Jackson (2004, 53–115), which itself reproduces the numbering in Bagchi (1938).
202. As Shahidullah (1928, 3) notes, Śāstrī did not number the often-fragmentary verses he found, but Shahidullah himself counts 114 in his predecessor's edition.
203. See Brunnhölzl 2023, 649–57.

204. See, for example, R. Jackson 2004, verses 1–14, 20, 22–23, 33, 35, 39, 44, 46, 50–51, 65, 103–6.
205. See, for example, R. Jackson 2004, verses 26–27, 37, 40, 49, 55–56, 68, 74, 76, 88, 93, 96–97, 100, 105.
206. See, for example, R. Jackson 2004, verses 13, 16–17, 20–22 26–29, 34–35, 37–39, 41, 44–45, 52, 54, 58, 60–62, 76–78, 79–81, 83, 96–97, 99–100, 103. These terms are analyzed in greater detail in chapter 3 of this book.
207. See, for example, R. Jackson 2004, verses 32, 34, 58, 64, 72, 74, 76–77, 84–87, 97, 100–101, 107–10.
208. See, for example, R. Jackson 2004, verses 19, 24, 26, 30, 45–49, 55, 64, 84–87, 89, 91, 94, 100.
209. See, for example, R. Jackson 2004, verses 18, 24, 38–39, 56, 57, 69, 95.
210. R. Jackson 2004, Saraha verses 15a–15b, 122, respectively.
211. See, for example, R. Jackson 2004, verses 18, 21, 31, 33–34, 37, 39, 41, 71, 92.
212. See Sāṃkṛtyāyana 1957; Bhayani 1997; Mathes and Szántó 2024, 21–22, 377–417.
213. For tables of correspondences, see Sāṃkṛtyāyana 1957, 459–67; Bhayani 1997, 63–64; see also Schaeffer 2005, 104–5.
214. See, for example, Bhayani 1997, verses 27–28, 75, 80, 96, 109–11, 116, 151.
215. See, for example, Bhayani 1997, verses 17, 53, 55–56, 80, 100, 104, 108, 113–14, 126, 131, 138, 143–49, 153, 159–60.
216. See, for example, Bhayani 1997, verses 43, 76, 97, 106, 111, 116, 157, 163.
217. See, for example, Bhayani 1997, verses 41–43, 123, 132–33, 156.
218. See, for example, Bhayani 1997, verses 78, 97, 102, 114, 129, 135, 153–54, 161.
219. See, for example, Bhayani 1997, verses 19, 54, 75, 120, 122, 134.
220. See, for example, Bhayani 1997, verses 95, 140, 141, 119, 139, 150, 103, 130, 134, 126, respectively.
221. See, for example, Bhayani 1997, verses 79, 106–7, 152, respectively.
222. For a general perspective on the collection, see, for example, Kvaerne 1977, 1–66; Bhayani 1997, 83–86; Brunnhölzl 2021, 13–15. For translations, see, for instance, Kvaerne 1977, 67–268; Brunnhölzl 2021, 285–418. The latter has the virtue of translating both the Indic and Tibetan versions of the songs, allowing readers unable to read both languages to get a sense of the similarities and differences between the two versions.

223. The language has often been identified by Bengali scholars as "Old Bengali," but others have classed them as old forms of Oriya, Maithlī, Bihāri, or Assamese. Its similarity to the language of Saraha's dohās makes it safest, perhaps, to simply describe it as an eastern Apabhraṃśa that served as the forerunner of numerous modern vernaculars; see Brunnhölzl 2021, 465n64.
224. Edited or translated in, for example, Śāstrī (1916); Shahidullah (1928, 229–34); Sāṃkṛtyāyana (1957, 355–61); Kvaerne (1977, 168–69, 199–200, 222–23, 226–27); Bhayani (1997, 81–139); Cleary (1998, 111, 137, 161, 165); Brunnhölzl (2021, 348–49, 387–88, 389–90).
225. See, for example, Beyer 1974, 258–61; Ray 1985; Kvaerne 1977, 100, 109, 113, 119, 122, 127, 130, 155, 214, 231, 238, 248; Snellgrove 1987, 1:158–59; R. Jackson 1992; Brunnhölzl 2021, 307, 312–13, 315–16, 318–19, 320–21, 323–24, 338–39, 340–41, 354, 382–83, 392–93, 397–98.
226. Bagchi 1938, 9–12.
227. See Bhattacharyya 1924, 45; 1925–28, 1:79–83; Sakuma 2002, 126–33.
228. Several of his dohās are quoted in Sanskrit in Nāropa's *Commentary on Consecration;* see above, n 37.
229. For Indic-language originals from the *Treasury of Performance Songs* (PS), see Kvaerne 1977, 71, 93, 102, 148, 157, 161, 166, 172, 194, 201, 205, 229, 243, 253, 256, 261; for translations from the *Treasury*, see Brunnhölzl 2021, 290, 302, 308, 337, 342, 344, 347, 353, 356, 365, 370, 374, 377, 392, 394, 401, 403, 407, 409, 411, 413, 416, 417; for Apabhraṃśa verses (with notes and some translation) from the *Compendium of Goods Sayings*, see Bendall 1905, 75, 77, 79, 80, 81, 84, 85. Bagchi (1938, 47–50) collects eleven dohās found in either the *Treasury* or the *Compendium* (or both) that he says are not attested elsewhere—although several of them actually are.
230. VY: PDM vol. 24, 1067–75.
231. CB: PDM vol. 13, 1145–1256. The first part of chapter 1 is translated in chapter 10 of this book.
232. BK: D 424 (rgyud, nga 143a1–167a5).
233. For an edition and translation of chapters 9–14, as commented upon by Abhayākaragupta, see Luo 2010. Luo (2010, xxvi) notes that Mae Isaacson will be revising a master's thesis covering chapters 1–8, but to the best of my knowledge, this has yet to appear.
234. Huntington and Bangdel 2003, 308.
235. Partially translated in Davidson (2002a, 248–50).

236. Translated in Wedemeyer (2013, 209–10); as noted, chaps. 9–14 are included in Luo (2010).
237. SB: PDM vol. 26, 1443–54; translated in chapter 11 of this book. See also Bhattacharyya 1924, 68–69; 1949, 47; Huntington and Bangdel 2003, 208–12.
238. ES: PDM vol. 26, 1455–58.
239. MB: D 1657 (rgyud, ra 230b2–243b5).
240. PD: PDM vol. 26, 193–210. English translations: Guenther 1993, 89–122; Schaeffer 2005, 129–73; Brunnhölzl 2024, 93–112; and chapter 6 of this book.
241. The *People Dohā* corresponds closely to the version of the *Dohā Treasury* commented upon by Mokṣākaragupta, which is available only in Tibetan, and whose Indic antecedents are unknown. See Mathes and Szántó 2024, 30, 443–548.
242. For the former, see IT vol. 2, 7–25; for a translation of that version, see Brunnhölzl 2024, 93–112.
243. AP: D 2256 (rgyud, wi 180b3–207a7). English translation: Brunnhölzl 2023, 325–88. See also the discussion at Brunnhölzl (2023, 40–42). For a critical edition and translation of the Sanskrit version, with Saraha's Apabhraṃśa verses included, see Mathes and Szántó 2024, 49–312.
244. See Brunnhölzl 2023, 41–42.
245. Brunnhölzl 2023, 42.
246. MP: D 2258 (rgyud, wi 265a2–283b). English translation: Brunnhölzl 2023, 389–429. See the discussion at Brunnhölzl (2023, 43–44). For an edition of the Tibetan and a translation, see Mathes and Szántó 2024, 443–548.
247. See Kajiyama 1966.
248. See Brunnhölzl 2023, 709–710n201, 710n204.
249. Brunnhölzl 2023, 44.
250. AV: D 2268 (rgyud, zhi 65b7–106b4). English translation: Brunnhölzl 2023, 523–602; see also the discussion by Brunnhölzl (2023, 48–55).
251. Brunnhölzl 2023, 48–55.
252. Brunnhölzl 2023, 654–56.
253. SO: D 2257 (rgyud, wi 207b1–265a2). English translation: Brunnhölzl 2021, 25–154. See also the discussion in Schaeffer (2005, 66–67, 105–15); Brunnhölzl (2021, 1–7). The verses themselves do not comprise a separate text in the Tengyur but are a distinct item in the Seventh Karmapa's *Indian*

Mahāmudrā Texts: IT, vol. 3, 380–406; English translation: Brunnhölzl 2023, 431–59; see also the discussion by Brunnhölzl (2023, 44–46).

254. Schaeffer 2005, 66–67, 105–15; Brunnhölzl 2021, 1–7.
255. Brunnhölzl 2021, 6.
256. KD: PDM vol. 26, 1013–19. Other Tibetan versions include those found in the commentaries by Rangjung Dorjé and Karma Trinlepa; for the latter, see KT, 195–233. Modern translations: Sāṃkṛtyāyana 1957, 83–97; Guenther 1969, 61–71; 1993, 89–122; Thrangu Rinpoche 2006, 141–55; Dowman 2020, 15–20; Brunnhölzl 2023, 317–23; and chapter 8 of this book. See also the discussions by Guenther (1969, 21–59); Thrangu Rinpoche (2006, 1–16); Brunnhölzl (2023, 37–40).
257. The commentary by Balpo Asu (a.k.a. Kyemé Dechen/*Ajamahāsukha) is found at D 2265, P 3112, and N 1913 and has been translated by Guenther (1969) and Brunnhölzl (2023, 603–48); the latter argues on terminological grounds that it is by the same author as Advaya Avadhūtipa's *Inexhaustible Treasury*, the commentary on the *People Dohā* summarized above.
258. For discussion, see Guenther 1969, 15–20; Schaeffer 2005, 73–75; Brunnhölzl 2023, 37–40.
259. See, for example, Guenther 1969, 75–202, which translates both the Balpo Asu and Karma Trinlepa commentaries; Thrangu Rinpoche 2006, 123–39, which sets a translation of the root verses within Karma Trinlepa's commentarial outline; and Brunnhölzl 2023, 40, 55–58.
260. QD: PDM vol. 26, 1020–34. Modern translations: Sāṃkṛtyāyana 1957, 99–125; Guenther 1993, 89–122; R. Jackson 2012, 173–84; Dowman 2020, 21–28; Brunnhölzl 2023, 509–22; and chapter 7 of this book. For discussion, see R. Jackson 2012, 162–73; Brunnhölzl 2023, 37–40, 45.
261. AD: PDM vol. 26, 1091–97. Modern translations: Sāṃkṛtyāyana 1957, 127–39; Brunnhölzl 2023, 245–50; chapter 13 of this book; and Braitstein et al. forthcoming. See also Brunnhölzl 2023, 34–35.
262. EA: PDM vol. 26, 1091–97. Modern translations: Brunnhölzl 2023, 251–65; Braitstein et al. forthcoming. See also Brunnhölzl 2023, 34–35.
263. Brunnhölzl 2023, 34.
264. BT: PDM vol. 26, 1221–37. Modern translations: Sāṃkṛtyāyana 1957, 141–83; Braitstein 2014, 125–49; Brunnhölzl 2023, 173–93; and chapter 17 of this book. See also the discussions in Braitstein (2014, 70–71); Brunnhölzl (2023, 31–32).

265. See Braitstein 2014, 66–68, 73–120.
266. Brunnhölzl (2023, 20) refers to the four as comprising the "tetralogy of vajra songs on body, speech, and mind."
267. Roerich and Gendun Chöpel (1949) 1976, 1010. See also Brunnhölzl 2023, 20–21.
268. See, for example, Lopez 1996, 202–15; Mathes 2019. On the four symbolic realizations or terms, see Guenther (1969, 29–41), who calls them *memory*, *nonmemory*, *unorigination*, and *transcendence*; Braitstein (2014, 92–119), who calls them *recognition*, *decognition*, *unborn*, and *beyond the intellect*; and Brunnhölzl (2023, 22–30), who calls them *minding*, *nonminding*, *unborn*, and *beyond mind*.
269. Braitstein 2014, 71; I have changed some of Braitstein's wording to reflect my own translation choices and occasionally expanded upon her descriptions.
270. ST: PDM vol. 26, 1238–45. Modern translations: Sāṃkṛtyāyana 1957, 185–201; Braitstein 2014, 150–60; Brunnhölzl 2023, 195–204; and chapter 18 of this book. See also the discussions by Braitstein (2014, 71–72); Brunnhölzl (2023, 32).
271. Braitstein 2014, 72. As before, I have changed some of Braitstein's wording to reflect my own translation choices and occasionally expanded upon her descriptions.
272. MT: PDM vol. 26, 1246–50. Modern translations: Sāṃkṛtyāyana 1957, 203–13; Braitstein 2014, 161–66; Brunnhölzl 2023, 205–10; and chapter 19 of this book. See also the discussions by Braitstein (2014, 72); Brunnhölzl (2023, 32).
273. Braitstein 2014, 72.
274. CD: PDM vol. 26, 1251–65. Modern translations: Sāṃkṛtyāyana 1957, 215–47; Brunnhölzl 2023, 211–26; and chapter 20 of this book. See also the discussion by Brunnhölzl (2023, 33).
275. Brunnhölzl 2023, 33. My numbering of the verses differs significantly from Brunnhölzl's.
276. MM: PDM vol. 26, 1266–32. Modern translations: Sāṃkṛtyāyana 1957, 249–67; Thaye 1990, 80–86; Stenzel 2008, 72–84; Brunnhölzl 2023, 229–36; and chapter 16 of this book. See also the discussion by Brunnhölzl (2023, 33–34).
277. In an earlier work (R. Jackson 2019, 48). I assigned the text to Śavari[pa], whereas here, upon reconsideration, I am treating it as part of the Saraha

corpus. It should be noted that Jamgön Kongtrul (DN, vol. 5, Contents, 1) credits the text to "Śabari," a name rather more unambiguously associated with Śavaripa, but his attribution is, so far as I know, quite unusual.

278. On this anthology (DZ), see Kapstein 2006. It is utilized for comparative purposes by Brunnhölzl in his translation of the Seventh Karmapa's edition of MM (2023, 229–36 and notes).
279. Brunnhölzl 2023, 33–34.
280. TV: PDM vol. 26, 1273–75. Modern translations: Sāṃkṛtyāyana 1957, 267–73; Brunnhölzl 2021, 241–43; and chapter 25 of this book. See also Brunnhölzl 2021, 10.
281. IT vol. 3, 157–65. Tibetan translator unknown. Modern translation: Brunnhölzl 2023, 237–43; see also the synopsis by Brunnhölzl (2023, 34).
282. Brunnhölzl 2023, 243, 824n1188.
283. SS: PDM vol. 26, 1276–79. Modern translations: Sāṃkṛtyāyana 1957, 275–83; Pathak 1994, 29–31; Brunnhölzl 2021, 237–40; and chapter 9 of this book. See also Pathak 1994, 26–29; Brunnhölzl 2021, 465n59.
284. Brunnhölzl 2021, 465n59.
285. SI: PDM vol. 26, 1280–83. Modern translations: Sāṃkṛtyāyana 1957, 285–95; Brunnhölzl 2023, 267–71; and chapter 23 of this book. See also Brunnhölzl 2023, 35.
286. Brunnhölzl 2023, 35.
287. VM: PDM vol. 27, 11–14. Modern translations: May n.d.; Brunnhölzl 2020, 61–63; and chapter 24 of this book.
288. OS: PDM vol. 27, 26–27. Modern translations: Sāṃkṛtyāyana 1957, 297–301; Brunnhölzl 2020, 45–46; and chapter 14 of this book.
289. Brunnhölzl 2020, 615n169.
290. US: IT vol. 5, 59–60. Modern translations: Schaeffer 2005, 83–84; Brunnhölzl 2020, 79–80; and chapter 21 of this book.
291. VS: PDM vol. 27, 290–308. Modern translation (Hindi): Sāṃkṛtyāyana 1957, 303–47. For analysis, see R. Jackson forthcoming-b.
292. Sāṃkṛtyāyana divides the sayings into 135 four-line verses, but there seems no thematic or metrical justification for doing so.
293. Schaeffer 2005, 89.
294. See, for example, Keith 1920, 227–65; Sternbach 1974; Olivelle 2006; Törzsök 2007.
295. PDM vol. 27, 291. For similar examples, see Schaeffer 2007, 25–28, 29–30, 37–38.

296. See Schaeffer 2007, 18, 25, 29, 44, 48, 53.
297. KI: D 2447 (rgyud, zi 81a2–82a7). Alternate edition (partial): Schaeffer 2007, 64–65. Modern translations: Schaeffer 2005, 94–95 (partial); 2007, 37–38 (partial); and chapter 26 of this book (complete). Like the *Vajra Secret Song*, it was excluded from the Seventh Karmapa's mahāmudrā anthology.
298. The reference here to Saraha as a "great hunter" (*mahāniṣāda*) is unusual but understandable. The Niṣādas were an Indian mountain tribal group renowned for their prowess in hunting and fishing—just as were the Śabaras, who of course provide the basis for a more common epithet for Saraha (or for his disciple or granddisciple Śavaripa), Mahāśabara.
299. SL: D 3164, D 3165, D 3371, D 3427, and D 3428. For a translation of D 3164 (rgyud, phu 182b2–183a6), see chapter 12 of this book. That version, along with D 3371, are preserved in Sanskrit; for the former, see Sakuma 2002, 126–28 and 252–53; for the latter, see Sakuma 2002, 129–33 and 252–54.
300. See chapter 2, text 4.
301. The other is attributed to Ānandagarbha (D 2519).
302. Chapter 2, text 4.
303. PM: This is missing from the Dergé Tengyur but is found in the Peking and Narthang editions. The order of sayings occasionally differs from one version to another.
304. CS 153b6–7. Cf. translations in Dowman (1985, 66); Brunnhölzl (2020, 283). This is also found in GG 83a3.
305. SM 67a1–2.
306. VJ 93a4–5. Alternative translation: Brunnhölzl 2020, 349. As Brunnhölzl (2020, 701n1135) notes, the title of this text in the Seventh Karmapa's Indian Mahāmudrā Texts (IT, vol. 5, 277) is confusingly listed as *Vajra Songs Sung by Forty Siddhas* (*Grub thob bzhi bcus rdo rje'i mgur bzhengs pa rnams*), but it is identical to the VJ found in the Tengyur (D 2543).
307. Chapter 2, text 11.
308. IT vol. 3, 380–406. Modern translation: Brunnhölzl 2023, 431–59. See also Brunnhölzl 2023, 44–46.
309. See, for the former, Schaeffer 2005, 121–77; for the latter, see KT.
310. Schaeffer 2005, 115–19, 187–89.
311. DT: IT vol. 3, 149–50. Modern translations: Brunnhölzl 2023, 227–28; and chapter 22 of this book. See also Brunnhölzl 2023, 33.

312. MD. I want to thank Charles Manson for drawing this text to my attention (personal communication, August 31, 2020) and Matthew Kapstein and Karl Brunnhölzl for providing additional perspective (personal communications, December 3, 2023). See also Manson 2022, 232n21.
313. Schaeffer 2007, 34; see also Schaeffer 2005, 184.
314. Kapstein 2000, 62–63; the verses in question are found at DN vol. 11, 94–95. Note that for the Tibetan *dran pa* (S. *smṛti*), Kapstein uses "remembrance" where I use "recollection."
315. Jo Nang Tāranātha 1983, 3.
316. Dakpo Tashi Namgyal 2019, 761. For a fuller discussion of citations of Saraha in Kagyu literature in general and *Moonbeams of Mahāmudrā* and the Ninth Karmapa's *Ocean of Definitive Meaning* (*Nges don rgya mtsho*) in particular, see Stenzel 2008, 85–115.
317. See R. Jackson 2019, 369–73, 489–94, 508–9, 513–14.
318. See, for example, PD 41, QD 24, CD 30.
319. For discussion of these practices, see, for example, Gellner 1992, 277–80, 285–87; Widdess 2004; Thapa 2015.
320. Or Apabhraṃśas, since there were, as noted in chapter 1, regional variations.
321. Shahidullah 1928, 57–66.
322. A. verse 43 (R. Jackson 2004, 78 = T. verse 53).
323. A caesura generally does occur, and the syllable count of a dohā line usually is around seventeen.
324. A. verse 55 (R. Jackson 2004, 84 = T. verse 66).
325. A. verse 54 (R. Jackson 2004, 83 = T. verse 65).
326. T. verse 53 (= A. verse 43; R. Jackson 2004, 78): *bcings bdag ni phyogs bcu ra 'gro la tshoms / thongs par gyur na mi g.yo brtan par gnas / go zlog rna mo lta bur bdag gis rtogs / bu khyod rnams kyang rang la char te ltos //.*
327. T. verse 66 (= A. verse 55; R. Jackson 2004, 84): *mthong dang thos dang reg dang dran pa dang / za snom 'khyam dang 'gro dang 'dug pa dang / cal col gtam dang lan smra gyur pa la / sems so shes na gcig gi rnam pa las mi bskyod //.*
328. T. verse 65 (= A. verse 54; R. Jackson 2004, 83): *dngos por skye ba mkha' ltar rang bzhin na / dngos po rnams spangs phyi nas ci zhig ske / gdod nas skye med rang bzhin yin pa la / de ring dpal ldan bla ma bstan pas rtogs //.*
329. As noted in chapter 3, the *Vajra Secret Song* (VS) provides no guidelines whatsoever on how it is to be interpreted, while *Key Instructions* (KI, translated in chapter 26) is divided by such common categories as view,

meditation, conduct, and fruit, but without ever explaining how any given line relates to the heading under which it is to be found.

330. The material in the remainder of this paragraph is found in R. Jackson (forthcoming-b).

331. TV, translated in chapter 25.

332. It should be noted that for metrical reasons, the Tibetan *de kho na nyid* (suchness) is sometimes contracted to *kho na nyid* (or even *kho na*) and both *de kho na nyid* and *de bzhin nyid* (thusness) may be contracted to *de nyid*. *De nyid*, however, also translates the Sanskrit *tattva*, which may be translated as "thatness" or "just that." Because we lack the Indic-language originals of most of Saraha's works, we cannot be sure in most cases whether *de nyid* reflects the Sanskrit *tattva* (thatness) or *tathatā* (suchness or thusness). I have generally opted to translate this contracted form *de nyid* as "thatness," recognizing that I may be mistaken in doing so.

333. For discussion, see, for example, Kvaerne 1975; Davidson 2002b; Loseries 2015.

334. See, for example, R. Jackson 2016, 2019.

335. The Sanskrit term *nija* is most accurately rendered "innate" (or "inborn") while the Tibetan *gnyug ma* describes something natural, fundamental, and continuous. I opt for "primordial" in part so it is not confused with "connate" (*sahaja*) but mostly because the word conveys a double sense of temporal and metaphysical precedence.

336. *Ngo bo gcig dang ldog pa tha dad*. The term *ldog pa*, which I translate as "contextual meanings," more precisely refers to a logical contrapositive.

337. Some of the material in the following three subsections appeared, in slightly different form, in R. Jackson (2022).

338. See, for example, Dasgupta (1946) 1976, 51–77.

339. Jo Nang Tāranātha 1983, 3; modified.

340. Kerouac 1959, 179.

341. The text in which the four terms are discussed most thoroughly is the *Body Treasury*, where it is a central theme, but at least the first two terms are also mentioned in the *King Dohā* (verses 23–30) and the *Queen Dohā* (verse 33). The best discussions of the four terms are in Guenther (1993, 30–34) and Braitstein (2014, 92–119).

342. See, for example, Higgins 2006; Mathes 2015a; Brunnhölzl 2020, 619–21n220.

343. Although there certainly were both male and female gurus among Indian

tantric Buddhists, Saraha most often defaults to seeing the guru as male, and I will follow that convention here.

344. See, for example, Simmer-Brown 2002; White 2003; Jacoby 2014.

345. See, for example, SB 1451; AD 6; BT 91, 94–95; ST 20; MT 14.

346. See, for example, KD 8; CB p. 1153; SB pp. 1444, 1451; AD 1, 9, 10, 12, 24, 27, 29.

347. See, for example, CB pp. 1153, 1154; AD 12.

348. *Madhyamakakārikā* 25:18–19.

349. See, for example, PD 30, 43, 120, 123, 131; QD 10; AD 19; PS 1:1; BT 6, 17; ST 2; CD 43, 49, 69; VM 1.

350. See, especially, Schomer and McLeod 1987; McDaniel 1989, 157–90; Lorenzen 1996; Urban 2001; Hawley and Jurgensmeyer 2008.

351. Schomer 1987, 67, adapted. (*bahuyaiṅ paduyaiṅ mūḍha para tālū sukkai jeṇa / ekku ji akkharu tan paḍhahu sivapuri jammai jeṇa //*.)

352. Schomer 1987, 71, adapted. (*nīṅjhara jharaṇaiṅ aṅimīrasa pīvaṇāṅ ṣaṭadala bedhyā jāi / chanda buhuṇāṅ chāṅdiṇāṅ tahāṅ dekhyā gorakha rāi //*.)

353. Schomer 1987, 69, adapted. (*chala dādū tahāṅ jāle jahāṅ chanda sūra nahiṅ jāi / rāto divasa ki gami nahīṅ sahajaiṅ kahi uesa //*.)

354. Schomer 1987, 82, adapted. (*kūkara kāka karaṅka pari pāka pūri taji jāṅhiṅ / tyoṅ rajjaba mana ki virati taji amṛta viṣa khāṅhiṅ //*.)

355. Hess and Singh 1983, 104; adapted. (Kabīr 1961, 595: *eka śabda guru devakā tāko anaṅta vicāra / thake paṇḍita muni janā veda na pāvaiṅ para //*.)

356. Hess and Singh 1983, 112; adapted. (Kabīr 1961, 597: *hada calai so manavā behada calai so sadha / hada behada donoṅ bejjai tako matā agadhā //*.)

357. Hess and Singh 1983, 122; adapted. (Kabīr 1961, 625: *yakasadhe savasādhīyā savasadhe yakajāya / ulaṭijo sīṃcai mūlako phalai aghāya //*.)

358. Hess and Singh 1983, 107–8; adapted. (Kabīr 1961, 589: *guru sikhilī gara kījiye manahi masakalā dei / śabda cholnā cholikai citta darpana karilei //*.)

359. Hess 2009, 68–69. (*śūnya śikhara para jhālara jhalake barasata amarita prema cuvā ji / kahe kabīrā suno bhāi sādho cākha cākha alamasta huvā ji //*.)

360. See R. Jackson 1996. On Milarepa, see Tsangnyön Heruka 2016; on Lingrepa, see Ewing 2017; on Godrakpa, see Stearns 2001; on Rangjung Dorjé, see Gamble 2020; on Pema Karpo, see Beyer 1974, 77–79; on Panchen Chögyen, see R. Jackson 2019, 226–35, 609–41; on Kalden Gyatso, see Sujata 2019; on Shabkar, see Sujata 2012.

361. On Chomden Raldri, see Schaeffer 2005; on Karma Trinlepa, see Guenther 1969, 1993; on Jamyang Shepa, see R. Jackson 2019, 375–78.

362. For early discussions, see, for example, La Vallée Poussin 1937 (Narada vs. Musīla); Bronkhorst 2019. For later debates, see, for example, Gregory 1987; Seyfort Ruegg 1989.
363. See R. Jackson 2019, 363–79.
364. See, for example, D. Jackson 1994.
365. Dakpo Tashi Namgyal 2019, 136–41. This tripartite analysis was suggested by any number of earlier Kagyupas, including Gampopa, but Tashi Namgyal seems to have been the first to explicate it quite so clearly.
366. See R. Jackson 2019, 363–79.
367. See, for example, R. Jackson 2019, 78–79; Tseten 2021.
368. See, for example, Hookham 1991; Stearns 2001; Sheehy and Mathes 2019.
369. See, for example, Thuken Losang Chökyi Nyima 2009, 197–212.
370. PD 43, which talks about mind as "the single seed of everything," is cited twice by Dölpopa in his magnum opus, *Mountain Doctrine:* Döl-bo-ba Shay-rap-gyal-tsen 2006, 240, 608.
371. For an excellent discussion of this tendency, see Davidson 2002a, 26–28.
372. Sāṃkṛtyāyana 1957, i.
373. See, for example, Pattanayak 2002.
374. For just one example, see Thrangu Rinpoche 2006.
375. For an interesting discussion of the place of Saraha in Kagyu ritual practices followed by Westerners in retreat in France in the early 2000s, see Stenzel 2008, 116–30.
376. Lopez 2009, 134–35.
377. Lopez 2009, 164–65. The Tibetan is in standard nine-syllable lines.
378. Trungpa 1983, 22–23. The Tibetan is in seven-syllable lines.
379. Trungpa 1983, 83–84.
380. Trungpa 1983, xi.
381. Trungpa 1983, xii.
382. For anthologies, see, for example, Johnson and Paulenich 1991; Tonkinson 1995; Gach 1998; Schelling 2005. For analysis, see, for example, Trigilio 2007 (on Allen Ginsberg); Gonnerman 2015, 213–57 (on Gary Snyder); R. Jackson forthcoming-a (on Jack Kerouac).
383. Guenther 1969, 23.
384. Guenther 1969, 28. I have changed parenthetical Tibetan terms from transliterated to phonetic form.
385. Guenther 1993, 15.
386. For further exploration of Saraha's status as a "philosopher," see Jackson

2022. I argue that Saraha is, like Nietzsche in the Western tradition, an "antiphilosopher" who points philosophy in a new direction—or perhaps points philosophy back toward its roots (in either Greece or India), where theory and praxis were inseparably combined.

387. PD: PDM vol. 26, 1091–97. For alternative translations of one or another version of the Tibetan, see Guenther 1993, 89–122; Schaeffer 2005, 129–73; Mathes and Szántó 2024, 485–544; Brunnhölzl 2024, 93–112. For further information, see chapter 2, text 1.

388. Equivalent A. verse 1a may be translated (cf. R. Jackson 2004, 53): "Brahmins don't know what's what," or "Brahmins don't know distinctions" (A. *bheu*; S. *bheda*). Cf. also Mathes and Szántó 2024, 196.

389. Equivalent A. verse 2a may be translated (cf. R. Jackson 2004, 53): "They incant, holding earth and water and kuśa grass." Cf. also Mathes and Szántó 2024, 199 (verse 2ab).

390. Equivalent A. verse 3b may be translated (cf. R. Jackson 2004, 54): "They pose as sages, imparting ascetic advice." Cf. also Mathes and Szántó 2024, 203.

391. Equivalent A. verse 3cd may be translated (cf. R. Jackson 2004, 54): "They're fakes—their error deceives the world; / they don't know right any more than wrong." Cf. also Mathes and Szántó 2024, 203–4.

392. Equivalent A. verse 6cd may be translated (cf. R. Jackson 2004, 55): "Jains mock the path by the way they look; / they deceive themselves in teaching freedom." Cf. also Mathes and Szántó 2024, 211. Note that the term "Jain" does not appear in A. 6c; the line simply mentions "fasting ascetics" (*khavana*), which most commentators take to refer to the Jains.

393. Equivalent A. verse 7b may be translated (cf. R. Jackson 2004, 56): "If baldness is perfection, then a young girl's bottom must have it." Cf. also Mathes and Szántó 2024, 211–12.

394. Equivalent A. verse 10d may be translated (cf. R. Jackson 2004, 57): "Others seek to dry up thought." Cf. also Mathes and Szántó 2024, 216.

395. Equivalent A. verse 11b may be translated (cf. R. Jackson 2004, 58): "Where scripture turns to sophistry and wordplay." Working from a different edition, Mathes and Szántó (2024, 217–18) omit this line.

396. These important and oft-quoted verses (A. 15a–15b, R. Jackson 2004, 61) are missing from the *locus classicus* for Saraha's Apabhraṃśa dohās, Advayavajra's commentary, and accordingly Bagchi (1938) omits them from

his edition of the *Dohākoṣa*; he does, however, include them elsewhere in his text among Saraha's uncollected dohās (Bagchi 1938, 48).

397. Equivalent A. verse 17 may be translated (cf. R. Jackson 2004, 62): "That's what's incanted, that's what's murmured, / and spoken in treatise and Purāṇa. / There is no seeing that doesn't perceive it— / but it's witnessed solely at the precious guru's feet." Cf. also Mathes and Szántó 2024, 223–24 (verse 16).
398. Equivalent A. verse 18b may be translated (cf. R. Jackson 2004, 63): "It's as if you've been handed assurance." Cf. also Mathes and Szántó 2024, 224 (verse 17b).
399. Equivalent A. verse 19d may be translated (cf. R. Jackson 2004, 63): "Saraha says, how can cognition be free?" Cf. also Mathes and Szántó 2024, 226 (verse 18d).
400. Equivalent A. verse 22a may be translated (cf. R. Jackson 2004, 65): "You're deceived by contemplation, so why meditate?" Cf. also Mathes and Szántó 2024, 229 (verse 21a).
401. For an explanation according to Karma Trinlepa, see Mathes 2019, 50–55.
402. Equivalent A. verse 25b may be translated (cf. R. Jackson 2004, 66): "There, fool, repose your mind! This is the teaching Saraha declares." Cf. also Mathes and Szántó 2024, 232 (verse 24cd).
403. This verse (A. verse 27, R. Jackson 2004, 67; Mathes and Szántó 2024, 233 [verse 26]) is equivalent to HT 2.5.68. Cf. Snellgrove (1959) 2010, 1:114, 2:84–85.
404. For an explanation according to Karma Trinlepa, see Mathes 2019, 56.
405. An alternate reading would be "fools must go into retreat."
406. Only the first and last lines of this verse are found in A., where they seem to form a unit (verses 30a, 31; R. Jackson 2004, 68). Cf. also Mathes and Szántó 2024, 234 (verse 29bcd).
407. Equivalent A. verse 32b may be translated (cf. R. Jackson 2004, 69): "Existence, nothingness, fortune: hey, fool, they're bondage!" Cf. also Mathes and Szántó 2024, 235 (verse 30b).
408. Equivalent A. verse 32c may be translated (cf. R. Jackson 2004, 69): "Think the inmost cognition completely, yogin." Cf. also Mathes and Szántó 2024, 236 (verse 30c).
409. I follow Mathes and Szántó (2024, 426) and IT (vol. 2, 11) in reading *sgyu 'phrul* (illusory display) for PDM's *sgyu lus* (illusory body).
410. Equivalent A. verse 33d may be translated (cf. R. Jackson 2004, 69):

"Saraha says, I've made my declaration." Cf. also Mathes and Szántó 2024, 237 (verse 31d).

411. For Karma Trinlepa's explanation, see Mathes 2019, 56–57.
412. In A., this is the last line of verse 34 (R. Jackson 2004, 70), but semantically, it seems to fit best with the following verse.
413. According to KT 43, these are (1) connate bodily appearance and emptiness, (2) connate expressive speech and emptiness, and (3) connate awareness and emptiness. Alternatively, they are (1) connate appearance and emptiness, (2) connate emptiness and nonarising, and (3) connate nonarising and beyond thought.
414. Equivalent A. verse 38a may be translated (cf. R. Jackson 2004, 72): "Another can't tell you your inmost nature." Cf. also Mathes and Szántó 2024, 242 (verse 36a).
415. Equivalent A. verse 38d may be translated (cf. R. Jackson 2004, 72): "It's purified, right and wrong both consumed." Cf. also Mathes and Szántó 2024, 243 (verse 36d).
416. Equivalent A. verse 40b may be translated (cf. R. Jackson 2004, 73): "When cognition is free, you reach the undeficient—utmost nirvāṇa." Cf. also Mathes and Szántó 2024, 246 (verse 38cd).
417. This verse (A. verse 42, R. Jackson 2004, 74; Mathes and Szántó 2024, 247 [verse 39cd]) partially echoes HT 1.9.19. Cf. Snellgrove (1959) 2010, 1:80, 2:34–35. Cf. PD 52, which is quite similar.
418. This verse partially echoes *Guhyasamāja Tantra* 2.3. Cf. Fremantle 1971, 36, 190–91.
419. For Karma Trinlepa's explanation, see Mathes 2019, 57–58.
420. Cf. PD 44, which is quite similar and also echoes HT 1.9.19.
421. Equivalent A. verse 44d may be translated (cf. R. Jackson 2004, 79): "Don't just wander around, bound by the lines of existence." Cf. also Mathes and Szántó 2024, 250 (verse 42d).
422. Equivalent A. verse 45a may be translated (cf. R. Jackson 2004, 73): "Releasing cognition and breath like unsteady horses." Cf. also Mathes and Szántó 2024, 250 (verse 43ab).
423. The equivalent A. verse, 47a (R. Jackson 2004, 80; Mathes and Szántó 2024, 251 [verse 45a]), simply has *jamuṇa*, making clear that the "Lunar River" is the Yamuna.
424. Equivalent A. verse 48b may be translated (cf. R. Jackson 2004, 81): "But

I've seen no place of pilgrimage more blissful than the body." Cf. also Mathes and Szántó 2024, 253 (verse 46cd).

425. Equivalent A. verse 49b may be translated (cf. R. Jackson 2004, 81): "Give up distinctions, fool, don't get hooked on lies!" Cf. also Mathes and Szántó 2024, 255 (verse 47cd).

426. Equivalent A. verse 50 may be translated (cf. R. Jackson 2004, 82): "Desire, indeed, is destroyed—ask the lowborn about it; / Brahmā, Viṣṇu, the triple cosmos—the whole world disappears." Cf. also Mathes and Szántó 2024, 255 (verse 48).

427. Equivalent A. verse 51 may be translated (cf. R. Jackson 2004, 82): "Hey, child! Study the alchemist's way, and you remain in ignorance; / reading their books, you don't know the world is pure." Cf. also Mathes and Szántó 2024, 256 (verse 49). This is a rare instance of a two-line Apabhraṃśa dohā being rendered in two Tibetan lines rather than four.

428. Equivalent A. verse 52 may be translated (cf. R. Jackson 2004, 82): "Hey, child! The real tastes wonderful—it's something that can't be described; / it's unconstructed, the place of bliss—a precious world rises there." Cf. also Mathes and Szántó 2024, 257 (verse 50).

429. Equivalent A. verse 54cd may be translated (cf. R. Jackson 2004, 83): "It transcends distinctions and leads to union— / the resplendent masterful guru declares, 'It's thus.'" Cf. also Mathes and Szántó 2024, 258 (verse 52cd).

430. Equivalent A. verse 55cd may be translated (cf. R. Jackson 2004, 84): "Throw off conventional nonsense— / give up cognition, don't move from the singular!" Cf. also Mathes and Szántó 2024, 259 (verse 53cd).

431. This verse is quoted in Atiśa's commentary to his own *Lamp for the Path to Awakening* (*Bodhipathapradīpa*); see Atiśa 1983, 118.

432. The Tibetan of this verse is nearly identical to that of verse 9a of Tilopa's *Dohā Treasury*; cf. R. Jackson 2004, 131.

433. Equivalent A. verse 58d may be translated (cf. R. Jackson 2004, 87): "Like a virgin's first taste of bliss." Cf. also Mathes and Szántó 2024, 262 (verse 56cd).

434. Equivalent A. verse 61 may be translated (cf. R. Jackson 2004, 89): "Don't think it's atoms or even subtle atoms— / it's bliss unceasing that spreads through existence. / Says Saraha, Such error is madness— / hey, lowborn,

comprehend the ultimate!" Cf. also Mathes and Szántó 2024, 264–65 (verse 59).

435. Equivalent A. verse 63ab may be translated (cf. R. Jackson 2004, 90): "What the guru declares—can you know it all? / Is freedom won without knowing everything?" Cf. also Mathes and Szántó 2024, 266 (verse 61ab).
436. Equivalent A. verse 64d may be translated (cf. R. Jackson 2004, 90): "Untroubled by things, enjoying things." Cf. also Mathes and Szántó 2024, 268 (verse 62d).
437. Equivalent A. verse 65 may be translated (cf. R. Jackson 2004, 91): "You worship a god, and even see signs, / but killing the self—what does that do? / Even that won't break up saṃsāra; / short of exertion, there is no escape." Cf. also Mathes and Szántó 2024, 269–70 (verse 63).
438. Reading *'chi* for *'ching*.
439. Perhaps following Mokṣākaragupta, Karma Trinlepa (KT 73) reads this as *yoginī* (*rnal 'byor ma*); cf. Guenther 1993, 174n87.
440. Equivalent A. verse 67ab may be translated (cf. R. Jackson 2004, 92): "As long as the village of senses and objects isn't destroyed, / inaction continues pouring forth on its own." Cf. also Mathes and Szántó 2024, 271–72 (verse 65ab).
441. Although separated in the Tibetan by a verse missing in A., lines 3 and 5 here of the Tibetan (equivalent to A. verse 68cd; R. Jackson 2004, 92; Mathes and Szántó 2024, 273 [verse 66d]) rhyme in Apabhraṃśa, hence were at some point "together" in the Indic tradition.
442. Equivalent A. verse 70a may be translated (cf. R. Jackson 2004, 93): "Not enjoying the purity of things, practicing emptiness only / [you're like . . .]." Cf. also Mathes and Szántó 2024, 275 (verse 68ab).
443. Following the reading of KT 78–79.
444. Equivalent A. verse 73 may be translated (cf. R. Jackson 2004, 95): "Told to whom? Who hears? What subsides here amid these doings? / Like noxious dust in a tunnel, what rises in the heart settles in the heart." Cf. also Mathes and Szántó 2024, 278 (verse 71).
445. Equivalent A. verse 74b may be translated (cf. R. Jackson 2004, 95): "Vices and virtues of mind, you fool—there is no conflict at all." Cf. also Mathes and Szántó 2024, 279 (verse 72cd). The A. of the entire verse is quoted by Bhavabhaṭṭa (tenth century) in his commentary on the *Four Seats Tantra* (*Catuḥpītha Tantra*), making it one of the earliest known citations of a verse by Saraha.

446. Equivalent A. verse 75a may be translated (cf. R. Jackson 2004, 96): "Bring things together in emptiness, consider them the same." Cf. also Mathes and Szántó 2024, 279 (verse 73ab).
447. For a discussion of Karma Trinlepa's interpretation of this verse, see Mathes 2019, 58–61.
448. This line, which is not reflected in A. 76 (R. Jackson 2004, 96) is read by Karma Trinlepa (KT 82–83) to teach that the ultimate (what "is like that") cannot be changed into the conventional (what "is not like that") any more than an elephant can be transformed into a pig, or vice versa.
449. Equivalent A. verse 76 may be translated (cf. R. Jackson 2004, 96): "That is thus: what's other is not like that: / it works just like a magic wishing gem. / Strange, how erring scholars are destroyed, / when great bliss dwells in their own awareness." Cf. also Mathes and Szántó 2024, 280–81 (verse 74).
450. This line, found only in Tibetan, has been interpolated into A. verse 77 (R. Jackson 2004, 97), which is quite coherent without it.
451. Equivalent A. verse 78b may be translated (cf. R. Jackson 2004, 97): "But outside great bliss, it's unheard of." Cf. also Mathes and Szántó 2024, 282 (verse 76b).
452. Reading *bzhin* for *gzhan*.
453. Equivalent A. verse 79 may be translated (cf. R. Jackson 2004, 99): "A single god is seen in many scriptures; / by your own will alone it clearly appears." Cf. also Mathes and Szántó 2024, 284 (verse 77).
454. This line (T. 99e), which is not reflected in the A. of equivalent verse 81 (R. Jackson 2004, 100), is difficult to place; Karma Trinlepa (KT 91) reads it together with T. 99cd and 100a.
455. Equivalent A. verse 82 may be translated (cf. R. Jackson 2004, 100): "If you don't give up coming and going, / how will you win the peerless coquette?" Cf. also Mathes and Szántó 2024, 287 (verse 80).
456. Equivalent A. verse 83a may be translated (cf. R. Jackson 2004, 100): "Mind shines, given up to the truth." Cf. also Mathes and Szántó 2024, 288 (verse 81a).
457. Equivalent A. verse 83cd may be translated (cf. R. Jackson 2004, 100): "If you don't break down body, speech, and cognition, / your connate nature will not shine." Cf. also Mathes and Szántó 2024, 288 (verse 81cd).
458. Reading *rnal 'byor ma* for *rnal 'byor pa*.

459. Equivalent A. verse 84 may be translated (cf. R. Jackson 2004, 101): "The mistress eats her husband: in a land of such misconduct, / O mother, what comes next? The yoginī's conduct is beyond compare." Cf. also Mathes and Szántó 2024, 289 (verse 82).

460. Equivalent A. verse 85 may be translated (cf. R. Jackson 2004, 101): "She's eaten her husband, relished the connate, destroyed attachment and detachment; / seated by her husband, mind destroyed, the yoginī appears before me." Cf. also Mathes and Szántó 2024, 290 (verse 83). For Karma Trinlepa's interpretation of the verse, see Mathes 2019, 61–65.

461. Equivalent A. verse 86 may be translated (cf. R. Jackson 2004, 101): "She eats, she drinks, she doesn't care what appears. / Hey, beyond cognition, the yoginī's way is past compare." Cf. also Mathes and Szántó 2024, 291 (verse 84). Between the last line here and the first line of T. verse 105 (in my enumeration), Schaeffer (2005, 163–64) interpolates two lines found in the Tibetan translation of Advayavajra's commentary: "Think upon this work alone. / The intellect which is indivisible in whatever endeavor/..."

462. Equivalent A. verse 87b may be translated (cf. R. Jackson 2004, 102): "It's mind perfected—know the connate sorcery of the yoginī!" Cf. also Mathes and Szántó 2024, 292 (verse 85cd). A. verse 87a—which may be translated as "Exalted both day and night, she creates the triple world"—is not found in the Tibetan.

463. Equivalent A. verse 88b may be translated (as per R. Jackson 2004, 103): "But resist words and you'll get past words." Cf. also Mathes and Szántó 2024, 293 (verse 86cd).

464. According to Karma Trinlepa (KT 99), the "mahāmudrā system" asserts that beyond the usual tenth bodhisattva level (the "dharma cloud"), there is an eleventh level, known as "all-illuminating," a twelfth level, known as "the unbreakable lotus-bearer," a thirteenth level, known as "the great collection of encircling syllables," and a fourteenth and highest level, known as "the level of great bliss."

465. Reading *bton* for *ston*.

466. Equivalent A. verse 90a may be translated (cf. R. Jackson 2004, 104): "I read the opening phrase, 'Let there be attainment.'" Cf. also Mathes and Szántó 2024, 294 (verse 88a). The Sanskrit phrase *siddhirastu* or *athasiddhi* is found at the outset of many Hindu treatises. Karma Trinlepa (KT 100–101) reads the four syllables (which are specified in A. but not in

T.) on several levels, adding an "inner" reading in which the four are *evaṃ mayā* ("thus [was heard] by me ," the phrase with which Buddhist sūtras begin) and a "secret" reading in which *evaṃ mayā* refers to the four stages of mahāmudrā realization: recollection, nonrecollection, nonarising, and beyond thought, or the four tantric seals, the four buddha bodies, or the four yogas of mahāmudrā.

467. This is most likely the syllable *a*, which is both the generative syllable of the whole Sanskrit language and also a privative prefix, which negates whatever follows. Each of these may be read as referring to emptiness. See KT 102.

468. For a discussion of Karma Trinlepa's analysis, see Mathes 2019, 65–66.

469. According to Karma Trinlepa (KT 102), the "three forests" refer to three conditions, those of the illusory body, expressive speech, and mental realization; the "single syllable" is *a*; the "three deities" are uncontaminated body, which is empty, uncontaminated speech, which is beyond expression, and uncontaminated mind, which is nonarising; and the one deity is the naturally luminous, inconceivable, and ineffable reality body or dharma sphere.

470. R. Jackson 2004, 106 (verses 92–93); cf. Mathes and Szántó 2024, 292–93 (verses 90–91). Given their summary tone, these two verses, which are missing from T., may possibly represent the conclusion of the text at some stage of its development. See Mathes and Szántó 2024, 26.

471. Reading *bstan* for *bden*.

472. Equivalent A. verse 94b may be translated (cf. R. Jackson 2004, 107): "Enjoying that, who in the triple world would not have their hopes fulfilled?" Cf. also Mathes and Szántó 2024, 298 (verse 92cd). As should be clear, the A. and T. convey almost completely opposite messages.

473. According to Karma Trinlepa (KT 105), these difficult lines refer to the blissful experiences induced by the sexual yoga involved in the third (wisdom-gnosis) consecration, which may be momentary or may lead on to full realization. For Advayavajra's interpretation, see Mathes and Szántó 2024, 299.

474. Equivalent A. verse 96a may be translated (cf. R. Jackson 2004, 108): "When you apprehend the profound, there is no self, nor is there other." Cf. also Mathes and Szántó 2024, 300 (verse 94ab).

475. Equivalent A. verse 101b may be translated (cf. R. Jackson 2004, 110): "But the yogin, like a skillful trainer, escapes and goes away." Cf. also Mathes

and Szántó 2024, 304 (verse 99cd). Cf. the rather different translations of the Tibetan by Guenther (1993, 118) and Schaeffer (2005, 168).

476. Equivalent A. verse 103 may be translated (cf. R. Jackson 2004, 112): "Don't stay home, don't go to the forest, just recognize cognition wherever you are." Cf. also Mathes and Szántó 2024, 305 (verse 101ab).

477. IT (vol. 2, 24) adds an extra line here, which may be translated: "Like dividing up what you see in the ocean." Semantically, it seems to me to fit with the following verse, but no A. equivalent has been found.

478. "Essentially pure" (A. *sahaveṃ suddha*; see A. verse 106b, R. Jackson 2004, 113) is quoted in verse 9:10 of the *Buddhakapāla Tantra*; see, for example, Luo 2010, 5, 59.

479. Equivalent A. verse 107b may be translated (cf. R. Jackson 2004, 114): "It bears compassion flower and fruit, though there is no other or doing good." Cf., however, Mathes and Szántó's (2024, 308 [verse 105cd]) translation, which is closer to the Tibetan.

480. Equivalent A. verse 108b may be translated (cf. R. Jackson 2004, 114): "Another's pleasure is its final fruit: mind intent on others' enjoyment." Cf. also Mathes and Szántó 2024, 309 (verse 106cd).

481. Reading *'chad* for *med*.

482. Equivalent A. verse 109b may be translated (cf. R. Jackson 2004, 114): "So if you prattle about it, your troubles will only grow." Cf., however, Mathes and Szántó's (2024, 309 [verse 107cd]) translation, which is closer to the Tibetan.

483. Cf. the rather different translations of line d by Guenther (1993, 122), and Mathes and Szántó (2024, 547).

484. QD: PDM vol. 26, 1020–34. Alternative translations: Sāṃkṛtyāyana 1957, 99–125; Guenther 1993, 89–122; R. Jackson 2012, 173–84; Dowman 2020, 21–28; Brunnhölzl 2023, 509–22. For further information, see chapter 2, text 13.

485. The nose tip is a common focal point of yogic meditation but in a tantric context may also connote the male sexual organ.

486. I follow KT 139 in reading *zhi ba* for *bzhi pa*.

487. The five lamps are the five "meats" consumed during tantric ritual feasts: bull, dog, elephant, horse, and human.

488. According to KT 167, these are the yoginīs connected to the six buddha families; in commentaries on *Hevajra Tantra* 1.5.9, they are identified as the wheel, jewel, chopper, lotus, sword, and vajra.

489. Although the Tibetan *ye shes* (S. *jñāna*) typically refers to higher wisdom, or gnosis, it also may simply refer to knowledge, and I translate it that way here so as to emphasize Saraha's contrast between mere knowledge and profound awareness.
490. In Indian tradition, these are construction, medicine, grammar, valid cognition, and inner science—that is, Buddhism.
491. See above, n. 464.
492. KD: PDM vol. 26, 1013–19. Alternative translations: Sāṃkṛtyāyana 1957, 83–97; Guenther 1969, 61–71; 1993, 89–122; Thrangu Rinpoche 2006, 141–55; Dowman 2020, 15–20; Brunnhölzl 2023, 317–23. For further information, see chapter 2, text 12.
493. *Kā ma rū pa* means sensuous forms but also refers to the South Asian region of Assam. KT 214 suggests that the term refers to the "contaminated" bliss induced by sexual practices performed with an action seal.
494. *E* typically stands for emptiness, *vaṃ* for bliss. The four moments (sometimes related to the four joys) are the diverse, the ripening, the dissolving, and the signless. The four seals, as we have seen, are the action, pledge, dharma, and great seals.
495. This line is missing from D—hence omitted from the main text of PDM—but, as per PDM vol. 26, 1018n12, is supplied by both N and Q.
496. SS: PDM 26, 1276–79. Alternative translations: Sāṃkṛtyāyana 1957, 275–83; Pathak 1994, 29–31; Brunnhölzl 2021, 237–40. For further information, see chapter 2, text 21.
497. Reading *gis* for *gi*.
498. BK: PDM vol. 13, 1145–58. For further information, see chapter 2, text 6. The translation of the commentary is interspersed with relevant passages (in italics) from *Buddhakapāla Tantra* (H 400): rgyud, nga 5b7–7b4; these largely overlap with the passages translated in Davidson 2002a, 248–50.
499. This reflects a scholastic subdivision of the four joys commonly discussed in the yoginī tantras.
500. This is drawn from HT 2.3.4; see Snellgrove (1959) 2010, 1:94, 2:252–53.
501. Source not found.
502. Source not found.
503. Source not found.
504. Source not found.
505. Source not found.
506. Or perhaps Mālava (*pū ṇi pū li ra*).

507. SB: PDM vol. 26, 1443–54. For further information, see chapter 2, text 7.
508. The text states clearly that Citrasenā has only two arms, which is hard to reconcile with the description of four objects in her hands.
509. Bhattacharyya (1949, 47) has Kapālinī.
510. This involves raising the right foot, with the leg mostly bent, and pointing it toward the left leg, which is partly bent and planted on the ground.
511. Bhattacharyya (1949, 47) has Mahodadhi.
512. Bhattacharyya (1949, 47) has Kāriṇī.
513. Bhattacharyya (1949, 47) has Sumālinī.
514. Bhattacharyya (1949, 47) has Mahāhāsā.
515. Bhattacharyya (1949, 47) has Sundarī.
516. Again, it is difficult to reconcile the description of the goddess as two armed with the statement here that she holds four implements.
517. Per P and N; D has *hāṃ hāṃ hāṃ* as the last three syllables.
518. Here, this mantra substitutes for the more common *jaḥ hūṃ vaṃ hoḥ*.
519. Perhaps, the uncreated, causal, and resultant.
520. Perhaps, the four bodhisattva applications: application of complete aspects, peak application, successive application, and instantaneous application.
521. Per P and N; D has *bho*.
522. SL (1): PDM vol. 39, 535–38. On the various versions of this sādhana attributed to Saraha, see the discussion in chapter 2, texts 4, 28.
523. The mix here of Sanskrit syllables and English reflects the fact that in this sādhana, many of the mantras involve a combination of Sanskrit and Tibetan; I have maintained the Sanskrit but translated the Tibetan.
524. AD: PDM vol. 26, 193–210. Alternative translations: Sāṃkṛtyāyana 1957, 127–39; Brunnhölzl 2023, 245–50; and Braitstein et al. forthcoming. For further information, see chapter 2, text 14. Prepared in consultation with Saraha's EA; the appropriate pages in the PDM version of that commentary are indicated in brackets after each of the syllables that structure the text.
525. As the reader will note, the key words in the following verse begin not with *ṅa* but *ṇa*—which also occurs as a separate entry in verse 14, below.
526. Possibly, the extremes of existence, nonexistence, both, and neither.
527. Those located at the crown, throat, heart, and navel cakras.
528. Note that the key words in the first, third, and fourth lines begin with *ṇa* rather than *jha*.

529. *Ṇa* also appeared earlier, in verse 5, under the (apparently) mislabeled rubric of *ṅa*.
530. As noted before, in tantric contexts, the "nose" may also refer to the vajra, or penis.
531. *Wa* is not a consonant found in Indic languages as such, although *va* often is pronounced as if it were a *w*. In the third line, *birā* (or *virā*), which might be pronounced *wīra*, might in some Indic languages be pronounced as if it were a *b*.
532. Note that the first, third, and fourth lines are actually keyed to words beginning with *sa* rather than *ṣa*.
533. Interpreted as *padma*, the lotus, or female organ.
534. The colophon to the autocommentary, attributed to Saraha (KT 1118), reads: "This *Written Explanation of the Alphabetical Dohās* composed by Saraha—who is like the crown jewel among all the lords of yoga—was translated orally on his own (*snga nas rang 'gyur du mdzad pa*) by the great lord of yoga, Śrī Vairocanavajra, who was born in the southern region, in Kośala, India."
535. OS: PDM vol. 26, 26–27. Alternative translations: Sāṃkṛtyāyana 1957, 297–301; Brunnhölzl 2020, 45–46. For further information, see chapter 2, text 24.
536. The Tibetan *gzhon nu* generally connotes a male, but as noted earlier, it is not outlandish to regard the voice in this song as female.
537. I follow Brunnhölzl (2020, 616n170) in this reading of *se bu* (*se 'bru*?).
538. As Brunnhölzl (2020, 616n172) notes, *sha ris pa* is unknown in either Sanskrit or Tibetan. It would seem to suggest a musician, but this is speculation.
539. Cf. Brunnhölzl's (2020, 45) reading: "The drawing falls down on me."
540. Reading *me* for *mo*.
541. PS: Kvaerne 1977, 168–69 (#1), 199–200 (#2), 222–23 (#3), 226–27 (#4); Shahidullah 1928, 229–31. Alternative translations: Shahidullah 1928, 233–34; Sāṃkṛtyāyana 1957, 355–61; Kvaerne 1977, 168–69, 199–200, 222–23, 226–27; Bhayani 1997, 81–139; Cleary 1998, 111, 137, 161, 165; Dowman 2020, 29–30 (#1 only); Brunnhölzl 2021, 348–49, 387–88, 389–90.
542. The A. equivalent to "unconcerned" (Kvaerne 1977, 168) lacks any negative qualifier. To me, this makes more sense than the Tibetan, but if Saraha is criticizing alchemists, a case could be made for the Tibetan reading too.

543. Instead of "far away," A. (Kvaerne 1977, 199) has "to Laṅkā," which Munidatta equates to saṃsāra.
544. Instead of "Saraha says," A. (Kvaerne 1977, 199) has "You think." Again, a case could be made for either reading.
545. The A. of this line may be translated (per Kvaerne 1977, 223): "The boatman tows the boat by means of a rope."
546. The A. of the first two lines may be translated (per Kvaerne 1977, 226): "O wonder—[you have] arisen from *hūṃ* [and entered] the sky. In Bengal, you have taken a wife."
547. The A. of this line may be translated (per Kvaerne 1977, 227): "Although there is nectar, you swallow poison." In the context of the verse, this makes more sense to me than the Tibetan.
548. The A. of this line may be translated (per Kvaerne 1977, 227): "Better an empty cowshed."
549. MM: PDM vol. 26, 1325–31. Alternative translations: Sāṃkṛtyāyana 1957, 249–67; Thaye 1990, 80–86; Stenzel 2008, 72–84; Brunnhölzl 2023, 229–36. For further information, see chapter 2, text 19.
550. If we read *yis* for *yi*, the line could be translated: "I, the hermit, entered realization."
551. These two lines also are found in PD 85.
552. This line echoes PD 27a.
553. Perhaps, the reference points of cognizer, the object of cognition, and the act of cognition.
554. As per DZ 6b5, reading *dga' zhing skyo* for *dka' zhing skye*.
555. This could be taken as referring either to the action, dharma, pledge, and great seals of tantric traditions or to the four doctrinal seals common to all Buddhist teachings: all compounded phenomena are impermanent, all contaminated phenomena are suffering, all dharmas are empty and selfless, and nirvāṇa is peace.
556. As per DZ 7a5, reading *pa* for *pas*.
557. BT: PDM vol. 26, 1221–37. Alternative translations: Sāṃkṛtyāyana 1957, 141–83; Braitstein 2014, 125–49; Brunnhölzl 2023, 173–96. For further information, see chapter 2, text 15.
558. Reading *la* for *dang*.
559. Reading *yid* for *yod*.
560. Cf. the reading by Brunnhölzl (2023, 179 and 792–93nn819–21).
561. Cf. the reading by Brunnhölzl (2023, 182 and 794n836), who has "oyster."

562. Cf. Braitstein (2014, 142), who reads it as "completion stage." See also Brunnhölzl 2023, 188 and 796n874.
563. Reading *rtogs* for *rtog*.
564. Reading *bzhin* for *bzhi na*.
565. Perhaps a vulture; see Brunnhölzl 2023, 797n909.
566. The identity of this animal is uncertain, but see Braitstein (2014, 147n382), who suggests that it may refer to some creature who lives in isolation in the mountains.
567. Perhaps a medicinal evergreen tree, perhaps a coconut tree. See Brunnhölzl 2023, 797–98n912.
568. PDM has *rgyu*, but *rgyud* (continuum) is an equally (or more) plausible reading.
569. ST: PDM vol. 26, 1238–45. Alternative translations: Sāṃkṛtyāyana 1957, 185–201; Braitstein 2014, 150–60; Brunnhölzl 2023, 195–204. For further information, see chapter 2, text 16.
570. For an alternate translation and analysis of this cryptic line, see Brunnhölzl (2023, 195 and 798n921), who suggests: "If you are on a lake out in the open, the range in the four directions is vast."
571. Reading *bstan* for *brtan* or *bsten*.
572. Pleasure, pain, loss, gain, shame, fame, praise, and blame.
573. See BT 31–32.
574. Reading *rtogs* for *rtog*. Cf. the reading by Brunnhölzl (2023, 199 and 799n940).
575. The "secret domain" might refer broadly to Vajrayāna as the secret-mantra vehicle, more specifically to the secret consecration, or to something entirely different.
576. Most likely, the openings at the crown cakra and the "secret" (or sexual) cakra, respectively.
577. *Rigs* may refer to a family or spiritual lineage, or to a social class or caste.
578. MT: PDM vol. 26, 1246–50. Alternative translations: Sāṃkṛtyāyana 1957, 203–13; Braitstein 2014, 161–66; Brunnhölzl 2023, 205–10. For further information, see chapter 2, text 17.
579. Reading *brjed* for *brjod*.
580. See Brunnhölzl 2023, 802n981 and above, n. 413. According to *Ajamahāsukha, the three are the connates of appearance, of emptiness, and of nonarising.

581. Compare the translation by Brunnhölzl (2023, 206): "when at the verge of death."
582. Reading *kyis* for *kyi*.
583. Cf. the translation at Braitstein (2014, 162).
584. Reading *dngos po* for *ngo bo*.
585. Which three are intended is unclear; Buddhists more typically eschew two or four extremes.
586. Cf. the translation by Braitstein (2013, 164). The threefold wisdom is that of hearing, reflection, and contemplation.
587. Cf. the rather different translation by Brunnhölzl (2023, 209). Braitstein's (2013, 165) reading is similar to my own.
588. CD: PDM vol. 26, 1310–24. Alternative translations: Sāṃkṛtyāyana 1957, 215–47; Brunnhölzl 2023, 211–26. For further information, see chapter 2, text 18.
589. With its mix of metaphors, this verse is quite difficult, and my reading conjectural.
590. Most likely either the śrāvaka, pratyekabuddha, and bodhisattva vehicles or the Mainstream, Great, and Vajra vehicles.
591. The three sufferings are the suffering of suffering, the suffering of change, and the suffering pervading all aggregates; the eight sufferings are those of birth, sickness, aging, dying, separation from the beloved, encounter with the unpleasant, not getting what one wants, and the five aggregates.
592. Cf. the translation by Brunnhölzl (2023, 214).
593. Reading *yan lag* for *yang dag*; see Brunnhölzl 2023, 807n1058.
594. This is a conjectural reading for *bse dri can*; cf. Brunnhölzl (2023, 220), who has "smelly armpits."
595. Reading *stong* for *stor*.
596. This is the first of the four stages of the path of preparation (S. *prayoga mārga*; T. *sbyor lam*), which is the second of the five paths recognized in Indian Buddhist scholasticism. It "prepares" for the direct realization of the truth—in this case, emptiness—attained on the third path, that of seeing (S. *darśana*; T. *mthong*).
597. These are eight similes for the nature of things, as expounded in the *Diamond Cutter* (*Vajracchedikā*) *Sūtra*: stars, a fault of vision, a lamp, a magic show, dewdrops, a bubble, a dream, a lightning flash, and a cloud.
598. It is tempting to read this as a reference to the third, or wisdom-gnosis, consecration of unexcelled-yoga tantra, but it may simply connote a more

general conferral of wisdom by the guru—or perhaps is another of way of describing the fourth, or word, consecration, which consummates the series, and is most connected with an attainment of the gnosis of emptiness.

599. Brunnhölzl (2023, 225 and 808–9n1084) reads *dbang* as referring to "consecrations" and the triple taint mentioned in the next line as implying the first three unexcelled-yoga-tantra consecrations—the vase, secret, and wisdom-gnosis—which are coarse in comparison to the fourth consecration. I find this explanation compelling but have opted for the simpler one.
600. US: IT vol. 5, 59–60. Alternative translations: Schaeffer 2005, 83–84; Brunnhölzl 2020, 79–80. For further information, see chapter 2, text 25.
601. DT: IT vol. 3, 149–50. Alternative translation: Brunnhölzl 2023, 227–28. For further information, see chapter 2, text 30.
602. SI: PDM vol. 26, 1280–83. Alternative translations: Sāṃkṛtyāyana 1957, 285–95; Brunnhölzl 2023, 267–71. For further information, see chapter 2, text 22.
603. This is similar to QD 24c.
604. This is a mode of Madhyamaka reasoning that analyzes things by way of parts and wholes. It is particularly associated with Śāntarakṣita (eighth century).
605. Reading *bdag* for *dag*.
606. VM: PDM vol. 27, 11–14. Alternative translations: May n.d.; Brunnhölzl 2020, 61–63. For further information, see chapter 2, text 23.
607. This term may connote undertaking retreat.
608. This may be a reference to a common Mahāyāna meditation in which one attempts to develop equanimity toward both friends and loved ones (visualized behind one) and enemies (visualized in front of one).
609. Reading *mi rtog* for *rnam rtog*, per IT vol. 5, 48.
610. Reading *yid la mi byed pa* for *yid la mi gzhag pa*, per IT vol. 5, 48. See Brunnhölzl 2020, 619–21n220.
611. TV: PDM vol. 26, pp. 1273–75. Alternative translations: Sāṃkṛtyāyana 1957, 267–73; Brunnhölzl 2021, 241–43. For further information, see chapter 2, text 20.
612. This line is missing from PDM and IT but is found in Sāṃkṛtyāyana (1957, 270–71).
613. Reading *ni* for *no*.

614. Reading *sbrul gis* for *sbrul gi*.
615. Reading *rtsi* for *rjes*; cf. Brunnhölzl 2021, 242.
616. See Brunnhölzl 2021, 536n985.
617. KI: D 2447 (rgyud, zi 81a2–82a7). Alternative partial translations: Schaeffer 2005, 94–95; 2007, 37–38. For further information, see chapter 2, text 27.
618. The translation is conjectural. Another possible rendering of *yid 'ong bral ba'i ma bzhin du* is "be like an unpleasant mother," but even in the world of symbol-songs, this seems far-fetched.
619. Reading *bskar* for *bskur*.

Bibliography

Indic and Tibetan Sources

Note: The entries are arranged alphabetically by abbreviation, not by author or text title.

AD: Saraha. *Alphabetical Dohās. Kakhasya doha-nāma. Ka kha'i do ha zhes bya ba*: PDM vol. 26, 1091–97; D 2266 (rgyud, zhi 55b3–57b2); P 3113 (rgyud 'grel, tsi 66a8–68b4); N 1914 (rgyud 'grel, tsi 55a1–57a3); IT vol. 3, 166–72. Tibetan translation by Vairocanavajra.

AP: Advayavajra. *Scriptural Commentary on the "Dohā Treasury." Dohakoṣapañjikā. Do ha mdzod kyi bka' 'grel*: D 2256 (rgyud, wi 180b3–207a7); P 3101 (rgyud 'grel, mi 199a7–231a5); N 1902 (rgyud 'grel, mi 193b7–222b5); IT vol. 3, 246–324. Tibetan translation by Vairocanavajra.

AV: Advaya Avadhūtipa. *Commentary on the Essential Meaning of the "Dohā Treasury." Dohakoṣahṛdayārthagītāṭikā-nāma. Do ha mdzod kyi snying po don gyi glu'i 'grel pa zhes bya ba*: D 2268 (rgyud, zhi 65b7–106b4); P 3120 (rgyud 'grel, tsi 97a6–138a1); N 1921 (rgyud 'grel, tsi 84a5–125b5). Tibetan translator unknown.

BK: *Buddhakapāla Tantra. Śrī-buddhakapāla-nāma-yoginī-tantrarājā. Dpal sangs rgyas thod pa zhes bya ba rnal 'byor ma'i rgyud kyi rgyal po*: D 424 (rgyud, nga 143a1–167a5); P 63 (rgyud, nga 126b4–153a6; N 388 (rgyud, nga 5b4–38b5; C 63 (rgyud, nga 136a6–166a6); H 400 (rgyud, nga 5b6–43b1). Tibetan translation by Gayadhara and Gyi jo Zla ba'i 'od zer.

BT: Saraha. *Body Treasury: An Immortal Vajra Song. Kāyakoṣāmṛtavajragītā. Sku'i mdzod 'chi med rdo rje'i glu*: PDM vol. 26, 1221–37; D 2269 (rgyud, zhi 106b4–113a2); P 3115 (rgyud 'grel, tsi 78a3–85a3); N 1916 (rgyud 'grel, tsi 66a5–72b3); IT vol. 3, 103–20. Tibetan translation (possibly) by Nag po sher dad.

CB: Saraha. *The Gnostic: A Commentary on the "Buddhakapāla Tantra." Śrībuddhakapālatantrasya pañjikājñānavatī-nāma. Dpal sangs rgyas thod pa'i rgyud kyi dka' 'grel ye shes ldan pa zhes bya ba*: PDM vol. 13, 1145–1256; D 1652 (rgyud, ra 104b1–150a2; P 2524 (rgyud 'grel, ya 119b1–168b2; N 1323 (rgyud 'grel, ya 120a4–169b7). Tibetan translation by Gayadhara and Gyi jo Zla ba'i 'od zer.

CC: Nāropa. *Commentary on Consecration. Paramārthasaṃgraha-nāmasekoddeśaṭīkā. Dbang mdor bstan pa'i 'grel bshad don dam pa bsdus pa zhes bya ba*. D 1351 (rgyud, na 220b1–289a7); P 2068 (rgyud 'grel, ga 258b3–337b4); N 862 (rgyud 'grel, ga 244a2–321a7). Tibetan translation by Dharmadhara and Grags pa rgyal mtshan; revised by Rin chen rgyal mtshan.

CD: Saraha. *Cognitive Disengagement from Body, Speech, and Mind. Kāyavākcittāmanasikāra-nāma. Sku gsung thugs yid la mi byed pa zhes bya ba*: PDM vol. 26, 1251–65; D 2272 (rgyud, zhi 117a3–122a3); P 3118 (rgyud 'grel, tsi 89b2–95a2); N 1919 (rgyud 'grel, tsi 76b3–82a1); IT vol. 3, 133–48. Tibetan translation by Kṛṣṇapaṇḍita (= Nag po Sher dad?).

CS: Vīraprakāśa. *Essential Realizations of the Eighty-Four Mahāsiddhas. Caturaśītisiddhasambodhihṛdaya. Grub thob brgyad cu rtsa bzhi'i rtogs pa'i snying po zhes bya ba*. D 2292 (rgyud, zhi 153a6–158b1); P 3140 (rgyud 'grel, tsi 168b3–174a1); N 1941 (rgyud 'grel, tsi 157a5–162b7). Tibetan translator unknown.

DN: 'Jam mgon kong sprul [I] Blo gros mtha' yas, ed. *Gdams ngag mdzod: A Treasury of Instructions and Techniques for Spiritual Realization*. 12 vols. Delhi: N. Lungtok and N. Gyaltsan, 1971.

DT: Saraha. *Special Mahāmudrā Instruction for Death Time. Mahāmudrāmārajālaupadeśa. Phyag rgya chen po 'chi kha ma'i man ngag*: IT vol. 3, 149–50. Tibetan translator unknown.

DZ: *Eight Dohā Treasuries. Do ha mdzod brgyad ces bya ba phyag rgya chen po'i man ngag gsal bar ston pa'i gzhung*. Darjeeling: Kargyu Sungrab Nyamso Khang, 1978–85.

EA: Saraha. *Explanatory Notes on the "Alphabetical Dohā." Kakhasya dohā-ṭippaṇa. Ka kha'i do ha'i bshad pa bris pa*: PDM vol. 26, 1098–1120; D 2267 (rgyud, zhi 57b2–65b7); P 3114 (rgyud 'grel, tsi 68b4–78a2); N 1915 (rgyud 'grel, tsi 57a3–66); IT vol. 3, 173–97. Tibetan translation by Vairocanavajra.

ES: Saraha. *Offering Rite for All Elemental Spirits. Sarvabhūtabalividhi. 'Byung po thams cad kyi gtor ma'i cho ga*: PDM vol. 26, 1455–58; D 1656 (rgyud, ra 229b3–230b2); P 2528 (rgyud 'grel, ya 256a3–257a4); N 1327 (rgyud 'grel, ya 257a4–25). Tibetan translation by Gayadhara and Gyi jo Zla ba'i 'od zer.

GG: Forty Mahāsiddhas. *Garland of Golden Drops: Vajra-Song Experiential Pith-*

Instructions. Vajragītibhāvanopadeśatilakakanakamālā. Rdo rje'i mgur bzhengs pa nyams kyi man ngag thig le gser gyi phreng ba: D 2449 (rgyud, zi 83a1–85b6); P 3277 (rgyud 'grel, tshi 104b4–108a4); N 2078 (rgyud 'grel, tshi 90b6–93b7).

HT: *Hevajra Tantra*. Sanskrit and Tibetan texts as found in Snellgrove ([1959] 2010), listed below under "Modern Sources."

IT: Chos grags rdo rje (Karma pa 7), ed. *Indian Texts on the Mahāmudrā of Definitive Meaning. Nges don phyag rgya chen po'i rgya gzhung*. In *Nges don phyag rgya chen po'i rgya gzhung dang bod gzhung*, vols. 1–6. Chengdu, China: Si khron mi rigs dpe skrun khang [Sichuan Minzu Chubanshe], 2008.

KD: Saraha. *Dohā Treasury: A Performance Song (King Dohā). Dohakoṣa-nāma-caryāgīti. Do ha mdzod ces bya ba spyod pa'i glu*: PDM vol. 26, 1013–19; D 2263 (rgyud, zhi 26b6–28b6); P 3110 (rgyud 'grel, tsi 31b3–34a2); N 1911 (rgyud 'grel, tsi 26b5–28b3). Tibetan translation by Balpo Asu.

KI: Saraha. *Key Instructions. *Marmopadeśa. Gnad kyi gdams pa*: D 2447 (rgyud, zi 81a2–82a7); P 3275 (rgyud 'grel, tshi 102a6–103b8); N 2076 (rgyud 'grel, tshi 88b6–90a3). Tibetan translator unknown.

KT: Karma Phrin las pa. *Do ha skor gsum gyi tshig don gyi rnam bshad sems kyi rnam thar gsal bar bston pa'i me long*. Sarnath: Vajra Vidya Institute Library, 2009.

MB: Saraha. *Illumining the Stages of the Offering Rite of Glorious Buddhakapāla. Śrībuddhakapāla-nāma-maṇḍalavidhikramapradyotana. Dpal sangs rgyas thod pa zhes bya ba'i dkyil 'khor gyi cho ga'i rim pa gsal ba zhes bya ba*: D 1657 (rgyud, ra 230b2–243b5); P 2529 (rgyud 'grel, ya 257a4–271b6); N 1328 (rgyud 'grel, ya 258a4–271b7). Tibetan translation by Gayadhara and Gyi jo Zla ba'i 'od zer.

MD: Karma Pakshi. *Melody of the Precious Reality Body beyond Thought. Rin po che'i blo 'das chos sku dbyangs*. In *Grub chen Pakshir yongs su grags pa'i rdo rje'i mgur*, in *Bod yul dmangs khrod kyi rtsa chen dpe rnying phyogs bsgrigs*, vol. 2, ff 45b–46a. Rare and Ancient Tibetan Texts Collected in Tibetan Regions Series. Chengdu: Institute of the Collection and Preservation of Ancient Tibetan Texts of Sichuan Province, 2016.

MM: Saraha. *The Mahāmudrā Pith-Instruction Called "Dohā Treasury." Dohakoṣa-nāma-mahāmudropadeśa. Do ha mdzod ces bya ba phyag rgya chen po'i man ngag*: PDM vol. 26, 1266–732; D 2273 (rgyud, zhi 122a3–124a7); P 3119 (rgyud 'grel, tsi 95a2–97a6); N 1920 (rgyud 'grel, tsi 82a1–84a5); IT vol. 3, 151–57. Tibetan translation by Vairocanavajra.

MP: Mokṣākaragupta. *Scriptural Commentary on the "Dohā Treasury." Doha-koṣapañjikā-nāma. Do ha mdzod kyi dka' 'grel zhes bya ba*: D 2258 (rgyud, wi 265a2–283b); P 3103 (rgyud 'grel, mi 295b1–317b8); N 1904 (rgyud 'grel, mi 288a3–308a7); IT vol. 3, 325–79. Tibetan translation by Rgyal ba'i lha and Rgya Lo tsā ba.

MT: Saraha. *Mind Treasury: A Vajra Song on Nonarising. Cittakoṣāmṛtavajragītā. Sku'i mdzod 'chi med rdo rje'i glu*: PDM vol. 26, 1246–50; D 2271 (rgyud, zhi 115b4–117a2); P 3117 (rgyud 'grel, tsi 88a2–89b2); N 1918 (rgyud 'grel, tsi 75a5–76b3); IT vol. 3, 129–32. Tibetan translation possibly by Nag po sher dad.

OS: Saraha. *Ornament of Springtime: A Dohā-Treasury Song. Vasantatilakadohakoṣagītikā-nāma. Dpyid kyi thig le do ha mdzod kyi glu zhes bya ba*: PDM vol. 27, 26–27; D 2351 (rgyud, zi 5b2–5b6); P 3179 (rgyud 'grel, tshi 6b4–7a2); N 1980 (rgyud 'grel, tshi 6b5–7a1); IT vol. 5, 32–33. Tibetan translator unknown.

PD: Saraha. *Dohā Treasury Song* (*People Dohā*). *Dohākoṣagīti. Do ha mdzod kyi glu*: PDM vol. 26, 193–210; D 2224 (rgyud, wi 70b5–77a3); P 3068 (rgyud 'grel, mi 74b6–81b8); N 1870 (rgyud 'grel, mi 73b5–80b2); IT vol. 2, 7–25. Tibetan translator unknown. For Apabhraṃśa editions, see Śāstrī 1916; Shahidullah 1928; Bagchi 1935, 1938; Sāṃkṛtyāyana 1957; R. Jackson 2004; and Mathes and Szántó 2024, all of which are listed below under "Modern Sources."

PM: Saraha. *Praise of Mahākāla. Mahākālastotra. Nag po chen po'i bstod pa*: P 4940 (rgyud 'grel, 'u 12b1–13a1); N 3729 (rgyud 'grel, 'u 14a2–14a7). Tibetan translator unknown.

PS: Munidatta. *Treasury of Performance Songs. Caryāgītikoṣa*. For Apabhraṃśa and Tibetan editions, see Kvaerne 1977, listed below under "Modern Sources."

QD: Saraha. *The Inexhaustible Treasury: A Song of Instruction* (*Queen Dohā*). *Dohakoṣopadeśagīti-nāma. Mi zad pa'i gter mdzod man ngag gi glu zhes bya ba*: PDM vol. 26, 1020–34; D 2264 (rgyud, zhi 28b6–33b4); P 3111 (rgyud 'grel, tsi 34a2–39b5; N 1912 (rgyud 'grel, tsi 28b3–33a3). Tibetan translation by Vajrapāṇi; revised by Asu.

SB: Saraha. *Sādhana of the Glorious Buddhakapāla. Śrībuddhakapālasādhananāma. Dpal sangs rgyas thod pa'i sgrub thabs zhes bya ba*: PDM vol. 26, 1443–54; D 1655 (rgyud, ra 225b3–229b3); P 2527 (rgyud 'grel, ya 251b4–256a3); N 1326 (rgyud 'grel, ya 252b4–257a3). Tibetan translation by Gayadhara and Gyi jo Zla ba'i 'od zer.

SI: Saraha. *The Summit of Instruction on Suchness: A Dohā Song. Tattvopadeśaśikharadohagīti-nāma. De kho na nyid kyi man ngag rtse mo do ha'i glu zhes bya ba*: PDM vol. 26, 1280–83; D 2276 (rgyud, zhi 126b6–127b1); P 3123 (rgyud 'grel, tsi 139b7–141a1); N 1924 (rgyud 'grel, tsi 127b5–128b7); IT vol. 3: 198–201. Tibetan translation by Kṛṣṇapaṇḍita.

SL: Saraha. *Sādhana of Lokeśvara Who Subdues the Three Worlds. Trailokyavaśaṃkaralokeśvarasādhana. 'Jig rten gsum dbang du byed pa'i 'jig rten dbang phyug gi sgrub thabs*:

- (1) PDM vol. 39, 535–38; D 3164 (rgyud, phu 182b2–183a6); P 3985 (rgyud 'grel, thu 224b8–225b6); N 2780 (rgyud 'grel, thu 213a4–214a2. Tibetan translation by Abhayākaragupta and Tshul khrims rgyal mtshan.
- (2) D 3165 (rgyud, phu 183a6–184a6); P 3986 (rgyud 'grel, thu 225b6–227a1; N 2781 (rgyud 'grel, thu 214a2–215a5). Tibetan translation by Ratnakara and Tshul khrims rgyal mtshan.
- (3) D 3371 (rgyud, mu 46b2–47a7); P 4192 (rgyud 'grel, du 59a8–60b3); N 2985 (rgyud 'grel, du 52b4–53b5). Tibetan translation by Amoghavajra (II) and Ba ri Lo tsā ba Rin chen grags.
- (4) D 3427 (rgyud, mu 88a1–88b3); P 4248 (rgyud 'grel, du 112a6–113a4); N 3041 (rgyud 'grel, du 102a1–102b5). Tibetan translation by Grags pa rgyal mtshan.
- (5) D 3428 (rgyud, mu 88b3–89b1); rgyud 'grel, du 113a4–114a7); N 3042 (rgyud 'grel, du 102b5–103b6). Tibetan translation by Grags pa rgyal mtshan.

SM: *Secret Songs of the Mind*. "Ḍākinīs." *Cittaguhyadoha-nāma. Thugs kyi gsang ba glur blangs pa zhes bya ba*: D 2443 (rgyud, zi 67a3–71a7); P 3271 (rgyud 'grel, tshi 85a1–90a8); N 2072 (rgyud 'grel, tshi 72b4–77b2).

SO: Advaya Avadhūtipa. *Song of the Overflowing Inexhaustible Dohā Treasury. Dohanidhikoṣaparipūrṇagīti-nāma-nijatattvaprakāśatīkā. Mi zad ba'i gter mdzod yongs su gang ba'i glu zhes bya ba gnyug ma'i de nyid rab tu ston pa'i rgya cher bshad pa*: D 2257 (rgyud, wi 207b1–265a2); P 3102 (rgyud 'grel, mi 231a5–295b1); N 1903 (rgyud 'grel, mi 222b6–288a2); IT vol. 3, 246–324. Tibetan translation by Prajñājñānakīrti.

SS: Saraha. *Stages of Self-Blessing. Svādhiṣṭhānakrama. Rang byin gyis brlab pa'i rim pa*: PDM vol. 26, 1276–79; D 2275 (rgyud, zhi 125a3–126a6); P 3122 (rgyud 'grel, tsi 138b4–139b7); N 1923 (rgyud 'grel, tsi 126b2–127b5; IT vol. 4, 245–48. Tibetan translation by Śāntabhadra and Rma ban chos 'bar.

ST: Saraha. *Speech Treasury: A Gentle Vajra Song. Vākkoṣāmṛtavajragītā. Sku'i mdzod 'chi med rdo rje'i glu*: PDM vol. 26, 1238–45; D 2270 (rgyud, zhi 113a3–115b); P 3116 (rgyud 'grel, tsi 85a4–88a2); N 1917 (rgyud 'grel, tsi 72b3–75a4); IT vol. 3, 121–28. Tibetan translation possibly by Nag po sher dad.

TR: Tsong kha pa. *Teachings Received. Rje rin po che blo bzang grags pa'i dpal gyi gsan yig.* In *Tsong kha pa'i gsung 'bum* [Zhol edition], vol. ka, 233–93 (31 folios). New Delhi: Mongolian Lama Gurudeva, 1978–79.

TV: Saraha. *Twelve Verses of Instruction. Dvādaśopadeśagāthā. Man ngag gi tshigs su bcad pa bcu gnyis pa*: PDM vol. 26, 1273–75; D 2274 (rgyud, zhi 124a7–125a3); P 3121 (rgyud 'grel, tsi 138a1–138b4); N 1922 (rgyud 'grel, tsi 125b5–126b1; IT vol. 4, 249–51). Tibetan translator unknown.

US: Saraha. *Two Untitled Songs. Sarahagītikā. Sa ra ha pa'i glu*:

· (1): D 2354 (rgyud, zi 6a5–6b1); P 3182 (rgyud 'grel, tshi 7b3–7b7); N 1983 (rgyud 'grel, tshi 7b1–7b4); IT vol. 5, 59. Tibetan translator unknown.

· (2): D 2355 (rgyud, zi 6b1–6b4); P 3183 (rgyud 'grel, tshi 7b7–8a3); N 1984 (rgyud 'grel, tshi 7b4–7b); IT vol. 5, 59–60. Tibetan translator unknown.

VJ: *Vajra Songs of the Siddhas. Sarvayogatattvāloka-nāma-sakalasiddhavajragīti. Rnal 'byor pa thams cad kyi de kho na nyid snang ba zhes bya ba grub pa rnams kyi rdo rje'i mgur*: D 2453 (rgyud, zi 92b1–115b3); P 3281 (rgyud 'grel, tshi 116b2–145b6); N 2082 (rgyud 'grel, tshi 101a4–125b6); IT vol. 5, 277–344. Tibetan translation by Dam pa rgya gar (most likely Pha dampa sangs rgyas).

VM: Saraha. *Dohā Song of View, Meditation, Conduct, and Result. Bhāvanādṛṣṭicaryāphaladohagītikā-nāma. Lta bsgom spyod pa 'bras bu'i do ha'i glu zhes bya ba*: PDM vol. 27, 11–14; D 2345 (rgyud, zi 3a5–4a2); P 3173 (rgyud 'grel, tshi 3b6–4b6); N 1974 (rgyud 'grel, tshi 4a6–5a5); IT vol. 5, 46–48. Tibetan translator unknown.

VS: Saraha. *Vajra Secret Song: A Pith Instruction on Mahāmudrā. Mahāmudropadeśavajraguhyagīti. Phyag rgya chen po'i man ngag rdo rje gsang ba'i glu*: PDM vol. 27, 290–308; D 2440 (rgyud, zi 55b7–62b6); P 3268 (rgyud 'grel, tshi 71a6–79a3); N 2069 (rgyud 'grel, tshi 60a1–67a5). Tibetan translation by Kamalaśīla and Zha ma ston pa Seng ge rgyal po.

VY: "Trisaraha." *Sādhana of the Glorious Vajrayoginī. Śrīvajrayoginīsādhana. Dpal rdo rje rnal 'byor ma'i sgrub thabs*: PDM vol. 24, 1067–75; D 1590 (rgyud, 'a 107a7–110a2); P 2301 (rgyud 'grel, pha 425a8–428b4); N 1096 (rgyud 'grel, pha 389a4–392a4). Tibetan translator unknown.

Modern Sources

Abboud, Gerardo, Adam Kane, and Sean Price, trans. 2017. *The Supreme Siddhi of Mahamudra: Teachings, Poems, and Songs of the Drukpa Kagyu Lineage.* Boulder, CO: Snow Lion.

Abhayadatta. 1979. *Buddha's Lions: The Lives of the Eighty-Four Siddhas*. Translated by James B. Robinson. Berkeley, CA: Dharma Publishing.

Abhinavagupta. 1989. *A Trident of Wisdom: Translation of "Parātrīśikā Vivaraṇa."* Translated by Jaideva Singh. Albany: State University of New York Press.

Atīśa. 1983. *A Lamp for the Path and Commentary*. Translated by Richard Sherburne. The Wisdom of Tibet Series 5. London: Wisdom Publications.

Avalon, Arthur, trans. (1913) 1972. *Tantra of the Great Liberation* (*Mahānirvāṇa Tantra*). New York: Dover.

Bagchi, Prabodh Chandra. 1935. "Dohākoṣa with Notes and Translations." *Journal of the Department of Letters* [*Calcutta University*] 28:1–180.

———. 1938. *Dohākoṣa* (*Apabhraṃśa Texts of the Sahajayāna School*). Calcutta Sanskrit Series, no. 25c. Calcutta: Metropolitan Printing and Publishing House.

Basham, A. L. 1959. *The Wonder That Was India: A Survey of the Culture of the Subcontinent before the Coming of the Muslims*. New York: Grove Press.

Beane, Wendell Charles. 1977. *Myth, Cult and Symbols in Śākta Hinduism*. Leiden: E. J. Brill.

Bendall, Cecil. 1905. "Subhāṣita-saṃgraha: An anthology of extracts from Buddhist works, compiled by an unknown author, to illustrate the doctrines of scholastic and of mystic (tāntrik) Buddhism." *Le Muséon* 4 (Part 1: 375–402) and 5 (Part 2: 1–46, 245–274).

Beyer, Stephan V. 1974. *The Buddhist Experience: Sources and Interpretations*. Belmont, CA: Dickenson Publishing.

Bharati, Agehananda. 1970. *The Tantric Tradition*. Garden City, NY: Doubleday.

Bhattacharyya, Benoytosh. 1924. *The Indian Buddhist Iconography, Mainly Based on the Sādhanamālā and Cognate Tāntric Texts of Rituals*. London: Oxford University Press.

———. 1925–28. *Sādhanamālā*. 2 vols. Gaekwad's Oriental Series 26, 41. Baroda: Oriental Institute.

———, ed. 1949. *Niṣpannayogāvalī of Mahāpaṇḍita Abhayākaragupta*. Gaekwad's Oriental Series 109. Baroda: Oriental Institute.

Bhayani, H. C. 1997. *Dohā-gīti-kośa of Saraha-pāda* (*A Treasure of Songs in the Dohā Metre*) *and Caryāgītikośa* (*A Treasure of the Caryā Songs of Various Siddhas*). *Restored Text, Sanskrit Chāyā and Translation*. Prakrit Text Series 32. Ahmedabad: Prakrit Text Society.

Braitstein, Lara, ed. and trans. 2014. *The Adamantine Songs* (*Vajragīti*). By Saraha. New York: American Institute of Buddhist Studies.

Braitstein, Lara et al., trans. Forthcoming. "Saraha's *Alphabetical Dohās*." The 84000 Project.

Bronkhorst, Johannes. 2019. "What Can We Learn from Musīla and Narada?" *Indian International Journal of Buddhist Studies* 20:1–19.

Brooks, Douglas Renfrew. 2000. "The Ocean of the Heart: Selections from the *Kulārṇava Tantra*." In *Tantra in Practice*, edited by David Gordon White, 347–60. Princeton Readings in Religions. Princeton, NJ: Princeton University Press.

Brunnhölzl, Karl, trans. 2019. *Luminous Melodies: Essential Dohās of Indian Mahāmudrā*. Somerville, MA: Wisdom Publications.

——. 2020. *Sounds of Innate Freedom: The Indian Texts of Mahāmudrā*. Compiled by His Holiness the Seventh Karmapa, Chötra Gyatso. Vol. 5. Somerville, MA: Wisdom Publications.

——. 2021. *Sounds of Innate Freedom: The Indian Texts of Mahāmudrā*. Compiled by His Holiness the Seventh Karmapa, Chötra Gyatso. Vol. 4. Somerville, MA: Wisdom Publications.

——. 2023. *Sounds of Innate Freedom: The Indian Texts of Mahāmudrā*. Compiled by His Holiness the Seventh Karmapa, Chötra Gyatso. Vol. 3. Somerville, MA: Wisdom Publications.

——. 2024. *Sounds of Innate Freedom: The Indian Texts of Mahāmudrā*. Compiled by His Holiness the Seventh Karmapa, Chötra Gyatso. Vol. 2. Somerville, MA: Wisdom Publications.

Campbell, John R. B., and Robert A. F. Thurman, trans. 2020. *The Esoteric Community Tantra (Guhyasamāja Tantra) by Vajradhara with The Illuminating Lamp (Pradīpoddyotana) by Candrakīrti), Vol. 1: Chapters 1–12*. New York: American Institute of Buddhist Studies.

Chimpa, Lama, and Debiprasad Chattopadhyaya, trans. 1970. *Tāranātha's History of Buddhism in India*. Simla: Indian Institute of Advanced Study.

Choephel, David Karma, and Michele Martin, trans. 2012. *The First Karmapa: The Life and Teachings of Dusum Khyenpa*. Woodstock, NY: KTD Publications.

Cleary, Thomas, trans. 1998. *Ecstasy of Enlightenment: Teachings of Natural Tantra*. Newburyport, MA: Red Wheel/Weiser.

Cort, John E. 1987. "Medieval Jaina Goddess Traditions." *Numen* 34 (2): 235–55.

——. 2000. "Worship of Bell-Ears the Great Hero, a Jain Tantric Deity." In *Tantra in Practice*, edited by David Gordon White, 417–33. Princeton Readings in Religions. Princeton, NJ: Princeton University Press.

Cozort, Daniel. 1986. *Highest Yoga Tantra: An Introduction to the Esoteric Buddhism of Tibet*. Ithaca, NY: Snow Lion Publications.

Dakpo Tashi Namgyal. 2019. *Moonbeams of Mahāmudrā, with "Dispelling the Darkness of Ignorance" by Wangchuk Dorje, the Ninth Karmapa*. Translated by Elizabeth Callahan. Boulder, CO: Snow Lion.

Das, Sarat Chandra. (1902) 1979. *Tibetan-English Dictionary*. Tokyo: Rinsen.

Dasgupta, Shashi Bhushan. (1946) 1976. *Obscure Religious Cults*. 2nd ed. Calcutta: Firma KLM.

———. 1958. *An Introduction to Tantric Buddhism*. 2nd ed. Calcutta: University of Calcutta.

Davidson, Ronald M. 1991. "Reflections on the Maheśvara Subjugation Myth: Indic Materials, Sa-skya-pa Apologetics, and the Birth of Heruka." *Journal of the International Association of Buddhist Studies* 14 (2): 197–235.

———. 2002a. *Indian Esoteric Buddhism: A Social History of the Tantric Movement*. New York: Columbia University Press.

———. 2002b. "Reframing Sahaja: Genre, Representation, Ritual, and Lineage." *Journal of Indian Philosophy* 30 (1): 45–83.

Davis, Richard H. 1997. "Introduction." In *Religions of India in Practice*, edited by Donald S. Lopez Jr., 3–52. Princeton Readings in Religion. Princeton, NJ: Princeton University Press.

Dimock, Edward C., Jr. 1989. *Place of the Hidden Moon: Erotic Mysticism in the Vaiṣṇava-Sahajiyā Movement of Bengal*. Chicago: University of Chicago Press.

Döl-bo-ba Shay-rap-gyal-tsen. 2006. *Mountain Doctrine: Tibet's Fundamental Treatise on Other-Emptiness and the Buddha Matrix*. Translated by Jeffrey Hopkins. Ithaca, NY: Snow Lion Publications.

Doniger, Wendy, and Brian Smith, trans. 1991. *The Laws of Manu*. New York: Penguin Books.

Dowman, Keith. 1985. *Masters of Mahāmudrā: Songs and Histories of the Eighty-Four Buddhist Siddhas*. Albany: State University of New York Press.

———, trans. 2020. *Mahamudra: The Poetry of the Mahasiddhas*. Monee, IL: Dzogchen Now! Books.

Ducher, Cécile. 2017. *Building a Tradition: The Lives of Mar-pa the Translator*. Collectanea Himalayika 5. Munich: Indus Verlag.

Dudjom Rinpoche. 1991. *The Nyingma School of Tibetan Buddhism*. Translated by Gyurme Dorje and Matthew Kapstein. Boston: Wisdom Publications.

Dundas, Paul. 2000. "The Jain Monk Jinapati Sūri Gets the Best of a Nāth

Yogi." In *Tantra in Practice*, edited by David Gordon White, 231–38. Princeton Readings in Religions. Princeton, NJ: Princeton University Press.

Edou, Jérôme. 1996. *Machig Labdron and the Foundations of Chöd*. Ithaca, NY: Snow Lion Publications.

English, Elizabeth. 2002. *Vajrayoginī: Her Visualizations, Rituals, and Forms*. Studies in Indian and Tibetan Buddhism.Boston: Wisdom Publications.

Ewing, Benjamin. 2017. "The Saraha of Tibet: How *Mgur* Shaped the Legacy of Lingchen Repa, Tibetan *Siddha*." Master's thesis, Kathmandu University.

Farrow, G. W., and I. Menon, ed. and trans. 1992. *The Concealed Essence of the Hevajra Tantra, with the Commentary "Yogaratnamālā."* Delhi: Motilal Banarsidass.

Flood, Gavin. 2000. "The Purification of the Body." In *Tantra in Practice*, edited by David Gordon White, 509–20. Princeton Readings in Religions. Princeton, NJ: Princeton University Press.

Fremantle, Francesca. 1971. "A Critical Study of the *Guhyasamāja Tantra*." PhD diss., University of London.

Gach, Gary, ed. 1998. *What Book!? Buddha Poems from Beat to Hiphop*. Berkeley: Parallax Press.

Gamble, Ruth. 2020. *The Third Karmapa Rangjung Dorje: Master of Mahāmudrā*. Lives of the Masters. Boulder, CO: Shambhala Publications.

Gellner, David N. 1992. *Monk, Householder, and Tantric Priest: Newār Buddhism and Its Hierarchy of Ritual*. Cambridge Studies in Social and Cultural Anthropology 84. Cambridge, UK: Cambridge University Press.

Gnoli, Raniero, and Giacomella Orofino, intro. and trans. 1994. Nāropa*: Iniziazione Kālacakra*. Milano: Adelphi Edizioni.

Gonnerman, Mark, ed. 2015. *A Sense of the Whole: Reading Gary Snyder's "Mountains and Rivers Without End."* Berkeley: Counterpoint.

Goudriaan, Teun. 1979. "Introduction, History, and Philosophy." In *Hindu Tantrism*, edited by Sanjukta, Dirk Jan Hoens, and Teun Goudriaan, 3–67. Leiden: E. J. Brill.

———. 2000. "The Wedding of Śiva and the Goddess in the *Kulālikāmnāya*. In *Tantra in Practice*, edited by David Gordon White, 184–94. Princeton Readings in Religions. Princeton, NJ: Princeton University Press.

Goudriaan, Teun, and Sanjukta Gupta. 1981. *Hindu Tantric and Śākta Literature*. Wiesbaden: Otto Harrassowitz.

Gray, David B. 2007. *The Cakrasamvara Tantra (The Discourse of Śrī Heruka): A Study and Annotated Translation*. New York: American Institute of Buddhist Studies.

——. 2023. *The Buddhist Tantras: A Guide.* New York: Oxford University Press.

Gregory, Peter, ed. 1987. *Sudden and Gradual: Approaches to Enlightenment in Chinese Thought.* Honolulu: University of Hawai'i Press.

Grünwedel, Albert. 1916. *Die Geschichten der vierundachtzig Zauberer (Mahäsiddhas).* Aus dem Tibetischen übersetzt von Albert Grünwedel. *Baessler-Archiv* 5:137–228 + 10.

Guenther, Herbert V. 1952. *Yuganaddha: The Tantric View of Life.* Varanasi: Chowkhamba Sanskrit Series Office.

——, trans. and annot. 1969. *The Royal Song of Saraha: A Study in the History of Buddhist Thought.* Seattle: University of Washington Press.

——. 1976. *Treasures on the Tibetan Middle Way.* Berkeley: Shambhala Publications.

——. 1993. *Ecstatic Spontaneity: Saraha's Three Cycles of Dohā.* Nanzan Studies in Asian Religions 4. Berkeley: Asian Humanities Press.

Gupta, Sanjukta, Dirk Jan Hoens, and Teun Goudriaan. 1979. *Hindu Tantrism.* Leiden: E. J. Brill.

Harper, Katherine Anne, and Robert L. Brown, eds. 2002. *The Roots of Tantra.* Albany: State University of New York Press.

Hatley, Shaman. 2016. "Converting the Ḍākinī: Goddess Cults and Tantras of the Yoginīs between Buddhism and Śaivism." In *Tantric Traditions in Transmission and Translation*, edited by David Gray and Ryan Richard Overbey, 37–86. New York: Oxford University Press.

Hawley, John Stratton, and Mark Jurgensmeyer. 2008. *Songs of the Saints of India.* 2nd ed. New York: Oxford University Press.

Hayes, Glen A. 2000. "*The Necklace of Immortality:* A Seventeenth-Century Vaiṣṇava Sahajiyā Text." In *Tantra in Practice*, edited by David Gordon White, 308–25. Princeton Readings in Religions. Princeton, NJ: Princeton University Press.

——. 2015. "Exploring the Uses of the Term *Sahaja* in Hindu Tantra: Studying Selected Texts of the Vaiṣṇava Sahajiyās of Bengal." In *Sahaja: The Role of Dohā and Caryāgīti in the Indo-Tibetan Interface*, edited by Andrea Loseries, 125–37. Delhi: Buddhist World Press.

Hess, Linda. 2009. *Singing Emptiness: Kumar Gandharva Performs the Poetry of Kabir.* Calcutta: Seagull Books.

Hess, Linda, and Shukdev Singh, trans. 1983. *The Bījak of Kabīr.* Delhi: Motilal Banarsidass.

Higgins, David. 2006. "On the Development of the Non-Mentation (*Amanasikāra*) Doctrine in Indo-Tibetan Buddhism." *Journal of the International Association of Buddhist Studies* 29 (2): 255–304.

Hookham, S. K. 1991. *The Buddha Within: Tathagatagarbha Doctrine According to the Shentong Interpretation of the Ratnagotravibhaga*. Albany: State University of New York Press.

Huntington, John C., and Dina Bangdel. 2003. *The Circle of Bliss: Buddhist Meditational Art*. Chicago: Serindia Publications.

Huntington, Susan L., and John C. Huntington. 1989. "Leaves from the *Bodhi* Tree: The Art of Pala India (8th–12th Centuries) and Its International Legacy." *Orientations* 30 (10): 26–46.

———. 1990. *Leaves from the Bodhi Tree: The Art of Pala India (8th–12th Centuries) and Its International Legacy*. Dayton, OH: Dayton Art Institute in association with the University of Washington Press.

Jackson, David P. 1994. *Enlightenment by a Single Means: Tibetan Controversies on the "Self-Sufficient White Remedy."* Beiträge zur Kultur- und Geistesgeschichte Asiens 12. Vienna: Verlag der Österreichischen Akademie der Wissenschaften.

Jackson, Roger R. 1992. "Ambiguous Sexuality: Imagery and Interpretation in Tantric Buddhism." *Religion* 22 (1): 85–100.

———. 1994. "Guenther's Saraha: A Detailed Review of *Ecstatic Spontaneity*." *Journal of the International Association of Buddhist Studies* 17 (2): 111–43.

———. 1996. "No/Responsibility: Saraha, 'Siddha Ethics' and the Transcendency Thesis." In *Felicitation Volume on the Occasion of the Sixtieth Birthday of H.H. the Dalai Lama*, edited by S. S. Bahulkar and N. Samten, 79–110. Sarnath: Central Institute of Higher Tibetan Studies.

———. 2004. *Tantric Treasures: Three Mystical Texts from Buddhist India*. New York: Oxford University Press.

———. 2009. "Archer Among the Yellow Hats: Some Geluk Uses of Saraha." *Indian International Journal of Buddhist Studies* 10:105–33.

———. 2012. "Saraha's *Queen Dohās*." In *Yoga in Practice*, edited by David Gordon White, 162–84. Princeton, NJ: Princeton University Press.

———. 2016. "Mahāmudrā in India and Tibet." In *Oxford Research Encyclopedia of Religion*. Last modified August 31, 2016. http://religion.oxfordre.com/view/10.1093/acrefore/9780199340378.001.0001/acrefore-9780199340378-e-184.

———. 2019. *Mind Seeing Mind: Mahāmudrā and the Geluk Tradition of Tibetan*

Buddhism. Studies in Indian and Tibetan Buddhism. Somerville, MA: Wisdom Publications.

——. 2022. "Saraha: The Anti-Philosopher as Philosopher." In *The Routledge Handbook of Indian Buddhist Philosophy*, edited by William Edelglass, Pierre-Julien Harter, and Sara McClintock, 124–37. London: Routledge.

——. Forthcoming-a. "American Dohās? Jack Kerouac's *Mexico City Blues* as a Modern Buddhist Poem." In *Between Philology and Faith*, edited by Jacob Dalton. Charlottesville: University of Virginia Press.

——. Forthcoming-b. "Great-Seal Text, or Not? Saraha's *Vajra-Secret Song*." In *Buddhist Minds and Bodies: Essays in Honor of José Ignacio Cabezón*, edited by Vesna Wallace and Rory Lindsay. Studies in Indian and Tibetan Buddhism. Somerville, MA: Wisdom Publications.

Jacoby, Sarah. 2014. *Love and Liberation: Autobiographical Writings of the Tibetan Buddhist Visionary Sera Khandro*. New York: Columbia University Press.

Jo Nang Tāranātha. 1983. *The Seven Instruction Lineages*. Translated and edited by David Templeman. Dharamsala: Library of Tibetan Works and Archives.

Johnson, Kent, and Craig Paulenich, eds. 1991. *Beneath a Single Moon: Buddhism in Contemporary American Poetry*. Boulder, CO: Shambhala Publications.

Joshi, Lal Mani. (1967) 1977. *Studies in the Buddhistic Culture of India*. Delhi: Motilal Banarsidass.

Kabīr. 1961. *Bījak Kabīr Sāhab*. Edited by Khemaraaja Śrīkṛṣṇadāsa. Bombay: Śrīvenkaṭeśvara.

Kajiyama, Yuichi. 1966. *An Introduction to Buddhist Philosophy: An Annotated Translation of the "Tarkabhāṣā" of Mokṣākaragupta*. Kyōto: Faculty of Letters, Kyōtō University.

Kapstein, Matthew T. 2000. "King Kuñji's Banquet." In *Tantra in Practice*, edited by David Gordon White, 52–71. Princeton Readings in Religions. Princeton, NJ: Princeton University Press.

——. 2006. "An Inexhaustible Treasury of Verse: The Literary Legacy of the Mahāsiddhas." In *Holy Madness: Portraits of Tantric Siddhas*, edited by Rob Linrothe, 49–61. New York: Rubin Museum of Art.

Karmapa. n.d. "The Lineage of Karmapas." Accessed December 11, 2023. https://kagyuoffice.org/karmapa/the-17-karmapas/#:~:text=Some%20of%20the%20most%20prominent,Buddha%20and%20benefited%20countless%20beings.

Keith, A. B. 1920. *A History of Sanskrit Literature*. London: Oxford University Press.

Kerouac, Jack. 1959. *Mexico City Blues (242 Choruses)*. New York: Grove Press.

Kittay, David, with Lozang Jamspel, trans. 2020. *The Vajra Rosary Tantra (Śrī Vajramālā Tantra): An Explanatory Tantra of the "Esoteric Community Tantra."* By Vajradhara. New York: American Institute of Buddhist Studies.

Kvaerne, Per. 1975. "On the Concept of Sahaja in Indian Buddhist Tantric Literature." *Temenos* 11:88–135.

——. 1977. *An Anthology of Buddhist Tantric Songs: A Study of the Caryāgīti*. Oslo: Universitetsforlaget.

La Vallée Poussin, Louis de. 1937. *"Musīla et Nārada: Le Chemin du Nirvāṇa." Mélanges Chinois et Bouddhiques* 5:189–22.

Lessing, F. D., and A. Wayman, trans. 1978. *Introduction to the Buddhist Tantric Systems: Translated from Mkhas grub rje's "Rgyud sde spyiḥi rnam par gźag pa rgyas par brjod," with Original Text and Annotation*. Delhi: Motilal Banarsidass.

Linrothe, Rob, ed. 2006. *Holy Madness: Portraits of Tantric Siddhas*. New York: Rubin Museum of Art.

Lopez, Donald S., Jr. 1996. *Elaborations of Emptiness: Uses of the "Heart Sūtra."* Princeton, NJ: Princeton University Press.

——. 2009. *In the Forest of Faded Wisdom: 104 Poems by Gendun Chopel*. Chicago: University of Chicago Press.

——. 2019. *Seeing the Sacred in Samsara: An Illustrated Guide to the Eighty-Four Mahāsiddhas*. Boulder, CO: Shambhala Publications.

Lorenzen, David N. 1972. *The Kāpālikas and Kālamukhas: Two Lost Śaivite Sects*. Berkeley: University of California Press.

——. 1996. *Praises to a Formless God: Nirguṇi Texts from North India*. Albany: State University of New York Press.

——. 2000. "A Parody of the Kāpālikas in the *Mattavilāsa*." In *Tantra in Practice*, edited by David Gordon White, 81–96. Princeton Readings in Religions. Princeton, NJ: Princeton University Press.

——. 2002. "Early Evidence for Tantric Religion." In *The Roots of Tantra*, edited by Katherine Anne Harper and Robert L. Brown, 25–36. Albany: State University of New York Press.

Loseries, Andrea, ed. 2015. *Sahaja: The Role of Dohā and Caryāgīti in the Indo-Tibetan Interface*. Delhi: Buddhist World Press.

Luo, Hong 2010. *Abhayākaragupta's "Abhayapaddhati": Chapters 9 to 14*. Critically edited and translated by Luo Hong with a preface by Harunaga Isaacson and Alexis Sanderson. Beijing: China Tibetology Publishing House.

Majumdar, R. C., ed. 1964. *The Struggle for Empire*. Vol. 5 of *The History and Culture of the Indian People*. London: George Allen and Unwin.

——, ed. 1966. *The Delhi Sultanate*. Vol. 6 of *The History and Culture of the Indian People*. London: George Allen and Unwin.

Manson, Charles. 2022. *The Second Karmapa Karma Pakshi: Tibetan Mahāsiddha*. Lives of the Masters. Boulder, CO: Shambhala Publications.

Mathes, Klaus-Dieter. 2015a. *A Fine Blend of Mahāmudrā and Madhyamaka: Maitrīpa's Collection of Texts on Non-Conceptual Realization (Amanasikāra)*. Vienna: Verlag der Österreichischen Akademie der Wissenschaften.

——. 2015b. "Saraha's Sahaja Tradition in the Light of the *Dohākoṣa* Commentary by a Nepalese (?) Advayavajra." In *Sahaja: The Role of Dohā and Caryāgīti in the Indo-Tibetan Interface*, edited by Andrea Loseries, 16–38. Delhi: Buddhist World Press.

——. 2019. "The Four Signs of Mahāmudrā Meditation—The Prevailing Topic in Karma Phrin las pa's Dohā Commentary." In *Techniques in Vajrayāna Buddhism: Proceedings of the Third Vajrayāna Conference*, 45–69. Thimphu: Centre for Bhutan and GNH Studies.

Mathes, Klaus-Dieter, and Péter-Dániel Szántó, eds. and trans. 2024. *Saraha's Spontaneous Songs*. Somerville, MA: Wisdom Publications.

May, Will, trans. n.d. "Saraha's *Song of the View, Meditation, Conduct, and the Result*." Unpublished manuscript.

McDaniel, June. 1989. *The Madness of the Saints: Ecstatic Religion in Bengal*. Chicago: University of Chicago Press.

Merendale, M. A. 1964. "Apabhraṃśa." In *The Struggle for Empire*, Vol. 5 of *The History and Culture of the Indian People*, edited by R. C. Majumdar, 348–51. London: George Allen and Unwin.

Mishra, Kamalakar. 1993. *Kashmir Śaivism: The Central Philosophy of Tantrism*. Portland, OR: Rudra Press.

Muller-Ortega, Paul E. 1997. "The Siddha: Paradoxical Exemplar of Indian Spirituality." In *Meditation Revolution: A History and Theology of the Siddha Yoga Lineage*, edited by Douglas Renfew Brooks et al., 165–221. South Fallsburg, NY: Agama Press.

——. 2000. "On the Seal of Śambhu: A Poem by Abhinavagupta." In *Tantra in Practice*, edited by David Gordon White, 573–86. Princeton Readings in Religions. Princeton, NJ: Princeton University Press.

Nālandā Translation Committee, under the direction of Chögyam Trungpa, trans. 1982. *The Life of Marpa the Translator*. Boulder, CO: Prajñā Press.

Nandy, Ashis. 2000. *The Tao of Cricket: On Games of Destiny and Destiny of Games*. New Delhi: Oxford University Press.

Newman, John [Ronald]. 1987. "The Outer Wheel of Time: Vajrayāna Buddhist Cosmology in the Kālacakra Tantra." PhD diss., University of Wisconsin-Madison.

———. 2000. "Vajrayoga in the Kālacakra Tantra." In *Tantra in Practice*, edited by David Gordon White, 587–94. Princeton Readings in Religions. Princeton, NJ: Princeton University Press.

Norbu, Thinley. 2022. *The Ruby Rosary: Joyfully Accepted by Vidhyādharas and Ḍākinīs as the Ornament of a Necklace*. Translated by Heidi Nevin. Boulder, CO: Shambhala Publications.

Olivelle, Patrick, trans. 2006. *Five Discourses of Worldly Wisdom*. By Viṣṇuśarman. Clay Sanskrit Library 28. New York: New York University Press.

Padoux, André. 1990. *Vāc: The Concept of the Word in Selected Hindu Tantras*. Translated by Jacques Gontier. Albany: State University of New York Press.

———. 2002. "What Is Tantra?" In *The Roots of Tantra*, edited by Katherine Anne Harper and Robert L. Brown, 17–24. Albany: State University of New York Press.

Passavanti, Marco. 2008. "The *Bla ma brgyud pa rim pa:* A Thirteenth-Century Work on the Lineage of Saraha." In *Contributions to Tibetan Buddhist Literature*, edited by Orna Almogi, 436–88. Halle, Germany: International Institute for Tibetan and Buddhist Studies (IITBS).

Pathak, S. K. 1994. "The Svādiṣṭhāna-krama of Sarahapā(da)." *Bulletin of Tibetology*. New Series 1:26–34.

Pattanayak, Subhas Chandra. 2002. "Chourashi Siddhacharyas of Orissa: New Light on the Authors of Bauddha Gana o Doha." Orissamatters.com. Last modified December 9, 2002. https://orissamatters.com/2002/12/09/doha/.

Pye, Michael. 2003. *Skilful Means: A Concept in Mahayana Buddhism*. 2nd ed. New York: Routledge.

Quintman, Andrew. 2015 [2013]. "Wrinkles in Time: On the Problem of Mi la ras pa's Dates." *Acta Orientalia* 74:3–26.

Qvarnström, Olle. 2000. "Jain Tantra: Divinatory and Meditative Practices in the Twelfth-Century *Yogaśāstra* of Hemacandra." In *Tantra in Practice*, edited by David Gordon White, 595–604. Princeton Readings in Religions. Princeton, NJ: Princeton University Press.

Ray, Reginald. 1985. "Reading the Vajrayāna in Context: A Reassessment of Bengal Blackie." *Buddhist-Christian Studies* 5:173–89.

Roerich, George N., with Gendun Chöpel, trans. (1949) 1976. *The Blue Annals.* Delhi: Motilal Banarsidass.

Sakuma, Ruriko. 2002. *Sādhanamālā: Avalokiteśvara Section; Sanskrit and Tibetan Texts.* Asian Icononography Series 3. Delhi: Adroit Publishers.

Sāṃkṛtyāyana, Rāhula. 1934. "Recherches Bouddhiques par le Bhikṣu Râhula Sàṅkṛtyâyana (de Bénarès)." Section 2: "L'Origine du Vajrayâna et les 84 Siddhas." *Journal Asiatique* 225:209–30.

——, ed. and trans. 1957. *Dohā-Koś. [Hindī-chāyānuvād-sahit].* Paṭnā: Bihār-Rāṣṭrabhāṣā-Pariṣad.

Samuel, Geoffrey. 2008. *The Origins of Yoga and Tantra: Indic Religions to the Thirteenth Century.* Cambridge: Cambridge University Press.

Śāstrī, Haraprasād, ed. 1916. *Hājaar Bacharer Purāṇa Bāṇgālā Bhāṣāy Bauddh Gān o Dohā.* Calcutta: Bagiya Saahitya Pariṣat.

Schaeffer, Kurtis R. 2005. *Dreaming the Great Brahmin: Tibetan Traditions of the Buddhist Poet-Saint Saraha.* New York: Oxford University Press.

——. 2007. "Crystal Orbs and Arcane Treasuries: Tibetan Anthologies of Buddhist Tantric Songs from the Tradition of Pha Dam pa sangs rgyas." *Acta Orientalia* 68:5–73.

Schelling, Andrew, ed. 2005. *The Wisdom Anthology of North American Buddhist Poetry.* Boston: Wisdom Publications.

Schmid, Toni. 1958. *The Eighty-Five Siddhas.* Stockholm: Statens Etnografiska Museum.

Schomer, Karine. 1987. "The *Dohā* as a Vehicle of Sant Teachings." In *The Sants: Studies in a Devotional Tradition of India,* edited by Karine Schomer and W. H. McLeod, 61–90. Delhi: Motilal Banarsidass.

Schomer, Karine, and W. H. McLeod, eds. 1987. *The Sants: Studies in a Devotional Tradition of India.* Delhi: Motilal Banarsidass.

Schopen, Gregory. 2004. *Buddhist Monks and Business Matters: Still More Papers on Monastic Buddhism in India.* Honolulu: University of Hawai'i Press.

Seyfort Ruegg, David. 1989. *Buddha-Nature, Mind and the Problem of Gradualism in a Comparative Perspective: On the Transmission and Reception of Buddhism in India and Tibet.* London: School of Oriental and African Studies, University of London.

——. 2010. *The Buddhist Philosophy of the Middle: Essays on Indian and Tibetan Madhyamaka.* Somerville, MA: Wisdom Publications.

Sferra, Francesco. 2003. "Some Considerations on the Relationship between Hindu and Buddhist Tantras." In *Buddhist Asia 1: Papers from the First Con-*

ference of Buddhist Studies Held in Naples in May 1991, edited by Giovanni Verardi and Silvio Vita, 57–84. Kyoto: Italian School of East Asian Studies.

Shahidullah, Muhammad. 1928. *Les chants mystiques de Kāṇha et de Saraha: Les Dohākoṣa (en apabhraṃsa, avec les versions tibétaines) et les Caryā (en vieux-bengali)*. Paris: Adrien-Maisonneuve.

Sheehy, Michael R., and Klaus-Dieter Mathes, eds. 2019. *The Other Emptiness: Rethinking the Zhentong Buddhist Discourse in Tibet*. Albany: State University of New York Press.

Simmer-Brown, Judith. 2002. *Ḍākinī's Warm Breath: The Feminine Principle in Tibetan Buddhism*. Boston: Shambhala Publications.

Snellgrove, David. 1954. "Saraha's Treasury of Songs." In *Buddhist Texts through the Ages*. Edited by Edward Conze et al., 224–39. New York: Harper and Row.

———. (1959) 2010. *The Hevajra Tantra: A Critical Study*. [2 vols. in one.] Bangkok: Orchid Press.

———. 1987. *Indo-Tibetan Buddhism: Indian Buddhists and Their Tibetan Successors*. 2 vols. Boston: Shambhala Publications.

Sorensen, Michele. 2011. "Padampa Sangye." The Treasury of Lives. Last modified March 2011. https://treasuryoflives.org/biographies/view/Padampa-Sanggye/P1243.

Stearns, Cyrus. 2001. *Luminous Lives: The Story of the Early Masters of the Lam 'bras in Tibet*. Boston: Wisdom Publications.

Steinert, Christian. n.d. *Tibetan-English Dictionary*. Accessed August 22, 2023. https://dictionary.christian-steinert.de/#home.

Stenzel, Julia. 2008. "From Radishes to Realization: Saraha and His Impact on the Mahāmudrā Tradition of the Tibetan Karma Kagyü School." Master's thesis, University of the West.

Sternbach, Ludwik. 1974. *Subhāṣita: Gnomic and Didactic Literature*. A History of Indian Literature 4, no. 1. Wiesbaden: Otto Harrassowitz.

Strong, John S., ed. 2002. *The Experience of Buddhism*. 2nd ed. Belmont, CA: Wadsworth.

Sujata, Victoria. 2012, trans. *Songs of Shabkar: The Path of a Tibetan Yogi Inspired by Nature*. Cazadero, CA: Dharma Publishing.

———, trans. 2019. *Journey to Distant Groves: Profound Songs of the Tibetan Siddha Kälden Gyatso*. Kathmandu: Vajra Publications.

Szántó, Péter-Dániel. 2012. "Selected Chapters from the *Catuṣpīṭhatantra*." PhD diss., Balliol College, Oxford.

Tagare, Ganesh Vasudev. (1948) 1987. *Historical Grammar of Apabhraṁśa*. Delhi: Motilal Banarsidass.

Templeman, David. 1994. "Dohā, Vajragīti and Caryā Songs." In *Tantra and Popular Religion in Tibet*, edited by Geoffrey Samuel, Hamish Gregor, and Elisabeth Stutchbury, 15–38. Śata-piṭaka series 376. New Delhi: International Academy of Indian Culture.

Thapa, Shanker, 2015. "Caryā Songs and Newār Buddhists: Ritual Singing in Vajrayāna Buddhism of Nepal." In *Sahaja: The Role of Dohā and Caryāgīti in the Indo-Tibetan Interface*, edited by Andrea Loseries, 99–117. Delhi: Buddhist World Press.

Thapar, Romila. 2002. *Early India: From the Origins to AD 1300*. Berkeley: University of California Press.

Thaye, Jampa. 1990. *A Garland of Gold: The Early Kagyu Masters of India and Tibet*. Bristol, UK: Ganesha Press.

Thrangu Rinpoche. 2006. *A Song for a King: Saraha on Mahamudra Meditation*. Edited by Michele Martin. Boston: Wisdom Publications.

Thuken Losang Chökyi Nyima. 2009. *The Crystal Mirror of Philosophical Systems: A Tibetan Study of Asian Religious Thought*. Translated by Geshe Lhundub Sopa et al. Edited by Roger R. Jackson. Library of Tibetan Classics 25. Boston: Wisdom Publications.

Thurman, Robert A. F., trans. 1982. *The Life and Teaching of Tsong Khapa*. Dharamsala: Library of Tibetan Works and Archives.

——, trans. 1995. *Essential Tibetan Buddhism*. San Francisco: HarperSanFrancisco.

Tonkinson, Carole, ed. 1995. *Big Sky Mind: Buddhism and the Beat Generation*. New York: Riverhead Books.

Törzsök, Judit. 2007. *Friendly Advice, by Narayana, and King Vikrama's Adventures*. Clay Sanskrit Series. New York: New York University Press.

Trigilio, Tony. 2007. *Allen Ginsberg's Buddhist Poetics*. Carbondale, IL: Southern Illinois University Press.

Trungpa, Chögyam. 1983. *First Thought, Best Thought: 108 Poems*. Boulder, CO: Shambhala Publications.

Tsangnyön Heruka. 2016. *The Hundred Thousand Songs of Milarepa*. Translated by Christopher Stagg. Boulder, CO: Shambhala Publications.

Tseten, Lama Migmar. 2021. *The Play of Mahamudra: Spontaneous Teachings on Virupa's Spiritual Songs*. Somerville, MA: Wisdom Publications.

Tsong Khapa Losang Drakpa. 2013. *Great Treatise on the Stages of Mantra (sngags rim chen mo): Critical Elucidation of the Key Instructions in All the Secret Stages of the Path of the Victorious Universal Lord, Great Vajradhara, Chapters XI–XII: The Creation Stage*. Translated by Thomas Freeman Yarnall. New York: American Institute of Buddhist Studies.

Tsong-ka-pa. 1977. *Tantra in Tibet: The Great Exposition of Secret Mantra*. Translated by Jeffrey Hopkins. The Wisdom of Tibet Series 3. London: George Allen and Unwin.

———. 1981. *The Yoga of Tibet: The Great Exposition of Secret Mantra—2 and 3*. Translated by Jeffrey Hopkins. The Wisdom of Tibet Series 4. London: George Allen and Unwin.

Tsongkhapa. 2017. *The Great Exposition of Secret Mantra. Volume 3: Yoga Tantra*. Translated by Jeffrey Hopkins. Boulder, CO: Snow Lion.

Tsuda, Shinīchi, ed. and trans. 1974. *The Samvarodaya Tantra: Selected Chapters*. Tokyo: Hokuseido Press.

Tucci, Giuseppe. 1930. "Animadversiones Indicae." *Journal of the Asiatic Society of Bengal*, n.s., 26: 125–58.

Urban, Hugh B. 2001. *Songs of Ecstasy: Tantric and Devotional Songs from Colonial Bengal*. New York: Oxford University Press.

———. 2003. *Tantra: Sex, Secrecy, Politics, and Power in the Study of Religion*. Berkeley: University of California Press.

van Schaik, Sam. 2020. *Buddhist Magic: Divination, Healing, and Enchantment through the Ages*. Boulder, CO: Shambhala Publications.

Wallace, Vesna A., trans. 2004. *The Kālacakra Tantra: The Chapter on the Individual, together with the "Vimalaprabhā."* New York: American Institute of Buddhist Studies.

———, trans. 2010. *The Kālacakra Tantra: The Chapter on Sādhanā, Together with the "Vimalaprabhā" Commentary*. New York: American Institute of Buddhist Studies.

Wayman, Alex. 1973. *The Buddhist Tantras: Light on Indo-Tibetan Esotericism*. New York: Samuel Weiser.

Wedemeyer, Christian K. 2007. *Āryadeva's Lamp That Integrates the Practices (Caryāmelāpakapradīpa): The Gradual Path of Vajrayāna Buddhism according to the Esoteric Community Noble Tradition*. New York: American Institute of Buddhist Studies.

——. 2013. *Making Sense of Tantric Buddhism: History, Semiology, and Transgression in the Indian Traditions*. New York: Columbia University Press.

White, David Gordon. 1996. *The Alchemical Body: Siddha Traditions in Medieval India*. Chicago: University of Chicago Press.

——, ed. 2000. *Tantra in Practice*. Princeton Readings in Religions. Princeton, NJ: Princeton University Press.

——. 2003. *Kiss of the Yoginī: "Tantric Sex" in Its South Asian Contexts*. Chicago: University of Chicago Press.

——. 2009. *Sinister Yogis*. Chicago: University of Chicago Press.

Widdess, Richard. 2004. "*Caryā* and *Cacā*: Change and Continuity in Newār Buddhist Ritual Song." *Asian Music* 35 (2): 7–41.

Williams, Paul. 2009. *Mahāyāna Buddhism: The Doctrinal Foundations*. 2nd ed. Cambridge, UK: Cambridge University Press.

Williams, Paul, with Anthony Tribe and Alexander Wynne. 2000. *Buddhist Thought: A Complete Introduction to the Indian Tradition*. London: Routledge.

Index

LIVES OF THE MASTERS

"Since the time of Buddha Shakyamuni himself, Buddhists have been accustomed to recollect the lives of great teachers and practitioners as a source of inspiration from which we may still learn. The Lives of the Masters series continues this noble tradition, recounting the stories, wisdom, and experience of many accomplished Buddhists over the last 2,500 years. I am sure readers will find the accounts in this series inspirational and encouraging."

His Holiness the Dalai Lama

"The lives of the most important Buddhist masters in history written by the very best of scholars in elegant and accessible prose—who could ask for more?"

José Cabezón, *Professor of Tibetan Buddhist Studies, University of California, Santa Barbara*

BOOKS IN THE SERIES

Atiśa Dīpaṃkara: Illuminator of the Awakened Mind
Dogen: Japan's Original Zen Teacher
Gendun Chopel: Tibet's Modern Visionary
Maitrīpa: India's Yogi of Nondual Bliss
S. N. Goenka: Emissary of Insight
Saraha: Poet of Blissful Awareness
The Second Karmapa Karma Pakshi: Tibetan Mahāsiddha
The Third Karmapa Rangjung Dorje: Master of Mahāmudrā
Tsongkhapa: A Buddha in the Land of Snows
Xuanzang: China's Legendary Pilgrim and Translator

Please visit www.shambhala.com for more information on forthcoming titles.